THE NOBILITY OF
LATER MEDIEVAL
ENGLAND

THE NOBILITY OF LATER MEDIEVAL ENGLAND

THE FORD LECTURES
FOR 1953 AND
RELATED STUDIES

BY

K. B. McFARLANE

*late Fellow of Magdalen College
Oxford*

OXFORD
AT THE CLARENDON PRESS
1973

Oxford University Press, Ely House, London W. 1

GLASGOW NEW YORK TORONTO MELBOURNE WELLINGTON
CAPE TOWN IBADAN NAIROBI DAR ES SALAAM LUSAKA ADDIS ABABA
DELHI BOMBAY CALCUTTA MADRAS KARACHI LAHORE DACCA
KUALA LUMPUR SINGAPORE HONG KONG TOKYO

PRINTED IN GREAT BRITAIN
AT THE UNIVERSITY PRESS, OXFORD
BY VIVIAN RIDLER
PRINTER TO THE UNIVERSITY

CONTENTS

Contents

INTRODUCTION

THE main purpose of this introduction is to explain how selection for publication from Bruce McFarlane's papers has been made. For this to be of any use or interest to readers, it must involve giving some general account of his papers and their relationship to what he himself published. The arrangement and listing of his papers after his death was done by Roger Highfield, Karl Leyser, Eric Stone, and myself. It so happened that I was the first to read a large part of the papers (mainly those from about 1945 onwards); consequently the preliminary plans for publication were based on general suggestions which I put forward. These were modified first as a result of general discussions between the four of us and then of more detailed proposals by James Campbell and Gerald Harriss, when the lines on which sections of the papers might be divided between individual editors had been agreed. The most obvious category for devolution was the lectures on Memling whose editing was eventually undertaken by Professor Edgar Wind.

Other decisions about how to treat the papers need to be seen in the context of some over-all view of his work and its development. It was generally easy to decide which was his latest view on a subject, since fortunately he almost always dated his lectures and papers to societies, but there were problems in deciding which was his most fully-developed exposition of some topics. There are also more general reasons for attempting some sort of conspectus, however inadequate. His lectures, tuition, and supervision influenced generations of undergraduates and advanced students, many of whom have become university teachers.

The papers fall into four main groups: transcripts, working notes, lectures, and papers prepared or in course of preparation for publication. From about 1938, or more certainly 1945, there are probably no original papers missing, apart from odd sheets mislaid, but there are some gaps in both the transcripts and the working notes. The great bulk of his own writings consist of courses of lectures, together with papers or lectures given to societies or as a visitor to other universities. From about the mid 1930s he almost invariably wrote out these in full, though he did not always keep slavishly to his written text. These lectures are not annotated, though very occasionally there are references given for quotations. There are also four papers (two of them unfinished) which are fully annotated, amounting to some 60,000 words. From the beginning of his academic career there is the uncompleted typescript of his fellowship dissertation 'Cardinal Beaufort's Financial Relations with Henry V and Henry VI', submitted in September 1927 and consisting of some 70,000 words. Connected with this is a chronological list of Beaufort's loans 1417–45, setting out the terms and history of each with full references, which was revised in 1931 and amounts to some 10,000 words.

The research on which the Beaufort typescript was based had been done in the two years since taking his Final Schools in 1925. Through this he laid foundations for the study of a whole series of problems which directly dominated his interests for the next ten years, while techniques and insights derived from them continued to influence his subsequent development. This study involved mastering the archives and administration of the Exchequer and to a lesser extent those of the duchy of Lancaster, since Beaufort was one of the feoffees of Henry V's will. Beaufort's actions as executor to Bedford and others were the starting-point for a long series of investigations into wills, testaments, and executors' accounts. He also began to investigate the administration of the estates and diocese of Winchester; though these investigations were not in the forefront of his immediate interests, he did later develop a wide-ranging interest in episcopal administration. More immediately he was concerned with the financial and political context of Beaufort's loans. The first involved him in a detailed analysis of Cromwell's 'budget' of 1433 and the whole question of the solvency of Lancastrian finances under Henry IV and Henry V. Studying the political context required detailed investigations into the attendance and work of the Council both during the minority of Henry VI and after 1437. His reactions to Poggio's account of his visit to England developed a lasting interest in late medieval culture which rejected the Procrustean categories of its humanist critics.

Beaufort's activities had also to be considered in a historiographical landscape dominated by the ruins of Stubbs's Lancastrian constitutional experiment. The great merit of Stubbs's account of Beaufort is that it went back behind the tradition established by Hall, which had equated Beaufort with Wolsey. Apart from Gloucester's complaints, there was relatively little contemporary criticism of Beaufort, so once Stubbs had discredited these he had a free hand. According to Stubbs the Lancastrian experiment was the result of both a genetic inheritance which was wiped out at Tewkesbury and a series of personal choices by Henry IV and Beaufort. Before Stubbs only Lingard had modified the traditional account of Beaufort by the silent omission of the usual anecdotes. 'To him can be traced the beginnings of a new and equally potent legend, for he wrote "His frugality multiplied his riches; but they were rendered subservient to the interests of his country" . . . it was left for Stubbs to work this up into an entirely new conception of Beaufort's career.' Stubbs proceeded to reverse the Tudor mythology: '. . . for fifty years he had held the strings of English policy . . . during the period in which the English nation tried first the great experiment of self government with any approach to success . . . he was ready to sacrifice his wealth and labour for the king . . . from the moment of his death everything went wrong . . .'[1] Thus 'Hall laid the blame for the two great catastrophes of the period on the life of Beaufort, Stubbs on his death'.

Already in his dissertation, McFarlane had argued that medieval biography was impossible, generalizing from the undoubted lack of personal material about Beaufort to the proposition that the medieval historian's province 'is rather the growth of social organization, of civilization, of ideas'.

In 1928 he wrote:

If there was ever a period when economic factors were masters rather than servants of man it was in the fifteenth and sixteenth centuries. . . .

---

[1] Stubbs, *Constitutional History*, iii (Oxford, 1878), 30; for the motives behind Beaufort's loans to the Crown now see G. L. Harriss, 'Cardinal Beaufort—Patriot or Usurer?', *T.R.H.S.*, 5th ser., xx (1970), 129–48.

All this was due to the influence of war finance . . . It was war finance that caused the Wars of the Roses, if any one factor is sufficient to explain them; it led to the fermentation of new social forces and destroyed the system based on an earlier conception of social order.

After 1928 he considered Beaufort's early career and was working towards a general view of Henry IV's reign and of the position and power of John of Gaunt. The study of warrants moving the seals and of the attendances at the Council seemed the best way of elucidating the character and working of Lancastrian government. But before considering how he first formulated his views on this, it is worth looking at his general approach to history, as revealed in a paper read to an undergraduate society in 1929.

This is the sort of paper which every teacher of history is likely to write at some time, if not in his twenties, then later, though nowadays the market has been inflated by the demands of publishers rather than by those of undergraduates. He commented on the unreliability of the eyewitnesses and on the impossibility of writing either absolutely true or truly scientific history. However valuable 'observation, measurements, statistics and all quantitative methods of study may be', the historian has to re-create the past by using imagination in Coleridge's sense of that word. He needs both self-knowledge and a sense of his own limitations. In accepting Croce's dictum 'what we do not understand, we do not dominate', he believed that self-knowledge will make the historian aware of bias, but cannot cure it. Confronted with a large mass of evidence, such as the judicial records of fifteenth-century England, some principle of selection is needed in investigation and this introduces bias. History is not the sum of individual biographies, its subject is 'man as a member of society', of which one of the foundations is 'the economic structure'. He then quoted Marx: '. . . legal and political conditions cannot be explained by themselves nor by the so-called general progress of the human mind, but they are rooted in the material conditions of civil society . . .' 'What is important is that the ideas and aims of society transform themselves.' He himself continued '. . . the manner and mode by which a community gains its existence will form its ideas as to the good life'. He rejected what he termed Michelet's liberal notion of history as a ceaseless struggle of 'man against nature, mind against matter, liberty against fatality', because there 'is no reason for regarding man as outside nature or thinking that he merely dominates a universe to which he is indifferent'.

What he emphasized was Marx's view that civil society and nature are part of a single system and the way this must affect our conceptions of man's part in historical change. In this paper there was no explicit mention of Marx's views on class or the relationship of stages in the development of production to changes in social structure. Nevertheless, some of his early lectures do touch on these concepts and he was actively associated with G. D. H. Cole in the dons' Pink Lunch Club in the early 1930s and was the senior member of the undergraduate October Club (dissolved in 1936). Most of the quotations from Marx in the 1929 paper come from an essay by A. L. Rowse.[1] While he may not have gone all the way with Rowse's later claim 'that Marxism is the intellectual system which has above all *relevance* and *significance* in modern conditions. And we may look to it therefore for the revivifying influence of a Renaissance',[2] this was more because of scepticism about cultural renaissance than because Marxism and many of Rowse's views did not influence him. There is no indication that he was attracted by the bogus analogies with biological evolution or the methodology of physical science which were then fashionable in the exegesis of Marx. His general attitude seems to have been nearer to that of the later apostles of alienation, inspired by Marx's then unpublished early writings; he found in Marx an illuminating hypothesis about man's fate in the world.[3]

In 1929 he appeared on the Lecture List as giving a course of sixteen lectures, 'The Lancastrians 1399–1471', but nothing seems to survive of them. Most of the next year's lectures on 'Some lesser Victorian politicians' do survive, as a reminder that much of his early teaching was of nineteenth- and late eighteenth-century

---

[1] *On History* (Psyche Miniatures, 1927), pp. 49–53.

[2] *Politics and the Younger Generation* (1931), p. 253, cf. p. 8.

[3] '. . . la structure conceptuelle de la pensée marxiste demeura jusqu'au bout marquée par le concept d'*aliénation*, par la vision, insistante et vague, de la reconquête par l'homme de sa propre humanité.' R. Aron, *Marxismes imaginaires* (Paris, 1970), p. 231.

history for the political history papers of the P.P.E. school. In 1931, 1932, and 1933, and for the last time in 1935, he lectured on 'The Lancastrian Constitution'. In 1932 these lectures were complemented by two other sets of lectures on social and economic questions, which included discussions not only of Beaufort's loans and royal finances, but also of commercial grievances and the *Libelle of Englyshe Policye*. In the course 'The De la Poles in English History 1327–1525' first given in 1934 (also in 1936 and 1938) he dealt with similar topics in the fourteenth century. This was eventually complemented by a course 'English Society in the Fifteenth Century' given in 1937 and 1939. Meanwhile the lectures on the Lancastrian constitution were transformed into general lectures on the reigns of the Lancastrian kings (the first course on Henry VI was in 1934, that on Henry IV in 1936). These were then complemented by a course in 1939 and 1940 on 'Parliament in the Later Middle Ages' which went back to Edward II. But even for didactic purposes he did not make strong distinctions between political, constitutional, or social history; thus the first two lectures of the 1937 course on Henry VI give a general picture of English society in 1422. The same themes were placed in different contexts and approached from different starting-points. This became typical of his way of working and is responsible for both the strength and weakness of what he left. In trying to show how this approach and his interpretations had developed by the later 1930s, it is necessary to try to define his starting-points.

An early influence was Tout's conception of administrative history as a record of struggle for control of departments of state between household and external influences. This influence dictated his early programme for discovering how the Lancastrian constitution really worked: 'We want to know more about the relations of King, Council, and Parliament; their relations with one another and with the executive machinery of government. By whose authority were the Great and Privy Seals attached to the mandates of government?' Another perhaps more lasting influence was Unwin's volume *Finance and Trade under Edward III*. He also bought Namier's first two books when they were published, but their influence was not very apparent for several years;

Tawney was a more immediate influence. The work on Beaufort's loans necessarily led to consideration of the problem of
usury. Attitudes to usury were then and for years to come a central
preoccupation of economic historians (not necessarily worse than
preoccupation with counter-factuals) seeming to offer the key to
understanding the development of capitalism. If McFarlane had
rejected Stubbs's constitutional experiment, he still implicitly
accepted the notion of a 'new monarchy' which had originally
been regarded as the product of that experiment's failure. The
phrase 'new monarchy' was Green's invention; Stubbs did not use
it, but his conception of developments after 1460 was similar.[1] But
if, as Tawney suggested, there were qualitatively revolutionary
economic and social changes in the sixteenth century, these must
have had some connection with the nature and success of Tudor
government. How far had such changes begun in, say 1399, and to
what extent was the social system sufficiently flexible to allow even
the possibility of solutions similar to those of Tudor government?

His formulations were naturally crude and superficial at first,
but they were clearly influenced by such conceptions and by the
notions of historical materialism revealed in his 1929 paper. In
1932 he believed it was necessary to study through economic and
social analysis 'the underlying conditions which made Lancastrian
society so unstable . . .'. Such general conceptions may be presumed to be behind what he wrote in 1935: '. . . acquisitiveness was
the predominating characteristic of Lancastrian England. . . .' 'Its
political unrest, though it often served the ends of ambitious
nobles, was not mere factiousness; it sprang from the efforts of a
new class to break through the cracking shell of medieval society.'
'. . . once fortunes could be made by trade and invested in land the
boundaries which had hitherto separated class from class rapidly
disintegrated and in a short time the old feudal aristocracy was
itself invaded by the *nouveaux-riches*.'[2] His original interest in the
history of the de la Poles was undoubtedly stimulated by such
considerations. It is also apparent that as his knowledge grew he

[1] See below, pp. 279–97.
[2] *Cambridge Medieval History*, vol. viii (1936), *The Close of the Middle Ages*,
pp. 380, 382.

found their rise less typical and less symptomatic of the general tendencies of English society. His treatment of their rise became a barometer of his changing views on how to interpret and analyse later medieval society.

Not surprisingly his views in 1931 on more specific matters sometimes expressed what he later regarded as fundamental misinterpretations. 'The Commons demanded it because they were the clients of the Lords.' 'Local administration was unable to stand the strain of the social revolution' so that not only did local justice become corrupt and ineffective, but 'the growth of justices of the peace in the place of stipendiary royal officials placed power more and more in the hands of the propertied classes'. 'Edward III had been content to govern through the propertied classes; he had in fact surrendered to them' (1934). But already by 1932 he allowed that the Commons did sometimes act independently. He acknowledged that knights were often members of baronial councils and instanced the Speakers in 1376 and 1377, but went on 'There are signs that in the fifteenth century knights, possibly from their contact with burgesses, were prepared to go further than the Lords in their demands for better government that... the Commons are definitely becoming a power to be reckoned with alone. However, these signs are rare.' He saw the burgesses as opposing 'government monopolies (in which barons often shared)' and foreign traders. They had business ties with lords and gentry and often owned land themselves, so that 'generally speaking the two houses represented the propertied interests of the country. . . . They made common cause against the Crown on the one hand and artisans and peasants on the other.' As to the Crown 'The evidence of the Council files leads one to see that Henry IV's conception of the royal power which he wished to maintain intact differed very little from that of his predecessors.'

Already in 1931 one of his main themes was 'bastard feudalism'. 'Social importance in the fourteenth and fifteenth centuries was no longer secured by status in the feudal scheme, it depended upon the number of clients a patron was able to attract.' Money 'had replaced the "feudal bond" by the "cash nexus"'. This forced barons to change methods of husbandry, to try to concentrate their estates and to seek control of royal patronage through the Council. By 1932 the emphasis on such hypothetical changes in estate management had gone and the emphasis was on the strain on royal finances caused by each magnate's quest for patronage to gain 'the support of the gentry of his district. To lead them in the king's wars, to offer them his protection in the law courts and his assistance in their careers. . . . The local ties of the great landholders only dwindle from English history in the nineteenth century.' Down to 1937 he also accepted the hypothesis that 'some barons were under pressure from falling incomes' as a result of the economic changes of the fourteenth century. 'A baron's importance depended on his power of attracting men to his service, however rich he was, nothing was so effective as influence at court.' Too much favouritism at the centre ensured local discontent; the ideal was achieved in the middle years of Edward III, under Henry V, and for most of Henry VI's minority.

The baronial conception of good government was that of a king guiltless of favouritism, employing and rewarding his natural councillors, leaving in their hands and in that of their servants and retainers, the administration of local affairs. It is a mistake to suppose that the barons objected to curialists as such . . . if the king's friends were dukes or cardinals, and the barons in any number were excluded from favour, the Suffolks, the Somersets, the Cardinals of England and of York, were as unpopular as Bushy, Green, or Bagot. . . .

These were his preoccupations when in December 1932 he was asked to revise a chapter on the Lancastrian kings for the *Cambridge Medieval History*, written by Miss C. J. Skeel in 1922 which Professor Waugh had been unable to revise before his death. The following January he was asked to write a new chapter and on 15 March he signed an agreement to deliver 15,600 words on 1 October next. Both parties seem to have been singularly unrealistic in supposing that an adequate chapter could be produced at this length and in this time. In fact he was seriously ill during the summer of 1933 and did not begin work on the chapter until September. The chapter as published, amounting to some 30,000 words, was delivered early in July 1935.

The narrative form of the *Cambridge Medieval History* and the need to offer a summary of what could be regarded as securely established meant that his own interpretations were often left out, or at most implied. The general account of bastard feudalism has some good phrases: 'Military service was no longer merely an incident of tenure, but also a commodity to be disposed of by sale.' The bond between lord and retainer 'was a contract voluntarily entered into by both parties',[1] but the implications of this were much less fully explored than in his lectures of 1932 and 1934. Their relationship to the political behaviour of the Commons is only hinted at. The account of the Parliament of 1406 emphasizes the independent role of the knights while that of 1422 claims 'The strength of those local ties which still bound the small landowners to their greater neighbours was felt as soon as the latter gained control of the royal patronage.'[2] The sections which depended most heavily on his own research were those on the reigns of Henry IV down to 1410 and of Henry VI until the fall of Suffolk.

In 1935, as he was finishing the chapter, he lectured for the last time on the Lancastrian constitution and there followed a reshaping of his views which became apparent in 1937–8. The chapter itself had given little indication of his concern with ecclesiastical history. This was first given some extended expression in his lectures on 'English Society in the Fifteenth Century' originally given in 1937, which were sub-titled in his preliminary notes 'Things that get left out of political and constitutional history'. These lectures made a general attack on the conception of the fifteenth century as 'a trough between the medieval and the modern worlds—a trough of low pressure between two high-pressure systems'. They also enunciate a general theme which was to be explained in detail in his later work on the Lollard knights and noble education: '. . . learning and the arts had ceased to be clerical monopolies, they flourished in the world. . . . Religion, like learning, was becoming secularized—it too produced its finest flowers in the world.' Lollardy was to be seen as the heretical left wing of a widespread movement of lay piety, most vividly illustrated by the experiences of Margery Kempe. He approached the higher clergy

[1] _Cambridge Medieval History_, viii (1936), 382.   [2] Ibid., pp. 371–2, 390.

through a detailed consideration of Gascoigne's criticisms, remarking more generally of the bishops 'As ecclesiastical governors, they had been taught to combine the wisdom of the serpent with the innocence of a dove—a combination so difficult that many . . . found it desirable to specialize.'

He also began to produce detailed criticism of assumptions that maintenance and local disorders were greater throughout the fifteenth century than in earlier periods. He also argued that 'one of the cardinal facts about the Lancastrian period is that the lower (not the lowest) classes were becoming increasingly restive at injustice; this restiveness dates back beyond the Peasants' Revolt but it grew in intensity. . . . Here again literacy plays its part. . . . What they were complaining of was nothing new; their complaints were new; that important distinction is not always realized.' However, his views on the implications of retainers' contractual relationships with lords remained the same as in 1934 and were not explored further until 1939. The way to this lay through reconsidering assumptions about the development of monarchical government which he had hitherto tacitly or openly accepted. These assumptions inherited from Stubbs and Green, elaborated by Pollard and with somewhat different and at times mutually contradictory emphases by Cunningham and Tawney, saw the Tudor monarchy as the saviour of society and order and the at least partially paternalistic promoter of progress, modernization, and the general interest of the nation. The Tudors asserted and strengthened the powers of the Crown in order to solve the problems which had beset England since the fourteenth century, yet they also preserved a tradition of national consent and constitutional legitimacy. As late as January 1937 he wrote of Henry VI's reign

oligarchy was given its chance and failed . . . Henry VII was not more absolute in theory than Henry V; he exercised few if any new powers. The difference is . . . of aim . . . rather than of method. Henry V was an 'Old Monarch' because his aims were those of the feudal aristocracy. . . . Henry VII was a 'New Monarch' because his aims chimed with those of the tradesmen and merchants. . . . The change is largely due to what happened in the reign of Henry VI.

Thus the rejection of the whole conception of a 'new monarchy' marks a decisive turning point in his views. It was first clearly presented in the paper 'Parliament in the Later Middle Ages' in November 1938, which also showed a decisive development in his analysis of the relationship between lords and retainers. This is why it seemed worth printing it as an annexe, although the most important points were developed in his paper 'Parliament and "Bastard Feudalism" '[1] and although since then further research, much of it arising from theses which he supervised, has shown some of his remarks about Edward IV to be ill founded. It is also a very good example of a genre, the paper for an undergraduate society, to which he devoted a great deal of time and which he often used to try out and develop hypotheses. The paper's immediate background was an increasing preoccupation with prosopography and the problems of producing biographies of members of Parliament. Syme's *Roman Revolution* was very much in his mind as an example of what could be achieved by such methods, while Colonel Wedgwood had provided an awful warning of how to abuse the method and reduce 'what is probably the correct answer to an absurdity by carrying it to impossible extremes'. Although he devoted much time to collecting materials for biographies of knights of the shire in Henry IV's parliaments, he eventually concluded that prosopographical methods were less rewarding than he had originally supposed.

The new orientation, outlined in his paper, produced twelve lectures on 'Parliament in the Later Middle Ages' in Hilary term 1940. They provide a remarkable justification of his repudiation of 'the point of view . . . of Anson rather than of Bagehot . . . more concerned to define the law of the constitution than to prove the realities of political power'.[2] In doing so they expounded his developed interpretation of the political and social implications of

[1] *T.R.H.S.*, 4th ser., 26 (1944), 53–79, read 15 May 1943; reprinted in *Essays in Medieval History*, ed. R. W. Southern (1968). Some of the remarks about the 'New Monarchy' were used as an introduction to 'Henry V, Cardinal Beaufort and the Red Hat', *E.H.R.* 60 (1945), 316–48, and below, pp. 282–7.

[2] *E.H.R.* 78 (1938), 707, reviewing S. B. Chrimes, *English Constitutional Ideas in the Fifteenth Century.*

bastard feudalism, of which the main parts appeared in the paper 'Bastard Feudalism'.[1] They also contained part of the material used in the paper on Parliament in 1944. In considering the relations between Lords and Commons he did not neglect the Lords, giving a careful account of the numbers summoned which pointed towards his later work on extinction and creations. Above all they offered a whole conspectus of the development of the English state and its ruling class. This was expounded more generally in two versions of a paper written during the first year of the war of which only parts survive and to which I shall return presently.

The lectures dealt with Parliament from the time of Edward II, but the discussion of the nature of government and society went further back. They gave a full discussion of sources and stressed the importance of monastic chronicles for the period 1376–1406. The town chronicles which succeeded them 'were meant for circulation and this may have imposed some circumspection'. He was prepared to guess that the Commons were at their most assertive in those years, but that the period 1439–50 'might have been a second period of almost as great significance'. He also claimed 'that in matters of constitutional theory the law is usually out of date; in the later middle ages it was probably more than usually so. . . . The Year Books thus are evidence only of the views of a profession and a class which on one very important occasion at least [1387] showed itself bitterly hostile to the pretensions of Parliament.' If the Commons 'had no legal right to refuse a grant', equally 'the king had no legal right to compel them'. 'Refused in principle in 1401 redress before supply was the almost invariable practice of the later middle ages.' If the Commons did not come to choose councillors for the king, they did in the first half of the fifteenth century come to develop the elements of a policy of aggressive economic nationalism, exemplified in the *Libelle of Englyshe Policye*, 'which was generally in flat opposition to that pursued by the government'. The most important general aim of the burgesses was the abolition of all 'privileges and monopolies granted to favoured bodies of merchants, either native or alien'. Parliament's main preoccupation was criticism and 'the

[1] *B.I.H.R.* 20 (1945), 161–80.

seventeenth century was right when it looked back to "that happy time" for its precedents'.

In considering the social background of Parliament he placed it in a perspective of the development of English society since 1066. In what survives of the other paper of 1940 he saw the study of the English ruling class as the most urgent task of English historians.

Government implies oligarchy; in no case can power reside solely in the hands of one man or equally in the hands of all; the prince has his councillors, the people their ministers. What matters is not government by the few, but how the few come to be chosen and how they are removed, because on the methods of choice and removal will depend very largely in whose interests the government is carried on. . . . The State is generally, if not always, as Marx asserted, an instrument by which one class imposes its will upon the rest. . . . It is a liberal delusion that the introduction of universal adult suffrage converted England from an oligarchy into a democracy. . . . If we wish to understand the nature of the English State, what is necessary is a study of the evolution of its governing class. For it is the peculiarity of the English governing class and the reason why, unlike that of other countries, it has remained in relatively undisturbed possession for nearly 900 years—that it has shown a special capacity for evolution. In most European countries aristocracies became, so to say, rigid at an early state in their history, maintained their feudal exclusiveness . . . proved incapable of adaptation to changed circumstances and therefore withstood change until it broke them. That did not happen in England, where the upper classes have always been the leaders of revolutions, not the victims. It is high time the history of England was written in these terms and indeed a beginning has been made chiefly in respect of the seventeenth and eighteenth centuries.

He proposed to sketch some of the earlier stages of that 'process of adaptation' which brought 'our governing class' 'from feudalism to industrialism and halfway to State Socialism without loss of continuity or tradition . . .'. Its distinctive feature was that it 'has not resisted invaders, it has absorbed them'. Land was 'the basis for power, but it was not necessarily the source of it, since the thirteenth-century English classes have not been watertight; it is doubtful whether they were even in the feudal period'.

The Conquest was decisive because it produced a strong monarchy, but did not produce compact autonomous fiefs which might have been the basis for a nobility of blood. It produced some 1,500 tenants-in-chief and continued the tradition that all men, whatever their status or tenure, owed service to the Crown. Henry I 'raised men from the dust to do him service' and had power to change men's inheritances. English earldoms were marks of social distinction without specific territorial powers or hereditary rights; the palatinates and marcher lordships proved to be exceptions without enduring significance. Barons might serve the king as sheriffs or justiciars, but the offices did not become hereditary. By the later thirteenth century baronial justice had decayed and it was ceasing to be worth while to hold courts for free tenants. 'The strength of the Crown was a greater leveller' and its demands for service from all men of property accustomed them to acting together. Political events in the thirteenth century also drew them together. Even Magna Carta was not the work of barons who ignored all interests but their own. The barons opposing Henry III were compelled to seek allies in the classes below them, among their tenants, their smaller neighbours, and even among the townsmen

. . . in the reign of Edward I there existed neither the idea of a *noblesse* of blood, nor circumstances favourable to the growth of a caste system. The military class had all kinds of subdivisions, but these cut across each other in every direction. Neither wealth nor rank provided a clear line of demarcation between high and low. The earl was not nobler than the knight . . . knighthood was itself no matter of blood, but of landed wealth. It may be that here we have a carry-over from the Anglo-Saxon period, when a ceorl who throve was, provided certain conditions were fulfilled, considered of thegn-right worthy.[1]

Thus the essential features of English society in the fourteenth century were 'its fluidity, its relative lack of social barriers and its competitiveness. . . . The peerage developed in a non-feudal world and it had few feudal characteristics. It was based on land,

[1] For a full discussion see F. M. Stenton, *Preparatory to Anglo-Saxon England* (Oxford, 1970), pp. 383–93, 'The Thriving of the Anglo-Saxon Ceorl'.

but in a society where land was the reward of service and the investment of the successful in all walks of life.'

The main sources for his views seem to have been Stubbs on the lack of an exclusive nobility of blood, Gneist and A. B. White[1] on the character of English local government, Stenton on the nature of earldoms and feudalism after 1066, Maitland on private jurisdiction, and Denholm-Young on the knights of Edward I. These were now used to try to explain how English society had reached the structure of landownership revealed by the income-tax of 1436. He had read the manuscript of Gray's article on this subject[2] for the *English Historical Review* and it undoubtedly had a decisive influence on his views of English society. His analysis of 1940 provided the general conceptual framework which he used until 1953 and for some years later. By now it may lack both novelty and persuasiveness. But in 1939 G. M. Trevelyan had assumed that the more mobile and less rigid features of English society developed under the Tudors.[3] Certainly McFarlane's views seemed novel enough to me as an undergraduate in 1940 and it is observable that many of his pupils concerned themselves with studying English and foreign nobles. He himself became dissatisfied with his original conception of an undifferentiated English nobility, comprehending peers, knights, and gentry, and stressed a growing exclusiveness which divided the peerage from the rest during the fifteenth century, so that they became identified as the only true nobles. This was accompanied by the growth of stratification inside and outside the peerage.[4] But he did not explicitly reconsider his assumptions about the differences between English and continental developments.

Later work has shown that these had exaggerated the differences between the relatively open, undifferentiated, and adaptable character of the English ruling class and the supposedly more rigid and closed groups, dominated by nobilities of blood on the continent

---

[1] I have in mind White's essay *Self-Government at the King's Command* (Minneapolis, 1933), which he regarded as stimulating, but exaggerated.

[2] 'Incomes from Land in 1436', *E.H.R.* 49 (1934), 607–39.

[3] *English Social History* (1944), pp. 124–7. The book was written before the Second World War.

[4] See below, pp. 221–4.

during the middle ages. But again we ought to remember that in 1940 Marc Bloch reached conclusions broadly similar to his, also based on the differences between English and continental usages of knighthood and argued that a closed, more caste-like, conception of nobility based on knighthood had developed in thirteenth-century Europe.[1] If Bloch's views on the increasingly closed character of the nobility, as shown by the restriction of knighthood to proven noble lineages, no longer command acceptance,[2] one major reason for this is the realization that extinction in the male line dictated recruitment of new men into nobilities on a considerable scale.[3] Similarly, Bruce McFarlane's own later work showed that the high incidence of extinction in the direct male line was a decisive factor in determining recruitment to the English peerage and in the descent of large landed estates.[4] Again the fifteenth-century distinction between English peers and non-peers is analogous to the drawing of lines between the high nobility and the rest found elsewhere especially in the Netherlands.[5] Recruitment from and into the nobility as a result of royal service was very much greater in France from the early fourteenth century onwards than was once supposed.[6] Military service to the Crown was a major source of wealth for the French nobility; in the first half of the fifteenth century it enabled many petty nobles and mercenaries to rise in status, though in the second half of the century it was again

[1] *La Société féodale: les classes et le gouvernement des hommes*, ii (Paris, 1940), 1–73, 'L'exception anglaise', pp. 73–7.

[2] G. Duby, 'La noblesse dans la France médiévalé', *Revue historique*, 226 (1961), 1–22; L. Genicot, 'La noblesse dans la société médiévale, à propos des dernières études relatives aux terres d'Empire', *Le Moyen Âge*, 71 (1965), 539–60, 'Naissance, fonction et richesse dans l'ordonnance de la société médiévale' in *Problèmes de stratification sociale*, ed. R. Mousnier (Paris, 1968), pp. 83–100; R. Boutruche, *Seigneurie et féodalité* (Paris, 1968), pp. 199–208 and *Revue historique*, 233 (1965), 199–203; G. Fourquin, *Seigneurie et féodalité au moyen âge* (Paris, 1970), pp. 203–43; E. Lourie, 'A Society Organized for War: Medieval Spain', *Past and Present*, 35 (1966), 54–76.

[3] E. Perroy, 'Social Mobility among the French *Noblesse* in the later Middle Ages', *Past and Present* 21 (1962), 25–38.

[4] See below, pp. 172–6.

[5] Genicot, *Le Moyen Âge*, 71 (1965), 115, 548; *Problèmes de stratification sociale*, p. 100.

[6] R. Cazelles, *La Sociéte politique et la crise de la royauté sous Philippe de Valois* (Paris, 1958), pp. 289–93; P. S. Lewis, *Later Medieval France* (1968), pp. 173–95.

the perquisite of a more closed and aristocratic group.[1] Thus developments elsewhere were more like those in England than was formerly assumed. Those assumptions had been too much dominated by legal definitions of nobility developed in the later middle ages and after. Lawyers alone are no better guides to social structures and behaviour than to political and constitutional ones.

Nevertheless, it remains true that in the fifteenth century a major difference between England and continental states was that legal definitions and privileges of nobility were confined to peers of Parliament; even they did not possess formal fiscal privileges and there were no restrictions on the alienation of fiefs to commoners. It is also true that the knights of Edward I were a group of much higher social status and wealth than those of Henry I and that thereafter the legal qualification for knighthood continued to be wealth not lineage. In later thirteenth century Picardy knights and seigneurs, though most of them were not from families of ancient lineage, were probably a more closed group in terms of social usage and legal definitions than their English counterparts. Seigneurial rights, in part originating from powers conferred by public authority, were a much more important source of wealth and status than in England.[2]

[1] *Revue historique*, 244 (1970), 561–3, Soutenance de thèses; Philippe Contamine, 'Guerre, État et Société à la fin du Moyen Âge. Études sur les armées du roi de France (1337–1494)'; Dr. Contamine's important essay 'The French Nobility and the War' in *The Hundred Years War*, ed. K. Fowler (1971), pp. 135–62 appeared after the present introduction had gone to press.

[2] R. Fossier, *La Terre et les hommes en Picardie jusqu'à la fin du XIII*e *siècle*, ii (Paris, 1968), 534–52, 560–4, 657–708, describes the emergence of a new nobility from the later twelfth century onwards based on the development of seigneurial rights over peasants and of feudal ties between nobles. This became a more stable and relatively exclusive group in the second half of the thirteenth century. This new nobility consisted of hundreds of lesser nobles, who held 40 per cent of the seign-euries, while magnates and middling families held a quarter and a third belonged to the Church and the Crown; its tendency towards a more caste-like exclusive-ness was checked by royal creations in the fourteenth century, ibid., pp. 662–5, 686. The contrast with England can be supported from the admittedly more impres-sionistic account of the west midlands in R. H. Hilton, *A Medieval Society* (1966). Of course there were regional differences; R. B. Smith, *Land and Politics in the Reign of Henry VIII* (Oxford, 1970), pp. 43–61, 254–8, claims that 'The lordship, much larger than a manor or a village, was the most fundamental element of control over land in medieval Yorkshire' and that the survival of these traditional

The privileges of the English gentry were tacit ones based on power and wealth without the sanction of legally defined status. The general direction of evolution towards greater differentiation and stricter definition was similar both in England and on the Continent, but the results were different. Again the view that the strength of royal administration, the nature of consent to taxation, and the decline of private jurisdiction (which had probably never been as considerable as it seems to have been on the Continent) were crucial in establishing English differences does get support from the fact that in many other countries the possession of *haute justice* became one of the distinguishing signs of higher nobility in the fifteenth century. In England hereditary rights of jurisdiction did not define status and had ceased to be an important source of income for great landowners, whereas in much of Europe the latter was still true until the eighteenth century or later. The English Crown had a financial interest in fining those who did not take up knighthood, but not in defining who was noble. Arguably, tacit expectations rather than legal privileges or prohibitions dominated English notions of status, so that this is an important difference in itself; even if actual results were not as completely different as had been supposed, expectations and attitudes were.

In 1940 McFarlane returned to the topic of inducement for loans to the Crown which he seemed to have laid aside since 1932. A paper delivered then, and revised in 1943, formed the basis of the published paper 'Loans to the Lancastrian kings'.[1] Some phrases and many examples in it derive from papers written around 1928. In May 1928 he wrote, 'I am convinced that interest and indeed a high interest was regularly paid on the royal loans.' He then cited Fortescue and Gaunt's statement reported in the *Anonimalle Chronicle*.[2] What seemed decisive evidence, cited then and in 1940,

categories in financial and administrative documents shows they were still important in the sixteenth century. He demonstrates the enduring importance of the administrative centres of these lordships in the historical geography of the region, but does not analyse their importance in terms of jurisdiction, power, and profit; the whole period from the twelfth to the sixteenth or even seventeenth century is seen as one of transition from 'lordship' to 'ownership'.

[1] *Cambridge Historical Journal*, 9 (1947), 51–68.   [2] Ibid., pp. 63–4.

1943, and 1946, were the loans made by Henry V's feoffees of the lands of the duchy of Lancaster in 1431/2. Between 1931 and 1940 he had added the record of Lyons's loans on the receipt roll.[1] Then between delivering the paper at Cambridge and publishing it, he rejected his long-standing interpretation of the feoffees' loans,[2] so that what had begun as a quest for greater certainty about economic behaviour ended by stressing the uncertainties of the evidence.

Shortly afterwards he wrote 'At the Deathbed of Cardinal Beaufort'[3] which proved to be his last published use of the Beaufort material which he had collected mainly in the 1920s. The immediate reason for this turning away was his preoccupation with Wycliffe which brought together wider interests in ecclesiastical history which had been nourished by his work on Beaufort. These had found comparatively little expression in his writing or lecturing hitherto, being represented explicitly by half a dozen lectures on the fifteenth century and implicitly by the paper on Beaufort's Red Hat. Before he undertook to write on Wycliffe in 1946–7, he had shown increasing interest in the study of ecclesiastical administration and bishops' registers during the last years of the war. The period to which he directed pupils who were interested in this kind of research was the first half of the fourteenth century. The picture of the 'possessioners' and the

[1] _Cambridge Historical Journal_, 9 (1947), p. 68 and n. 91.

[2] What seems first to have directed his attention to the possibility of '"bastard" usury' was the discrepancy between loans and repayments in one of Beaufort's transactions in 1433–4 (ibid., p. 65). His first full discussion of these in 1927 allowed that they might be the result of clerical error. What in 1928 and 1932 seemed decisive evidence were two loans of £1,333. 6s. 8d. and of £2,133. 6s. 8d. by Henry V's feoffees accounted for in John Leventhorpe's account. There are six such loans assigned to the clerical tenth in the Receipt Rolls for 9 and 10 Henry VI. As Leventhorpe's certificate of account is for 10 Henry VI, McFarlane's original assumption seems to have been that both loans would be found on the Receipt Rolls for the tenth year, where in fact three loans of £1,000, £800, and £2,500 repaid by forty-seven tallies are entered. But he ultimately excluded the last loan and included one of £1,000 and two of £333. 6s. 8d. in the Receipt Rolls of the ninth year, giving a total of twenty-three tallies (ibid., p. 68 and n. 92). This has the merit of simplicity and plausibility, but in neither case did the number of tallies agree with that in Leventhorpe's account.

[3] _Studies in Medieval History presented to F. M. Powicke_, ed. R. W. Hunt, W. A. Pantin, R. W. Southern (Oxford, 1948), pp. 405–28.

relationship of Church and State in his *Wycliffe* is certainly based on knowledge and interests which had already occupied him for some time. His work on Wycliffe (finished in 1951), followed by that for the Ford Lectures of 1953 began a new epoch; he gradually abandoned the courses on the Lancastrian kings which had been his main concern in the 1930s, lecturing on Henry IV for the last time in 1953.[1]

The turning away from the Lancastrian kings meant the abandoning of a considerable amount of material on the Council and its attendance and on warrants moving the seals which he had collected from 1927 to about 1935. This abandonment of earlier projects was confirmed by his supervision of Dr. A. L. Brown's thesis on the Privy Seal 1399–1425[2] which laid the foundations for accurate detailed study of the Lancastrian Council and the king's part in the business of government. Apart from Henry IV's reign, the period to which he had devoted most attention was that of Henry VI and again in those years he was concerned with two other doctoral theses which dealt effectively with fundamental aspects of the period, one by his pupil G. L. Harriss[3] (supervised by Mr. C. A. J. Armstrong) dealing with the most critical years of the reign and the other which he himself supervised by B. P. Wolffe, a pupil of Mr. Armstrong, dealing with a crucial issue over a longer period.[4] This turning away from earlier projects was of course partly a matter of temperament, of an inability to bring long-term projects to what he regarded as a worthwhile conclusion. But it is also related to his desire to see late medieval English political society in a general perspective of development in time and to see churchmen and laymen in authority functioning

[1] In 1959 he lectured to post-graduates on 'Late Medieval Financial Records'; the five lectures on the Exchequer included work from his early researches in producing a critique of misunderstandings of the Receipt Rolls and of the functioning of the Lower Exchequer together with an illuminating account of the work of the Upper Exchequer.

[2] 'The Privy Seal in the Early Fifteenth Century' (unpublished Oxford D.Phil. thesis, 1954).

[3] 'The Finances of the Royal Household 1437–60' (unpublished Oxford D.Phil. thesis, 1953).

[4] 'The Crown Lands and Parliamentary Acts of Resumption 1399–1495' (unpublished Oxford D.Phil. thesis, 1954).

in a wider context than that of the routines and formalities of administration. He still regarded government finance and its repercussions as of fundamental importance, while believing that 'The deleterious effects of assignment on the stability of the king's finances . . . have been exaggerated . . .'; but his interest in men's attitudes to money, wealth, and opportunities for profit became predominant in his own work.

The pattern which lies behind his first four articles[1] is important. They were only a sample of a much wider body of research, but they are also related to a wider framework of method and interpretation. This had been developed over a dozen years, though the main ideas and direction had emerged by about 1940. The programme then envisaged meant the revision of many assumptions which had lain behind his earlier work. The Ford Lectures can be seen as the carrying out of a major part of that programme. They were partly based upon sources upon which he had been working for some years, but of which he had made relatively little use in his published papers. This is particularly true of the private accounts of noble families. His work on these probably began with the accounts of John of Gaunt and of Bolingbroke, most of which he transcribed before the war, being then chiefly interested in the light they cast upon political history. In the years before 1953 he worked on many other noble accounts, above all, but by no means exclusively, on those in the British Museum and at Longleat.[2] He continued to search out and transcribe such accounts until nearly the end of his life. Another element in his work which found fuller expression in the Ford Lectures than previously was his wide knowledge of topographical and genealogical literature.[3] Very few academic historians who had worked on the later middle ages had made much critical use of the mass of local and genealogical information which their predecessors had, for more than three centuries, been printing. The deficiency is as apparent in Tout as it had been in Stubbs. McFarlane did much more to bridge the gap between old and modern learning.

---

[1] I am excluding 'Anglo-Flemish Relations in 1415/16', *Bodleian Quarterly Record*, 7 (1932), 41–5.

[2] See below, p. 17, nn. 2 and 3. [3] See below, p. 2.

The long delay in preparing the Ford Lectures for publication was due to temperament and habit which prolonged his search for further evidence. But already by 1956 and still more after 1960 he had modified some of his general ideas about the nobility and their relationship with other groups. His last lectures on the subject in 1965 and 1966 show him working towards a new synthesis.

The first extension of the Ford material was in a series of lectures to postgraduates in 1954 on 'English seignorial administration and its records'. These discussed many of the sources used in 1953 in detail and gave particularly interesting accounts of the way receivers-general and magnates' councils functioned. In 1955 he gave a course on 'Livery and Maintenance' and another in 1957 on baronial opposition which developed the themes of the sixth Ford lecture. In 1955 and 1956 he was also writing the papers on Fastolf's profits of war[1] and on William Worcester.[2] Both were the fruit of some of the work on Fastolf and Worcester which had intermittently engaged him since before 1939. His interest had probably been first aroused by the large and little-used collection of relevant materials in the archives of his own college. The first was an extended demonstration of conclusions briefly indicated in the Ford Lectures and the second was a study of sources with a remarkable assessment of Worcester's services both to Fastolf and to learning. In 1958 he gave a course on the Hundred Years War and English society whose main conclusions were given in a paper written in 1961[3] when he was also writing a fully documented account of the partnership between Molyneux and Winter[4] discussed in the Ford Lectures.

This recital might suggest that he had concentrated exclusively upon the theme of war and its profits. Yet in these years he was also compiling elaborate statistics on the rate of extinction among the peerage and had written papers on the development of uses

[1] *T.R.H.S.*, 5th ser., 7 (1957), 91–116.
[2] 'William Worcester: A Preliminary Survey', *Studies Presented to Sir Hilary Jenkinson*, ed. J. Conway Davies (Oxford, 1957), pp. 196–221.
[3] 'England and the Hundred Years War', *Past and Present*, 22 (1962), 3–13.
[4] 'A Business Partnership in War and Administration 1421–1445', *E.H.R.* 78 (1963), 290–310, cf. pp. 20–1 below.

and the growth of settlement in tail male which were the starting-point for an elaborate study of the descent of earldoms. Moreover, from 1955 he had been working on the Lollard movement and produced a series of lectures and papers on the Lollard knights between then and 1966. In 1961 Professor Edgar Wind persuaded him to draw together his work on Memling (which he had begun in 1946 when he had interested himself in dating the Done triptych) and to give eight lectures in Trinity Term 1962. By then he had also begun an elaborate study of those impeached by the Good Parliament in which he had intended to collaborate with Dr. G. A. Holmes. The immediate origin of this was his teaching of a Special Subject on John of Gaunt and Richard II, though it also marks a resumption of his interest in the impeachment of Lyons and in the political connections and behaviour of merchants from before 1939.

In 1963 he developed another theme sketched in the Ford Lectures in his paper on the education of the nobility.[1] Both the Raleigh Lecture of 1964[2] and the paper on Edward I and the earls[3] arise from his various lectures on baronial opposition[4] and his work on extinctions. In 1963 he finished a fully annotated paper of about 25,000 words on the descent of earldoms in the fourteenth century. By 1965 and 1966 he was drawing together the various themes which he had been pursuing towards new syntheses both in his major work on the nobility and the lesser one on the Lollard knights. This latter depended on a detailed re-examination and reinterpretation of evidence whereby he revised Waugh's views which he himself had accepted in 1951. He thus directed his Lollard studies back towards prosopographical problems and showed how they could throw fresh light on old evidence. This is also true of the unfinished paper on the Good Parliament. Both developed from his work on Wycliffe and from teaching the Special Subject on Richard II; both exemplified a favourite theme, the rashness of rejecting the evidence of chroniclers without careful testing and consideration.

[1] See below, pp. 228–47.
[2] 'The Wars of the Roses', *Proceedings of the British Academy*, 50 (1964), 87–119.
[3] 'Had Edward I a "Policy" towards the Earls?', *History*, 50 (1965), 145–59.
[4] He lectured on this topic in 1957 and produced a revised course in Michaelmas 1962.

Both dealt with topics relatively restricted in time. Part of his work on the nobility was to have been founded on similar particular studies, as the articles on the Molyneux partnership and Fastolf show, the rest on more general and even more laborious inquiries exemplified in the work on extinction and the paper on fourteenth-century earldoms. His most general conclusions from these last were given in a paper for the International Congress of Historical Sciences at Vienna in 1965.[1] Finally, the fourteen lectures on the nobility in Hilary and Trinity Terms 1965 and the seven on lords and retainers in Trinity Term 1966 gave a review and elaboration of the themes and materials which had concerned him since 1953. The treatment of the general effects of war and of the political activities of the nobility is less full than in some of the earlier series, though considerable portions of the Ford Lectures and of some subsequent lectures were included. They were to have been the draft for the full study which he intended to write in the next year. It should be emphasized that they were somewhat quickly composed and that they should be regarded as outlines of the views which he was forming at that time, not as his last word in anything more than a literal and tragic sense. For example, the figures given for noble incomes (below, pp. 177–212) are not, so far as can be seen, the result of so exhaustive an analysis as he would have made for publication. They are approximate figures worked out with sufficient accuracy to illustrate the main line of his argument. These lectures should not be regarded as a definitive statement of his views.

If he believed more strongly than ever that it was necessary to defend the nobility against the ultra-royalist prejudices of most historians, this was not out of love of lords, but because he believed that the assumptions behind those prejudices were ill founded and led to misunderstanding of important historical problems and developments. In 1962 he denied that 'oligarchy—the capture of the royal administration' was ever a baronial objective; 'the baronage favoured a strong monarchy rather than a weak'.

Some of their number were always no doubt as vain and foolish as some kings, because like them they were products of primogeniture.

[1] *XII Congrès Int. des Sciences Historiques, Vienna; Rapports*, i (Vienna, 1965), 337–45.

But some were as wise as the wisest of kings; and they might hope to lead or influence their fellows. The baronage *as a whole* had something which a succession of individual kings might lack; something which made for moderation, balance. It contained all sorts of men, together they made up something like an average. They possessed corporate traditions as well as a sense of their own interests. Their rank forced them to be active; membership of the baronage was not then a sinecure; it imposed obligations. The vagaries of a personal monarchy were to some extent counterbalanced and corrected by the existence of a class of hereditary councillors—who preserved the means to impose their will, but only if they could carry the people with them. Such a polity may seem to some unworkable, or merely clumsy, but was it more so than the only practicable alternative: a personal monarchy unchecked and therefore absolute?

In wishing to see justice done to the nobles, he pointed out that 'justice is not the same thing as exculpation'. He did not lose his eye for injustice, though he did not think it necessary for historians to set themselves up as judges. He believed that great landowners' exactions caused increasing resentment from the later fourteenth century onwards, so that by 1500 the nobility were hated by their tenants. Nevertheless, he thought that excessive concentration on the problems of 'the peasants' treated in relative isolation had hindered the understanding of how society functioned and changed. His own prejudices were usually for minority causes and it was the weight of Wycliffite hagiography which inspired his excessive indulgence towards Courtenay. As he became increasingly pessimistic about man's capacity for remaking himself by faith in general theories, whether Marxist or any others, he did not weaken in rejecting the consolations of religion. He did not believe that any sect had a monopoly of either hypocrisy or virtue, but he did believe in the importance of showing that some accounts of men and the circumstances in which they lived were truer than others.

The lectures on lords and retainers represent the greatest expansion of what had originally been only a part of the last Ford Lecture. They went beyond the elaboration and revision of earlier views to offer new conceptions about the development of retaining and the giving of liveries. He stressed that retaining, like maintenance, was to be found before the fourteenth century and that its emphasis was on service in peace rather than in war, developing what is only hinted at in a primarily prosopographical article which was his last published work on the subject.[1] In 1966 he concluded 'The fourteenth century was the century of retaining as it was of liveries. Retainers shrank after 1399, not because the great landowners could not afford them, nor because like liveries they were subject to legislation, but . . . because they failed to buy the *exclusive* loyalty which was their principal object.'[2] He was also considering introducing a new topic which would have brought together the two main aspects of his work since 1947; among the papers on his desk at his death was a page of notes for the plan of a chapter on the nobility and the Church.

In the last eighteen months of his life he seemed to be reviewing most of the problems which had concerned him since 1940. In a paper on parliamentary electioneering in November 1965, he was consciously looking back to his paper on Parliament and bastard feudalism. It was mostly concerned with fifteenth-century shire elections, but also offered general reflections about boroughs, 'Management may have been necessary and proper feelings had to be respected, but these small corporations and even some larger ones were willing to be led.' He also went back to an example which had figured largely in his lectures in 1940, Mathew Crowthorne's parliamentary career and his petition against the Devonshire election of 1318. He urged that in the fourteenth century, as later, just as many sought the honours as avoided the burdens of membership of the Commons and that historians had too readily dismissed the possibility that Gaunt and Richard II could ever have influenced the composition and proceedings of the Commons. He ended with the example of Robert Fry, clerk of the Council under Henry IV, writing to accept an offer of election by Wilton and promising to follow their instructions in a tone that 'could hardly be more abject. When one remembers that this is the clerk of the king's Council, writing to the fathers of what was little more than

---

[1] 'An Indenture of Agreement between two English Knights for Mutual Aid and Counsel in Peace and War', *B.I.H.R.* 38 (1965), 201–8.

[2] See below, p. 107 n. 3.

C

an impoverished up-country market town, one begins to realize how deep-rooted, how almost as old as the Commons itself are the conventions, the traditional hypocrisies, what are often called the decencies, of English public life.' Thus if much of his work stressed the growing individualism of men's choices in religion and piety, or in the relationships between lords and retainers, he also stressed the sense of belonging to local communities and the existence of a political consciousness founded upon, but also transcending, the communities of shire and borough.

The purpose of this survey was to explain how a group of his former pupils have tried to deal with his unpublished work. I myself must bear a somewhat heavier share of responsibility than the rest, since I was the first to attempt to read through what was left and to put forward suggestions for a plan of publication. Some of our decisions were simple enough—that the Memling lectures and those on the Lancastrian kings and Lollard knights should be published separately. The real problems concerned the material relating to the nobility. The only certain result of any editorial choice was that it would be unsatisfactory in some respect.

Apart from published and unpublished papers on various related topics, there were eight sets of lectures later than the Ford Lectures. At first the most obvious solution seemed to be to print the last two sets of lectures, given in 1965 and 1966. But careful rereading of the 1965 lectures showed that, although they did record important changes in emphasis and analysis, they were sometimes hurriedly written. As a result there were some tentative or ambiguous statements which either failed to express accurately or were inconsistent with what are known to have been parts of his later arguments and findings. The text of the Ford Lectures, although no longer a completely satisfactory or full account of his knowledge and interpretations, was carefully composed and polished for an important occasion by an author who was always fastidious about what he wrote for publication or for a wider audience. Thus we eventually decided that it would be better to publish the original text of the Ford Lectures with only very minor emendations, while indicating how his ideas had changed by using extracts from the 1965 lectures in notes and appendices where they directly supplemented or modified what had been written in 1953. In addition three studies of topics which were not originally discussed at any length have been taken from the 1965 lectures and accompany the unpublished paper on the Education of the Nobility (itself an expansion of one of the original topics), together with a full conspectus of his statistics on extinctions. The paper written for the Vienna Congress in 1965 is included because this was the last work he published on its subject and because the printed version is both full of printers' errors and not easily accessible.

A further problem was that of the other published and unpublished papers deriving from the Ford Lectures. After much hesitation, we decided not to include the papers on Fastolf and on the Molyneux partnership, as they are readily accessible, and to leave the paper on the descent of earldoms for a second volume, as it is a very detailed treatment of a topic peripheral to the main themes of this volume. On the other hand, the paper on Edward I and the earldoms is clearly related to the Vienna paper and does show in finished form one of the more important directions in which his views had developed since 1953. It was also a problem which had long interested him and on which he had regularly set essays since 1939. These decisions left for a second volume, the lectures on lords and retainers, the papers on the descent of earldoms, and the Good Parliament, and some selection from the papers and lectures on parliamentary electioneering.

The most obvious and serious objection is that we may have failed to represent adequately the more developed and complex structure of argument which he had achieved by 1965 and that the putting of the lectures on retainers into another volume divorces what properly belongs together. The latter is undeniable, but the overriding consideration has been to print as much as possible from his unpublished work, and to have tried to include everything in one volume would either have produced a very large and miscellaneous volume or have increased the probability of ultimately excluding some items from publication. If the 1965 lectures had been made the basis of the present volume, the amount of editorial manipulation of the text would have had to be much greater. It is also arguable that the present arrangement is of some use in so far as it shows how his views developed.

However, it would be an act of self-delusion to pretend that Bruce McFarlane would ever have approved of most of this volume or published it in this form. The standard of documentation which he set can be seen in the papers on Fastolf and the Molyneux partnership. Moreover, it is not certain that we have succeeded in conveying his final views adequately. It is also easy, though less profitable, to point out his shortcomings. He liked plans and beginnings, but failed to finish the important projects which he began. He was a generous, stimulating, and usually successful supervisor of research, but he found it impossible to collaborate with others, though he realized that this was the most certain means to carry out some projects. He rightly despised any notion of the supervisor acting as an entrepreneur in the division of historical labour, retaining rights of patronage and marketing in the work of his research students. But he seemed to go to excessive lengths in the opposite direction, since in his own work he rarely used material from theses which he had supervised, though he was very willing to point out their relevance and merit to others. It is also arguable that he was in danger of accumulating more material than he could control and that an obsessive search for completeness in recovering magnates' accounts hindered their analysis. He undoubtedly spent much time in rewriting lectures and papers in order to make comparatively minor changes.

It is also clear that he found great enjoyment in the mechanics of prosopographical research, in the construction of genealogies and the transcription of detailed accounts. These were the aesthetic satisfactions of the skilled craftsman and the technical virtuosity with which he could rapidly and accurately transcribe the most crabbed accounts, or date undated fragments of household accounts by his recognition of ages and relationships, can still be seen in his transcripts. For him the pleasures and rewards of acquiring knowledge dangerously outweighed those of publishing it. But readiness to publish is not necessarily a virtue in itself, or even a benefit to readers. An important function of historical research is to discover what topics are unprofitable, what particular applications of a method unrewarding, and what bright ideas produce no dividend commensurate with the capital sunk in them. Such investigations can be turned into elaborate discussions of methodology, but it is arguably better to consign them to a footnote or a file. Examples of such investments of his time were the search for significant chronological variations in the rates of years' purchase in the manuscripts of a doggerel about buying land[1] and the classifying of patterns of tiled floors in Memling's pictures in an attempt to establish distinctive features which would be of use for dating or attribution.

What he looked for from prosopographical studies was some glimpse, however fleeting, of thinking, living individuals, apprehended dimly, but not romanticized and above all not to be patronized. His preoccupation with deathbeds and the diseases of Henry IV and Wycliffe has sometimes been mistaken for some crude kind of physiological determinism. But the attempt to diagnose their maladies emphasizes the poorness of the evidence which makes even the most eminent opaque and relatively undifferentiated as individuals; yet in so far as their physical condition can be established with some probability this links them to us as human beings more surely than anything else. Similarly he agreed with traditional antiquaries in finding in funeral monuments, heraldic achievements and wills, if read aright, the most important evidence of men as individuals.

He himself wrote, 'Few of us would care to be judged posthumously by the evidence of our note-books alone, least of all for our prose style.'[2] But, like William Worcester, he comes well out of this test and left a body of transcripts, comparable to those left by Dodsworth and Dugdale; I do not think he would have disdained to be remembered for this and in such company.

16 April 1971 J. P. C.

---

[1] *T.R.H.S.*, 5th ser., 7 (1957), 112, notes 1 and 2.
[2] *Studies Presented to Sir Hilary Jenkinson*, p. 218.

EDITORS' NOTE

Of the unpublished lectures, McFarlane left that on 'The Education of the Nobility in Later Medieval England' with its annotation almost complete.[1] The remainder, that is to say the Ford and 1965 lectures, were virtually unannotated and the annotation to them has been provided by the editors. An effort has been made to provide references to sources for all statements which seem to require them. In a few cases we have been unable to find a reference. The references given to manuscripts nearly always depend on McFarlane's transcripts, which have generally not been checked with the originals. When a source has been printed or re-edited since a lecture was written, references are given to the printed or later text. When other scholars have written on a subject of which McFarlane treated, using the same materials, references are sometimes given to their published work rather than to the original sources. (The place of publication has not been given for books published in London.) Although very many of the footnotes are known to refer to the sources upon which McFarlane himself based a statement, this is not always so. Some of the statements for which we have given references to secondary authorities probably in fact derived from independent work on manuscript sources. Obvious slips have been corrected. A few changes have been made in the light of McFarlane's own later work or following changes which he made in parts of the Ford Lectures which were reused in later series. A handful of statements for which no source could be found and which it was thought might perhaps derive from a slip or an oversight have been deleted. One paragraph (below, pp. 197–9) has been almost completely rewritten. Most of the editorial changes relating to matters of detail in the text have been made in the 1965 lectures, which were somewhat hastily composed. A different problem was posed by more general questions of interpretation. As has been pointed out above McFarlane altered

[1] The following notes were missing and have been supplied: p. 242 nn. 2, 3, 4; p. 243 n. 5; p. 244 nn. 4, 6; p. 245 nn. 1–3, 5–7; p. 246 nn. 1–3.

some of his views considerably after 1953. So far as possible such changes have been indicated in the annotation to the Ford Lectures and to the appendices but the original text has not been modified. It is likely that had McFarlane come to publish a final version of his work on the nobility other changes would have been introduced; for example his account of enfeoffment to uses might well have been modified to take more recent work into account. In such cases we have thought it wrong to change the original text but have provided references to the work of other scholars. We have not attempted to ensure that the apparatus contains a complete bibliography even of modern works on the English nobility in the later middle ages; our aim has been simply to provide the necessary references and to indicate the more important modern works. The early paper on 'Crown and Parliament in the Early Middle Ages' which has a different status and is printed for somewhat different reasons than the rest has deliberately been left almost unannotated. The Introduction was written by J. P. Cooper. The great majority of the notes were compiled by J. Campbell, who was also largely responsible for checking the text. A number of colloquialisms, italicizations, etc., which would not normally appear in a printed text have been left as they stood in McFarlane's manuscripts of the original lectures; they remind the reader of the nature of the text before him. E. S. Stone gave much help in correcting the proofs. Thanks are due to the following owners of manuscripts: Mr. R. J. R. Arundell, the Most Hon. the Marquess of Bath, the Right Hon. the Lord Bagot, the Right Hon. the Lord Brooke, the Right Hon. the Lord de l'Isle and Dudley, the Right Hon. the Lord Stafford, the Corporation of Warwick, the Dean and Chapter of Westminster. The paper 'Had Edward I a "Policy" towards the Earls?' is reprinted by permission of the Editor of _History_.

ABBREVIATIONS

B.I.H.R.	*Bulletin of the Institute of Historical Research.*
B.M.	British Museum.
C.C.R.	*Calendar of Close Rolls.*
C.F.R.	*Calendar of Fine Rolls.*
C.I.P.M.	*Calendar of Inquisitions Post Mortem* (14 vols., 1904–1952).
C.S.	Camden Society.
D.N.B.	*Dictionary of National Biography.*
E.E.T.S.	Early English Text Society.
E.H.R.	*English Historical Review.*
Econ. H.R.	*Economic History Review.*
Foedera	*Foedera, conventiones, litterae et cuiuscunque generis acta publica,* ed. T. Rymer (20 vols., 1704–35), except where the Record Commission edition of 1816–69 is specifically cited.
G.E.C.	G. E. Cokayne, *The Complete Peerage,* ed. V. Gibbs and others (12 vols. in 13, 1910–59).
H.M.C.	Historical Manuscripts Commission.
P.R.O.	Public Record Office.
R.O.	Record Office.
R.S.	Rolls Series.
Rot. Parl.	*Rotuli Parliamentorum,* ed. J. Strachey and others (6 vols., n.d. (1767–77); index, 1832).
T.R.H.S.	*Transactions of the Royal Historical Society.*
V.C.H.	*Victoria County History.*

The following classes of documents in the Public Record Office have been cited by number:

DL 28	Duchy of Lancaster, Accounts (Various).
DL 29	Duchy of Lancaster, Ministers' Accounts.
DL 40	Duchy of Lancaster, Returns of Knights' Fees.
E 36	Exchequer Books.
E 101	Accounts, Various (K.R.).
E 368	Memoranda Rolls (L.T.R.).
E 401	Receipt Rolls.
E 404	Warrants for Issues.
PL 3	Palatinate of Lancaster; Warrants, Privy Seals and Writs (Chancery).

SC 1   Ancient Correspondence.
SC 6   Ministers' and Receivers' Accounts.
SC 11   Rentals and Surveys, General Series (Rolls).
SC 12   Rentals and Surveys, General Series (Portfolios).
SP 1   State Papers, Henry VIII, General Series.

I

The English Nobility, 1290–1536[1]

I. GENERAL CONSIDERATIONS

JUST over a century ago, in 1850, the living of Navestock in Essex changed hands. Old Mr. X died and young Mr. Y was instituted in his place. The late vicar had held an Essex living for forty-two years and is described by the *Annual Register* as 'a zealous local antiquarian'. He had made a 'large collection' for a new edition of Morant's *History* of the county. But he seemed to have been rather a Mr. Casaubon, for none of this was published in his lifetime, and all is probably now lost. Eccentric in a harmless sort of way and a bit ineffective, he had a very different successor. The latter, it is true, celebrated his arrival, as was his wont, by a poem of the *Keepsake* variety, which he duly copied into his notebook; but there was nothing romantically poetic about him. Industrious, level-headed, knowing what he wanted, seeing his way quickly—and usually rightly—where others had wavered, a self-confident though wary Yorkshireman of twenty-five, he too meant to be a scholar. Historian rather than antiquary, he was to have his way. When—at the age I am now—he deserted scholarship for administration, he had stamped English medieval historiography so deeply with his image that we have hardly escaped the imprint yet. If we are still too preoccupied with that far from helpful abstraction, constitutional history, it is thanks to the powerful mind of—let me utter his name for the last time in these lectures—William Stubbs.

It isn't likely that I shall be obliged to name his predecessor at Navestock much more often, but it is for reasons other than mere

[1] The Ford Lectures delivered in the University of Oxford in Hilary Term 1953.

piety that I do so once. He was called James Ford and it was he and not, as one of my pupils supposed, Henry Ford who founded these lectures. Believing perhaps that Regius Professors were a somewhat doubtful quantity, he wished to endow a chair of English history. But £2,000 in the 3 per cents were only enough to provide an annual lecturership. It was a fortunate mischance, giving us more books for fewer pounds than any other scheme yet devised. The man who made that possible, however unintentionally, should not be forgotten. At the same time, his own obvious reluctance to publish may help to commend him to many English medievalists. (I for one must love him for it.)

His memory can be invoked for yet another reason: for his antiquarian tastes. These tastes he shared with centuries of scholars before him, but until fairly recently the devotion of university-trained historians—a breed unknown to him—was given to other and higher things. Heraldry, genealogy, and the study of manorial descents are even now slightly disreputable occupations; the best that the charitably inclined will say of them is that they are amiable, harmless follies, fit pastimes for the doting and slippered amateur. In my raw youth I doubt if I was as kind as that. Yet these same follies were the serious and daily concern of those about whom I am going to speak; and I am happy to offer amends in lectures founded by an antiquary of the old school. Let me hastily add that I am not going to offer you a diet of heraldry, pedigrees, and manorial descents; but they *have* been used in the cooking.

An excessive addiction to constitutional issues has, it seems to me, made nearly all current interpretations of our early history much too royalist. Medievalists, that is to say, have usually been 'King's Friends'; critical on occasion of rulers who failed, but deeply and often blindly attached to the kingly office itself. To make the Crown strong, to impose order, to pulverize faction, that was virtue; the only vice was to be weak. It is easy for such thinking to slip into totalitarianism. 'What England needed' after 1485, we have often been assured, was the revival of authority. Possibly true, but is that any reason for trying to excuse judicial murder? If Henry VIII inherited some of the less amiable characteristics of his great-uncle Richard III, they are rendered no more attractive by talk of reasons of state. Habitual charity towards tyrants may seriously distort our understanding of the problems that they faced—or more often failed to face. Needless to say those who exercise it are generally quite unfair to that much-maligned body of far-from-average men, the landed aristocracy of medieval England. Even if *some* of its members were just as capable of savage crimes as were *some* of its kings, that is no ground for damning the class as a whole. Yet for the last century, and perhaps longer, the magnates have been the victims of a strong prejudice in favour of the Crown. They have not even been seen through the eyes of those who actually ruled them and might therefore be presumed to have known their qualities, good and bad. As usual, the apologists for monarchy are more royalist than Richard II.

Need I do more than remind you of the sort of judgements I mean? How often have you not read of those 'over-mighty sub-jects', if not factious then feeble, politically and even mentally backward, greedy for power yet incapable of any sustained appli-cation to business, frivolous and untrustworthy, hiding an inner void under an ostentation that was as extravagant as it was taste-less? How fortunate that they killed each other off in the Wars of the Roses and that the Tudors decapitated the survivors!

Now it is not my intention to answer these attacks with a defence of the English baronage in the two centuries before Henry VIII. But it seemed to me that it was time that an attempt were made to find out something about these men. We historians have been very free with our views; it would be nice for a change to know. There is something odd and, I suppose, significant about the fact that much more work has been done upon the fourteenth-century villein than upon his noble master. What, for example, is the evidence for Mr. Conway Davies's unqualified statement that 'the barons' administration of their lands (sc. in the time of Edward II) was not efficient'?[1] I do not think he had examined their estate accounts, for these do not bear him out. Nor is it on the face of it likely that the baronial Despensers, whose talent for

---

[1] J. Conway Davies, *The Baronial Opposition to Edward II* (Cambridge, 1918), p. 66.

the king's service is so properly insisted on, were any less competent in the management of their own affairs. Indeed we know that
they were not. Why again should Professor Galbraith suppose
that Richard II's magnates had a low I.Q., except upon the
assumption that it is difficult to account otherwise for their dis-
agreeable behaviour towards the king?[1] Yet one of them, Bolingbroke, was intelligent enough to outwit poor Richard and to
succeed where he had failed. Indeed, I should be prepared to argue
that Henry of Lancaster was the better educated and, *pace* the
Divine Right school, the greater connoisseur and patron of the
two. And it is more than doubtful whether his training (which
enabled him to write in Latin, French, and English) was unusual
for his class.[2]

Finally, Professor Mackie cites two examples to support a general
charge of 'baronial extravagance' at the end of our period.[3] One,
the *Northumberland Household Book*, might more easily be used as
evidence of the careful husbanding of his resources by one of the
abler members of the house of Percy.[4] The other, a list of guests
and food consumed on 6 January 1508 at the Duke of Buckingham's manor of Thornbury, may seem at first sight to carry
greater weight. Yet the total bill for this entertainment, on one
of the major holidays of the year—Epiphany—was only just over
£13 while the host's gross income from his lands alone (and at
that date he could still draw profit from the royal favour) exceeded £6,000; on almost every other day recorded in his household 'journal' expenditure was far less lavish; during Lent it was
meagre.[5] It still remains, therefore, to be seen whether Buckingham was living beyond his means.

[1] V. H. Galbraith, 'A New Life of Richard II', *History*, 26 (1941–2), 227.

[2] K. B. McFarlane, *Lancastrian Kings and Lollard Knights* (Oxford, 1972),
pp. 20–3.

[3] J. D. Mackie, *The Earlier Tudors* (Oxford, 1952), pp. 16–17.

[4] Professor Mackie was under a misapprehension about the financial position
of the fifth Earl of Northumberland; for he confused (p. 17) the debts of the fifth
earl with those of his thriftless son, apparently following in this E. B. de Fon-
blanque, *Annals of the House of Percy* (2 vols., 1887), i. 379–80; see J. M. W. Bean,
The Estates of the Percy Family 1416–1537 (Oxford, 1958), pp. 137, 142–3, 152–3,
155–7.

[5] Buckingham's household journal for Nov. 1507–Mar. 1508 is now in the

Altogether too much remains to be seen; hence this attempt at exploration. The task is one that must now be more closely defined. In the first place I owe you an apology for my title. In order not to fill more than one line in the Lecture List, I was reduced to calling it 'The English Nobility, 1290–1536', but the noun is ambiguous and the dating eccentric.

'1290–1536' is only shorthand for 'from the statute of Westminster the Third to the end of the Reformation Parliament'. In 1290 Edward I's legislation was virtually complete. In the Parliament that sat from 1529 to 1536 changes were projected that were to leave an even deeper mark on English landed society. The terminal date might have been 1529, but there were other reasons for preferring 1536; for one thing it included the Statute of Uses. In any case my treatment will not be chronological, but topical. Many of the topics were not new in 1290 nor done with by 1536, but it is necessary to begin and end somewhere. The dates are in short not terribly significant, but if their choice can do anything to break the old tyranny of 1485 and the new tyranny of 1307 in our School, so much the better.

Nevertheless the period has, roughly speaking, a sort of unity. It could, for example, be described, most reasonably, as the first great revolutionary epoch in English history. During it kings were seven times driven from the throne by force, while five rulers and two heirs presumptive met with violent ends. It was *filled*, too, by what we have agreed to miscall the *Hundred* Years War, fought from the time of Edward I to that of Henry VIII and Wolsey, most expensively, by armies organized upon the basis of indentured retinues. But if the outlook and occupations of the English landed families seem to have changed little in those dozen or so generations, the impression is superficial. For one thing the laity had become in the fullest sense of the word literate; they were no longer dependent upon the clergy for secretaries and accountants; they could—and often did—manage for themselves.

Staffordshire R.O., Stafford (Bagot Collection, Stafford MSS.), D (W) 1721/1/5. Extracts from it were printed by J. Gage, *Archaeologia*, 25 (1834), 311–41. Professor Mackie used selections from Gage's selections in C. A. Sneyd, ed., *Relation . . . of England* (C.S. xxxvii, 1847), pp. 92–7. For Edward, Duke of Buckingham's financial position see pp. 207–12 below.

That change happened early in the period. The landed families had also been threatened by a social revolution from below and although they had weathered it, it had not been without cost. And their relation to the land had been profoundly affected by the entail and the use. My topics should be obvious enough: War, the Land and the Family, Lordship and Service, Maintenance, Revenue and Expenditure, ending with Politics. But Nobility itself has not yet been defined.

It will have to be taken to mean what is in French *noblesse*; its members cannot be contrasted with the gentry because they include them; the baronage is merely their upper layer. In this sense the word is obsolete and may have been never quite so used. But there is good medieval authority for attributing nobility to those well below the rank of lord and it is convenient as well as illuminating to revive it. Even as late as the seventeenth century, at least among genealogists, it preserved more than a trace of its earlier meaning. When in 1626 Edward Gwynne complimented Sir Simon Archer on 'the wondrous and generous care of yor Auncesters who . . . have ab origine et in progressu bin so tenacious of theyre nobility', he was speaking of a family long settled on its own land indeed, but rarely even knighted.[1] Two centuries earlier his language would have been perfectly normal. Thus Nicholas Upton, in writing that 'many poor men by their service in the French wars have become noble', had no intention of suggesting that they had necessarily received a personal summons to Parliament.[2] One actual instance, not of a soldier, but of a man of business, may be allowed to drive the point home. Robert Whitgreave, a teller of the Exchequer and trusted servant of Humphrey, Earl of Stafford, was on 13 August 1442 granted a coat of arms by his grateful master. In Stafford's patent he was described as a 'noble man' and the object of the grant was to augment him in honour and 'noblesse'.[3] Yet the highest rank Whit-

[1] P. Styles, *Sir Simon Archer 1581–1662*, Dugdale Soc. Occasional Papers, no. 6 (1946), p. 18.

[2] *De Studio Militari* (1654), p. 258: 'ut hiis diebus aperte videmus quomodo multi pauperes in guerris *Francie* laborantes facti sunt nobiles'.

[3] Staffordshire R.O., D (W) 1721/1/1, p. 123; W. Camden, *Remaines of a greater worke concerning Britaine* (1614), p. 9.

greave ever attained to was that of esquire and sometimes he had to put up with being called mere gentleman.

Now this, in my view, is not just a matter of a choice of terms. In a sense the English nobility in 1442 actually included such men as Whitgreave. There was something which he and his employer, soon to become a duke, had in common and in which the vast majority of their countrymen had no share. To say that they belonged to the same class is not helpful; talk of class rarely is. But between the armigerous there still lingered a tradition of chivalrous fellowship, and it was into that select, if oddly recruited, company that Whitgreave had now arrived. Whether his family went further would depend, as always, upon opportunity and skill. But a barrier of sorts had been crossed, the barrier, to adopt Upton's categories, between the noble and the poor.

It would certainly be impossible to draw a useful line any higher in society.[1] Neither tenure nor rank assists it. To adopt, as some have done, the easily recognizable distinction between barons of Parliament and knights is surely no solution. For there were many thriving knights wealthier and more worshipful than those who formed the baronial tail: Sir Nigel Loraine, Sir Robert Knollys, Sir Humphrey Stafford of the Silver Hand, and Sir John Fastolf may serve as examples.[2] Still less can knighthood itself be taken as a handy guide to consequence, for it is easy to think of men who remained all their busy lives esquires and yet had the rule in their own countries to the discomfiture even of great lords: Thomas Chaucer, for instance, or Thomas Daniel.[3] To cast them out with

[1] McFarlane later modified his views on this subject. In his 1965 lectures, while continuing to hold that 'in a sense, though it may have been a disappearing sense, the English nobility still included such men as Whitgreave', he came to lay stress on the development in the fourteenth and fifteenth centuries of a parliamentary peerage, distinct, and distinguished by contemporaries, from the gentry. For his later views see Appendix A, pp. 122–5 below.

[2] This argument is developed at rather more length in K. B. McFarlane, 'Parliament and "Bastard Feudalism"', *T.R.H.S.*, 4th ser., 26 (1944), 53–73 esp. 65–70; for Stafford see ibid. 66–7, for Loraine G. F. Belz, *Memorials of the Order of the Garter* (1841), pp. 65–7, for Knollys *D.N.B.* xi. 281–6.

[3] J. S. Roskell, *The Commons in the Parliament of 1422* (Manchester, 1954), pp. 165–7 (Chaucer); J. C. Wedgwood, *History of Parliament. Biographies of Members of the Commons House 1439–1509* (1936), pp. 253–5 (Daniel).

the goats is to lose some of the fattest sheep. Rank is not a work-
able criterion. And as for tenure, well it was so confused as to have
become quite meaningless in such a context before, possibly long
before, the end of the thirteenth century.

This is not to deny the existence of such things as estate or
degree with which it is fashionable to endow the contemporary
world-picture. A man's degree, what used to be called his station,
was a matter of considerable importance to himself and to his
fellows. On his degree would depend his rate of pay in lordly
households to say nothing of the royal array. Dukes and earls
squabbled violently about precedence. All lords were to be loved
or feared; some men preferred to keep out of their way altogether.
'As for my lord of Norwych', wrote John Paston, 'I suppose ye
know I have not usid to meddel with Lordes maters meche forther
than me nedith.'[1] To judge from the books of courtesy, degree
strictly regulated the seating at feasts and other social occasions.
From the Pope who 'hath no peer' down to the 'gentlemen well-
nurtured and of good manners' each had his place.[2] But it was not
an immovable place. Respect for degree was compatible with a
great deal of mere oppugnancy and offered very little defence
against appetite. Degree never kept a good man down. On the
contrary if he got too rich, he would have to pay to avoid knighthood. By all the tests that have yet been thought of, the nobility,
in the wide sense I have given the term, remains one. But its
indivisibility does not of course prevent one from being able
to chart a man's position within it by reference to his power,
connections, and income.

Of these income is most easily measurable. To say that its
influence was decisive would not be true. Yet given it and the
ability to use it, the rest would in time follow. To be noble, as
Upton implied, a man could not be poor. 'Gentility', said Lord
Burghley, 'is ancient riches.' The more ancient the better no doubt,
but rather new than not at all. A chronicler might grumble that
Michael de la Pole was less at home in the camp than in the

---

[1] *Paston Letters*, ed. J. Gairdner (Library edn., 1904), iii. 46.
[2] *The Babees Book*, ed. F. J. Furnivall (E.E.T.S., vol. xxxii, 1868), pp. 186–94
(John Russell's *Book of Nurture*), cf. pp. 284, 381.

counting-house,[1] but that did not discourage Hugh, Earl of
Stafford, from marrying his daughter—on the cheap naturally—
to de la Pole's eldest son.[2] Those who lived in the world could
not afford to be as snobbish as the monks. Nobility was always for
sale.

It is easy to see why in a new family's rise to prominence the
last stages are the most obvious. The origins are bound to
be obscure and for that reason cry all the more strongly to be
covered up. At the same time their obscurity to us must not be
mistaken for an obscurity *per se*. The recruitment of the nobility
is much more difficult to study than the upward motion of those
who have already entered its lower ranks. No one has yet been
successful in tracing Michael de la Pole's grandfather; all that is
known is that he was not the Sir William, merchant of Hull,
described by Tout, for there was no such person.[3] What is certain
is that Michael's father was William de la Pole, a Hull merchant
who first appears in the reign of Edward II. To take another
case: the founder of the baronial house of Moleyns, John,
who grew immensely rich in Edward III's service, had a father
called Vincent; but although the family's cartulary survives,
crammed with transcripts of title-deeds, indentures, and grants,

---

[1] *Chronicon Angliæ*, ed. E. M. Thompson (R.S., 1874), p. 367.

[2] The marriage contract, made on 1 Feb. 1383, laid down that Katherine
Stafford's portion was to be £1,000; 500 marks to be paid on the wedding day
and the balance by annual payments of 200 marks for five years, *C.C.R. 1381–5*,
pp. 249–50. For her jointure see C. D. Ross, 'Forfeitures for Treason in the Reign
of Richard II', *E.H.R.* 71 (1956), 568. See also G.E.C. xii, pt. i, p. 442 n. *d*.

[3] For the origins of the de la Pole family see G.E.C. xii, pt. i, p. 434 and
especially A. S. Hervey, *The de la Pole Family of Kingston-upon-Hull* (East Yorks.
Local History Society, 1957). McFarlane did a great deal of work on the de la
Pole family, upon which he gave more than one course of lectures. The Ford
lectures were, however, composed before the appearance of Mr. Hervey's book.
The final sentence of the account of the family in the original manuscript of the
lectures indicated that McFarlane accepted that William de la Pole's mother was
Elena who became by a second marriage the wife of John Rottenherring. It is not
known whether he had evidence of this beyond Rottenherring's will and the text
has been modified in deference to Mr. Hervey's discovery that the will does not,
in fact, prove Elena to have been William's mother (*De la Pole Family*, p. 10).
It is not impossible that the family were of gentle, or even better, origins. John
Paston's dark remarks (ibid., p. 2) would indicate that the family had been discovered to be of very low, or very high, descent.

nothing can be discovered about Vincent Moleyns except that his famous son inherited no land from him.[1] The de la Poles and Moleynses soared high and rapidly; but others—and these were the majority—who built themselves up by stages, are often worse-documented at the start.

Yet the number of different ways in which nobility in that period might be achieved or enhanced were few; and they are easy to recognize. I doubt if there were more than five of real importance. One likely candidate may be quickly eliminated. The mere possession of land was not a road to wealth; it was rather the evidence that so much wealth had been achieved. By saving and scraping a husbandman might succeed in adding one field to another; and our Marxists are doubtless right to emphasize the process by which one village kulak surpassed his neighbours. But for his betters, land, though a safe investment which gave its buyer social and political consequence, was a very slow means of increasing his principal. There were ways by which the soil could be made to yield more; but the improving landlord was only too often one whose assets were in danger of shrinking and whose other traditional outlets were barred.

Then there was marriage. I shall have more to say on this subject in a later lecture, but since it was occasionally the method by which a poor man became rich without effort, it must be mentioned here. The time when kings disparaged their vassals' defenceless women was over and most heiresses were protected from the imprudence of marrying beneath them. But accidents did happen and it was not unknown for a family to have to make the best of a runaway match. What most parents would do to prevent one, even when their daughter did not stand to inherit anything, is familiar to all readers of the *Paston Letters*. A series of untimely deaths might create expectations that were too remote to be thought of when the contracts were drawn up and sometimes these expectations bore fruit. It was one of the effects of the entail and still more of the use that the speculative element in marriage

---

[1] For John Moleyns see G.E.C. ix. 36–9; W. Dugdale, *The Baronage of England* (2 vols., 1675–6), ii. 145–7. The cartulary referred to is that in the custody of the Somerset Archaeological Society at Taunton.

was curtailed, though it could not be entirely brought under control. The great loophole was the susceptibility of dowagers, their tendency to disparage themselves. Again and again you will find a widow, whose attractions resided less in her face than in her fortune—especially if it were her very own by grant or inheritance—choosing to throw herself away upon a social inferior. The latter's advantages are easy to guess. These marriages for love—at any rate on one side—could upset the best calculations. They happened even within the royal family, to Joan of Acre, for example, Edward I's daughter, and to Elizabeth, the sister of Henry IV. The Woodvilles and the Tudors were the products of two such *mésalliances*. The former, having captured a royal dowager in one generation, did nearly as well in the next. It was the union of John Woodville aged about twenty with Katherine Nevill, widow of John Mowbray, Duke of Norfolk, a lady well over sixty, which made a chronicler write indignantly of *maritagium diabolicum*.[1] Thanks to the fortunes of war and the toughness of the Nevill women, the bride was the survivor by more than a dozen years.

Marriage must, therefore, be admitted as a possible sixth road to success. The five certain ones were (1) the Church, (2) the law, (3) service, (4) trade (including industry and finance), and (5) lastly war. Not being sure of their precise order of importance I have arranged them alphabetically—and of course they often overlap. Since two lectures will be largely taken up with service and war, I will say nothing further about them now. There remain the Church, law, and trade, each of which can be quickly dismissed. As social groups, both churchmen and merchants have received adequate study and, although the early history of the legal profession remains to be written, the successful lawyers are visible enough. All three, I think, were less important than the servants and the soldiers.

With the possible exception of war, the shortest cut to great

[1] *Letters and Papers Illustrative of the Wars of the English in France*, ed. J. Stevenson (R.S., 2 vols., 1861–4), vol. ii, pt. ii, p. 783 (in the annals attributed to William Worcester, for which see McFarlane, 'William Worcester. A Preliminary Survey', pp. 206–7). Cf. J. R. Lander, 'Marriage and Politics in the Fifteenth Century: the Nevilles and the Wydevilles', *B.I.H.R.* 36 (1963), 135–6.

(though not all transmissible) riches was through the Church. The qualification is, however, vital. The incomes of the highest clergy were princely, the prizes were open (but not equally open) to all who received the tonsure. Those who gained them were drawn from many levels in society and it may be said in general that the lower his origins the greater were the services that a prelate could do his kinsmen. The cheapest for him was a share in his often large ecclesiastical patronage; if his nephews were clerks he could advance and endow them. It is not surprising therefore that most bishops' families ran to priests and that archdeacons were often bound by ties of blood as well as gratitude to their diocesans. But if a bishop was disposed to help his lay relations also, this had to be done out of income. It *was* done, but the scale on which it *could* be practised was generally small and it competed with the other objects of the donor's bounty or self-indulgence: the founding of colleges for example. Those who could afford to be most lavish were generally more than bishops. Their sees were the reward of service and the service too had helped to swell their private fortunes. It was William Wickham, one at least of whose parents was unfree, who could afford both to endow a pair of colleges and to provide a great-nephew with a castle and lands worth some £400 a year.[1] Robert Burnell, Edward I's minister, did even better for his brother's son to whom his vast estates passed at his death in 1292.[2] Thanks to this the Burnells were transformed from a family of impoverished Shropshire knights into one of the richest baronial houses of the fourteenth century.

Law too was a form of service. It was the king's justices rather than those who practised before them who made, it seems, the most considerable fortunes. Nor can it be without significance that it was from the early part of our period, when the judiciary was scarcely differentiated from the other branches of administration —council and counsel being nearly indistinguishable—that the best examples come. Then the baronage was entered by the Scropes of Bolton and the Scropes of Masham, issue of two

---

[1] R. Lowth, *Life of William of Wykeham*, 3rd edn. (Oxford, 1777), pp. 268–9; *V.C.H. Oxfordshire*, ix (1969), ed. M. D. Lobel and A. Crossley, 88, 89.

[2] T. F. Tout in *D.N.B.*, s.n.; Dugdale, *Baronage*, ii. 60–1.

brothers, chief justices to Edward II and Edward III, by the Bourchiers, the Norwiches, and the widely ramified clan of Cobhams. Then also Sir William Howard laid the foundations upon which later generations of Howards were to build. But the fifteenth century, if it failed to show the like, made up for quality by the number of well-to-do families that were sired by its judges: Gascoigne, Paston and Fortescue, Yelverton, Littleton, Catesby, Fairfax. Men went to law much in those years not because they were temperamentally litigious, but because uncertainties of title were thrusting litigation upon them. Naturally the lawyers prospered.

The same pattern, a few early giants followed by 'a larger number of smaller men . . . respectable, prosperous',[1] but preferring safety to adventure, has been imposed, rather roughly, upon the facts of contemporary trade. The contrast between the 1330s and the 1340s on the one hand and the subsequent century and a half on the other strikes me as overdrawn, indeed wrongly drawn. It is surely idle to measure the traders of the fifteenth century to their detriment beside William de la Pole, in the first place because he was a freak and secondly because the sphere of his more spectacular achievement was finance rather than trade. His career was made possible by Edward III's idea that he could split the profits derived from the export of English wool with a syndicate of merchants. As soon as the king had been cured of that delusion and the merchants had been taught the danger of investing heavily in unsecured royal loans, that sort of career could not be repeated. De la Pole himself went back in the end to straight trade, though the adjective rather flatters him. He deserves to be regarded as a freak, if for no other reason, because he was the *only* member of his class in our period to found a baronial house. The address of his eldest son carried him to the estate of earl, but the first, decisive stage was due to the gambler's courage of old William from the pool of Hull. It is no accident that after him the two biggest known lenders to the Crown were an earl and a cardinal, men, that is, who were in a better position than a mere townsman to secure prompt

---

[1] M. Postan, 'The Trade of Medieval Europe: the North', *Cambridge Economic History of Europe*, vol. ii, ed. M. Postan and E. E. Rich (Cambridge, 1952), p. 219.

repayment. It was safer to lend to fellow subjects who could be dunned in the courts, while the risk was more widely spread.

Ruling out the de la Poles as the great exception, the other merchant aspirants to gentility seem to be distributed fairly evenly over the two centuries; if anything, the timing was, I believe, crescendo, and as far as the Londoners were concerned it was so unmistakably. Their transplantation to the land can be studied in Dr. Thrupp's useful appendices.[1] The increase in the number of citizen knights would not by itself signify much, for a few of the most prosperous—Henry Picard, Richard Whittington, and John Hende—were never knighted, but there is plenty of other evidence that it *was* symptomatic of the city's growing wealth. From the days of Sir Richard de la Pole and Sir John Pulteney to those of Sir Thomas Seymour, Sir Richard Gresham, and Sir Thomas Kitson, London fortunes provided more and more recruits for the landed nobility. A formidable list could be quoted, but not here. And this in spite of the fact that an unusually large number of the most successful merchants left no sons to inherit from them: Henry Picard, for instance, Richard Lyons, Sir William Walworth, Sir Nicholas Brembre, Richard Whittington, Henry Barton, Sir William Eastfield, and Sir John Plummer; while there were others like Sir John Pulteney whose issue quickly perished. Was town life so insanitary? Probably that is the answer. But some stocks emerged to flourish in country air.

It has been remarked that there were fewer citizen dynasties than in the thirteenth century, that those who prospered brought up their children to other and more gentlemanly pursuits. As far as this was true, it is doubtful whether it will support the deductions that some would base upon it; in particular the view that those who were lucky enough to make their pile rushed at once for the safety of investment in land. When this view is combined with another, for which there is greater warrant, that land was a wasting asset it comes near to making nonsense. As if any indirect explanation were necessary for an affluent merchant's desire to found a noble house! If he were able to get out quicker in the four-

[1] S. L. Thrupp, *The Merchant Class of Medieval London* (Chicago, 1948), pp. 321–87.

teenth than in earlier centuries it may be because piles had become easier to make. In any event from Gervase of Cornhill to Alderman Beckford and beyond is this not one of the most persistent features of English society?

So far we have been concerned with an upward movement, with rising rather than sinking families. Yet there can be no question that the ranks of the nobility were thinner at the top in 1400 than a century earlier and by 1500 thinner still. That this was the case not only in the higher ranges but also lower down is suggested by the fall in the number of knights, real and 'potential' (i.e. those with an adequate property qualification who evaded knighthood), which Mr. Denholm-Young has called to our attention.[1] There are a number of causes for this shrinkage, so great that the general movement upwards was never enough to fill the gaps.

Firstly, of course, extinction by natural or violent means. Here the Wars of the Roses have not deserved their textbook prominence. It is doubtful whether the rates of extinction among the nobility was higher in the half-century 1450–1500 than in any other half-century since the Conquest. A count of the number of 'peerages' that either lapsed by failure of heirs or were transmitted through the female line, arranged in fifty-year periods from 1300 to 1500, shows no great fluctuation.[2] There had after all been wars before; *and* political miscalculation ending on the scaffold or the battlefield. The rate in fact was always high. But men married young and were often fathers of sons before they were old enough for knighthood. Struck down at the beginning of their active lives, they left heirs to succeed them. Even in civil war it was not usual to slaughter children. But forfeiture or partial forfeiture made political miscalculation expensive. Even many revolutions of the wheel of fortune could not restore to some families all they lost by being on the wrong side.

Rarely did they owe their ruin to the inability of their members to manage their own affairs. One is hard put to it to collect more

[1] N. Denholm Young, 'Feudal Society in the Thirteenth Century: the Knights', *Collected Papers* (Cardiff, 1969), pp. 83–94. McFarlane's later view was that the number of lesser landowners was more stable after 1300 than this paragraph might seem to imply, see p. 268, n. 2 below, but contrast p. 151.

[2] Cf. pp. 172–6 below.

than a handful of landowners who parted with their estates in order to meet their obligations, fewer still who went under altogether for this one reason alone. Not even the crazy traitor, Thomas Fauconberge, who spent most of Richard II's reign in prison, did so much damage that a Nevill was unwilling to marry his congenital idiot of a daughter for the sake of her lands.[1] Prodigality such as that of the sixth Percy Earl of Northumberland has no parallel.[2] Long minorities often helped to repair extravagance, to pay off old debts, and to extinguish mortgages; and there were other influences at work. If any but a tiny section of the nobility foundered from an incapacity to pay its way, I have yet to see the evidence.[3] The laws by which land was inherited often worked against them. Partition between coheirs, the separation of entailed lands from those held in fee simple, were more potent causes of decline than mismanagement. For the most part, survival was what counted: the rich got richer as they got fewer.

The history of such families is very unevenly documented. Although evidence is scattered widely among the public records, much on this subject is inaccurate. It has long been known that the testimony of witnesses when a tenant-in-chief proved his age was untrustworthy; but it has not always been realized that this element of trouble-saving fiction runs through other classes of record, where the king's interests were not at stake. Even where they were, as in assessments for taxation, historians could have avoided grave error by being less credulous. Nevertheless, many private archives found their way into the government's hands and there is enough on the dorse of the Close Rolls alone to illustrate many aspects of their lives; but it can hardly be claimed for them that they allow one to see the private concerns of the nobility from within or to see them whole. This can only be done from their own records, from their title-deeds or private cartularies, their household and estate accounts, their valors and inventories, their correspondence and their wills.

Time has dealt savagely with such deposits. It began doing so at

---

[1] G.E.C. v. 276–80, 281–2.

[2] Bean, *Estates of the Percy Family 1416–1537*, pp. 144–57.

[3] Cf. p. 48 below.

once. We have, for example, two great rolls of accounts belonging to Henry Lacy, Earl of Lincoln, who died in 1311: they are two isolated survivals from a great series, but we happen to know that they were already the only survivals in 1322.[1] Few families were immune from the results of civil commotion, even when they themselves were not destroyed along with their records. For some of the greatest, there is virtually nothing left. The fate that has wiped out or scattered the contents of so many castle muniment-rooms has not been more sparing of their humbler neighbours.

What can still be found, fragmentary, often illegible from neglect, and difficult to interpret, is perhaps enough, more, certainly, than at first seemed likely. More, also, than could be easily listed here. In any case there is only time now for the briefest of surveys. Apart from John of Gaunt, whose already depleted archives came into the possession of the Crown in 1399, the land-owner whose papers have most successfully defied oblivion—though they have come to rest in several different collections—is Edward Stafford, third and last Duke of Buckingham.[2] The Staffords as a whole are well covered; so are the Mowbray Dukes of Norfolk, the Lancastrian Thomas, Duke of Clarence, and, more patchily, the descendants of Edmund Langley, Duke of York; among earls, the Veres of Oxford, the Beauchamps of Warwick, and the Courtenays of Devon; and among lesser barons Ralph, Lord Cromwell, and the Bourchiers. Sir John Fastolf, if only because so much more of his estate correspondence has been preserved, must stand at the head of the commoners, followed by the Din-hams of Hartland, the Ferrerses of Chartley, and the Staffords of Grafton.[3] Lack of time has prevented me from so far examining

[1] J. F. Baldwin, 'The Household Administration of Henry Lacy and Thomas of Lancaster', *E.H.R.* 42 (1927), 195.

[2] McFarlane made use of documents relating to Duke Edward in the collections at the Public Record Office, the British Museum, Berkeley Castle, Westminster Abbey, Longleat, and the Staffordshire Record Office (Stafford).

[3] McFarlane made use of documents and transcripts relating to the families listed above in the following collections: those listed in n. 2 immediately above, the Northamptonshire Record Office and the Bodleian Library (Stafford); British Museum, College of Arms, Berkeley Castle, Norwich Public Library (Mowbray); Westminster Abbey (Clarence); British Museum, Longleat, Westminster Abbey, Public Record Office (descendants of Edmund of Langley); British Museum, Essex

the accounts of the Willoughbys of Wollaton; and there are doubtless others which I have overlooked.

Evidence derived from such sources as these cannot readily be made palatable *viva voce*. In planning these lectures, my concern has been to distil my impressions, to generalize broadly, drawing upon the facts as sparingly as possible and only by way of illustration.

Record Office, Longleat (Vere); British Museum, Public Record Office, Longleat, Warwick Castle, Shakespeare's Birthplace (Coughton MSS.), Throckmorton MSS. (Coughton Place), Warwick Corporation (Beauchamp); British Museum, Westminster Abbey, Public Record Office, Wardour Castle (Courtenay); Public Record Office, Magdalen College, Oxford, Penshurst (Cromwell); Longleat (Bourchier); British Museum, Magdalen College, Oxford (Fastolf); Wardour Castle (Dinham); Longleat, Westminster Abbey (Ferrers); British Museum (Stafford of Grafton). (The Arundell of Wardour MSS. are no longer at Wardour Castle, but are in the possession of Mr. R. J. R. Arundell, Hook Manor, Donhead St. Andrew, Wilts.)

II. THE NOBILITY AND WAR

THE French wars of Edward I and his successors, though they may still, for all I know, be used to incite patriotism in the nursery, have rarely in modern times escaped heavy condemnation by those who write history for adults. Glorious they may have been, runs the common indictment, but the glory was barren. The 'foolish policy and selfish designs' of Edward III ended in 'economic exhaustion'.[1] France was ruined and devastated, but not for England's benefit. For she too had been 'bled white' by 1340; and even when her king returned in triumph after Crécy and Calais in 1347 he was 'full of glory, but almost empty-handed'.[2] 'Futile and expensive' *chevauchées* succeed one another monotonously in the years after 1369, while from 1372 until 1387 the English fleets even 'lost control of the Channel'.[3] In the general writing-down of this age of 'pseudo-chivalry', Henry V's union of the crowns fares hardly better. He left his brother Bedford a 'vain and hopeless task' as well as an England on the edge of bankruptcy.[4]

I am reminded of an incident described by the Oxfordshire chronicler, Geoffrey le Baker of Swinbrook.[5] It was in October 1338 and at Southampton, when the town had been surprised and occupied one Sunday morning during Mass by a fleet of French privateers. Among these latter was a young knight, the King of Sicily's son, and when next day the townsmen, with the help of their country neighbours, quickly turned the tables on the invaders, he was clubbed to the ground by a rustic. Prostrate, he cried for quarter: 'Rancon' (i.e. 'ransom'). But, 'Yes, I know you're a Francon', the man replied and killed him; for, says Baker, 'he did not understand the other's lingo (*idioma*), nor had he been taught to hold gentlemen prisoners for their ransom'. With few

[1] W. Stubbs, *Constitutional History*, vol. ii (4th edn., 1906), p. 394; *Finance and Trade under Edward III*, ed. G. Unwin (reprint, 1962), p. xiii.
[2] E. Perroy, *The Hundred Years War* (transl. W. B. Wells 1951), pp. 112, 120.
[3] A. Steel, *Richard II* (Cambridge, 1941), p. 19.
[4] Perroy, *Hundred Years War*, p. 258.
[5] *Chronicon*, ed. E. Maunde Thompson (Oxford, 1889), pp. 62–3.

exceptions historians seem to have shared his ignorance; they have failed to grasp the first essential point of medieval warfare; its *idioma* has quite escaped them, while they have clung obstinately to their own. Yet it was not for lack of evidence.

Take for example an agreement made on 12 July 1421 by two English esquires, Nicholas Molyneux and John Winter, in the church of St. Martin at Harfleur.[1] Wishing to augment the love and fraternity already growing between them, they engaged themselves to become sworn brothers-in-arms, 'loyal one to the other without any dissimulation or fraud'. They then set out what this was to mean in detail. If either were taken prisoner by the king's enemies—'which God forbid'—the other was bound to secure his liberation, provided that the ransom did not exceed £1,000; if it did then the free brother-in-arms was to become a hostage for eight or nine months in order to allow the prisoner to go home to raise the larger sum. These arrangements were to be made at the common expense of the two parties. Should both be taken captive at the same time one was to remain as hostage, while the other went to procure the money for both. Capture was the disaster they feared, but they also dreamed of fortune. All the gains of war that each could spare were to be pooled and sent home to await their return in a coffer deposited in St. Thomas Acon's church, London. Whichever reached England first was to invest their accumulated capital in heritages as wisely as he could to their joint profit. When they married and came to live on this side of the Channel, their property was to be divided equally. If only one survived he was to have all, allowing a sixth part for her life to the dead man's widow, if there were one; but he was to 'nourish' his comrade's children, pay for their schooling, and give them a start in life by dividing among them a rent (for their lives only) of £20 a year. If both parties to the bargain died without issue, all was to be sold to endow masses for their two souls and those of their parents.

Brotherhood-in-arms, as defined in this agreement, was thus a business partnership, an insurance against the greatest financial

---

[1] K. B. McFarlane, 'A Business Partnership in War and Administration, 1421–45', *E.H.R.* 78 (1963), 290–308.

misfortune that could befall a soldier—to be taken alive—and a gamble on survivorship, a kind of rudimentary tontine.[1] It reveals very clearly—and that is why I have cited it at some length—an attitude towards war as a speculative, but at best hugely profitable trade that was shared by all who joined the mercenary armies of Edward III and Henry V—as their contracts of service show. These retainers made no pretence of fighting for love of king or lord, still less for England or for glory, but for gain; and since they staked their lives it is evident that they thought the prizes worthy of their strife. It is time that the degree of their success or failure was measured by the standard they themselves applied. The wars with the French are usually judged as national conflicts and nothing more. So since they resulted in a defeat for 'England', in territorial losses for her kings and in a heavy internal debt, their disastrous outcome is taken as proved. The verdict, if right, has been arrived at on the basis of only part of the evidence. It is by no means clear to me that all the king's subjects did badly out of war, even at its least successful, even in defeat; nor that on balance the national wealth was diminished. There is a case, and it seems to me a strong case, for thinking that while 'England' was beaten the English were enriched.

The two esquires certainly were. Their fraternal alliance prospered under the captaincy of Sir John Fastolf, grand master of the Regent Bedford's household. I cannot tell you if it was ever necessary to invoke those clauses of their agreement concerning ransoms. But the brothers-in-arms can be traced as late as 1436, when, remember, the war was no longer going particularly well for Henry VI, remitting money home and using it for the joint purchase of several manors and other properties in what is now south London; their most famous and perhaps most valuable acquisition was the Boar's Head tavern in Southwark, which was sold to Fastolf for £214 after Winter's death. This occurred in 1445; his will shows that the compact made nearly a quarter of a century before at Harfleur was still being honoured. Of the two Nicholas Molyneux had the longer and more distinguished career in

---

[1] For brotherhood-in-arms in general, see M. H. Keen, 'Brotherhood in Arms', *History*, 47 (1962), 1–17.

France. For twelve years at least before 1447 he was Master of the king's Chamber of Accounts at Rouen and then, described as a royal councillor and—wrongly—as a knight, he presided over a commission to arrange for the surrender of Maine. Henry VI's French possessions might be lost and his Exchequer emptied, but Nicholas Molyneux was still able to salvage a competency for himself. We last hear of him in 1456 or thereabouts being addressed as 'right trusty brother' by no less a career soldier than his old employer John Fastolf. By 1461 he was dead.

Early Tudor tradition, preserved for us in the *Itinerary* of John Leyland, bears out the impression that those who did well out of the war were numerous and widely spread. Visiting Beverstone in Gloucestershire, Leyland writes: 'Thomas, Lorde Barkeley, as old Syr William Barkeley . . . told me, was taken prisoner in Fraunce, and after recovering his losses with Frenche prisoners and at the Batail of Poyters, buildid after the castell of Beverstane thoroughly, a pile at that tyme very preaty.'[1] Nor are the examples he mentions all or mostly from the fourteenth century. Indeed in describing Bolton castle in Wensleydale, finished in Richard II's reign at a cost of £12,000, he does not so much as refer to the fact that its builder was one of the most notable captains of his generation, Richard Scrope.[2] It is rather to the castles

---

[1] *The Itinerary of John Leland*, ed. L. Toulmin Smith (reprint, 1964), iv. 133. Lord Berkeley's belief that his family had gained from the war may well have been justified. But the details of Leyland's story are suspect. There is no reliable evidence that Thomas, Lord Berkeley (d. 1361) was captured. Froissart, in the commonest version of his *Chronicles*, does indeed say that he was captured at Poitiers (ed. Luce, v. 49–51) and so has misled Dugdale (*Baronage*, i. 358) and others including, it may be, old Sir William Berkeley. A surviving ransom-agreement (I. H. Jeayes, *Catalogue of the Charters and Muniments . . . at Berkeley Castle* (Bristol, 1892), pp. 167–70) makes it practically certain, however, that Baker (ed. Thompson, pp. 149–50) was right in stating that it was not Thomas, but his son and heir Maurice, who was captured at Poitiers. This loss makes it *prima facie* implausible that the Berkeleys gained from this particular battle, though it is not impossible that Maurice made prisoners before he was himself captured and it may be that, as Hewitt (*The Black Prince's Expedition*, p. 157) suggests, Berkeley made money by dealing in Poitiers prisoners captured by others. Such evidence as is in print on the rebuilding of Beverstone suggests that it was done in 1348–9 (J. Smyth, *Lives of the Berkeley's*, ed. J. Maclean (2 vols., Gloucester, 1883), i. 309).

[2] *Itinerary of John Leland*, i. 79; iv. 27; v. 134, 139–40; cf. L. F. Salzman, *Building in England* (revised edn., Oxford, 1967), pp. 454–6.

and houses of the Lancastrian period, nearest to his own time, that Leyland freely ascribes an origin in the spoils of war. 'Syr William Bowes that was in Fraunce with the Duke of Bedeford did build *a fundamentis* the manor-place of Stretlam in the Bisshoprik of Dirham';[1] 'There is a commune saying that one of the Hungrefords buildid this part of the castelle (of Farleigh in Somerset) by the praye (i.e. the ransom) of the duke of Orleaunce',[2] taken with his peers at Agincourt; the immense and luxurious palace of the Botillers at Sudeley, Gloucestershire, came 'ex spoliis nobilium bello Gallico captorum';[3] Stourton in Wiltshire, with its two great courts, the front of the inner court 'magnificent, and high embatelid castelle lyke' was also built 'ex spoliis Gallorum'.[4] Sir Rowland Lenthall took prisoners under Henry V and spent the proceeds on Hampton Court near Monmouth;[5] while Ampthill, Bedfordshire, was the work of 'a man of greate fame in owtewarde warres' ... 'of such spoiles, as it is saide that he wanne in Fraunce.'[6] Was Leyland deceived by baseless fictions or did many, like eighteenth-century nabobs, return from Henry VI's French possessions laden with plunder? And if in Henry VI's time why not still more in his father's and in that of Edward III? John Winter and Nicholas Molyneux were minnows; were there any sharks? On the number of war profiteers and on the scale of their gains the interpretation of a whole phase of English social history may depend.

A soldier had then three fairly distinct sources of profit: his pay, his prisoners, and what in the indentures were lumped together under the heading: gains of war. The first, his pay, seems to have been the least important, but it must not therefore be regarded as trivial. The wages of war offered by the king, either directly or through the agency of the various captains, were so far stereotyped that in most indentures of service it was enough to define them as 'usual'. Graded according to rank and military function from a mark a day for a duke to a shilling a day for a man-at-arms below the estate of knight, these accustomed rates might on occasion be multiplied by one and a half or even doubled. Thus in 1370 Sir

---

[1] *Itinerary of John Leland* ii. 9.   [2] Ibid. i. 138.   [3] Ibid. v. 221.
[4] Ibid. 106, 223.   [5] Ibid. ii. 72.   [6] Ibid. v. 8; i. 102.

Robert Knollys, though only a banneret, was offered wages at 8*s.*
a day or £146 a year. Captains of retinues normally received
twice as much as others of their degree who served under them. It
was customary also to pay a 'regard' or extra reward at the rate
of 100 marks for every thirty men-at-arms for each quarter of a
year's service; this too was often increased to £100 for a specially
favoured captain, and almost as often doubled.[1] No one could
grow rich on such pay alone. Yet, when it was forthcoming, it
was more than enough to cover the reasonable expenses of a
soldier; and if, as was generally the case, he lived as far as possible
off the enemy's country—one of the advantages of fighting
abroad—it could be a useful supplement to other sources of profit.

However modest the amounts received by individuals may
appear, the payment of a lordly retinue of some hundreds of
men-at-arms and archers involved entrusting their captains with
enormous sums. Take, for example, the case of Lancaster's expeditionary force which landed at Calais towards the end of July 1373.[2]
Of the 5,000 to 6,000 troops under the duke's command, only 780
men-at-arms and 800 mounted archers were of his own retinue.
Service was for a year and in Lancaster's indenture, sealed on
1 March 1373, wages were fixed at the usual rate and regard at
double, a quarter payable in advance. Between the date of the
indenture and August, when the army started on its long march,
Lancaster drew from William Airmyn, the royal clerk who acted
as paymaster, just short of £19,000.[3] Edward, Lord Despenser,
the Earls of Warwick and Stafford, and others bringing their own
retinues were dealt with proportionately; and it was agreed that
the troops should be 'refreshed' at the end of half the year by a
new advance to the duke's receiver of £12,000.[4] To send another

[1] A. E. Prince, 'The Indenture System under Edward III', *Historical Essays in
Honour of James Tait*, ed. J. G. Edwards, V. H. Galbraith, E. F. Jacob (Manchester,
1933), pp. 283-98, esp. pp. 291-4.

[2] J. W. Sherborne, 'Indentured Retinues and English Expeditions to France',
E.H.R. 79 (1964), 727-30.

[3] B.M. Add. MS. 37494 (William Ayremyn's counter-roll for wars 1 Dec.
1372-31 Jan. 1374); prests on 5 Mar., 23 Mar., 9 May, 20 June, 16 July, 16 Aug.,
totalling £18,948. 7*s.* 2½*d.*

[4] For the indentures in which these conditions are specified see p. 727 of Mr.
Sherborne's paper, n. 3.

Earl of Stafford, Ralph, with 143 men-at-arms and 234 archers to Aquitaine as Lieutenant there for less than eight months in 1352 cost Edward III a little over £6,100, of which about £4,400 represented wages and regard; the balance was needed for victuals and shipping. The earl was granted half the money in advance and the rest in July 1353 when he tendered his account.[1] Between Christmas 1488 and Easter 1491 Henry VII's captains in Brittany in precisely the same way received over £108,000.[2]

Innumerable such accounts have been preserved. Reading them, one can hardly be surprised that the duty of handling and answering for these large sums of money should have led some, if not 'most, great lords to create a separate department of their private administration to cope with their military finance. Thus, as soon as Sir Richard Nevill, later Earl of Salisbury and father of the 'kingmaker', came of age in 1421 he retained one Thomas Stockdale to be of his and his mother's council for life. For nineteen years thereafter it was to be Stockdale's job to act as Nevill's attorney in the royal Exchequer and there 'to pursue and receive payments and assignments of wages, fees and regards' on his behalf;[3] from 1420 until 1435 Sir Richard's employment as Warden of the West March against the Scots must have given his servant plenty to do.[4] On the other hand, his brother-in-law, John Mowbray, Earl Marshal and soon to be restored to his father's dukedom of Norfolk, seems to have entrusted his ordinary receiver-general, at any rate in the year 1422–3, with the financing of the retinue he took to France.[5] (If others had followed his example, the historian's troubles would be less. This practice of assigning responsibility for each branch of a magnate's complex economy to a different official makes an over-all survey of his financial position nearly impossible. For it is almost too much to

---

[1] Staffordshire R.O. D (W) 1721/1/1 (Great Cartulary), f. 368, 368ᵛ (copy of the earl's account at the Exchequer); P.R.O. E 101/26/25 (his indenture, a transcript of which is in Bodleian Library, Dugdale MS. 2, p. 252; for details see Dugdale, *Baronage* i. 160–1).

[2] Westminster Abbey Muniment 12240. (Account of the costs and expenses incurred on the king's behalf before Easter 1491 in connection with the agreement between the king and the Duchess of Brittany.)

[3] T. Madox, *Formulare Anglicanum* (1702), p. 144.

[4] G.E.C. xi. 396.   [5] B.M. Add. Roll 17209.

hope that in any given year all the accounts of all the branches have been preserved together.)

How different from Mowbray's was the policy of Thomas of Woodstock, Duke of Gloucester. For he employed a separate 'treasurer of wars', whose accounts for some four and a half months in the summer of 1392 raise some interesting problems.[1] The duke was appointed the king's Lieutenant in Ireland on 21 April and during the next three weeks Edmund Broxbourne esquire, his treasurer of wars, obtained 9,500 marks from the tellers of the Exchequer. By 15 June 409 soldiers, including fourteen knights, had been retained for a year and paid some £1,340 for their first quarter's service. Further small amounts—less than £300 in all—went on artillery and other necessary expenses of the voyage, and £200 more on silver plate for the duke's own use in Ireland. This leaves £4,500 unaccounted for. It had in fact all been spent on a variety of things irrelevant to the expedition; on buying a manor, for example, in paying the duke's debts and the expenses of his household, not to mention those of his duchess. Yet by 23 July Richard II had changed his mind and cancelled Gloucester's appointment.[2] There is no evidence that the Exchequer recovered any of its money.

But that is not the only noteworthy feature of this affair. Broxbourne's account was a private one, intended only for his master's use. It encourages a suspicion that the financial statements tendered by captains for audit at the Exchequer may not always have contained the whole truth. Their very tidiness is itself a ground for mistrust. It is possible that there was nothing improper in John of Gaunt's ability to transfer thousands of pounds received for the wages of his troops to objects as far removed from war as Gloucester's purchase of a manor; but such operations must raise doubts. At least one of those who fought under him suffered from a guilty conscience. For it was only on his deathbed in 1390 that an esquire named Richard Fotheringay left orders to his executors to distribute among those who had been retained with him on

[1] B.M. Add. MS. 40859A.
[2] G.E.C. v. 724, cf. J. F. Baldwin, *The King's Council* (Oxford, 1913), pp. 500, 503.

Lancaster's Spanish voyage the 200 marks of which 'from too great cupidity' he had defrauded them; his other legacies show that he had plenty more to leave.[1]

On the other hand, retainers may sometimes have been too ready to accuse their captains of peculation. A case in point comes from another soldier's testament: that of Sir Andrew Ogard, a noble Dane who entered Henry VI's service, prospered, was naturalized, and ended by representing Norfolk in the House of Commons. He died in 1454; and his testament contains a long and solemn protestation from which I can only quote these few words: 'I declare in discharge of my conscience that such money as I have had and received for them (his garrison at Caen) of the king and his officers, I have duly and truly contented and paid.' This may be allowed to ring true; but if Sir Andrew's men, as he says, 'came out of Normandy in great necessity as starving beggars', it is only fair to record that he had done very well for himself.[2]

One reason why Henry V and the Duke of Bedford developed an extraordinarily elaborate system of 'muster and review' was the captains' tendency to claim pay for absentees and even for non-existent soldiers.[3] A thorough and periodic check was to be kept upon retinues. How many dead souls, one vainly wonders were on the books of their fourteenth-century predecessors, undetected when control was lax? Yet had there been no disease, the cure would have been unnecessary. All that can be safely asserted is that if wages made any soldier's fortune, it was because it was possible for the captains, illegally, to help themselves. There is a little evidence that some did.

The most considerable source of profit for the fighting man was probably the ransom money he extorted from his prisoners. Here there doesn't seem to have been any generally accepted tariff. Chivalrous theory favoured moderation; a ransom should not be so great as to disinherit the captive's wife, children, family, or friends; 'for justice demands that they should have the wherewithal

---

[1] *Collectanea Topographia et Genealogica*, ed. J. C. Nichols, vol. iii (1836), p. 101; Prerogative Court of Canterbury, Reg. Rous f. 54 (called 53).

[2] Prerog. Court of Cant., Reg. Stokton, ff. 13ᵛ–14.

[3] R. A. Newhall, *Muster and Review* (Cambridge, Mass., 1940).

to live after the ransom has been paid.'[1] Chivalrous practice was less lenient. The matter was one for individual bargaining in which the captor had the whiphand; he even made his prisoner pay for his keep. In writing on 13 May 1374 to excuse himself to his wife for having consented to pay £2,000, Sir John Bourchier made great play with the argument that ill health was endangering his life when he agreed.[2]

The proportions in which the ransom money was divided between the actual captor and his military superiors varied according to the terms of their indenture.[3] It was usual for the king to reserve for his own disposal a captured commander of the opposing army and any prince of the French blood royal who fell into his soldiers' hands, though he promised something handsome to the men who actually made them prisoner. A favourite lieutenant might be granted all the ransoms he could gain, but as a rule the king asked for a third or a quarter of the profits of his indentured captains. The latter in their sub-contracts normally claimed a third of their men's winnings and a third of such thirds as the men in their turn exacted from their humbler followers. But like the king, the greater chieftains were wont to reserve certain distinguished classes of prisoners for themselves—in return for a liberal gratuity. It was on this ground and out of no high-handed disregard for the rights of his two esquires that the Black Prince could obtain possession of the Count of Denia, taken at Najera.[4] Should one of his own servants be put to ransom, the king or the captain had a moral, rather than a contractual, duty to help him recover his freedom. There is plenty of evidence that it was an obligation both frequently and generously fulfilled.

The workings of this somewhat complicated system can be

[1] *The Tree of Battles of Honoré Bonet*, trans. and ed. G. W. Coopland (Liverpool, 1949), pp. 152–3.   [2] Muniments of the Marquess of Bath, Longleat, 396.
[3] Cf. D. Hay, 'The Division of the Spoils of War in Fifteenth Century England', *T.R.H.S.*, 4th ser., 4 (1954), 91–109; M. H. Keen, *The Laws of War in the Late Middle Ages* (1965), esp. pp. 137–85; H. J. Hewitt, *The Black Prince's Expedition, 1355–7* (Manchester, 1958), pp. 152–60.
[4] E. Perroy, 'Gras profits et rançons pendant la Guerre de Cent Ans: L'Affaire du Comte de Denia', *Mélanges . . . Louis Halphen* (Paris, 1951), pp. 573–80; A. Rogers, 'Hoton versus Shakell', *Nottingham Medieval Studies*, 6 (1962), 74–108, 7 (1963), 53–78.

traced in many surviving documents. One group that is perhaps more than usually revealing concerns the expenditure incurred by Lady Margaret Hungerford on behalf of her son and heir, Robert, Lord Moleyns, wounded and taken prisoner in Gascony in July 1453.[1] The ransom demanded and paid was £6,000, but this already considerable figure was swollen to more than £9,800 by a number of extras. These included the loss (some £1,100) consequent upon borrowing the money, a charge of 10 per cent made by the merchants who negotiated the exchange, and the cost of supplying the prisoner and his attendants with meat, drink, and apparel until their enlargement in 1459.[2] These heavy outgoings were a source of embarrassment to the Hungerford family for years. When Margaret's husband Robert, Lord Hungerford, died in 1459 he mentioned in his will that in order to raise £2,000 of the ransom money, 'borrowed of divers gentlemen and merchants', he had had to put most of his lands in feoffment on his creditors' behalf.[3] Margaret's own will drawn up in 1476, about eighteen months before her death, sets out in illuminating detail why 'myne heires have none occasion to grudge for that I leve not to theyme so grete enheritaunce as I myght and would have done, if fortune had not been so sore against me'.[4] Her feoffees were ordered to discharge any debts still owing for her son's ransom, although at that time the prisoner on whose account all these efforts were being made had been executed a dozen years ago. That was, indeed, her final misfortune, Moleyns's attaint and forfeiture; it is to it rather than to the battle of Castillon that she referred when she wrote that her debts and alienations were 'not done by foly, nor bycause of any excesse or undiscrete liberalite, but oonly I haue been arted and caused by necessite of fortune, and mysaventure, that hath happend in this seasons of trobill

---

[1] For these documents see G.E.C. vi. 618–19 and Appendix B, pp. 126–8 below.

[2] These expenses occur among those listed in a schedule appended to Margaret Hungerford's will, printed by R. Colt Hoare, *Modern Wiltshire. Heytesbury Hundred* (1824), pp. 100–2 and abstracted by Dugdale, *Baronage* ii. 209–10.

[3] *Somerset Medieval Wills (1383–1500)*, ed. F. W. Weaver (Somerset Rec. Soc. xvi, 1901), pp. 186–93, esp. 191–3.

[4] Colt Hoare, *Heytesbury Hundred*, p. 99; *Testamenta Vetusta*, ed. N. H. Nicolas (2 vols., 1826), i. 321 and see n. 2 above.

tyme late paste'. She had been hard put to it to keep a hold on her own and her husband's estates following the political revolution of 1461; for those of Hungerford alone she had been obliged to pay a composition of £2,155.[1] But there can be no doubt that Moleyns's capture began her troubles.[2]

A few other examples may be cited. In 1340 Sir Walter Mauny after a successful raid on the Low Countries sold his prisoners to Edward III for £8,000.[3] One of the earliest important captures in France was made at Caen in July 1346: the Count of Eu and the hereditary chamberlain of Normandy, the former by Sir Thomas Holland, the latter by one of the Black Prince's bachelors.[4] Next year Holland sold his count to the king for 20,000 marks.[5] In January 1347 John Coupland who had with his own hand taken David Bruce, King of Scots, was made a banneret and endowed with £500 a year in tail—the equivalent of something like £10,000.[6] Poitiers was naturally the scene of a rich harvest for all ranks: 'you might see many an archer, many a knight, many an esquire', wrote an eyewitness, 'running in every direction to take prisoners'.[7] Thomas Beauchamp, Earl of Warwick, ransomed the Archbishop of Sens, rounded up on that crowded field, for £8,000.[8] Warwick, indeed, seems to have had most luck with the non-combatants, since he also won three-quarters of another prelate, Le Mans, the actual captor of whom, an esquire named Robert Clinton, disposed of his share to the king for £1,000.[9] Edward also bought three of the Black Prince's own prisoners at Poitiers for £20,000.[10] To cut what could easily become a tedious

---

[1] *Heytesbury Hundred*, 101; some of this expenditure may have been incidental expenses rather than part of the composition itself.

[2] In his 1965 lectures McFarlane gave a longer account of the effect of war on the fortunes of the Hungerford family. The additional material is printed in Appendix B, pp. 126–8 below.

[3] *Foedera*, v. 183.

[4] *Adae Murimuth Continuatio Chronicarum*, ed. E. Maunde Thompson (R.S., 1889), p. 203.

[5] *C.P.R. 1345–8*, pp. 337, 538–9, 550; *Foedera*, v. 568.

[6] *A History of Northumberland* (15 vols., 1893–1940), xi. 219 (by K. H. Vickers).

[7] *The Chandos Herald's Life of the Black Prince*, ed. M. K. Pope and E. C. Lodge (Oxford, 1910), ll. 1395–7.　　　　　　　　　　　　　　　[8] *Foedera*, vi. 359.

[9] *Foedera* (Record edn.), ii. ii. 399; *C.P.R. 1358–61*, p. 167; ibid. *1361–4*, p. 323.

[10] *C.P.R. 1358–61*, p. 300.

list short, let me note four famous professional soldiers with their ways to make in battle who drew splendid prizes in this game of ransoms: in 1348 it was agreed that Sir Thomas Dagworth should receive nearly £5,000 for Charles of Blois;[1] that was the sum Jean de Laval in 1365 agreed to pay Sir Mayhew Gurney for his freedom;[2] while from the period after 1369, when the fortunes of war were less obviously in the English favour, we find, for example, Ralph Bassett of Drayton receiving £2,000 for a captive in 1375[3] and John Harleston and Philip la Vache receiving £2,500 in 1376 for their share in two others.[4] The victories of Henry V and Bedford yielded them and their retinues similar fruit.

But Englishmen, like Robert Moleyns, were also taken prisoner. Since theirs was the defeated side, it might be thought that the contest ended to their disadvantage—or, at best, all square. There is no hope that we shall ever have anything like complete figures, but on the evidence available I do not believe this to be true. Down to 1369 the balance of advantage was overwhelmingly in favour of the English; and even after that date it does not seem to have turned at all decisively against them. From 1412 to the spring of 1429, with the single exception of Baugé, a run of victories gave them an immense lead which even the later disasters—and those in the field were after all few—could not catch up. In any event, the conditional surrenders with which the war in the north ended deprived the French of ransoms; on the contrary it was the English who were being bribed to go away; another advantage of fighting your wars abroad. It was a repetition, but on a grander scale, of what had happened at Saint-Sauveur in 1375 when the garrison was offered over £9,000 to march out.[5] The aggressor in medieval warfare, even when finally expelled from his conquests, was not always the loser. An indication of England's probable advantage on balance in the matter of ransoms can be derived from comparing the number of princes, dukes, and earls captured by each side. The English bag was far the larger; it

[1] *Foedera* (Record edn.), iii. i. 170.
[2] D. Gurney, *Supplement to the Record of the House of Gournay* (1858), p. 1071.
[3] *Foedera*, vii. 81–2. [4] Ibid. 103, 121.
[5] C. C. Bayley, 'The Campaign of 1375 and the Good Parliament', *E.H.R.* 55 1940), 376, 382–3.

included three kings, one of France and two of Scots, as well as many nobles of the bloods royal; on the other hand, of the King of England's near kinsmen only the Beaufort brothers, taken when their stepfather Clarence was slain for his rashness in 1421, fell into French hands, and by comparison very few earls. Country for country the advantage in prisoners was overwhelmingly in favour of the invaders, whose numbers were fewer and who did not scruple to take and hold to ransom any civilians they could lay their hands on. When they *were* defeated in the field, in the naval battle off La Rochelle in 1372, at Baugé in 1421, Patay in 1429, and Castillon in 1453, their numbers were small. In all the great pitched battles of the war in which the prisoners included most of the defeated they were the victors. The Earl of Pembroke, taken at La Rochelle, died in the enemy's hands before a penny of his ransom of £20,000 had been paid.[1] Most of the nobles who fought at Baugé were killed outright. John Holland, Earl of Huntingdon, who survived, had to produce 20,000 marks, the precise sum his ancester Sir Thomas Holland had received for the Count of Eu, taken by him at Caen in 1346. He had himself been at Agincourt and through Henry V's conquest of Normandy. For his services he received the county of Ivry from the Regent Bedford.[2] An inventory of his goods, made at the time of his death as Duke of Exeter in 1447 with its scores of cups made of fine gold, its beds and tapestries, does not encourage the view that his finances were crippled by his one disaster.[3] That an English magnate was able to raise 20,000 marks and yet not be noticeably poorer is itself a fact worth underlining; part of the explanation is that in captive's ransoms, as in much else, the balance of payments was highly favourable to the English.

Prisoners were only the most valuable of 'the advantages of war'. A soldier was justified in seizing anything he could. The Black Prince, that paragon of chivalry, had no scruple in taking for himself the French king's jewels found in his camp after

---

[1] G.E.C. x. 393; *Anonimalle Chronicle*, ed. V. H. Galbraith (Manchester, 1927), p. 71.

[2] G.E.C. v. 206, n. *h*.

[3] Westminster Abbey Mun. 6643 (this document is incomplete).

Poitiers; he used some of them later as securities for borrowed money.[1] Criticism of English generalship often misses its mark from not taking the great plundering *chevauchées* as seriously as did those who led and profited by them. I know of no document more revealing of the spirit in which the war was fought than a letter which the great Earl of Salisbury wrote to Henry V on 21 June 1421:[2]

> And liketh your Hinesse to wite that, the Saterday afore the Date of this, I, your humble Liege Man, com hom from a Journe, woch I hadde mad into Aungow and Mayne, where as I hadd Assemblid with me gret Part of the Capteines of your Lond; And Blessed bee God wee spedde right well; for your Peple is gretly Refreshed with this Rood; For as they seien in commune, they woueir neure more in no such Roode. And we browghten Hom the fareste and gretteste Prey of Bestes, as alle tho seiden that saw hem, that euer they saw.

Letters from the captains of Edward III's armies, preserved in Avesbury's chronicle, tell the same exultant story of organized and highly successful pillage.[3] Booty was one of the chief military objectives, and no one, peasant or townsman, clerk or knight, was immune from loss at the hands of enemy raiders; civilians were as fair game as combatants. It is not easy to calculate, even roughly, what these 'gains of war' amounted to. But we have one man's estimate of his own from a single battle: Sir John Fastolf noted that he had made 20,000 marks at Verneuil in 1424—the sort of profit that must have made up for a good deal of arrears in his wages bill.[4] Clearly the plunder of France was no small matter; and equally clearly the English got far more than they gave. Fighting most of the time on alien soil, they could and did strip it of everything movable in the line of march. It was their good fortune that the nobility of France went on campaign laden with

---

[1] *Register of Edward the Black Prince* (4 vols., 1930–43), iv. 302, 333.

[2] *Foedera*, x. 131.

[3] *De Gestis . . . Edwardi Tertii*, ed. E. Maunde Thompson (R.S., 1889), pp. 372–6, 388–90, 416–17, 439–49. (For a general account of plunder in Edward III's wars, see H. J. Hewitt, *The Organisation of War under Edward III* (Manchester, 1966), esp. pp. 104–10.)

[4] K. B. McFarlane, 'The Investment of Sir John Fastolf's Profits of War', *T.R.H.S.* 5th ser., 7 (1957), 95, and n. 2.

jewels and gold plate. But when these did not offer, many an English yeomen was content to despoil a Norman peasant of his hack, not to mention his purse.

Fortresses and towns captured, fell, by the terms of most indentures, to the king's share. But if they were to be held, they had to be garrisoned. To be made captain of Calais or Brest or any of the innumerable strongholds of the *pays de conquête* was to be given a source of income that asked to be exploited. The indenture sealed between Richard II's government and Sir William Windsor on 20 December 1382 by which Alice Perrers's husband obtained the keeping of the castle and town of Cherbourg may do as an example.[1] He was to have all ransoms and other gains of war by land and sea as well as £4,000 a year; the king was to provide him with the necessary shipping, artillery, masons, and a thousand marks' worth of victuals. Windsor seems to have done his service by deputy: so too did William, Lord Latimer, his as Captain of Becherel, by which he was accused in the Good Parliament of making an illegal profit of £83,000.[2] No doubt the amount was exaggerated, but the Commons were at least not ill informed about the sale of Saint-Sauveur with which the charge was linked. The thirty years following Henry V's conquest of north-west France saw the largest number of such captaincies at the disposal of the English leaders. There was hardly a knight, or indeed an esquire, of Henry V's army that was not given one or more of these offices of responsibility *and* profit under his son. Not mere towns or castles but whole provinces of France were committed to their rule. It was something to be Lieutenant of Normandy or Governor of Maine and Anjou. The list of preferments, including both of these, enjoyed by Sir John Fastolf between 1413 when he became deputy constable of the castle and town of Bordeaux and his final return home

[1] Bodleian Library, Dugdale MS. 2, p. 258.

[2] *Rot. Parl.* ii. 324–5; Bayley, 'The Campaign of 1375 and the Good Parliament', 372, n. 4. For the exploitation of Brittany by English captains see M. C. E. Jones, *Ducal Brittany 1364–1399* (Oxford, 1970), esp. pp. 161–9 and for the exploitation of occupied territories in general, K. A. Fowler, *The Age of Plantagenet and Valois* (1967), pp. 165–72 and 'Les finances et la discipline dans les armées anglaises en France an XIVe siecle', *Actes des Colloque International de Cocherel, Les Cahiers Vernonnais*, iv (1964), 56–74.

in 1440, after eighteen years of being Henry VI's councillor in France (at an annual fee of £110 sterling), amounts to at least twenty, several of which he held for long stretches of time in plurality.[1] If the expression 'bled white' was at any time accurate, it best describes the state of the conquered provinces of France under the English garrisons.

Henry V's conquest of France was indeed very like the Norman conquest of England. In both cases the more important landowners were expropriated and their estates divided up among the conqueror's lieutenants. One conquest, it is true, lasted a great deal longer than the other, but all the same for a quarter of a century the English captains collected the revenues, still valuable though depleted by war, of scores of French fiefs from great duchies like Anjou and Touraine down to baronies and seigneuries all over the *pays de conquête*. In 1418 and 1419 Henry V granted six counties in Normandy to his principal captains and his example was followed, almost indiscriminately, by the Regent Bedford. Nor did the latter stint himself; at one time he possessed in tail male the duchies of Alençon and Anjou, the counties of Maine, Mortain, Harcourt, and Dreux, the viscounty of Beaumont and many lesser lordships.[2] Most of the earls employed under him could boast a French county to set beside their English earldom: the Earl of Warwick and Aumale, the Earl of Salisbury and Perche, the Earl of Shrewsbury and Clermont. These were not empty titles. As late as 1447-8, on the eve of the collapse of the English occupation, Humphrey, Duke of Buckingham, estimated the revenues of his French county at 800 marks per annum in time of peace.[3]

By this princely *largesse* the royal income from the conquered territories was not affected. The forfeited lands and revenues of Dauphinist supporters were merely transferred to English lords

[1] McFarlane, 'The Investment of Sir John Fastolf's Profits of War', pp. 94–5. The date of the appointment as deputy constable of Bordeaux has been modified in accordance with M. G. A. Vale, *English Gascony, 1399–1453* (Oxford, 1970), pp. 67, 247.

[2] For land held by Englishmen in Normandy see now C. T. Allmand, 'The Lancastrian Land Settlement in Normandy', *Econ. H. R.*, 2nd ser. 21 (1968), 461–79.

[3] Longleat Mun. 6410 (Valor of the lands of Humphrey, Duke of Buckingham, Michaelmas 1447–Michaelmas 1448), m. 21.

and knights. It is not often possible to determine the value of these concessions; most of the greater beneficiaries employed a separate receiver for their Norman lands. Two comparatively minor examples will suggest the scale. According to William of Worcester, Sir Andrew Ogard held lordships in France (which he specifies) worth £1,000 sterling per annum.[1] Sir John Fastolf's were estimated to have a clear annual value of £401 sterling at Michaelmas 1445, when the annual value of his English lands was put at £1,062. By then he had disposed of some of his French lands and the value of the remainder had been much diminished by the effects of war.[2] Fastolf was lucky enough to have sold out of a few before the crash; but in any case he had enjoyed most of them for twenty years and more, long enough for him to grow rich, though that did not console him for their loss. And besides these and his many offices in Normandy and the *pays de conquête*, he received fees as grand master of the Regent's household, as a royal councillor, and as member of other, private, councils as well. It was his proud boast in old age that he had been the councillor of Thomas, Duke of Clarence, Thomas, Duke of Exeter, Humphrey, Duke of Gloucester, Richard, Duke of York, John, Duke of Somerset, and John, Duke of Norfolk; he didn't bother to mention anybody of lesser rank![3] How much of his continental earnings he sent home it is difficult to say. Acknowledgements of the receipt of various sums by his English agents together with a receiver-general's account for the not very favourable year 1433–4 suggest that they were considerable.[4] He was able both to spend £6,000 on Caister castle and to increase his East Anglian holdings fourfold.[5]

The advantages which the English derived from the war have only to be enumerated to be seen to be large. Where did they come from? In the case of the ransoms, the plunder, the lordships, and offices in France, the question is easy to answer: the enemy

---

[1] *Itineraries*, ed. J. H. Harvey (Oxford, 1969), p. 48.

[2] McFarlane, 'The Investment of Sir John Fastolf's Profits of War', pp. 105–6; for some additional details Allmand, 'The Lancastrian Land Settlement in Normandy', pp. 469–71, 473–5.

[3] Magdalen Coll., Oxford, Fastolf Papers, 69, m. 5.

[4] McFarlane, 'The Investment of Sir John Fastolf's Profits of War', pp. 96–9.

[5] Ibid., pp. 103, 105.

paid. And he paid in one other important respect so far unmentioned. The *pays de conquête* was taxed and taxed heavily, over and above its ordinary revenues, to support the garrisons it required. In the sixteen years 1419–35 the Norman estates alone voted some £350,000 sterling, although perhaps only two-thirds of this large sum was actually raised; in addition to this the duchy's contribution from other sources amounted to nearly another £330,000 during the same period.[1] And the rest of the occupied provinces were similarly squeezed. Almost all this money went to pay the wages and regards of the troops quartered on the country. Finally, the invaders had to be paid to go away. I have already mentioned Saint-Sauveur and the final capitulations. But Clarence's insignificant expedition of 1412 was another example. In order to get rid of the unwanted English the Duke of Orleans agreed to give them £35,000 sterling. How this sum was to be shared out among the commanders and their retinues is known from a document written, partly if not wholly, in Orleans's own hand.[2] Although this document was drawn up in 1417, when Orleans was himself a prisoner, it does not concern his own ransom—he was too important to be released until 1440 when he was ransomed for £40,000— but that of his younger brother John, Count of Angoulême. Count John was not captured in battle, but handed over by Orleans in the capitulation of Buzançais in 1412 as one of seven hostages for the payment to the Duke of Clarence's army to withdraw from France. A third of the £35,000 was handed over in cash and jewels and by 1417 some £19,000 had been paid. Orleans's memorandum contains the lists of English captains with the amounts each was owed. But the duke's own capture in 1415 delayed further payment, while his own expenses were being met, and after 1417 many of his estates in Normandy and elsewhere from which his brother's ransom money was to come either passed under Henry V's control (their revenues being confiscated) or ceased to produce their expected income. Angoulême was twelve years of age in 1412; he was in his forties when Orleans's release in 1440 enabled him to pay the balance of his brother's ransom.

[1] McFarlane, 'England and the Hundred Years War', p. 10.
[2] B.M. Add. MS. 31359.

Between them the brothers had contributed £75,000 towards the gains of the English.[1] The pensions received by Edward IV under the treaty of Picquigny and by Henry VII after 1491 had respectable precedents. The Spanish too made their contribution, when they bought out John of Gaunt for £100,000 and a pension of 10,000 marks a year.[2] Among the receipts recorded in his accounts for the half-year February to August 1394 will be found £2,700 forwarded from Bordeaux 'from the treaty of Spain'.[3]

The gains of war, and some of the wages, were paid by the enemy. The rest of the wages and the cost of equipping the troops was borne by the English Exchequer. Not, it must be emphasized, by the English king, but by taxation for which the war was the excuse. When Edward III won advantage by his arms, he didn't pay it into the Exchequer; he treated it as he treated John of France's ransom; he put it in his own pocket.[4] It was the same with his gambling; if he lost his servants paid, his winnings were his own. When expenditure on the war was called for, his subjects had to find the price.[5] During the period 1337–1453 there were occasional 'fancy taxes', taxes *in* wool, poll-taxes, and graduated taxes on landed incomes, but the main sources for the huge sums needed were, as is well known, the tenths and fifteenths, the clerical tenths, customs, subsidies, tonnage, and poundage. To direct taxes in the period 1290 to 1334 the tenants of most manors contributed a sum greatly in excess of that due from their lord; the bulk of the tax, that is to say, was levied on the movables of the villagers of

---

[1] G. Dupont Ferrier, 'La Captivité de Jean d'Orléans, Comte d'Angoulême (1412–45)', *Revue historique*, 62 (1896), 42–74; J. H. Wylie, *History of England under Henry IV* (4 vols., 1884–98), iv. 81–6; J. H. Wylie and W. T. Waugh, *The Reign of Henry V* (3 vols., Cambridge, 1914–29), i. 119–30, iii. 39, 40, 417; P. Champion, *Vie de Charles d'Orléans* (Paris, 1911), pp. 155–208, 272–312, 353.

[2] P. E. Russell, *The English Intervention in Spain and Portugal in the Time of Edward III and Richard II* (Oxford, 1955), p. 506.

[3] P.R.O. DL 28 28/32/21 (certificate of account of the duke's receiver-general).

[4] D. M. Broome, 'The Ransom of John II', *Camden Misc.*, vol. xiv (C.S., 3rd ser. xxxvii, 1926), pp. xiv–xxvi.

[5] A later and more extended account of the themes dealt with in the remainder of this lecture is to be found in McFarlane's paper on 'England and the Hundred Years War'. Two sentences from this paper have been substituted for two in the original manuscript of the Ford Lectures.

England.[1] Although man for man the townsman paid at a rate half as high again as that of the countryman, a tenth as against a fifteenth, townsmen were by comparison scarce. There is no reason to think that the assessment of 1334 altered this distribution in any significant way. Even if the financial history of the war were no more than 'a circular tour of rural wealth' as it has been called, taxation sucked up by the sun to descend later as a rain of soldiers' and contractors' earnings, but much 'shrunk and depleted' in the process, the circuit still appears to have several segments missing.[2]

And how about the indirect taxation? A rough calculation suggests that this yielded more than the direct over the whole period of the war.[3] It is thus of some importance to be sure who paid these taxes. The most remunerative of them was the export tax on raw wool, woolfells, and leather. It used to be thought, in the words of Thorold Rogers, that wool was 'the only article . . . on which an export duty could be put, the whole of which was paid by the foreign consumer'.[4] Lately this view has been abandoned and we are told that 'the greater part' of the tax was passed on by the merchants 'in the form of lower payments' to the native grower.[5] There *is* a little evidence that some merchants said and some producers believed that had there been no subsidy the graziers would have been better off. But I find it difficult to believe that an interest strongly represented both in the Commons *and* the Lords would have taken kindly to such an arrangement or that the producers would have been content with so feeble a protest. When Edward III decided to experiment with the block purchase of his subjects' wool by means of syndicates he took care to mollify opposition by fixing agreed minimum prices.[6] Yet we are asked

[1] J. F. Willard, *Parliamentary Taxes on Personal Property, 1290 to 1334* (Cambridge, Mass., 1934), pp. 163–4.

[2] Cf. M. M. Postan, 'Some Social Consequences of the Hundred Years War', *Econ. H.R.*, 1st ser., 12 (1942), 10–11.

[3] McFarlane later calculated that between 1336 and 1453 direct taxation yielded approximately £3¼ million and indirect taxation nearly £5 million, 'England and the Hundred Years War', p. 6 and nn. 7, 8, 9.

[4] J. E. Thorold Rogers, *Six Centuries of Work and Wages* (1912), p. 79.

[5] E. Power, *The Wool Trade in English Medieval History* (Oxford, 1941), p. 71.

[6] E. B. Fryde, 'Edward III's Wool Monopoly of 1337: a Fourteenth Century Royal Trading Venture', *History*, new ser. 37 (1952), 12.

to suppose that it was possible for him to impose a tax which had the effect of cutting deep into the grower's profits without any such guarantee. It just does not make sense. Nor does it explain the phenomenal expansion of the native cloth industry which accompanied the war. If this was not due to the fact that the English manufacturer was able to undercut his Flemish competitor in the European markets precisely because the latter was paying the wool tax and he was not, then at least some other explanation is needed; and so far none has been offered.[1] It was, I maintain, the foreigner who made the largest contribution towards the cost of the Hundred Years War; and, if my estimates are anywhere near right, the wealth of England in 1450 was greater—and probably very much greater—than in 1300.

One last point: who were the beneficiaries? Not, to be sure, the king; at any rate after 1422; though it cannot be said that up to then he had not enjoyed his share. But the nobility of England and those on whom they threw away their winnings had had the means to achieve a standard of living, indeed of luxury, of which I shall give you evidence anon. And among those who had done best out of the war were the great landed families. It is not my intention to minimize the part played by needy adventurers of obscure birth and no inherited property; scores of them made notable fortunes. But it is the unbroken service of the greater baronage from Crécy to Castillon that is in danger of being taken for granted and ignored. There is no truth in the theory that the aristocracy started the war and left the professional mercenaries to finish it off.[2] The names of the captains, from Bohun, Fitzalan, and Stafford to Beauchamp, Montagu, Mowbray, and Talbot, would be recognized for what they are by any English schoolboy.

[1] E. B. Fryde, *The Wool Accounts of William de la Pole* (St. Anthony's Hall Publications, 25, 1964), pp. 14–15, has evidence suggesting that the tax was not passed on to the Flemish consumer at least in the years immediately after 1338.

[2] Contrast Postan, 'Some Social Consequences of the Hundred Years War', pp. 7–8.

III. THE NOBILITY AND THE LAND

LAST week we were saying 'Ha, ha' among the trumpets; but now we must leave the thunder of the captains and the shouting, if not for the soil of England, then for the dust of the conveyancer's office. Here we shall find ourselves keeping very much the same company. For the captains, as I must repeat, were also the lords of land; most of them by inheritance, some by purchase (or, as they characteristically described it, conquest). Only a physical infirmity, like Edward, Earl of Devon's, blindness, could excuse an English magnate from taking a part in the war equal to his rank. Tough and greedy prize-fighters half their time, they had need of other qualities than their virility and a thick skull. Even in war itself they had to be business men and rulers as well as active combatants. Those who reached eminence in France were more likely to resemble Odysseus than Ajax; and that would be specially true of those who, like Odysseus, returned home.

The first question to be asked, therefore, must be: what equipment had these men for the tasks of peace, for the management of their estates, directing and keeping a close watch upon a host of subordinate officials, and for taking their natural share, the share their birth imposed on them, in the government of the shires and in the work of the parliaments and councils of the kingdom? Little thought has been given to the education of the English nobility; the general assumption is that it was neglected.[1] A little singing, dancing, and table-manners acquired in lordly households under the tutelage of women, followed by intensive training in the serious business of life: riding, fighting, and hunting, directed by superannuated knights like Sir Simon Burley; that is the common picture. The impression I derive from a variety of sources is that it is neither an accurate nor a credible one.

As far as the second half of the fifteenth century is concerned the evidence is clear. The five sons of John Paston the eldest, who

[1] Cf. 'The Education of the Nobility in Later Medieval England', pp. 228–47 below.

died in 1466 and was himself educated at Cambridge and the Inner Temple, after being taught their letters at home by the domestic chaplain, went on either to Cambridge, Oxford, Eton, or the Inns of Court.[1] Of their contemporary, Thomas Howard, afterwards the second Duke of Norfolk of his family, it was recorded on his tomb that he 'was in hys yong age, ofter he had been a sufficient season at the gramer schole, hencheman to Kyng Edward the iiii';[2] and, as we know from that king's household ordinances his henchmen were provided with a master 'to teche them sondry langages'; for 'we will that the sons of nobles, lords and gentlemen, being in household . . . be virtuously brought up and taught in grammar [i.e. Latin], music and other cunning and exercises of humanity according to their births and after their ages'.[3] By that date such a grounding was looked upon as normal; the only question is how long it had been so.

Sir John Fortescue was probably looking back to his own youth —and he entered Lincoln's Inn as a student about 1402—when he described, in over-rosy language very likely, the advantages of a legal training. The most interesting thing about his account is its evidence that long before the sixteenth century the inns were being used as a secular university by members of the upper classes who had no ambition of being called to the bar: 'knights, barons and also other magnates and nobles of the realm place their sons in these inns, although they do not intend them to be imbued by a professional knowledge of the laws nor to live by its practice, but upon their patrimonies alone'.[4] Unfortunately the earliest surviving list of admissions, that to Lincoln's Inn, only begins with those already members in 1420 and leaves many of them unidentifiable.[5]

There is more—and earlier—evidence of education at home.

---

[1] H. S. Bennett, *The Pastons and their England* (Cambridge, 1922), pp. 102–10.

[2] Dugdale, *Baronage*, ii. 269; J. Weever, *Antient Funeral Monuments* (1767), p. 554.

[3] *The Household of Edward IV*, ed. A. R. Myers (Manchester, 1959), p. 126, cf. pp. 137–8. We cannot identify the second quotation, which does not appear to be from the 'Black Book'.

[4] *De Laudibus Legum Anglie*, ed. S. B. Chrimes (Cambridge, 1942), p. 118.

[5] *The Records of . . . Lincoln's Inn* (2 vols., 1896), vol. i, pp. v–vi, 1–3.

The household accounts of Henry, Earl of Derby, in the 1390s when his young family of four sons and two daughters was growing up, mention their tutors by name, as well as some of their schoolbooks, and enable us to gain some idea of their studies and even rate of progress. In February 1396, when he was eight and a half, seven books of Latin grammar bound together were bought for the eldest, Henry; they cost 4s.[1] Exactly a year later, the third son John, aged seven and a half, was given his Donet or Latin primer. At the same time his sisters, five minus and two and a half respectively, had their first spelling-books: 'Et pro duobus libris de A.B.C. pro iuvenibus dominabus erudiendis emptis', 1s. 8d. It may be objected that this was an exceptional family; it is certain that it was an exceptionally able one. But the fact that its head soon afterwards usurped the throne is immaterial; for it can hardly be supposed that in 1396 or even in February 1397 these children were being educated as kings and princes-to-be. At that time John of Lancaster, the future Regent of France, was merely a cadet of a cadet branch of the royal house and it is unlikely that there was anything abnormal in his learning Latin. How *far* back it may be necessary to push the beginnings of such instruction is suggested by entries in the accounts of the semi-baronial Roches (de Rupe) from distant—and one might have assumed, backward—Pembrokeshire. In 1325 William de la Roche was paying Sir John 'le scolmaistir' of Haverfordwest 10s. a quarter for his services.

The efficacy of such teaching can best be judged by the uses to which it was put. Again the fifteenth century offers the bulkier evidence, though some of it is not of much value. It merely establishes the fact that members of the nobility could sign their names. Thanks to the royal minority there are for the period after 1422 hundreds of warrants attested by the signature of the lords of the council present when the decision was taken. By the middle of the century it was becoming usual for such sign manuals to be placed, in addition to the seal or signet, at the foot of *private* instruments, such as grants, indentures, bonds, and receipts; and they had begun to appear on accounts. Henry VII's habit of signing each page of his account-books has been cited as proof of his

[1] For the remainder of this paragraph see pp. 243–4 below.

exceptional interest in financial detail; but he was not the first to adopt this somewhat laborious, if absolutely certain, method of approving the conduct of his agents. It would be nearer the truth to say that he introduced into the royal administration what was the ordinary practice of his magnates. His adviser, Sir Reynold Bray, had after all done long service with the Stafford house before 1485. The third Duke of Buckingham carried this financial centralization to almost excessive lengths; his sign manual seems to have been required on everything.

As evidence of literacy these signatures may not be thought to take us very far. Nor are private letters much more helpful. Busy men in the fifteenth century like busy men today preferred to save time by employing a secretary. Unless there is internal evidence that the hand throughout is the signatory's own, it is best to assume that it is not. In any case, although the accounts show that the nobility received and dispatched a mass of letters, very few have survived. Muniments of title were carefully preserved, but for a long time no permanent value was attached to letters. An odd one here and there escaped destruction by accident. It took an antiquary to realize their interest; and it is, therefore, I would suggest, no coincidence that the first landowner, the originals of whose private correspondence have come down to us in any number, employed the father of English antiquaries, William of Worcester, as his secretary.[1] Fortunately he did not always employ Worcester but wrote long letters for himself. No one could say that Sir John Fastolf led a particularly studious or inactive life; the fact that this hard-bitten fighting man was able to express himself fluently on paper in a practised and legible hand should warn us against dismissing lay literacy as superficial. His correspondence shows Fastolf as a good deal more than merely literate, for he controlled every detail of estate business from a distance and was perfectly at home in a discussion of accountancy or law.

Since he was born in 1380, Fastolf's education must have been

---

[1] For whom see McFarlane, 'William of Worcester, a Preliminary Survey', pp. 196–221; William Worcestre, *Itineraries*, ed. J. H. Harvey (Oxford, 1969); K. B. McFarlane, 'William Worcester and a Present of Lampreys', *Medium Aevum*, 30 (1961), 176–80.

well advanced before the end of the fourteenth century. His ancestors had long been merchants of Great Yarmouth, but Sir John himself was the only son of an esquire of Edward III's household and the nephew of Hugh the under-admiral. If he be thought too marginal an example of nobility, John, Lord Bourchier, whose letter of 1374 I have already mentioned, is not open to the same objection. Although the grandson of a mere judge, he was the son of a distinguished soldier who was also the first lay Chancellor of England; both he and his father received personal writs of summons to Parliament. In his Breton prison, Bourchier could employ no amanuensis; his letter to his wife is in his own hand throughout and there is nothing halting or half-baked about its neatly written, idiomatic French.[1] Nor is there about the last will and testament which Sir William Mowbray, cadet of an ancient baronial house, drew up for himself at York on 30 July 1391; it is the handiwork of a trained draftsman who may well have been a practising lawyer.[2] It is well to remember that as early as the first day of 1259 the testament of no less a person than the great Simon de Montfort was written out for him by Henry, his eldest son.[3]

Edward III's choice of Sir Robert Bourchier for the chancellorship in 1340 may have been prompted by a merely transitory irritation with clerks, but it was none the less the signal that the literate layman had arrived in government. The precedent was soon and often followed. Edward III himself frequently employed his barons in diplomatic and other business, sending, for example, those veteran soldiers Guy, Lord Brian, and John, Lord Cobham, at the head of embassies to the papal court.[4] That they were not simply figureheads, behind whom clerks did the real work, is proved by the letter which William Wickham sent Cobham in 1366, reproduced in facsimile in the bishop's life by Moberly.[5]

[1] Longleat Mun. 396; cf. p. 241 above. Another, damaged, letter, Longleat Mun. 400, is apparently written in the same hand.

[2] *Testamenta Eboracensia*, vol. i, ed. J. Raine (Surtees Soc., 1836), pp. 158–61.

[3] Facsimile facing p. 278 of C. Bémont, *Simon de Montfort*, trans. E. F. Jacob (Oxford, 1930).

[4] L. Mirot and E. Deprez, *Les Ambassades anglaises pendant la Guerre de Cent Ans* (Paris, 1900; an offprint from *Bibliothèque de l'École des chartes*, 1898, 1899, 1900), nos. CLXVIII, CCLXVII.

[5] G. H. Moberly, *Life of William of Wykeham* (1887), frontispiece.

Others, such as Sir William Burton and Sir Nigel Loraine, were similarly used.[1] Thenceforward the practice was general. So Henry V entrusted John Tiptoft with an unusually confidential mission to the Emperor Sigismund in January 1417. Though damaged in the Cottonian fire, the instructions which the king wrote for this occasion can still be read. This is how they begin: 'Tiptoft, I Charge yow by the Feith that ye owe to me that ye kepe this Matere . . . from al Men secre save from my Brother Th'Emperor owne Person . . . Kepeth this Charge, as ye wil Kepe all that Ye may forfet to Me'; and end: 'for the secrenesse of this Matere, I have writen this Instruccion wyth myn owne Hande'.[2] Born about 1375 of ancient baronial stock, Tiptoft, by turns household official, Commons' Speaker, royal Treasurer, diplomat, and soldier, might well stand as the epitome of the new literate *noblesse*. He received his summons to the Lords in 1426 and was the father of that butcher and humanist, John, Earl of Worcester.[3]

It has been my purpose so far to emphasize the practical rather than the literary side of these men's education. But it is not wholly irrelevant to remind you, as the name of Worcester should have done, that some of their number were ambitious to be scholars, authors, and collectors; that William de la Pole, Duke of Suffolk, was not only the gaoler of Charles of Orleans but also his fellow poet;[4] that John Montagu, Earl of Salisbury, dabbler in Lollardy, and friend of Richard II, was commended for his verses by no less a judge than Christine de Pisan;[5] and that the brilliant and warlike Henry, Duke of Lancaster in 1354 sat down and wrote a long devotional treatise in French.[6] Anyone who is tempted to dismiss the fourteenth-century aristocracy as wanting in intellectual depth should be given the *Book of Holy Medicines* to digest as a penance. We are dealing with men not only of tested capacity in action, as

[1] Mirot and Deprez, *Les Ambassades anglaises*, nos. CXLVII, CLI, CCIX, CCCXXIII, CCXI, CCXV, CCXXVIII (Loraine's christian name is wrongly given as Nicholas).

[2] B.M. Cottonian MS. Caligula D v, ff. 13–14, printed *Foedera*, ix. 427–430.

[3] For Tiptoft see J. S. Roskell, *The Commons and their Speakers in English Parliaments 1374–1523* (Manchester, 1965), pp. 367–8.

[4] Below, p. 241 and n. 4.

[5] Wylie, *History of England under Henry IV*, i. 100, n. 2.

[6] See below, p. 242.

their record in war and government shows, but also, in not a few cases, of quite remarkable versatility, accomplishments, and taste. It would not be wise altogether to forget this when considering their achievements in the most traditional of all their roles, that of landlords.

It is only necessary to read through their estate papers and household bills and accounts to be reminded that the exercise of authority, whether by king, baron, or knight, was an exacting discipline. Most in evidence the whole time is the extent to which everything (in the long run) depended upon the initiative of the lord himself. He was advised by his principal ministers, his council, and his lawyers; he delegated the execution of his policy to subordinates; and there were many things done *de cursu* which did not require his specific order. But at every turn a decision by him was needed. In the kingdom, as most of us realize, the source of all authority was a personal monarch; his servants were there to carry out his desires, but the responsibility was his alone; their first rule of business—and he gave it them—was: do nothing without a sufficient warrant; and unless the king was ill, absent, or a child, that meant in the last resort at least an oral command from him. He gave government its momentum. Although in certain events the machine would continue to function without him, it was bound before long to run down; the driving force was entirely his. The same was true of seignorial governments; each was a monarchy; and as the varied records demonstrate beyond question, the lord's will was the source of decision. Action was taken in response to his express wish—in writing, *per litteram domini de warranto*, or by word of mouth, *par sa bouche de mesme*. An existing file of John of Gaunt's warrants to his chancellor leaves one in no doubt who was the mainspring of his vast administration.[1] But so it was with others: nothing without a sufficient warrant. When a lord went on pilgrimage or to the wars, his place might be taken by his eldest son or by his wife, assisted by his council; but they were still answerable to him, and, if he were no further away than Normandy, constantly and directly answerable as in 1417–21 the

---

[1] P.R.O. PL 3/1 (indexed *43rd Report of the Deputy Keeper of the Public Records*, App. I, pp. 363–70).

English Council was to Henry V.[1] In one respect the subject was a great deal more successful than the king: namely in making provision for the management of his estates after his death, during the minority of his heir. Once his wishes became his last will, his *ultima voluntas*, they had the force of law; and the courts both royal and Christian would see that they were observed. Neither Henry V nor Henry VIII was able to achieve as much for himself.

Some kings were better business men than others, and it may be presumed that heredity worked as uncertainly among their vassals. The evidence for it is singularly hard to find. We are reduced to the dangerous conclusion that the accounts of well-regulated families have alone survived. Even where some indebtedness might appear to indicate neglect or mismanagement there was generally an external cause. I have found no example of proved indebtedness on a really large scale. Slight embarrassment was frequently the occasion for careful overhaul and strict economy. There are signs that in his great age and last illness, Sir John Fastolf's inability to reach his outlying Yorkshire manors had resulted in peculation and waste; and he lost grip nearer home as well.[2] There are a number of baronial families whose decline *may* have been due to the extravagance or inefficiency of their temporary head. When we find the fifth John Mohun of Dunster selling some manors and mortgaging others it is scarcely rash to assume that he was in difficulties, though the fault may not have been his own.[3] His public career was notably distinguished and he had married an able wife. A fairly short list of other suspected cases of bad management can be compiled. It would include such north-country families of ancient settlement as the Herons of Ford[4] and the Darcies of Knaith,[5] and less certainly the Lisles of Rougemont.[6]

---

[1] R. L. Storey, *Thomas Langley and the Bishopric of Durham 1406–1437* (1961), pp. 36–7.

[2] *Paston Letters*, iii. 72, 90–1, 129; B.M. Add. MS. 39848, no. 46.

[3] H. C. Maxwell Lyte, *A History of Dunster* (2 vols., 1909), i. 46–53.

[4] G.E.C. vi. 486–7; *A History of Northumberland*, xi (1922), 375–85 (by K. H. Vickers).

[5] C. D. Ross, 'The Yorkshire Baronage 1399–1435' (unpub. Oxford D.Phil. thesis, Bodleian Library), ff. 294–309, esp. ff. 300–1, 309.

[6] G.E.C. viii. 76–7.

There is no sign whatever that even a single one of the comital houses, though a few like those of Vere and Courtenay had never been over-rich, came to disaster by any other road than political miscalculation.

If a general charge had to be preferred, it would rather be one of harsh efficiency; the commonest impulse detectable was to exploit every imagined right, to push every promising advantage to its limit. Hardly a collection of private papers fails to offer some piece of vivid evidence of lordly high-handedness or extortion in which neither tenants nor servants were spared. No sooner was a landowner dead than complaints began to reach his executors. Thus Elizabeth Bourchier, widow of Sir Lewis Robsart, was petitioned between 1431 and 1433 by John Elde 'sutyme' yowr ffermer' at Stanford Revers and at all tymys yowr seruant'. Elde had a long tale of wrongs, of constant surcharges, of imprisonment in the Marshalsea and of the confiscation of his goods, which if only a quarter true would still be monstrous. It ends: 'Also þe same John Elde . . . & othyr' personys haue ryde for' to sewe to my lord and to my lady for theze materys þe sume' of vii c mylys and mor', that ys to seye to Wyndesor', to Badewe, to Stanstede, to London', to Stanforde & to many othyr' places, in costes to John' Elde, xls. and mor'.' The 'rey3t worthy lady' was implored 'to do restytycon' & remedye in relevyng' of my lordes sowle'.[1] An instruction, commonly found in late medieval testaments, to the executors that they should try to undo all the injustices committed by the testator, was no mere form. It will be found in the testament of Ralph, Lord Cromwell who died in 1455. On that occasion it was found necessary to refund to their lawful owners lands worth £5,500 with which he had wrongfully made away; 'as full greatly it moved the conscience of the said executors'.[2] It is a little difficult to subscribe to H. L. Gray's judgement that Cromwell was an example of 'integrity in high office'.[3]

---

[1] Longleat Mun. 235. Cf. pp. 221-2 below.

[2] Magdalen Coll., Oxford, Misc. 359 is a copy of Cromwell's will. Another copy is abstracted *H.M.C. Report on MSS. of Lord de L'Isle and Dudley*, i. 210; the executors' accounts, Magdalen Coll. Misc. 355 (Cromwell Papers 432). show that restitution was made, mm. 1ʳ, 4ʳ, 5ʳ, 3ᵛ, 5ᵛ.

[3] H. L. Gray, 'Incomes from Land in England in 1436', *E.H.R.* 49 (1934), 612.

The Fastolf papers inevitably continue the tale. A list of bad debts owing to the fierce old knight in *c.* 1459 shows that at different times half his estate officials had been gaoled for being in arrears with their dues. Thomas Newton, lately bailiff of Saxthorpe, was down £5. 6s. 7d.; here is the note on him: 'This det is arrer' of his last accompt, wherupon he was commytted to prison in Norwich & ther lay ner' two yere & than my mayster grauntyd hym daye of payment [i.e. time to pay] w^t sufficient suertie to be bounde for the seyd duetye.' Bartholomew Hulver, ex-bailiff of Guton, still owed 40s. 8d. after ten years: 'for whiche dutye a vii yeer passed he was sewed at þe common lawe, and þan the lord Beaumond spake for hym; and than my maister graunted hym yerys of payment; and so he payed all' except the seid some' for whiche he fonde suerte sufficient, and hise obligacon' is sewed [afresh?] at London.' As for the 'trespacys' committed by Henry Pidgeon 'in my maister's wode', the penalty was twenty times the damage.[1] Henry Windsor's well-known judgement on Fastolf's character was true enough: 'Cruell and vengible he hath byn euer, and for the most parte w^toute pite and mercy.'[2] There is also John Bocking's description of 'the sharp' bittre ansueres by the said knyght' with which the humble petition of an old and once trusted servant was rebuffed.[3]

This is the sort of conduct that gentlemen of the old school expect from parvenus. But Ralph Cromwell was no parvenu. Nor was Edward Stafford, third Duke of Buckingham, ninth Earl of Stafford, Earl of Hereford, Buckingham, and Northampton, thirteenth baron of Stafford in the male line, lord of Brecon, Tonbridge, and Holderness. His close supervision of his finances has already been mentioned. Not only did he countersign the accounts of his receiver-general and his cofferer; he is the first member of the nobility whom I have found keeping detailed records of his financial position with his own pen. A series of rolls entitled 'creditor rolls . . . made of mine own hand' records what was owed by him to various persons from May 1518 until his death three

---

[1] Magdalen Coll., Oxford, Fastolf Papers, 62, mm. 3, 4.
[2] *Paston Letters*, iii. 89.
[3] Magdalen Coll., Oxford, Fastolf Papers, 98, m. 3.

years later; and there are remains of a parallel series dealing with debts owing to him.[1] But among all the various accounts and other estate memoranda preserved from these last years of Buckingham's life, two are of particular interest. The first, consisting of some twenty-four paper folios, is described on the cover as 'a booke of informations geven by diverse by [*sic*] my lordes graces officers of diverse his lordeships'.[2] It is largely devoted to answers received in response to a systematic inquiry held in the month of May 1516, but there are also entries from other years. The second and much larger manuscript is a notebook kept as he perambulated his master's estates during the year 1518–19 by John Pickering the duke's receiver-general.[3] Both books were intended for Buckingham's own perusal and both have marginal evidence that he had read and considered them before referring particular items to his council for legal action. Their purpose was to keep a better check upon local officials, to make it more difficult for them, the tenants, and their neighbours to profit at the lord's expense and to exploit every available source of revenue. The duke's ministers were encouraged to spy upon one another, to report any instances where bribes had been taken or collusive bargains made. Entry fines were to be pushed as high as possible, tenants forced to maintain their buildings in repair, prosperous bondmen were to be detected and squeezed, and every waste of the lord's timber, every evasion of his right of wreck, every poaching of his woods and warrens to be smartly punished. Here are some extracts from Pickering's notebook:

'Item I have seesed your bondman' John' Dyx of Padbury and takyn' suerty for hys body and gooddes by obligacion' in forty li. as more playnly doythe apere by ye obligacion' and also a Invitory of hys goodes as herre after doyth apere more at large.' The inventory shows that Dix's chattels were worth £18. 6s. 0d.; he offered to pay £2. 13s. 4d.[4]

[1] B.M. Royal Rolls 14 B XXXV; A 1, A 2, A 4, A 5, A 7–12. For these rolls and for a further account of Edward, Duke of Buckingham's finances, see pp. 208–12 below.

[2] Staffordshire R.O. D (W) 1721/1/6 (one of several items bound together in this unfoliated miscellany). Cf. pp. 223–5 below.

[3] Westminster Abbey Mun. 5470.   [4] Ibid., ff. 3ᵛ–4ʳ.

'Item Lonkester the bayly of Haverell' says that m' Cade haythe doyn' hyme' gret wrong' . . . m' Cade had of hyme' on' geldyng' price xls. and iiij geldryngges of hys syster to make hyme' bayly ther. He promysed me to come' to London' and schew yt to you^r g^a ce hyme' selfe, mervelyng gretly he dyd nott.'[1]

'I have resoned both w^t certen' of yor ten^a ntes and also w^t othir gentilmen' & yomen' for yor fynes in euery particuler place and they haue saide to me that they have no joye to offer.'[2]

And these are from the 'book of informations':

'Nicholas Clerk oone of the kepars of my lordes fforest of Hathefeld . . . seith that the seid John' Burrell' made grete wast of wodd in the park of Hatfeld wherof he ys keper.'[3]

John Lyttley of Rokeby 'hath by his bill supplicatory informed my lordes grace that he woull shewe unto his grace and his counsell' when his grace shall comaund' hym certen' grete Iniuries and wronges concelid to the disheritaunce of my seid lord' in the lordeship of Rokeby', and the bill is annexed.[4]

Edmund Paris, bailiff of Ratcliff-upon-Soar 'seith that oone Martyn' Pyes of Kegw^r the . . . in the counte yoman destroyeth my lordes waren' of Ratclyff w^t grehoundes and fferettes.' A marginal note runs: 'matter in the lawe'.[5]

The practice of taking informations by what amounted to an inquest by a private landowner was not new. In 1451 Sir John Fastolf 'communed' with his tenants at Dedham in Essex to discover 'who were the chieff councell of brekyng my milledam, wherby I hafe lost xxli. by yeare. And they seyn Sir John Squyer was chieff, but John Waryn was of councell and court halder there. Also Sir John Buk, parson of Scratton was off councell and doer also, whych physshyd my stankes and waters . . . and destroyed the grete quantite of physsh to the damage' of xxli.'; he ordered his council to go to law.[6]

A lord in short needed to look well to his own if he were to keep it. His ministers could only be trusted if they were efficiently

[1] f. 37^r.   [2] f. 56.
[3] ff. 2, 4. (The foliation here used counts the first folio of the 'Book of Informations' as f. 1.)
[4] f. 7^v and attached schedule.   [5] f. 12^v.
[6] B.M. Add. MS. 39848, no. 12.

watched and made to watch one another. All the evidence suggests that most of the landowners of our period—*all* who have left any records—were well able to take care of their property, and if they got the chance, of their neighbours' also. The indolent, the vacillating, or the feebly good-intentioned would not long have had any estates to enjoy. Yet the number of misfits, wastrels, and victims of circumstance was not so great as to bring much business to the market in land.

That at any time in the two and a half centuries after 1290 that market was ever, even temporarily, in danger of glut is improbable. The question should be rather how *small* was the fraction of England that then changed hands by sale. This was not, I believe, a result of either *Quia Emptores* or even *De Donis*; the restraints on alienation by laymen to laymen were never crippling; and most families were as tenacious of their lands in fee simple as of those that were entailed.[1] One reason was, of course, the Church; its vast lands, or at least most of them, were out of reach of buyers, it seemed for ever. Not all of them, because there were the lands of alien priories, houses dependent upon abbeys under the obedience of the king's enemies. During the fourteenth century a good many manors belonging to these monasteries passed by sale or royal grant into the hands of the laity. For example, Sir William de la Pole the financier set up his three surviving sons, Michael, Thomas, and Edmund as landowners in 1354 by the purchase of eight manors belonging to the Norman mother-house of Wilmington Priory in Sussex.[2] But the scale of such transactions can

[1] In his 1965 lectures McFarlane attributed more importance to the effect of entails in restricting the land market. He then pointed out that sales of land by noble houses seem to have been fewer in the fifteenth century than in the fourteenth and suggested that this was 'not because the crisis was deepening and the landowners clinging even more desperately to their capital but because by then the practice of entailing land had still further restricted their powers of sale, even if they had wanted to sell'. In a later lecture in the same series he added that some great estates came into the market in Henry VII's reign.

[2] The manors were acquired via the German merchant, Tideman of Lymburg, who had bought them from Wilmington's Norman mother-house of Grestain in 1348 (McFarlane suggested in an unpublished lecture that Tideman may have been acting as de la Pole's agent from the beginning), *C.C.R. 1354–60,* pp. 659–60; *C.P.R. 1348–50,* pp. 221, 441–2, 515; *C.P.R. 1354–8,* pp. 158, 217; *C.F.R. 1347–56,* p. 139; *Cal. Pap. Reg., Papal Letters,* iii. 276, 338.

hardly have been great enough to balance the gifts of land which Englishmen, in spite of the Statute of Mortmain, continued to make to Holy Church.

Nevertheless, the Statute did profoundly affect the land market. Piety, whether real or conventional, was not so easily thwarted. To obtain a licence to alienate land in mortmain was expensive; it was as it were a tax on charity. How heavily it pressed on donors a letter of Henry Fillongley to Sir John Fastolf bears witness: 'And, Sir, my brother Paston and I have comened togeder as touchinge to your colage that ye would have made; and, Sir, it ys too gret a good (i.e. price) that ys axed of yow for youre lycens; for they ax for every C. marc that ye wold amortyse, D. marc3, and woll gef hit noo better chepe.'[1] The licence cost at least the equivalent of five years' income. No wonder that would-be founders hesitated! One solution was to establish a chantry out of income: to lay the duty upon one's heirs to pay the chaplains a regular salary for ever; as the Percies did the five priests they maintained in their great family chantry at Beverley, with a sixth at Topcliffe.[2] But for most men this was too uncertain; heirs might forget and heirs were liable to extinction. The best and commonest solution was to make a will ordering certain manors to be sold, the proceeds either to be given to one church, or, more often, to be distributed among a number. In most wills the residuary legatee was the Church; if heirs failed, all the testator's lands were to be sold for pious uses. A man's friends or more distant kinsmen might be given the chance of buying them cheap. Thus William Street, king's sergeant, controller of Edward III's wardrobe, and afterwards chirographer of the common bench, making his will in Rome in 1383, said that Sir John Cheney might have his manor of Mereworth for 3,000 marks or £100 'better cheap than any man'; Nicholas Carew might have Nutfield, for £800 but a stranger was to pay £900; Grantchester was to be offered to one friend for £900, but if Sir Richard Burley 'will have it he must agree with

[1] *Paston Letters*, iii. 98.

[2] Payments to these priests, 'my lord's chantry priests', are recorded in the Earl of Northumberland's cofferer's account for 1514–26 (E 36/226), e.g. pp. 153, 208. Each received £5 annually.

my executors', of which as it happens Burley was one; Coldham manor was 'to be sold and bestowed for the soul's health of Edward III'.[1] We gather that Street had no children. Since failure of issue was all too frequent, a steady break-up of estates was thus ensured. The Statute of Mortmain, though it succeeded in its purpose of hindering the transfer of land to the Church, had the unexpected result of greatly increasing the area for sale to laymen.

Not all childless landowners waited until they made their wills. Some sold their estates for cash down either with immediate seisin to the purchaser or in reversion after the vendor's death. In either event they had the pleasure of spending part of their capital in their own lifetime; their collaterals went without. So Joan, Lady Mohun, left a widow without heirs male in 1375, and having married off her daughters, sold the reversion of her late husband's barony of Dunster in the following year to the Luttrells for 5,000 marks; and then kept them waiting almost thirty years while she enjoyed herself at court on the proceeds.[2] Her contemporary and son-in-law, William Montagu, Earl of Salisbury, followed her wise example. Having killed his only son in a tilting-match he parted with the reversion of two valuable Somerset manors to John of Gaunt for 5,000 marks[3] and sold the Isle of Man outright to the Scropes of Bolton for twice that sum.[4]

A number of similar cases could be cited. Almost always when a man is found dispersing his inheritance, it turns out that he was childless or at least without male issue. Fathers of sons only very rarely were reduced to such a sacrifice. The great mass of lay estates descended by inheritance or by will without ever coming into the market at all. If a man had money and wanted to buy he had to wait his chance. It might come as it came to William Street's friends and to many like them. Executors and feoffees could

---

[1] *Collectanea Topographica et Genealogica*, iii. 100.

[2] Maxwell Lyte, *History of Dunster*, i. 50, 52–5.

[3] P.R.O. DL 28/32/21 (Certificate of account of the Duke of Lancaster's receiver-general, 2 Feb. 1394–12 Aug. 1395): payment of 4,000 marks to the Earl of Salisbury in full payment of 5,000 marks for the reversion to the manors of Martock and Curry Rivell and their appurtenances; cf. p. 84 below.

[4] G.E.C. xi. 386, n. *g*.

generally be relied upon to use their influence on behalf of their connections, lords, or kin. Those in the way to know, especially the London attorneys, were quick to send hasty warning to country clients that a sale was likely. As a result, estates tended to remain, even when often sold, in the hands of men with the same kind of social ties. It will be found, for example, that the lands bought by a London merchant, if they came into the market again, would probably find a London purchaser; and so with the townsmen of other boroughs.

It did not seem to matter greatly if the lands for sale were conveniently placed. They might after all be later exchanged. Fastolf's many manors, apart from those in Wiltshire and Yorkshire in which he acquired a life interest by marriage, all lay in the east of England. Yet William of Worcester in Southwark, living next door to Winchester House, when he heard a rumour that Cardinal Beaufort might sell Canford in Dorset in 1444, wrote at once to interest his master.[1] Good chances, at any rate in the mid fifteenth century, did not arise every day. And since escheats were rarely allowed to happen, one route by which land might come into the market had been closed.[2]

Evidence on price is easily come by; that is to say, the amount actually paid is known; what is generally lacking is a reliable estimate of the annual value of the purchase. It is not possible, therefore, to state definitely what return an investor in land received on his money. For the fourteenth century the number of cases where both price and return are known is too small for generalization. With the fifteenth there is some improvement. In 1444–5, for example, Sir John Fastolf caused a valuation to be made of all his estates in which were luckily included notes of the

[1] Magdalen Coll., Oxford, Fastolf Papers, 40.
[2] In his 1965 lectures McFarlane added to his account of the land market above. He pointed out that kings 'just occasionally' sold land, giving as instances Edward III's sale of most of Holderness to William de la Pole and Henry V's of Chirk to Cardinal Beaufort. (It should also be observed that forfeitures for treason from time to time brought considerable quantities of land on to the market. C. D. Ross, 'Forfeitures for Treason in the Reign of Richard II', *E.H.R.* 71 (1956), 564–5, 570–1; J. R. Lander, 'Attainder and Forfeiture, 1453–1509', *Historical Journ.* 4 (1961), 147, n. 109.)

original cost to him of each property acquired.[1] At about the same time Ralph Cromwell's executors were valuing *his* lands, partly for division among his heirs and partly for sale.[2] These and other smaller pieces of evidence indicate a number of rough conclusions:

(1) That it was generally *assumed* that land would fetch about twenty times its annual *net* revenue, its revenue, that is, after deducting all outgoings in wages, tithe, taxation, repairs, and works. In other words, that an investor in land aimed at a return of a clear 5 per cent on his money.

(2) That in practice manors changed hands at both more and less than this ratio. Fastolf made a number of highly profitable purchases which brought him in considerably more than 5 per cent; in one or two cases he was unlucky and a defective title involved him, in addition, in heavy legal expenses. Lord Cromwell's executors aimed at obtaining the equivalent of twenty years' rent and generally did so.

(3) That a fixed rent charge was almost always sold for precisely twenty times its annual value—and this seems to be true not only of the fifteenth century but of the whole period. Where this rule was departed from—as in the Cromwell valor[3]—the price was greater and not less than twenty times the rent.

(4) That reversions, the mere expectation of a perhaps remote enjoyment, varied in price, perhaps upon a rough estimate of the probable delay, from as little as twelve to as much as eighteen times the clear annual return.

Now a clear 5 per cent is what Fastolf also obtained from the loans he was in the habit of making to a number of London and Yarmouth merchants.[4] These were safe investments and his interest was paid regularly and punctually. His investments in land, thanks perhaps to the shrewdness of his buying, were just as safe and slightly more profitable—at any rate on the comparatively short run of one man's long life. This is relevant to my final theme

---

[1] Magdalen Coll., Oxford, Fastolf Papers 69, cf. McFarlane, 'The Investment of Sir John Fastolf's Profits of War', pp. 101–2.

[2] Magdalen Coll, Oxford, Misc. 355 (Cromwell Papers 432).

[3] The executors valued one quit rent at twenty-four times its annual value (Magdalen Coll., Oxford, Cromwell Papers 432, mm. 3ᵛ, 5).

[4] McFarlane, 'The Investment of Sir John Fastolf's Profits of War', p. 100.

for today: the fall in agricultural profits. The evidence that there was such a fall in our period meets one on every hand; but the answers to the questions WHEN?, WHERE?, and HOW MUCH? are not so easily given, even approximately. Of the estates called manors in the later middle ages there were a great many and they were on the increase; I am not sure whether the total number in England was nearer 50,000 than 30,000; but I doubt whether a sample of 400 or even ten times that figure, however carefully chosen in type and distribution, will provide us with very reliable data. That there was a serious fall after the Black Death seems reasonably certain; that there was any comparable collapse in the fifteenth century does not accord with what evidence I have myself seen. The case of Fastolf's estates has been mentioned. The valors made for Lord Cromwell, one in 1429–30 and the other after his death in 1455,[1] tell the same story; and the accounts of the west-country Staffords of Grafton confirm it.[2] Not even serious *political* disturbance affected the stability of agriculture. The accounts of the estates of Richard, Duke of York in the eastern counties for various years between 1447 and 1460 show no signs that their lord was engaged in civil war.[3]

On the other hand, one rarely finds a manor that was giving a higher yield at the end of, say, fifty years than at the beginning. But this is to some extent deceptive. By the end of the fourteenth century on most great lay estates the 'casualties' as they were called, such sources of revenue as entry fines, wood-sales, and the profits of mining, quarrying, and brick-kilns—precisely in fact those sources which were being most systematically and gainfully exploited—were being collected not by the manorial officials but by trusted servants of the lord direct. Since they were often paid straight into the lord's coffers, they are not even recorded in the accounts of his receiver-general and hence are omitted from the valors for which that officer was responsible. It is impossible to obtain a *complete* picture of the financial operations of a great *lay*

[1] *H.M.C. Report on MSS. of Lord De L'Isle and Dudley*, i. 207–10; Magdalen Coll., Oxford, Cromwell Papers, 356.

[2] B.M. Add. Rolls 74129, 74158–65, 74168–78 (various Stafford of Grafton accounts from the period 1430–61).

[3] Westminster Abbey Mun. 12165–8.

magnate, even where the exploitation of his estates is concerned, from his manorial accounts alone.[1] It is not for me to say whether this is equally true in the case of the large ecclesiastical landowners also.

But even allowing that agricultural profits were stationary at best and generally falling, had this any marked effect upon the solvency or upon the morale of the governing families? Were they threatened by ruin? Were they incommoded by debt? Did they have to reduce expenditure? The answer to all these questions is a most emphatic NO. In the first place they did not rely upon their lands alone for revenue. For example, John of Gaunt's receiver-general in the year Michaelmas 1376 to Michaelmas 1377 received less than £7,000 from the estates of the duchy, but he met expenses amounting to £8,700 and he ended the year with £4,000 in hand—because he had received more than £6,000 from the Exchequer in wages of war.[2] Late medieval kings did not need to 'live of their own'; because they had plenty of taxes. Their magnates shared their good fortune; they too had no need to 'live of their own'.

But that is not the only reason. Their landed incomes were rising, not steadily but, more accurately, by leaps. The cause is a simple and obvious one: wealth attracted wealth; land married land. Any family that continued to produce male heirs could scarcely fail to increase its inheritance by marriage with an heiress —or a series of heiresses. Earlier I recited the titles of the last Duke of Buckingham; their accumulation represents the result of his ancestors' marriages. Take two other examples, chosen very much at random: the heads of the family of Lovel of Titchmarsh married rich baronial heiresses three times in five generations; the last of the line who perished at Stoke in 1487 could therefore be styled Viscount Lovel, Lord Holland, Deincourt, Burnell, and Grey of Rotherfield.[3] The Mortimer Earls of March were still more fortunate: the first married the heiress of Geneville: his eldest son a coheiress of Badlesmere; the third earl—most successfully of all— the heiress of both Clarence and Ulster—and indeed ultimately of

---

[1] Cf. Appendix C, pp. 129–35 below.
[2] P.R.O. DL 28 3/1.   [3] G.E.C. viii. 2, n. *h.*

England itself; and the fourth a coheiress of the Holland earls of Kent. But heiresses were not the only profitable matches; their portions made most daughters of magnates a means of gain to their husbands. If the nobility had had nothing else but its lands, there would have been no need for anxiety. On the *long* run they were bound to profit, on the short—and indeed also on the long— they could command other sources of supply. Whatever else may have brought them low, there is no call to mention the secular slump.

IV. THE LAND AND THE FAMILY[1]

So far the emphasis has been upon acquisition and accumulation, the getting and piling rather than the spending of wealth. And that is where, until at least quite near the end of the period, the emphasis should properly come. The members of the nobility had earned the means to spend more. Except when they failed to produce a direct male heir in each generation, or committed political suicide—things that happened fairly often—the curve of most individual and family incomes was upward. This was partly because the total available was divided among fewer persons, but not entirely; not, I think, mainly. For the reasons which I have already urged it seems to me certain that the same upward movement was true for the group as a whole. The total available was larger. If the rate of dispersal had not been *almost* as great as the rate of accumulation, the number of noblemen would have fallen much more rapidly than it did.

The most efficient cause of dispersal was, without serious doubt, parental love, the desire to make as large a provision as justice—or even injustice—and circumstances allowed, for children other than the legal heir. Such provision might take the form of either land or cash. The latter can best be considered in my next lecture along with the other objects upon which money was spent. But land, the descent and alienation of which were limited and

---

[1] McFarlane later changed the emphasis of his arguments on some aspects of this subject. His subsequent writings attach more importance to the effect of entails, especially in tail male, in maintaining the unity of inheritances. He also changed his view on the importance of *De Donis*. An outline of his later views will be found in 'The English Nobility in the Later Middle Ages', pp. 268–78 below. Important modifications of the views expressed in 1953 made in the 1965 lectures are noted in footnotes to the present chapter. G. A. Holmes, *The Estates of the Higher Nobility in Fourteenth-Century England* (Cambridge, 1957), pp. 41–57, is an important account of the ways in which the descent of great estates was governed. J. M. W. Bean, *The Decline of English Feudalism 1215–1540* (Manchester, 1968), gives a more recent account of many of the same problems; see also J. L. Barton, 'The Medieval Use', *Law Quarterly Rev.* 81 (1965), 562–77 and S. F. C. Milsom, *Historical Foundations of the Common Law* (1969), pp. 140–210.

governed by its own complicated law, gave rise to special problems if fathers wished to transfer it to their younger children. The satisfaction of this natural impulse was the cause of much bitterness; a number of obstacles, not always devised for the purpose, arose to thwart its most obvious expression; and its over-indulgence in *one* generation had sometimes the result of making it wholly impossible in the next. Yet there is no denying that it was a social force of great power. Since its influence has been the cause of little but misunderstanding, this lecture will be devoted to the land and the family.

It is still a widely held belief that the law of primogeniture, by driving younger sons from the ancestral home into trade and the professions, was a main factor in giving to English society, at least in its higher ranges, that mobility, that lack of rigid stratification, which was its chief virtue, indeed its vital principle. 'When we balance the account of our primogenitary law,' wrote Maitland, 'we must remember that it obliterated class distinctions.'[1] It would be easier to subscribe to this attractive doctrine if the law had in fact been rigorously and *continuously* applied. In our period, for example, the tendency towards primogeniture was greatest at the beginning and at the end; because in Edward I's reign the way to evade the enforcement of the law had not yet been discovered;[2] while by the Tudor period the gradual increase in the amount of entailed land and the introduction of stricter marriage settlements had begun to limit the freedom enjoyed in the interval. Broadly speaking, the expectations of an eldest son—or of daughters as against the collateral male heir—were assured in 1300; as far as the son was concerned they were fairly safe in 1500; but for some time before 1400 they had become precarious, dependent upon the goodwill of parents and public sentiment rather than on law; already by 1400 a better time for the eldest son was in sight. Why was this?

What, at the opening of our period, afforded the heir his (or her) strongest protection was the lack of any means by which land

---

[1] F. Pollock and F. W. Maitland, *History of English Law* (2nd edn., 1911), ii. 274.

[2] But cf. pp. 69 and 276–7 below.

outside boroughs could be devised by will.[1] Alienation was comparatively easy *inter vivos*; but when a landowner died his heir inherited; if he wanted to benefit his younger children he had to do it in his own lifetime. There was nothing much to prevent him when that was his wish. If the land affected was held in chief, a royal licence was necessary; but it was the more readily and cheaply given since the king lost nothing by it and was almost certain to be in full sympathy with its purpose, if that were the endowment of a younger son.[2] The only effective check on dispersal was not attachment to the rights of heirs, but the more selfish—and on that score no less determined—reluctance of most men to divest *themselves*. Members of the medieval nobility did not often fall into King Lear's error. As long as alienation was only possible *inter vivos*, heirs could count on receiving the bulk of their ancestors' lands.

Some inroads were made upon their security as a result of the first chapter of the Statute of Westminster the Second (1285), *De Donis*. The purpose of this enactment was clearly their protection; if it did not always work out as its creators intended, this was not altogether their fault, though in so far as the statute was carelessly drawn perhaps it was. The intention, if we are to believe Chief Justice Bereford—and I think we must—was to ensure that should a man grant lands to his younger sons, or to his daughters in free marriage, these should not be alienated by them until after the third generation; if the line failed before a third heir (i.e. the fourth generation) had entered, then the estate was to revert to the head of the family or his right heir.[3] That is to say that the issue of the younger sons and of the daughters had to earn the

[1] See now M. M. Sheehan, *The Will in Medieval England* (Toronto, 1963), esp. pp. 266–81. While in general agreement with the position stated above, Dr. Sheehan argues that freedom of devise was not unknown even outside boroughs (pp. 278–9) and that something not unlike a bequest of land could be accomplished by the device of the donor's enfeoffing the intended recipient and the recipient's then granting the donor a life interest in the land concerned (p. 273).

[2] For royal control over alienation *inter vivos* and for attempts by mesne tenants to gain or regain control over such alienation in the thirteenth and fourteenth centuries, see Bean, *Decline of English Feudalism*, pp. 40–103.

[3] T. F. T. Plucknett, *The Legislation of Edward I* (Oxford, 1949), pp. 132–4; cf. p. 64, n. 1 below and Milsom, *Historical Foundations of the Common Law*, pp. 140–6.

right to dispose freely of their share of the family lands by surviving into the fourth generation; if as happened in a great many cases, they failed before that, their lands came back to the main line. In the interests of the heir, grants of land to his brothers and sisters were entailed for three generations; that was the intention of *De Donis*.[1]

As far as the daughters were concerned the statute was obsolete almost from birth. For the practice of granting a *maritagium*, a marriage portion *in land*, practically died out before the end of the thirteenth century. Thenceforward the portion took the form of a sum of money. As such it falls outside the scope of this lecture. Daughters, unless they were heiresses, were not, in the later middle ages, an occasion for the dispersal of land.

As far as the estates granted to younger sons were concerned, the statute in the main fulfilled its purpose. The heir's right as reversioner was protected. Yet the entail could be, and soon was, used to deprive the eldest son in whole or in part of the enjoyment of his inheritance. For it provided a means of devising land after death. A man might for example entail lands upon himself with remainder after his death to a younger son and that son's issue in preference to his own heir. And since this did not deprive him during his lifetime of the enjoyment of the land, he was often tempted to greater generosity than he would have been, had the only way been a grant *inter vivos*.

Another factor that helped to weaken the heir's position was the growth of the jointure. I use the word in its strict, original

---

[1] In his 1965 lectures McFarlane pointed out that when Hubert de Burgh was created Earl of Kent on 19 Feb. 1227 the grant was on terms which made the earldom one in fee tail with special remainder to the children of Hubert's third wife, Margaret, only. He continued: 'Hubert de Burgh's only child by Margaret of Scotland predeceased him. So when he died in 1243 his earldom became extinct. Its brief life should, however, warn us that the clause in the second Statute of Westminster 1285 known as *De Donis Conditionalibus* did not originate *estates tail*; it is a good deal later than an outstanding example of one. Even in the fourteenth century the law courts were teaching bad history, as they and their inmates usually do. Entails are older than 1285 and the purpose of *De Donis* was a different one, one which we can fortunately ignore.' For de Burgh's earldom see G.E.C. vii. 137; S. H. F. Johnson, 'Lands of Hubert de Burgh', *E.H.R.* 50 (1935), 430; F. M. Powicke, *King Henry III and the Lord Edward* (2 vols., Oxford, 1947), ii. 767.

sense: that is to say, land held in joint tenancy for their two lives .
by husband and wife and by the survivor alone after the death of
one partner. Early marriage contracts are so rare that it is difficult
to say how old this practice was. Not much older than Edward I's
reign certainly. But in most marriage contracts of the fourteenth
and fifteenth centuries the wife was made sure of a jointure in
part of her husband's lands. If she were an important match, a
great heiress for example, he might have to promise her a jointure
in all he had in order to secure her hand. Many husbands not so
compelled did the same out of pure affection or uxoriousness. The
Lady Mohun who sold Dunster to the Luttrells in reversion owed
her ability to do so to the fact that her late lord had given her a
jointure in all his lands.[1] Without going as far as alienation, a
mother could, merely by surviving, keep her son out of his
inheritance for most of his life; and meanwhile carry it with her
to a second and a third husband. Hence the peculiar prominence of
dowagers in late medieval England. They did not enjoy merely a
dower right in the traditional third of their late husbands' landed
property; they often held it all in jointure, or if not all, at any rate
the greater part. Not every one of them was tempted into second
marriage with a handsome nobody. Many indeed survived more
than one noble—and wealthy—husband, and made better bargains for themselves each time they gave their hands. Others
preferred to keep their freedom in perpetual widowhood. Rich
and respected—or feared—they kept the heirs waiting often as
much as half a century. Horace Walpole writes ungallantly somewhere of 'a dozen antedeluvian dowagers whose carcasses have
miraculously resisted the wet'. It would be easy to match his
collection at any time in our period, from Isabella de Fors to the
Lady Margaret. Think for example of those foundresses of Cambridge colleges, the Lady of Pembroke and the Lady of Clare; of
Margaret, the Countess Marshal, the first woman and apart from
royal mistresses one of the very few to be made a duchess in her
own right; of Joan, Lady Mohun and that other Joan, Lady
Bergavenny whom Adam of Usk called a 'second Jezabel';[2] of

---

[1] Maxwell Lyte, *History of Dunster*, i. 46–8.
[2] *Chronicon*, ed. E. Maunde Thompson (2nd edn., 1904), p. 63.

Joan, Countess of Hereford, the grandmother of Henry V, of Anne, Countess of Stafford and her daughter-in-law Anne, Duchess of Buckingham, of the thrice-widowed Alice Chaucer, Duchess of Suffolk who lies buried out at Ewelme under the finest alabaster effigy of our period; and finally of those two survivors into the reign of Henry VII, Maud, Lady Willoughby, and Cecily, Duchess of York.

What their obstinate survival meant to the expectant heir is brought home to us pointedly enough by the case of Margaret the Countess Marshal. Born sometime in the 1320s, she became by the death of her only brother coheir with her sister to their father, Thomas of Brotherton, Earl of Norfolk, fifth son of Edward I. Between the brother's death in 1337 and her father's the following year she was married to John, Lord Seagrave.[1] For such a chance Seagrave paid by giving her a jointure of nearly all his lands.[2] He died in 1353 when his so-called 'heir' was their daughter Elizabeth, wife of John Mowbray of Axholme. But his widow enjoyed nearly the whole Seagrave inheritance long after the death of her daughter and son-in-law, saw her own second husband Walter, Lord Mauny into his grave, and survived, by then her father's sole heir,[3] until 1399. It was not until November 1413 that her *great-*grandson, another John Mowbray, coming of age, at last entered upon the lands of both Seagrave and Brotherton exactly sixty years after John Seagrave's death. If in this period dowagers had a new and sometimes disproportionate weight in society it was thanks largely to the jointure.

Jointure and entail combined with a second marriage could do

---

[1] G.E.C. ix. 599–601; xi. 609–10.

[2] This appears from his inquisition post mortem (*C.I.P.M.* x, no. 116). The great majority of the Seagrave properties were held jointly with Margaret. All that appear to have remained for his daughter and her husband were a manor in Northants. and, two in Warwicks. and a number of small properties elsewhere. Cf. *C.C.R. 1369–74*, pp. 374–7 for the Seagrave property in Margaret's possession after the death of her second husband.

[3] Margaret became sole heir to Thomas of Brotherton's lands on the death of her niece, Joan, Countess of Suffolk, in 1375. She had earlier succeeded to half the dower lands held by her stepmother, who died in 1361 or 1362 (*C.C.R. 1360–4*, p. 444). For an indication of the extent of her estates at her death see *C.I.P.M.* iii (Rec. Comm., 1821), 271–2.

most damage to the chances of an heir. An actual case will make this clear; I choose a fairly early one. Maud, only sister and heir of Edward Burnell, who died without issue in 1315, had two husbands: John Lovel who was killed at Bannockburn in 1314 and John Hadlow, a creature of the younger Despenser's, who survived her and lived until 1346. Maud had children by both husbands, a daughter and a posthumous son John by Lovel and two or more sons by Hadlow. Between her second marriage in 1315 and her death in 1341 much of her enormous inheritance was entailed upon herself and Hadlow in jointure with remainder to the heirs male of their two bodies, with only a reversion, them failing, to her eldest son and legal heir, John Lovel, and his issue. Fortunately for the latter he had his father's inheritance already, though this was not as valuable as his mother's. By this perfectly legitimate use of jointure and entail, he was excluded from most of the Burnell estates unless and until the Hadlow male line failed.[1]

But men also were widowed and agreed to marry again. If like Maud Burnell they reared a second family some of them were inclined to do as she did. One of the most famous examples was that of Ralph Nevill, first Earl of Westmorland, who under the influence of his ambitious, determined, and well-connected second wife, Joan Beaufort, stripped his heir for the benefit of *her* eldest son, Richard, later Earl of Salisbury.[2] In that case not only propriety but also legality was sacrificed, since a part of the lands thus diverted from the second Earl of Westmorland was itself already

[1] For the entailing of much of the Burnell inheritance on Hadlow see *Sir Christopher Hatton's Book of Seals*, ed. L. C. Loyd and D. M. Stenton (Oxford, 1950), no. 358; *C.P.R. 1313–17*, pp. 554–5; *C.P.R. 1317–21*, p. 601. Nicholas, Hadlow's son by Maud, changed his name to Burnell on succeeding to the Burnell lands (G.E.C. ii. 435). The male line from Hadlow and Maud ran out with the death of Hugh Burnell in 1420 and William, Lord Lovel, made good his claim to most of the Burnell estates; his succession to some was impeded by a further, and illegal, settlement which had been made by Hugh Burnell in 1416 ('Exul', 'Cases from the Early Chancery Proceedings', *The Ancestor*, 8 (1904), 170–183; *V.C.H. Shropshire*, vol. viii, ed. A. T. Gaydon, p. 7; *Lincoln Diocesan Documents*, ed. A. Clarke (E.E.T.S., orig. ser., no. 149), pp. 73, 81–6; P. Morant, *History and Antiquities of Essex* (2 vols., 1768), ii. 12–13, 92. Cf. G.E.C. viii. 217–23).

[2] T. B. Pugh and C. D. Ross, 'The English Baronage and the Income Tax of 1436', *B.I.H.R.* 26 (1953), 7–8; J. R. Lander, 'Marriage and Politics in the Fifteenth Century: the Nevilles and the Wydevilles', *B.I.H.R.* 36 (1963), 137 and n.

entailed upon him; but the times of Henry VI's long minority were, as we shall see, bad for a friendless and impoverished claimant to prevail against the might of Beaufort.

Nevertheless, even where the entail was employed without scruple to deprive the heir of the practical enjoyment of his inheritance, its influence was always in favour of securing his reversionary rights. During the fourteenth century, as judicial interpretation was employed upon *De Donis*, the scales were tipped still more to the profit of the reversioner. The limitation to three generations disappeared and the entail became perpetual. Its irrevocable character and, until effective ways of breaking it had been discovered, its almost infinite survival were felt to be irksome, at least by some holders of entailed lands. What to them were disadvantages were of course precisely the reverse to those who wished, as too many ancestors always do, to impose their will upon unborn generations of their issue; from their point of view the idea of their descendants suffering from their bonds was not altogether distasteful; that was what the bonds were for; the fact that an entail was unbreakable was its virtue. But it had some vices for them also. They could not change their minds; circumstances during their own lives changed, but the entail tied *their* hands as effectively as it did their descendants'. Again an entail, even when limited to male issue of a particular marriage, committed them to doing more for the family of a younger son than they always thought necessary; a life-interest just for one generation seemed to many parents a sufficient provision; it gave the cadet line a start and the chance to make good. The case could be met by a cash payment similar to that which had replaced the *maritagium* and often was so met. But money was perhaps too easily squandered. For these reasons most men were attracted to something of shorter duration and greater adaptability than the entail and which at the same time enabled each to distribute his land after his death in accordance with the promptings of his heart. He found what he wanted in the use.

This device owed its origins to no statute and it is possible that the occasion of its first appearance might repay careful search. Maitland, looking through volume I of *Testamenta Eboracensia*, noted as 'about the first' case of its employment to devise land, the will made by William, Lord Latimer in 1380; and a very interesting will it is, though it is far from being the first of its kind.[1] There are many surviving from every decade of Edward III's reign. The earliest I have noticed, though, wills of that period being scarce, I should hesitate to describe as even 'about the first', belongs to the year 1323 and we can carry its history at least as far back as 1297, to the arrangements made by William de Vescy to convey his Yorkshire manors to his bastard son.[2]

Whenever, and still more whatever, its origins, the use was a simple, but flexible, means of devising land by will; as early as Edward III's reign its value was widely recognized and by the end of the fourteenth century it was almost universally resorted to, even to transmit land to the heir at common law because it had the over-riding advantage of excluding the lord from wardship during a minority. And like the entail it protected the lands from forfeiture for treason.[3] All that was necessary was that a man should grant his lands, or any part of them, to a number of his friends, usually called his feoffees, to hold to his *use* as long as he instructed them and to dispose of when he was dead in accordance with his *last* will. The feoffees were bound in equity to obey his wishes and were answerable in Chancery for any default.[4] By

[1] F. W. Maitland, *Equity and the Forms of Action at Common Law* (Cambridge, 1909), p. 30.

[2] G.E.C. xii, pt. 2, 282; cf. Bean, *Decline of English Feudalism*, pp. 118–19. Dr. Bean (pp. 104–79) sees the beginnings of the practice of employing enfeoffment to uses to control the disposition of land after the feoffor's death as lying in the thirteenth century. His researches among the *Inquisitiones Post Mortem* have produced a number of instances from the reign of Edward II and have shown the practice to have been of growing popularity in the reign of Edward III. Enfeoffment to uses was, he believes, to begin with largely confined to mesne tenants and 'the practice . . . appears to have begun among the lower orders of feudal society', becoming popular among great lords after 1340.

[3] Enfeoffment to uses gave such protection until 1388 (Ross, 'Forfeiture for Treason in the Reign of Richard II', pp. 569–70); entails gave it until 1398 (Lander, 'Attainder and Forfeiture, 1453–1509', p. 119). Cf. p. 270 n. 2 below.

[4] The development of Chancery jurisdiction over feoffees to uses is very obscure. Mr. Barton ('The Medieval Use', p. 569) suggests that 'it would seem most probable . . . that *cestuy que use* first obtained his remedy in equity in the early years of Richard II', cf. Holmes, *Estates of the Higher Nobility*, p. 55. M. E. Avery, An Evaluation of the Effectiveness of the Court of Chancery under the Lancastrian

two or more conveyances *inter vivos* a landowner was thus enabled to make a *post obit* distribution of his estates; just as, by means of his testament, he could already of his goods. And he could combine the use and the entail in whatever proportions he pleased. His freedom was thereby much enlarged. How did he use it?

To please himself, of course. For that very reason no generalization is possible. Practice varied from a flat endorsement of primogeniture to the virtual disinheritance of the common law heir, from an obvious partiality for one son to an equal partition among many. Since the last of these courses, if widely followed, would have resulted in the greatest dispersal, it merits first attention. Although primogeniture had been the prevailing rule in England, at any rate since the Conquest, the survival of other customs must not be wholly ignored, ultimogeniture or Borough English, for example, and partibility, or, as it is generally called, gavelkind. The first, at any rate where the nobility was concerned, did not matter, but partibility, in Kent and its neighbourhood at least, was still widely prevalent down to the end of the middle ages. It is often said that Kentish gavelkind was restricted to men of low estate and of no concern to members of the knightly class. This is quite untrue. Although Edward I disgavelled the lands of Sir John Cobham in 1276, the latter's descendants, forming one of the most notable and prolific families in the county, were still partitioning many of their lands a century and more later.[1] Not all had earned the royal gratitude by such service as Sir John Cobham's. It is only necessary to look at the history of any prominent Kentish family —for example the Savages of Bobbing, who gave a Speaker to the Commons and a wet-nurse to Richard II—to find knightly owners of gavelkind lands.[2] This they could not help, but parti-

---

Kings', *Law Quarterly Rev.* 86 (1970), 84, indicates that the great growth in Chancery business between 1420 and 1450 was due mainly to litigation over enfeoffment to uses. 'By the 1450s 90 per cent of all cases coming before the Chancellor were concerned with uses'; cf. M. E. Avery, 'The History of the Equitable Jurisdiction of Chancery before 1460', *B.I.H.R.* 42 (1969), 129–44.

[1] Pollock and Maitland, *History of English Law*, ii. 273. For later members of the family holding in gavelkind see, e.g. *Collectanea Topographica et Genealogica*, vii. 335, 340.

[2] Bodleian Library, Dodsworth MS. 71, f. 11^{r-v} records the partition of the

bility was also adopted voluntarily by others. Thus Sir John Archdeacon of Ruan Lanihorne in Cornwall in 1365 divided his estates into eight portions and settled one of them in tail male on each of eight sons.[1] Lest this should be thought a piece of Cornish eccentricity, take the case of that immensely wealthy peer, William, Lord Lovel, whose family, as I described last time, amassed in its hands the heritages of five baronial houses. He certainly did his best to scatter this accumulation in the will he made on 18 March 1455.[1] At his death, which followed on 13 June, his scores of manors were to be partitioned, if not equally, yet with a generous share for each, among his four surviving sons.

But that went a good deal further than most parents thought right. At least two convictions or principles guided their actions. One was of ancient origin: the tradition that distinguished between inheritance and conquest, that laid down what a man received from *his* father ought to go undiminished to his eldest son, but that what he acquired by purchase, marriage, or the like he might distribute how he thought best. It was on this principle that Robert received Normandy in 1087 and Rufus England. The other principle was scarcely less ancient: that to leave *any* son unprovided for was a sign of failure. Whatever may have seemed to Maitland the virtues of primogeniture, they were not recognized by medieval parents; it was no part of *their* social theory that their younger sons should be de-classed. For a time the law that whatever land they died in possession of *must* go to their heir or heirs thwarted their efforts to make a handsome provision for their cadets. Now the use allowed them to follow their bent. The effects of this are too obvious: in the number of younger sons of magnates, even bastard sons of magnates, who themselves became magnates in their own right. Late medieval society is full of them: John Fitzalan, Lord Maltravers; William Beauchamp, Lord Bergavenny; Hugh Stafford, Lord Bourchier; John, Lord Devereux; Thomas Percy, Earl of Worcester; or John Beaufort, Earl of Somerset and Marquess of Dorset, to name merely a few

lands of Sir Roger Savage between his two sons temp. Edward II. Cf. F. R. H. Du Boulay, 'Gavelkind and Knight's Fee in Medieval Kent', *E.H.R.* 77 (1961), 504–10.
[1] p. 277 below.

alive in the last years of Richard II's reign. In the fifteenth century the prominence of cadet members of such families as the Nevills, the Percies, the Staffords, and the Bourchiers needs no emphasis. And yet both Edward I and Edward III have been heavily and continuously blamed by historians for what is called their 'appanage policy', for creating earldoms and duchies for *their* younger sons. As if they would not have been condemned by public opinion both abroad and in England if they had done anything else! They could do no less for their cadets than their noble subjects did for theirs; that they could do much more was evidence of their wealth. And before they are dismissed as short-sighted, please remember that Henry VII created (in 1494) a new cadet royal house of York in the person of his second son; only the death of Arthur undid the effects of that day's work. But neither kings' sons nor knights' sons could be cast landless upon the world without being reproaches to their fathers. There was no question of allowing cadets to be de-classed.

If, on the other hand, a common law heir was to be disinherited, it was likely to be a woman. An heiress carried her inheritance out of the family; *co*heiresses in addition broke it into fragments. Their occurrence was understandably disliked. Both use and entail were employed to retain the estates in the hands of a family's male members, or at least to give them a preference; only in the event of a total failure of heirs male were they to 'fall among the spindles'. To make certain of this was the commonest purpose of the entail. Thus on 24 April 1344 Thomas Beauchamp, Earl of Warwick, with Edward III's licence, entailed the major part of the lands of his earldom.[1] Not content with that, he put everything into the hands of feoffees before making his will on 6 September 1369.[2] His concern was justified, since on 28 April 1360 his eldest son Guy had died leaving only two daughters, who for the greater security of their uncle were quickly made to take the veil.[3] This enabled Earl Thomas to bequeath lands worth 400

---

[1] For this entail and that of Gower in 1356 see Holmes, *Estates of the Higher Nobility*, pp. 48–9; G.E.C. xii, pt. 2. 374.

[2] *C.C.R. 1369–74*, pp. 108–9; cf. Holmes, *Estates of the Higher Nobility*, p. 49. For the will see p. 187, n. 4 below.

[3] Katherine, the elder of Guy's daughters, was aged seven in 1360 and a nun by

marks per annum (probably about a twelfth of the whole) to his younger surviving son, William, and the rest to the elder, his successor and namesake.[1] Katherine Beauchamp, by then a nun of Shouldham, who but for her grandfather's actions would have inherited all (her sister was dead), received a gold ring and £20. It was no rare thing for the women of noble houses to be thus cynically thrust aside. Yet as a rule a landowner put his daughter's interests above those of his brother or his brother's son. The de la Poles owed their Wingfield estates in Suffolk to Sir John Wingfield's preference for Katherine, his only child, as against his brothers.[2] It took the male Wingfields until the sixteenth century to recover from the loss. When the heir male was still more distant, his chances were correspondingly reduced. Inheritance by females, though less usual, continued to happen.

Thanks to the freedom conferred by the use, every conceivable alternative to straight inheritance had its devotees. Bastard children, for example, could be more liberally provided for; in default of legitimate issue, they would stand a much better chance of receiving the unentailed lands than, say, a distant cousin. The rise in the social status of bastards towards the end of the middle ages was due to no invasion of continental morals from France, but to the fact that, whereas a natural child could not legally inherit, he could by then receive a bequest of land under his father's will.

Here the use was a means of transferring land to someone who in no conceivable circumstances (short of an act of Parliament) could have become the heir. It was also commonly employed to benefit friends and relations suffering from a like disability. Of this the case of the Malmains inheritance may serve as an example, for it well illustrates a tendency that has spread confusion among

the time of her grandfather's death in 1369 (G.E.C. xii, pt. 2. 375, n. *c*.). The younger, Elizabeth, was aged one in 1360 and died in 1369 (ibid.); we cannot trace the reference to her having been a nun.

[1] Cf. p. 191 below and notes.

[2] For the passage of most of Sir John Wingfield's lands to his daughter and so to the de la Poles see G.E.C. xii, pt. i. 440 and notes; *C.I.P.M.* xiv, no. 217; *C.P.R. 1388–92*, pp. 209–10; *C.C.R. 1389–92*, pp. 41–2, 116–18. For the Wingfield pedigree, T. Blore, *History . . . of Rutland* (Stamford, 1811), pp. 65–9; J. M. Wingfield, *Some Records of the Wingfield Family* (1925).

peerage lawyers and muddled even John Horace Round. On 1 November 1375 Sir Thomas Grandison, the last male of his baronial family, died childless. His heirs-at-law to the Grandison part of his inheritance were the issue of his three aunts and to them most of it descended. But Sir Thomas was also the son and heir of Beatrice Malmains, herself a coheiress of a rich Kentish family. Instead of the Malmains lands going to their rightful Malmains heir, they were entailed upon a certain Sir William Brian. The beneficiary, a younger son of Guy, Lord Brian, was a distant cousin of Grandison's through the latter's father and had no blood relationship with the family of Malmains at all.[1]

What happened on the death in 1389 of the last Hastings Earl of Pembroke may seem even more irregular, as it is certainly more complicated. John Hastings was childless and under age. His heir was his second cousin once removed, Reynold, Lord Grey of Ruthin.[2] There was a still more distant heir male, Hugh Hastings of Elsing, but he was disabled by being of the half-blood only, so that his brother, and heir, Edward's attempt to intervene in the case was both futile and expensive; he was kept for twenty years a prisoner in the Marshalsea for refusing to pay the costs.[3] Reynold Grey's danger came not from him, but from William Beauchamp, that younger son of the Earl of Warwick who was left 400 marks of land in his father's will.[4] For in 1369 John Hastings's father had

---

[1] For the disposal of Grandison's lands and the entails which, upon his death without heirs of his body, benefited Sir William Brian, see *C.I.P.M.* xiv, no. 141, esp. pp. 137–8, cf. G.E.C. vi. 68 and *Minutes of Evidence . . . before the Committee for Privileges . . . [on] . . . the Petition to determine the Abeyance of the Barony of Grandison* (1854), esp. p. 313. Brian was the grandson of Katherine, Thomas Grandison's father's sister, being the son of her daughter Elizabeth (G.E.C. ii. 361). At least some of the Malmains lands which ultimately went to Brian appear to have been entailed by Thomas Grandison's mother's father, Nicholas Malmains, upon her and her husband, Otto Grandison, with remainder to Otto's heirs (*C.I.P.M.* ix, no. 418; *C.F.R. 1347–56*, p. 215).

[2] This case has now been discussed at length by R. I. Jack, 'Entail and Descent: the Hastings Inheritance', *B.I.H.R.* 38 (1965), 1–19. See also Holmes, *Estates of the Higher Nobility*, pp. 38, 42, 54; G.E.C. i. 24, n. *b*; vi. 155 and n. *h*; x. 394–7.

[3] G.E.C. vi. 352–9; G. C. Young, *An Account of the Controversy between Reginald, Lord Grey of Ruthyn and Sir Edward Hastings* (priv. printed, 1841); A. R. Wagner, 'A Fifteenth Century Description of the Brass of Sir Hugh Hastings at Elsing, Norfolk', *Antiquaries Journ.* 19 (1939), 421–8.

[4] Above, p. 72.

made an enfeoffment of all his lands in England and Wales,[1] and three years later he had made his will.[2] If he died without heirs of his body Pembroke itself was to go to the king. Everything else was to be offered to Sir William Beauchamp, his cousin on the distaff side (their mothers were sisters), upon two far from heavy conditions: (1) that he should take the entire arms of the Hastings family and (2) that he should do his best to induce the king to grant the title of Earl of Pembroke to him and his heirs. If he refused, the same offer was in turn to be made to a friend and connection who was not even a kinsman, Sir William Clinton. In 1375 after Pembroke's death, Beauchamp came before the king's Council and averred his willingness to abide by the conditions; this eliminated Clinton.[3] But for the moment the matter was in abeyance since the earl who had made the will had left an infant son. That was still the weakness of Beauchamp's position in 1389, when that son was dead; its strength lay in the fact that the child had never had possession and died under age. Reynold Grey could claim that he had died intestate and that everything, including Pembroke, went to his legal heir. Here he found himself in conflict with the king, who had been bribed with that valuable Welsh county to side with Beauchamp. The parties wisely decided to split the spoils. Richard II kept Pembroke but leased it to Beauchamp for life; Beauchamp received the great lordship of Bergavenny and a number of English manors, mostly in the west midlands; Grey was left with the rest, including the arms of Hastings.[4] For the heir this can hardly have been much consolation. Had there been no power to devise land, had, that is to say, the position

[1] *C.P.R. 1367–70*, p. 223; *C.P.R. 1374–7*, p. 78, cf. p. 437; *C.C.R. 1374–7*, pp. 286–8.

[2] *C.C.R. 1374–7*, p. 287. Cf. *Catalogue of Ancient Deeds*, iii, A 4890; G.E.C. i. 24, n. *b*. This will is distinct from those printed by J. Nichols, *Royal Wills* (1780), pp. 92–5 (corrected G.E.C. x. 394, n. *a*), though of the same date, 5 May 1372, as the first of them.

[3] *C.C.R. 1374–7*, pp. 286–8.

[4] See also Dr. Jack's important article (above, p. 74, n. 2), where it is shown that Abergavenny was probably sold to Beauchamp by Grey; though it is unclear whether the price was a concessionary one or not. Besides the sources cited above and by Dr. Jack there are documents relating to the case of the Hastings inheritance in Westminster Abbey (Mun. 1976, 1978).

not changed radically since 1290, Reynold Grey would have succeeded to the earldom of Pembroke, just as the Hastings family had succeeded the Valences and the Valences the Marshals. The law of primogeniture had been thrown to the winds.

And so it often was. Except for its size this was not an exceptional case. The same means were employed by Ralph, Lord Basset of Drayton, in 1390 to deprive his heirs, Thomas, Earl of Stafford and Alice Chaworth, his second cousins once removed, in favour of Hugh Shirley, the son of his uterine and possible bastard sister.[1] It was used again in 1430 to convey the Latimer estates and peerage away from the lawful heir, Elizabeth Willoughby, to George Nevill.[2] Although the injured parties were naturally furious, there was nothing illegal in these alienations; a man had no legal duty, only a moral one variously interpreted, to leave his heir anything. The most that the disinherited could hope for was a bribe to abstain from being a nuisance to their supplanters in the courts. The weaker the title, the larger the bribe; thus William Beauchamp's shaky hold made it necessary for him to buy Grey off. A settlement by arbitrators was usually the best plan; if reinforced by quitclaims with warranty all round it might last.

But in most cases the result was not dispersal. In that of Basset of Drayton, for example, a single nephew, had been preferred to two more distant coheirs. Only to the extent that it was necessary to buy off dangerous claimants did these practices threaten the integrity of the great estates. It is noteworthy that in all the examples I have cited the testator was childless. His lands, slowly built up by a series of marriages with heiresses, had as a result several heirs; the use and the entail often kept them together.

They did other and mightier things as well; mightiest of all, they kept them, sometimes permanently, out of the hands of the overlord and particularly those of the chief of all overlords, the king. Entailed estates were not forfeit for treason or felony; their tenant was in law only a life tenant and the rights of remainderman and reversioner were not affected. It was for this reason and

[1] G.E.C. ii. 3–6.   [2] G.E.C. vii. 477.

not from weakness or good nature that kings restored the heirs of traitors to their *entailed* lands; their fees simple and their chattels were at the king's mercy, not so what they held in tail or for life.[1] Some rulers did not honour this distinction fully, but when they did not it was they who were law-breakers. Then again, the man to whose use lands had been enfeoffed was not the tenant in law; his feoffees were. It followed that his lord was deprived of wardship and marriage when he was a child and of escheat when he died without heirs. With the introduction of the use there was a rapid decline of seignorial incidents. A family retained control of its estates (and of their revenues) during a minority and could marry the heir, his brothers, and sisters, without interference from above. But believing in making doubly sure, most landowners hastened to arrange marriages for their children when the latter were still in the nursery—or indeed in the cradle. There was always the chance that a flaw might be discovered in their enfeoffments for use; and the king for one was on the look-out for a wardship if the opportunity offered. It was as well to be quick; the brides were sent home after the wedding to wait until they were husband high. (These were not child marriages in the Hindu sense.)

Everything, however, conspired to deprive the lord of his traditional privileges. Only the unwary died leaving their families exposed to his exploitation. In so far as they were lords men suffered, but since they were also someone's tenants they benefited. The only general sufferer was the Crown, though its right to license an enfeoffment at least in part safeguarded its position. It was content until 1485 to let the nobility have its way without demanding heavy compensation. For the time had not come when kings worried desperately about the fall in their seignorial revenues; they found taxation preferable. It is one of the ironies of history that it was those 'new monarchs' the Tudors who were so afraid to tax that they had once more to exploit the incidents of tenure. One might say 'how medieval of them!' had not the middle ages in fact been more modern. But since the nobility in the fourteenth and fifteenth centuries paid less than their fair share—

[1] But cf. p. 69, n. 3 above.

far less—of taxes, the king's preference for taxation was doubly favourable to them. They kept a tighter hold than ever before over their own lands. If there was any dispersal it was in accordance with their choice.

To judge from the hundreds of wills for lands that survive the balance of choice was in favour of dispersal. Had all these wills taken effect as their makers intended, the total result would have been a considerable break-up of the great estates. But intention was one thing and effect another. What made their wills in the long run inoperative was the failure of most families to breed. I do not mean that they were sterile; in each generation there were as a rule large numbers of children; but few reached manhood, fewer still had male children of their own. With a few rare and notable exceptions, the junior branches of the nobility failed to strike roots of their own. It is not generally realized how near to extinction most families were; their survival was always in the balance and only a tiny handful managed to hang on in the male line from one century to another.

This was true after all of the royal family itself. Edward I had six sons; yet by 1338 there was only one stock among them left in the male line, that of Edward III himself. Again, Henry IV had four sons and two daughters who outlived childhood; a fifth son was stillborn; yet by 1450 his only living descendant was the sickly Henry VI. From the Conquest to the end of the fourteenth century the only junior branch of the royal house to last for as much as a century was the first house of Lancaster; and that perished after achieving only 116 years.

The house of Anjou was not unlucky; on the contrary it was tougher than most. Its span—in England—from 1154 to 1499, when Edward, Earl of Warwick, perished in the Tower, was surpassed by few among the greater baronage. Of these the Vere Earls of Oxford were the longest lived, but they also often came near to extinction and as far as our period is concerned established only two cadet branches, each of which, by the extinction of the main line, inherited the earldom. Take two other great families of ancient settlement: the Staffords of Stafford and the Beauchamps of Warwick. The Staffords became earls in 1351, dukes in

1444, and were deprived in 1521; during that period of 170 years they produced no cadet branch that survived for more than two generations. Yet Hugh, the second earl, had five sons and Humphrey, the first duke, had three; in vain, for only the single line endured. The Beauchamps became Earls of Warwick by inheritance from the Mauduits in 1268; the male line failed with the death of Henry, Duke of Warwick, in 1445. There were six generations only in this long span of 177 years and once at least there were four hopeful sons. Yet, as in the case of the Staffords, there was no cadet branch founded during that period which survived for more than two generations. If a link is wanted between the various contemporary Staffords and Beauchamps and their parent stock it is necessary to go further back than the first earls. How many baronial families lasted for so long? The answer is: very few. If each succeeded in establishing a junior line once in a while it was lucky. The chances against a spreading family tree of many branches seem to have been heavy. Even the unusually prolific stocks the Fitzalans and the Courtenays in the fourteenth century, the Nevills and the Bourchiers in the fifteenth, were heavily lopped soon enough. Ralph Nevill, first Earl of Westmorland, boasted of twenty-three children, of whom eleven were sons. Yet four of these were never reared and the number of descendants of the remainder shrank steadily; there were only three male Nevill lines left by 1500, but seventy-five years after the patriarch Ralph's death. On such a scale has the wastage to be reckoned.

However generous, therefore, fathers may have been in endowing their younger sons, death and the entail conspired to bring the greater part of the dispersed lands back to the male heirs. Nor does the evidence suggest that the mortality rate was any lower among the inferior *noblesse* than it was among the baronage. Provision for cadets, however lavish it may at times have been, cannot therefore be safely relied upon as a potent influence in favour of dispersal. What is more, the reason for the fall in the number of magnates as well as in the number of knights ('real' and 'potential') throughout the middle ages has by now become clearer. By the laws of inheritance, lands were becoming concentrated in fewer and fewer hands, the hands of those lucky enough to survive the danger of extinction, threatened partly by violence but largely by natural causes. The recruits to the nobility, though many, were not sufficient to fill the gaps; and what is more they had further to go to reach the top as those above them added estate to estate, the few profiteers of survival.

Such was the position when the long-term effects of *De Donis* began to make themselves felt. By the middle of the fifteenth century a great deal of the land held by the older nobility had become entailed. Long before then a series of attempts had been made to bar an entail (or in non-legal language, to break it); various devices were resorted to with that intention; some, assisted by bribery and maintenance, though illegal, were partially successful. The right solution was at last found in the action known as 'common recovery'. There seems to be no historical reason for quarrelling with the legal tradition that this dates from *Taltarum's Case*, 1472.[1] It was certainly not much older.

Entails henceforward could be barred. But that does not mean that they were. In most cases they were irksome but not intolerable. So long as each successive tenant left an heir male of his own body to inherit, he was unlikely to make any effort to bar the entail. Trouble might arise when there was a prospect of the estate being carried to a distant kinsman in preference to the tenant's own daughter or daughters. But for the most part the claims of the heir male were rated higher than any woman's; and many men were content to let the entail run its course unbarred. There is no evidence that during this period it was ever barred in order to provide for younger sons and daughters out of the land that ought to have gone in tail to the eldest. If *Taltarum's Case* ultimately made dispersal easier, its first effects in that direction were negligible. It did not threaten the primogenitary law—

[1] T. F. T. Plucknett, *Concise History of the Common Law* (5th edn., 1956), pp. 620–2; and more recently A. W. B. Simpson, *Introduction to the History of the Land Law* (Oxford, 1961), pp. 122–7 and Milsom, *Historical Foundations of the Common Law*, pp. 147–59, who brings out the uncertainties and obscurities of this subject. M. Hastings, *The Court of Common Pleas in Fifteenth Century England* (Ithaca, N.Y., 1947), p. 13, maintains that the common recovery was well established before Taltarum's case.

which was at this time being strengthened by help from another quarter.

The interests of eldest sons had fallen into safe hands: those of their prospective fathers-in-law. Freedom of dispersal, as permitted by the use, had alarmed those with daughters to marry, as well it might. What was the point of a man's offering a large portion in order to secure for his daughter the hand of an heir, if the value of the match could be subsequently depreciated by an excessive provision for the heir's younger brother? There are signs of this uneasiness in some fourteenth-century marriage contracts, where the father of the heir was sometimes obliged to take an oath 'not to alienate his lands and tenements'[1] after the contract had been sealed. Or he might agree to entail most of his estates. But until about 1450 such a clause is rarely found; thereafter it becomes increasingly common. A good simple example occurs in the contract between Thomas Howard, Earl of Surrey and Elizabeth, Henry VII's queen, dated 12 February 1495, for the marriage of his eldest son with her sister Anne of York. The earl covenants that he 'shall not alien ne discontinue any of the manors, castles, lands', etc., 'whereof he or any other to his use is now seised . . . but that he shall die sole seised of the same . . . of estate of inheritance of the same'; though it was allowed that he might give any future wife he might himself marry a jointure of £200 a year.[2] Many instances could be quoted of fathers thus made to promise to leave nearly the whole of their estates 'discharged of all statutes of the Staple, statutes merchant, recognisances, dowers, jointures, annuities, grants or other encumbrances' to their lawful heirs. They lost their freedom when they married their eldest son, as Sir William Plumpton painfully discovered.[3] By 1485 primogeniture, after a century and a half of uncertainty, was once more enthroned. The time was gone when a man could devise his estate

[1] *Catalogue of Ancient Deeds*, iv, no. A 8768, a marriage agreement of 1349 between Thomas de Dutton and Adam de Moldeworth, whereby Thomas's sister was to marry Adam's son; one of the terms was that Adam was to take such an oath.

[2] Madox, *Formulare*, pp. 109–10.

[3] *Plumpton Correspondence*, ed. T. Stapleton (C.S., 1839), pp. lxvii–v, lxxvii–xcv.

in equal parts between his sons. It was gone, but it had happened; and it deserves to be remembered.[1]

---

[1] The corresponding lecture in the 1965 series ended: 'Our primogenitary law, in danger of fading away, was thus restored. But in the interval freedom to devise land by will had seemed likely to give England a *noblesse*. The entail and the marriage settlement made sure that it would only have a peerage.'

V. EXPENDITURE

ON what did the late-medieval nobility spend its money? Once again the evidence allows no more than some very tentative answers. In bulk that evidence is considerable; but apart from the long, though by no means complete, series of testaments, it is made up of chance and isolated survivals, an occasional household or wardrobe account, tradesmen's receipts and bills of servants' expenses, miscellaneous contracts and bonds, and a few detailed inventories of furniture, jewels, and plate. Sometimes the discovery of a single new document may radically alter our knowledge of a man's financial interests or status. It is clearly dangerous to generalize on so personal a matter as expenditure from even a large number of separate examples. It is still more dangerous when in no single case is the evidence complete, rarely indeed even full. Nevertheless, these random glimpses *are* instructive, if only about individuals. And there are so many of them that in the end it is difficult not to reach some hesitant conclusions about the spending habits of the group as a whole.

Not, of course, that all men behaved alike. When it came to buying land, for example, practice varied widely. Nothing could be further from the truth than the impression that once a noble captain had made money he invariably hastened to sink it in real estate. Some did and some did not. Those with the most unquenchable appetite for land were most often men who had been born without much of it, the parvenus. Sir John Fastolf's patrimony when he came of age in 1401 was small; it consisted of some tenements in Yarmouth and a few farms to the north of the town at Caister. His marriage while on active service to the widow of another captain, a woman much his senior in age, put him in life possession of an estate of about £240 a year. By 1433 he had increased his English holdings so that they brought him annually a clear £600. Twelve years later, when he caused a valor to be made, his landed income had risen to close upon £1,000. By then the pace was slackening and the last decade of his long life was overshadowed by trouble with his lawless neighbours, expensive litigation, and failing health. Even so he died a very rich man.[1]

It is unusual to find a *baronial* family increasing its acreage at this rate, except by marriage. Yet William, Lord Latimer, who was born in 1330, fought beside the Black Prince at Crécy and ended his active military career less than a year before his death in 1381, lists in his will the dozen manors in five counties he had bought to add to his already considerable patrimony.[2] Another example is that of Fastolf's younger contemporary and sometime comrade-in-arms, Ralph, Lord Cromwell; this peer, though he spent immense sums on other things, more than doubled his net income from land—excluding his wife's inheritance—between 1429 and 1456, the year when he died.[3]

On the whole, however, members of the greater baronage were slow to add to their estates by purchase. For one thing, marriage was a cheaper step to the same end. If an earl or a duke bought land, it was sometimes perhaps for the benefit of himself and his heir (like the Scropes's acquisition of the lordship of Man), but more often in order to provide for his younger sons. When John of Gaunt paid the childless Earl of Salisbury 5,000 marks for the reversion of those two manors in Somerset, it was in order that they might be settled on his bastard son John Beaufort.[4] This and an act of legitimation made possible the latter's marriage to a daughter of the Earl of Kent. But the object could have been achieved just as easily by a grant of some of the duke's own lands; Gaunt's reluctance to diminish his eldest son's expectations may have been unusually scrupulous; in any case it was yet another proof of his abundant wealth.

Among the first claims on his pocket which no self-respecting father thought it right—or wise—to shirk was the provision of adequate marriage portions for his daughters. To possess dis-

---

[1] For Fastolf's wealth see McFarlane, 'The Investment of Sir John Fastolf's Profits of War'.

[2] *Testamenta Eboracensia*, i. 113–16; a slightly different version is in Lambeth Library, Reg. Sudbury, f. 108ᵛ.

[3] McFarlane, 'The Wars of the Roses', p. 97, n. 1.

[4] For the purchase see p. 55, n. 3 above; for the settlement *C.P.R. 1391–6*, p. 529 (involving some other Somerset lands also).

tinguished sons-in-law added greatly to his worship, his worldly repute. The disposal of the hand of a daughter was his chief opportunity to forge a valuable connection; for him, therefore, a marriage contract was in the nature of a treaty of alliance. He could either buy a royal ward or deal directly with the boy's own family. For unlike the obsolete *maritagium*, the portion went neither to the bride herself nor—except in the rare case when he was his own master—to her future husband, but to the latter's father or guardian. It was not really a portion but the price of a husband. Its amount, which was the subject for prolonged bargaining, depended both on the circumstances of the parties, including their prospects, and, to a lesser degree, upon the size of the jointure. This latter was only important if the bridegroom failed to live long enough to inherit his father's lands, or if he were not the heir. If he *were* the heir and *did* live to inherit, his widow's dower rights entered the calculation. For this reason, probably, it is impossible to establish any direct, invariable relation between portion and jointure. What dictated the choice of one figure rather than another can be only matter for guesswork.

Many of these contracts survive though often in isolation. I therefore choose as illustrations four relating to marriages of children of Ralph, first Earl of Stafford. Ralph himself was born about 1299, had livery of his father's lands in 1323, was made an earl in 1351, and died in 1372. The first contract was sealed on 15 December 1343 for the marriage of his daughter Joan to John, grandson and heir of John, Lord Charlton of Powys. The portion was £800 and the jointure £100 a year.[1] Next, on 12 March 1347, Elizabeth Stafford was betrothed to Fulk, son and heir of John, Lord Lestrange of Blackmere; the portion was £1,000 and the jointure 200 marks a year.[2] The third daughter, Beatrice, was promised on 20 April 1350 to Maurice, son and heir of the Earl of Desmond; the portion was again £1,000, but this time the jointure had risen to £200.[3] Finally on 20 July 1353 Ralph

---

[1] Bodleian Library, Dugdale MS. 15, p. 62.
[2] Madox, *Formulare*, pp. 92–4; *C.C.R. 1346–9*, pp. 246–7, cf. G.E.C. xii, pt. i. 343–4.
[3] Bodleian Library, Dugdale MS. 15, p. 63.

contracted his only surviving son, Hugh, to Philippa Beauchamp, daughter of the Earl of Warwick; for this match he was given £2,000; what jointure he offered is not recorded.[1] Thus he paid out more for three daughters than he received in exchange for his heir. Had he younger sons to marry as well he would have been still more out of pocket. There were advantages in doing what the Earls of Arundel and Northampton did in 1359, when each married his heir to the other's daughter and no portions were needed.[2]

The marriages of two successive Mortimer Earls of March, namely Edmund who died in 1381 and his son Roger who was killed in Ireland in 1398, were sold outright without conditions. This may explain why they fetched such unusually high prices. The former was bought by Edward III from the family for his granddaughter, Philippa of Clarence, before 1359 for 5,000 marks.[3] Roger's marriage fell to the Crown, owing to his father's unexpected death; in 1384 Richard II granted it to Thomas Holland, Earl of Kent, for £4,000.[4] Had Holland not been the king's half-brother, he might reasonably have been asked to pay more; for Roger was his mother's heir as well as his father's. It was similarly

[1] The sum of the portion is stated in a receipt for payment of 200 marks of it in Whitsun Term 1353 (Bodleian Library, Dugdale MS. 15, p. 294 (transcript)). For the estates reversion to which was settled on the pair see *C.P.R. 1350–4*, p. 67. (Stafford's eldest son, Ralph, who had died in 1348, had been married on 1 Nov. 1344 to Maud, daughter of Henry of Grosmont, Earl of Lancaster. The marriage agreement is calendared, *35th Report of the Deputy Keeper of the Public Records*, p. 12.)

[2] *C.C.R. 1354–60*, pp. 633, 658; *Cal. Papal Letters*, iii. 606; *C.P.R. 1358–61*, pp. 274, 304. Northampton's son ultimately also inherited the earldom of Hereford from his uncle.

[3] P.R.O. E 404 6/36, 28 Jan. 1359, 2,000 marks to be paid to the Earl of March in payment of 3,000 marks for the marriage of his son Edmund, which he should have received from the Earl of Arundel, according to a bargain made between March and Arundel; March to receive a further 2,000 marks because the inheritance has become more valuable through an escheat. (The bargain with the Earl of Arundel referred to is one for the marriage of his daughter Alice to Edmund, *C.C.R. 1354–60*, pp. 92–4.) On 25 July 1369 500 marks was paid to March in part payment of 4,000 marks which Edward III had ordered should be paid to him for the marriage of his son (P.R.O. E 403/396, s.d.; inaccurately translated, F. Devon, *Issues of the Exchequer* (1837), p. 171).

[4] *C.C.R. 1381–5*, p. 572.

the favour of Henry IV that secured for Ralph, Earl of Westmorland, the marriage of John Mowbray, heir of Norfolk, Nottingham, and Seagrave, in 1411 for 3,000 marks;[1] but when the
Council allowed Westmorland to buy for another of his daughters
a still greater marriage, that of Richard, Duke of York, for the
same amount in 1423, it was guilty of neglecting Henry VI's
financial interests.[2]

The king's treatment of his wards was influenced by different
considerations from those present in the minds of the fathers. In
no marriage contract between parents known to me was a portion
of as much as £4,000 offered. The largest sum that I have noticed
was the 4,700 marks paid by Richard Nevill, Earl of Salisbury, in
1434 in order to obtain for his daughter Cecily the hand of Henry,
son and heir of Richard Beauchamp, Earl of Warwick.[3] Up to
that date the size of portions had tended to rise steadily. Thereafter there may have been some decline though the evidence for
the latter part of the fifteenth century is unaccountably thin.
When the Duke of Buckingham married a daughter to Viscount
Beaumont's heir in 1452, he promised only 2,300 marks and took
a long time even to pay that.[4] For a time all the money the nobility
could collect was needed for other objects. Whether after the civil
wars there was any recovery I am not sure. But about 1500 Sir
Reynold Bray gave 1,000 marks with his niece Elizabeth on her
marriage to the grandson and heir of Sir William Norris.[5] This
was certainly as much as a minister and councillor of his rank
would have thought generous a century before. For want of
enough other early Tudor evidence, the question remains open.

Portions were generally paid in a number of instalments spread
over several years. They could therefore be met out of income.

[1] *C.P.R. 1408–13*, p. 307.　　　　[2] *C.F.R. 1422–30*, p. 64.
[3] Bodleian Library, Dugdale MS. 15, p. 76, cf. W. Dugdale, *The Antiquities of Warwickshire* (ed. W. Thomas, 2 vols., 1730), i. 414. Higher portions (of 10,000 marks each) were provided for Edward IV's daughters Elizabeth and Mary in 1475 in certain contingencies; R. Somerville, *History of the Duchy of Lancaster*, i. (1953), 239.
[4] The marriage took place 6 Aug. 1452. On 16 Aug. 1459 Buckingham still owed £442. 14s. 2½d.; Staffordshire R.O., D (W) 1721/1/1 ('Great Cartulary' of the Stafford family), f. 395ᵛ.
[5] Westminster Abbey Mun. 9197 (part of the actual contract).

This may have been convenient, though it was not always necessary. Apart from the masses of plate and other rich gear bequeathed by John of Gaunt in his testament, the cash legacies to
his family and intimates amounted to nearly £5,000; when it was
drawn up on 3 February 1399 he had already done his duty by his
many children.[1] To take a less obvious case, the combined will and
testament of John, Lord Devereux, who died in 1393, with its
large bequests of gilt and silver plate, shows what could be
achieved by a successful military adventurer. He gave his widow
a life-interest in all his lands; to his only son John he left 2,000
marks 'to help him to purchase and marriage', to his daughter
Joan 1,100 marks for her portion; as a result both children secured
the hands of baronial heirs, Brian and Fitzwalter.[2]

Testaments, however valuable the information they contain,
do not necessarily tell everything. In the first place, they offer no
clue to the value of the *articles* bequeathed and often only the
barest description. Another omission may be even more serious;
if there was any residue of either cash or goods left over after the
legacies had been paid, there is no way of deducing its size. How
incomplete an impression even the most detailed testament may
give is proved by the few surviving inventories. The cases of Sir
John Fastolf or Ralph Cromwell might be cited, but you have
heard enough of them already. Take rather a less familiar example:
Richard Fitzalan, Earl of Arundel and Surrey, known as 'Copped
Hat', who was born about 1306 and whose active career coincides
almost exactly with the reign of Edward III. His father had been
one of the victims of Isabella and Mortimer's revolution in 1326
and Earl Richard therefore succeeded to a disrupted and wasted
inheritance. As some compensation for this, he was later granted
the Mortimer lordship of Chirk. In 1347 and 1361 he succeeded
his uncle and aunt in most of the southern estates of the house of
Warenne. His territorial wealth was unquestionably large, but an
active career of nearly half a century in the king's service added
much to it. There were few of Edward III's campaigns in which

[1] S. Armitage Smith, *John of Gaunt* (1904), pp. 420–36; *Testamenta Eboracensia*,
i. 223–39.
[2] Prerog. Court of Cant., Reg. Rous, ff. 20–1; G.E.C. iv. 299–301.

he did not take a conspicuous part. In the 1330s he was captain-general of the royal armies in Scotland, he fought at Sluys, Crécy, Calais, and Espagnols-sur-Mer and made his last appearance in the field in 1372. More than once in his early days he came to Edward III's assistance financially also, lending £1,600 in Flanders in 1340, 1,200 marks in 1345, 4,000 marks to the Chamber in 1351, £2,000 in 1357, and £3,000 in 1359.[1] He even helped out his old enemy Isabella the queen mother with an occasional loan.[2] At the same time he was advancing money to the Black Prince, small sums at first, rising to £2,000 in 1359 and £1,000 three years later.[3] With the renewal of the war in 1369 his loans to the king became really important, 10,000 marks in 1369,[4] £20,000 in 1370,[5]

[1] These are the loans recorded on the Patent Rolls, *C.P.R. 1340–3*, p. 38, *C.P.R. 1343–5*, p. 528, *C.P.R. 1350–4*, p. 106, *C.P.R. 1354–8*, p. 511, *C.P.R. 1358–61*, p. 241. The Receipt Rolls before 1370 were not searched and other loans may be recorded there. (This note and the six immediately following are derived from McFarlane's notes to an unpublished paper on the financial background to the Good Parliament which it is hoped to publish in a later volume.)

[2] She seems to have pawned one of her crowns to him for £300 (Devon, *Issues of the Exchequer*, pp. 170–1) and was £100 in his debt at her death (F. Devon, *Issue Roll of Thomas de Brantingham* (1835), pp. 424–5).

[3] *Black Prince's Register*, iii. 354, 364, 449; iv. 99, 159, 163, 302, 319, 333.

[4] *Antient Kalendars and Inventories of the . . . Exchequer*, ed. F. Palgrave (3 vols., 1836), i. 221.

[5] He lent £6,000 on 1 July (E 401/501, s.d.). On 28 June he advanced a further 20,000 marks. Half was received from his ministers in Shropshire and half 'per manus Gauteronis de Barde', the London representative of the Florentine company with which he had long had dealings (E 401/501 s.d.). The indenture of this loan was deposited in the treasury of the Exchequer on 18 June (*Antient Kalendars and Inventories of the . . . Exchequer*, ed. Palgrave, i. 226–7). For 10,000 marks coming from Shropshire, see Devon, *Issue Roll of Thomas de Brantingham*, p. 228. For Arundel's connections with the Bardi, see *C.C.R. 1341–3*, pp. 535, 542; *C.C.R. 1343–6*, pp. 460, 462; A. Beardwood, *Alien Merchants in England 1350–77* (Cambridge, Mass., 1931), pp. 129, 130. By 1 July he had agreed to lend £20,000 in all, for on that day the Abbot and Prior of Westminster were ordered to deliver to him the king's vessels of silver as security for a loan of that amount (*C.P.R. 1367–70*, p. 451). On 4 Sept. he found the 1,000 marks necessary to make up the balance (E 401/501, s.d.). While repayment for most of the other creditors making loans in this year took the usual form of a speedy, though not always effective, assignment on future revenue, the earl was granted 2½ marks on every sack of wool laded in the port of London from 3 Aug. 1370 until his whole claim had been discharged. He was to have custody of one part of the cocket seal. Several prelates, earls, lords, knights, and others bound themselves to him in the king's name to guarantee repayment by midsummer 1371 (*C.C.R. 1369–74*, pp. 149–50).

and further large sums in the following years.[1] The evidence for his financial dealings at this time with the Prince of Wales is lacking, but the surviving register of John of Gaunt for 1372–6 refers to some half-dozen occasions when the duke borrowed from him sums between 1,000 and 4,000 marks.[2] Finally, there is evidence that Arundel was investing money with London merchants. As early as 1350 Thomas Batsford received £300 from him 'to traffic therewith to the earl's advantage'[3] and during the next quarter of a century his connections with the city were extended. For some time before his death his agent was John Philipot.[4]

Meanwhile he had been settling his family. I have already mentioned how he married his heir and his daughter Eleanor to the two Bohuns.[5] In 1364 he found a husband for another daughter, Alice, by paying the Black Prince 4,000 marks for the young heir of Kent, Thomas Holland.[6] His second son John, himself a distinguished soldier, he partly provided for by marrying him to a coheiress of the baronial house of Mautravers.[7] Finally, he obtained the see of Ely for his youngest son Thomas, aged twenty, from a complaisant Gregory XI.[8] The terms of the bull of provision suggest that a great deal of money had been distributed in the Curia.

Arundel predeceased his king by less than two years. His and his wife's 'high tombs of marble' by Henry Yeaveley were on their way to Lewes priory in January 1375;[9] on the following 5 December he made his will.[10] To his daughters, younger sons,

---

[1] In the winter of 1370–1 he lent 5,000 marks (*C.C.R. 1369–74*, p. 207); on 15 Apr. 1371 2,000 marks (E 401/505, s.d.); on 16 Aug. 1372 5,000 marks (E 401/508, s.d.), and on 18 Sept. 1374 £10,000 (E 401/515, s.d.).

[2] *John of Gaunt's Register 1371–5*, ed. S. Armitage Smith (2 vols., C.S., 3rd ser. xxi–xxii, 1911), i. 74–5, 77, 79; ii. 36, 62–3, 93–4, 154–5, 189, 296–7, 303.

[3] *C.C.R. 1349–54*, pp. 205–6.

[4] *John of Gaunt's Register 1371–5*, i. 79; ii. 36; B.M. MS. Harl. 4840, f. 393–393ᵛ (for which see p. 91 n. 1 below). Philipot was one of Arundel's executors (Lambeth Lib., Reg. Sudbury, f. 94ᵛ) and disposed of wool worth £2,041. 13s. 4d. belonging to him after his death. [5] Above, p. 86.

[6] *C.P.R. 1361–4*, p. 480; *Black Prince's Register*, iv. 558–9.

[7] G.E.C. viii. 585–6; *C.C.R. 1354–60*, pp. 614, 616–17, 629; *C.P.R. 1354–8*, p. 595.

[8] M. Aston, *Thomas Arundel* (Oxford, 1967), p. 8.

[9] Ibid., p. 16, n. 1.

[10] Lambeth, Reg. Sudbury, ff. 92ᵛ–95ᵛ; an incomplete abstract is printed by

and grandsons his legacies in money came to nearly £11,000 and there were in addition markedly large bequests to servants, the poor, and to other pious uses. But his executors soon found that his liquid assets were far greater, when they came to make an inventory after his death on 24 January 1376.[1] The list begins thus: 'Firstly there was in the high tower of Arundel on the said day of his death in a coffer in divers bags, both in silver and gold, the sum of 44,981 marks and 20 pence.' Further, there were in chests at St. Paul's, London, under the care of John Philipot, 27,150 marks; and on the Fitzalan estates in the Welsh march another 16,471 marks. Altogether Arundel had at his death, in actual cash or bullion, the impressive sum of 90,360 marks or over £60,000. Nor had he succeeded in calling in all the money out on loan, amounting to some £4,500. Many notable people were still in his debt: Richard Scrope owed him 1,500 marks. 'Madame la Princesse', Joan of Kent, 1,000 marks, John Philipot £600, and so on. It is doubtful whether Henry Beaufort, the 'Rich Cardinal', had as much. In 1376 the approach of death had led Arundel to recall his capital. He was no miser hoarding his gold; a few months later 5,000 marks was lent to Edward III from his estate.[2]

The inventory is unfortunately not complete, since it contains no mention of the earl's personal wardrobe, his jewels, or the furnishing of his castles and houses; all items which, to judge from other inventories, would have added greatly to the total. And what was probably only a fraction of his plate is included. Nevertheless, it is enough to suggest that Edward III's companions had reason to be content with his policy of aggression. It is impossible to say how much Arundel had multiplied his capital by skilful investment, but its original source was almost certainly the war. He was not the only baron to turn moneylender. Here is a more modest example: a will of Ralph Basset of Drayton, made in September 1383, contains a reference to 200 marks, which were

N. H. Nicholas, *Testamenta Vetusta*, i. 94–6 and the part of the will relating to Thomas Arundel by Aston, *Thomas Arundel*, pp. 379–80.

[1] B.M. Harleian MS. 4840, f. 393, 393ᵛ. (A transcript by Peter le Neve.) Cf. L. F. Salzman, 'The Property of the Earl of Arundel 1397', *Sussex Archaeolog. Coll.* 91 (1953), 33–4.

[2] *C.P.R. 1374–7*, p. 441.

'in the hands of John Philipot'.[1] A petition to the Parliament of January 1390 shows that the wife of the great captain Sir Robert Knollys had deposited £2,000 with a London grocer to merchandise with and was alleged to be a most exacting creditor.[2] In the single financial year 1392–3 the Duke of Lancaster recovered £3,100 which he had lent to merchants, his fellow magnates, and, in small amounts, to his retainers.[3] At other times he found it necessary, as we have seen, to borrow; and so did other peers, often at heavy cost to themselves. These were all short-term loans, repayable in a year or less and made on good security. They were not, as far as one can judge, large enough to be ruinous.[4] On the same moderate scale they are found regularly in the accounts of such early Tudor magnates as the fifth Percy, Earl of Northumberland.[5] Those who had the capital did not allow it to lie idle. One of John Fastolf's most profitable undertakings—and he had many—was to buy up corn all over East Anglia in a year of shortage and then to hold it until the price rose. Being the owner of several ships and the sleeping-partner of other merchants, he was able to take the corn where it was most needed. On more than one occasion, by this means, he cleared a profit of several hundred pounds.[6]

Apart from buying land and making as large a provision as possible for their children, the members of the nobility spent their gains as they had always spent them—only they had more to spend. One of the chief objects of peaceful expenditure was building. The period of the Hundred Years War, as Leyland correctly realized, saw the first great flowering of English *domestic* architec-

---

[1] Bodleian Library, Dugdale MS. 15, p. 10.

[2] *Rot. Parl.* iii. 258b–259a.

[3] P.R.O. DL 28/3/2 (receiver-general's account 2 Feb. 1392–2 Feb. 1393), ff. 5r–6v. Most of the loans had been made in the previous year. Two thousand marks had been lent to the Duke of Gloucester and £1,000 to the London merchant William Venour and his son.

[4] For Lancaster's borrowings see p. 90 n. 2.

[5] In his cofferer's account for 1514–26, E 36/226, pp. 50, 62, 81, 96, 97, 115, 140, 161, 200, 232–3, 282. Some of the 'borrowed money' recorded in these accounts seems to be advance payments by the earl's officials, but there are many genuine loans. Cf. Bean, *Estates of the Percy Family 1416–1537*, pp. 140–1.

[6] McFarlane, 'The Investment of Sir John Fastolf's Profits of War', pp. 115–16.

ture. Immense sums were spent by the heads of baronial families
in making the bleak, ill-lit castles of their ancestors comfortable,
almost luxurious, by the addition of halls, withdrawing-rooms,
and ranges of private apartments with glazed and traceried win-
dows and chimneyed hearths; as Lancaster did at Kenilworth and
elsewhere, the Beauchamps at Warwick, the Fitzalans at Arundel,
and the Percies at Alnwick, to take a few examples of buildings
still partially extant from what could easily become a wearisome
list. Elsewhere the work of conversion was still more radical as at
Raby, Skipton, Wingfield in Suffolk, Brancepeth, Lumley, and
Sheriff Hutton. Old castles were transformed; but many huge and
expensive piles were raised on largely new sites: Penshurst, Maxstoke, Beverstone, Bolton-in-Wensleydale, Cooling, Bodiam,
Wressel, Drayton (Northamptonshire), Wardour, and Darting-
ton. Nor should the palatial town houses like Gaunt's Savoy or
Sir John Pountney's Coldharbour be forgotten. Time has dealt
particularly savagely with these urban mansions, but they were
objects on which much care—and wonder—were lavished. Hardly
a receiver-general's account survives that has no reference to
expenditure on building. Spread over many years the total costs
of these works are rarely known. But Leyland's statement that
Bolton of the Scropes took eighteen years to build at the rate of a
thousand marks a year seems well founded; £12,000 compares
reasonably well with Professor Edwards's figures for the Welsh
castles of the late thirteenth century.[1]

So far I have chosen all my examples from the reigns of Edward
III and Richard II. But *pace* Dr. Joan Evans, the Lancastrian period
saw no marked falling-off in the amount of domestic building.[2]
The contrary opinion is based upon the steady decline in the
number of royal licences to crenellate—without which castle-
building was illegal—after 1399. This was never a very safe
statistical guide and the later the date the more unsafe it becomes.
By the accession of Henry IV it was a formality that could be
dispensed with. It would be easy to make a long list of fortified

[1] Leland, *Itinerary*, v. 139; J. G. Edwards, 'Edward I's Castle Building in Wales',
Proc. Brit. Acad. 32 (1946, published 1951), 15–81.
[2] J. Evans, *English Art 1307–1461* (Oxford, 1949), pp. 118–19.

houses erected thereafter for which there is no record of a licence. Fastolf spent more than £7,000 on building; there can be no doubt that Caister, upon which the greater part of this sum was spent, though made of brick, was moated and crenellated, castle-wise; but no licence is known.[1] Nor is there one for any of Ralph Cromwell's several splendid edifices. Tattershall castle, like Caister of brick, took more than twelve years to build and for the four years for which accounts are available expenditure was about £450 per annum.[2] The huge freestone manor house that Cromwell built at South Wingfield in Derbyshire must have cost much more. One account of 1442–3 tells us the name of the architect, John Enterpas, and that by then the chambers on the west side of the inner court were complete, the undercroft of the hall vaulted, and the great chamber and kitchen in process of erection.[3] Not content with these works, Cromwell about the same time began work at another great house at Colly Weston,[4] rebuilt the manor place at Lambley,[5] and bought for 5,000 marks the castle that Lord Fanhope had built at Ampthill.[6] The many other captains who were also great builders cannot be mentioned here; a few examples

---

[1] Magdalen College, Oxford, Fastolf Papers 69, mm. 1, 3; H. D. Barnes and W. D. Simpson, 'The Building Accounts of Caister Castle, A.D. 1432–1435', *Norfolk Archaeology*, 30 (1952), 178–88 and 'Caister Castle', *Antiquaries Journal*, 32 (1952), 35–51.

[2] W. Douglas Simpson, *The Building Accounts of Tattershall Castle, 1434–1472* (Lincoln Record Soc., 55, 1960), pp. 1–37.

[3] Muniments of Lord de L'Isle and Dudley at Penshurst 57, roll 5 (account of John Ulkerthorp, supervisor and clerk of the works at Wingfield, 1 Nov. 1442–25 Dec. 1443). Expenditure in this period was £229. 6s. 3½d.

[4] Leland, *Itinerary*, i. 22; iv. 91; William Worcester, *Itineraries*, ed. Harvey, p. 72; there are references to the expenditure of small sums on new buildings there in accounts of 1443–4 (Penshurst Mun. 43), 1445–6 (ibid. 44, 53 (m. 2d.), 64 (roll 3), 115) and 1453–4 (ibid.59, roll 1), cf. *H.M.C. Report on MSS. of Lord de L'Isle and Dudley*, i. 210, 219. Nothing now remains of the house.

[5] Particulars of expenditure of £19. 8s. 8½d. on new building there 1444–5 are contained in Penshurst Mun. 63, roll 14 (*H.M.C. MSS. of Lord de L'Isle and Dudley*, i. 217) and of up to £40. 4s. 1½d. in 1445–6 in Penshurst Mun. 12, m. 4 and 13. Nothing remains of the manor, but the church which Cromwell built at Lambley survives; N. Pevsner, *Nottinghamshire* (Harmondsworth, 1951), pp. 91–2.

[6] William Worcester, *Itineraries*, ed. Harvey, p. 72. Worcester adds that Cromwell had to spend £2,000 in half a year defending his right to Ampthill against the Duke of Exeter.

are Sir Ralph Boteler whose castle at Sudeley was coveted by
Edward IV, Sir Roger Fiennes of Hurstmonceux, Sir Walter
Hungerford of Farleigh, and Sir William ap Thomas of Raglan.
Many of these new houses have not survived. There is little left of
the Duke of Suffolk's palace at Ewelme; or of Sommaries in
Luton, the home of that active soldier-of-fortune, John, first Lord
Wenlock; or of the Rye House near Ware, scene of a famous plot,
to which Sir Andrew Ogard retired after the loss of Normandy.
But at nearby Hunsdon rather more still exists of the large mansion
begun by another of the Duke of Bedford's councillors, Sir
William Oldhall, unfinished at his death, though it had already
eaten up some 7,000 marks.[1]

The church-building in the perpendicular style is less easily
forgotten, though it is too often set to the credit of the merchants
rather than the soldiers. In some cases the staplers were responsible, but besides the wool-churches there were also the war-
churches: those great collegiate establishments such as Leicester,
Fotheringay and Pleshey, Arundel, Wingfield, Warwick, and
Tattershall, in which the war-profiteers invested heavily for the
good of their souls, as Edward III himself did at St. George's,
Windsor; not to mention such regular foundations as the Charter-
house in London and Michaelhouse at Hull. The later middle ages
were not less generous than the earlier in their pious works. The
Statute of Mortmain merely tended to deflect alms from landed
endowment to building and altar funds; and even it could not put
an end to endowments altogether.

But if the soul's health was not neglected, it was not indulged
at the expense of the body in this world. In the eyes of such
moralists as Bromyard, the balance was still too much in favour
of the flesh. 'Where,' he asks with the conviction that he knows
the answer,

where are the evil princes of the world, the kings, earls and other lords
of estates, who lived with pride and with great circumstance and
equipage, who used to keep many hounds and a numerous and evil
retinue, who possessed great palaces, many manors and broad lands . . .,
who nourished their bodies in delicacies and the pleasures of gluttony

[1] Ibid., p. 50.

and lust . . ., [with their] scented baths . . ., drunkenness . . ., and excessive gambling?

'In the deep lake of Hell' of course.[1] And given his premisses, Bromyard was doubtless right. But in spite of the Puritans, the quality that that age most admired was called *largitas, largesse*; which may be translated 'open-handedness', though that does not perhaps sufficiently emphasize its ostentatious character, what the economists call 'conspicuous waste'. The greater part of the earnings of the nobility was neither hoarded nor invested; it was used to achieve a higher standard of luxury. Those roomy new houses were splendidly furnished as the surviving inventories prove, with their long lists of beds of estate, arras and other hangings, carpets for floor and table, chapel vestments, and great open cupboards in which to display the lord's collection of gold and silver vessels. Several of these inventories have been printed. May I suggest that you at least glance at four of them, four which in their varied and detailed contents give the best possible idea of late medieval luxury? A list of the contents of Thomas of Woodstock's castle of Pleshy at the time of his arrest in 1397 was edited for the *Archaeological Journal*, volume 54; the property forfeited by Henry Scrope of Masham in 1415 will be found in volume 70 of *Archaeologia*; Sir John Fastolf's inventory for 1459 is printed in the *Paston Letters*;[2] while, also in *Archaeologia*, volume 66, will be found that of John Vere, Earl of Oxford at his death in 1512.

The richness of many of these articles certainly helps to explain the denunciations of the moralists. Thomas of Woodstock's best bed of cloth of gold, with valances of blue satin and curtains of tartarin, was, for example, reckoned to have a second-hand value of over £180, equivalent to the annual stipends of about thirty mass-priests or to the landed income of quite a substantial knight.[3] Ralph Cromwell's executors sold a similar bed to Sir John Din-

---

[1] G. R. Owst, *Literature and the Pulpit in Medieval England* (Cambridge, 1933), pp. 293–4.

[2] *Paston Letters*, iii. no. 388.

[3] Viscount Dillon and W. H. St. John Hope, 'Inventory of the Goods and Chattels belonging to Thomas, duke of Gloucester . . .', *Archaeolog. Journ.* 54 (1897), 277, 289.

ham for £122.[1] Most of Cromwell's movable goods were, however, pillaged by his heirs 'and other straunge persones' before the executors could take possession; it was estimated that objects worth just under £16,000 disappeared in this way.[2] Later in the unquiet 1450s much the same fate befell Fastolf's property.

Chapel furnishings were also expensive and many lords maintained a large staff of priests and choristers. Thomas of Lancaster, Duke of Clarence, for instance, had a dean and at least fifteen clerks attached to his household. Their wages and fees for celebrating during the last two and a quarter years of his life (November 1418 to March 1421) amounted to over £200.[3] Two of Thomas of Woodstock's many copes were valued at as much as £60 each.[4] Henry Scrope's inventory contained no less than ninety-two copes as well as other vestments; to judge from their descriptions, many were sumptuously embroidered, but unfortunately no values were given.[5] Again the largest arras at Pleshy, depicting the history of Charlemagne, 72 feet long by 12 feet high, was priced at over £48 and another, shorter, one at £45.[6]

The biggest item of expenditure, however, was almost certainly upon plate and jewellery. Every lord had a stock of gold, gilt, and silver cups, ewers, salvers, and candlesticks, such as John, Duke of Bedford kept in the piece of furniture described in his executors' accounts as his 'Riche coupbourde'.[7] This practice was not, as some have suggested, a form of hoarding in a period of economic

---

[1] Magdalen College Misc. 355 (Cromwell Papers 432, a draft account of Cromwell's executors), mm. 3^r, 4^r, 4^v.

[2] Ibid., m. 1: 'Item ther' was taken fro the seid executours by myght ayenst lawe ("consciens" interlineated) and the wille of the seid late lorde as well by the heires seru^{a}ntes and other straunge persones as particlerly it may be shewed in a boke thereof made xv^{ml} ix^c lxxiiij li ijs. vd.'

[3] Westminster Abbey Mun. 12163, f. 14^{r-v}.

[4] Dillon and Hope, 'Inventory . . .', pp. 279, 295.

[5] C. L. Kingsford, 'Two Forfeitures in the Year of Agincourt', *Archaeologia*, 70 (1920), 77–8, 92–3, cf. 76. Ninety-two copes are listed among those of Scrope's goods received by Richard Knyghtely. A further fourteen appear on another list, pp. 81, 98–9.

[6] Dillon and Hope, 'Inventory . . .', pp. 276, 288.

[7] P.R.O. E 101 411/7, f. 1.

recession. If that were all there would have been no call to waste money upon having them elaborately worked, chased, and enamelled. These pieces might when necessity arose be pledged for loans, but their sole purpose was display like the rich personal jewellery in which the nobility delighted. Reckoning gold at 40s. the ounce troy and silver at 2s. 10d., it is obvious that quite apart from the costly workmanship a lord's plate was usually worth many thousands of pounds. His jewels were fewer, but individually more expensive. Richard, Duke of York, for example, had a collar 'called in English "a White Rose"', studded with precious stones, which he gave to Fastolf partly in repayment of a loan, partly as a gift; its value was estimated at £2,666.[1] This was, perhaps, exceptional, though it was surpassed at least by Henry V's 'rich collar'.[2] But even men of inferior rank spent considerable sums on their personal adornment; thus Lord Fanhope's executors were able to obtain £540 for two of his jewelled clasps (*ouches*).[3] As a last instance of expenditure upon goldsmiths' work, let me cite a clause in the will of Richard Beauchamp, Earl of Warwick, who died in 1439. He commanded his executors to order 'iiij ymages of golde, everych of hem of the weyght of xx pounde of golde, to be maad after my similitudeo [*sic*] figure, with myn armes, holding an Anker betwene the handes so figured'.[4] These were to be set up in the shrines of St. Alban, of St. Thomas at Canterbury, St. John at Bridlington, and St. Winifred at Shrewsbury. The material alone before casting must, I estimate, have cost £1,280 at least.

There remain the current expenses of maintaining a great household. In some cases there was a fixed annual allocation, which might only be exceeded by the lord's order. In 1392–3, for example, the treasurer of the Duke of Lancaster's household was allowed £5,000 a year; beyond that 2,000 marks were allowed

[1] McFarlane, 'The Investment of Sir John Fastolf's Profits of War', pp. 108–9. (For the values given to gold and silver above see ibid., p. 108 and n. 3.)

[2] The collar was valued at £5,162. 13s. 4d. in the list of Henry V's jewels, etc., contained in an indenture made between his executors and the Treasurer in 1423 (*Rot. Parl.* iv. 214).

[3] Palgrave, *The Antient Kalendars and Inventories of . . . the Exchequer*, ii. 257.

[4] Prerog. Court of Canterbury, Reg. Rous, f. 148; summarized Dugdale, *Baronage*, i. 246–7.

annually to the duke's great wardrobe and another 1,000 marks to the duchess's chamber.[1] At about the same date the household of Gaunt's son, Bolingbroke, was receiving an allocation of 1,000 marks per annum, and so also was his great wardrobe.[2] The treasurer of the household was mainly concerned with the purchase of foodstuffs, wine, beer, napery, towels, and other domestic linen, with the catering and with the management and wages of a host of menial servants. The keeper of the great wardrobe bought and saw to the tailoring and embellishment of the clothes of the lord and the members of the family and household, received and stored such things as armour and harness, and bought and distributed his master's New Year gifts. But there was little differentiation of function in the households of lesser men. The accounts, when they survive, are full of information, some interesting, much trivial. Humphrey Stafford of Grafton is found buying presents for Joyce Middlemore, presumably his mistress.[3] The Earl of Devon, Henry Courtenay, gives a boy 4*d.* for his cap when Henry VIII and his lords were playing at snowballs.[4] There are scores of gratuities given to minstrels, mimes, tumblers, and fools. We learn the price of night-caps and of sending a boy to the university; and we find occasional references to improved sanitation and the provision of baths,[5] for which a precedent had

---

[1] These are the annual allowances stated in the receiver-general's account for 1392–3, DL 28/3/2, ff. 9^r, 10^r. Neither the treasurer of the household nor the clerk of the great wardrobe had in fact received his full allowance during the period of this account.

[2] The evidence for these allocations comes from Bolingbroke's receiver-general's accounts for 1391–2 (DL 28/3/3, m. 3) and 1392–4 (DL 28/3/4, ff. 5^v, 19^v). There was some variation in the allocations and they were not always paid in full. Cf. the accounts of Bolingbroke's great wardrobe for 1391–2, 1393–4, and 1395–6 (DL 28/1/3–5).

[3] B.M. Add. Roll 74173 (Humphrey Stafford's receiver's account Michaelmas 1453–Michaelmas 1454), m. 2, 74174 (ibid. 1454–5), mm. 3, 4.

[4] *Letters and Papers . . . of the Reign of Henry VIII*, vol. iii, pt. i, ed. J. Brewer (1867), p. 50.

[5] e.g. Westminster Abbey Mun. 6630, m. 5^v, expenditure by Sir Thomas Charlton, *c.* 1465 on 'baynes to bath in', and Muniments of Lord Arundel at Wardour Castle, Ministers' Accounts 430, m. 2 (Dinham inventory) 'And ij vatis for the lordys bathyng ymad of a bot of malmesyn'. (This inventory of the goods of Sir John Dinham is slightly damaged and it is uncertain whether it was dated 5 Jan. 13 Henry IV or 5 Jan. 13 Henry VI. McFarlane's notes suggest that he

been set when Edward III installed one with hot and cold water at Westminster in 1350.[1]

Above all there is further evidence of conspicuous waste. From one of Bolingbroke's accounts it appears that the embroidery upon one of his garments, forget-me-nots on black velvet, alone cost £29;[2] from another that the horse-cloth with which he proposed to enter the lists at Coventry in 1398 was embroidered with his arms, the bill being 70 marks or more.[3] An inventory of Sir John Dinham's goods of 1412 shows that the arrows he used in hunting were bound with gold.[4] As for household expenses let me quote the case of Margaret, the widowed Countess of Norfolk, whose total landed income in 1394–5 was £2,840; although she had no kinsman living with her at Framlingham, she was not saving money. In that one year she spent £122 on wine and £111 on spices and preserved fruit.[5] It was the duty of the great to maintain a large household and to offer lavish hospitality. When Sir John Dinham came up to London from Devon in 1382 for Richard II's marriage, he gave his friends a *convivium*;[6] Bolingbroke entertained the king to a banquet in the house of the London Carmelites at the time of the 1397 Parliament and spent £29 on cloth-of-gold for a canopy to the royal throne.[7] The few surviving household journals, in which the number of guests and meals served were daily noted, tell the same tale. That belonging to Richard, Earl of Warwick, from March 1431 to March 1432, for the greater part of which time the Beauchamps were living at Rouen, has evidence of constant visits from other great lords and their trains, sometimes

inclined towards the earlier date because the preamble is in French, but regarded the later date as possible.)

[1] *The History of the King's Works*, ed. H. M. Colvin, i. 550.

[2] P.R.O. DL 28/1/6 (account of the keeper of the Duke of Hereford's great wardrobe 1 Feb. 1397–1 Feb. 1398), f. 27r.

[3] Ibid., f. 47v.

[4] Wardour Castle, Ministers' Accnts. 430, m. 2v, for which see p. 99, n. 5 above.

[5] College of Arms, Arundel MS. 49 (Countess of Norfolk's treasurer of the household's account 1 Oct 1394–1 Oct. 1395), ff. 27v, 34v, 35r.

[6] Wardour Castle Muniments 416 (accounts of the expenses of John Dinham the younger on going to London for the marriage of the king and queen, Dec. 1381–Jan. 1382), m. 1 and the fifth of the attached schedules.

[7] DL 28/1/6, f. 9v.

to dinner or supper, often merely to drink; a frequent caller was the young Henry VI.[1]

Yet food was cheap. Dinham's *convivium* at which over ninety birds of various kinds were eaten, as well as much beef and mutton, only cost him some 30s. *Largesse* of this sort was quite compatible with a careful husbanding of resources; indeed thrift was almost as much admired as open-handedness. Tradesmen were the chief sufferers, though no doubt they knew how to recoup themselves; they often had to wait years for the settlement of their accounts. But there seems to be no evidence that magnates owed these creditors as much as one year's income. Though some gambled—the Black Prince is said to have lost as much as £100 to his father on a single day's play[2]—there is really little sign of that riotous living which naturally arouses the disapproval of all serious-minded economic historians. The music, the theatricals, the hunting, and even the tournaments seem all to have been on a very modest scale. Hospitality, however generous, could be reckoned to yield a practical return; like the liberal rewards for service, the universal bribes, it was a way of building up and maintaining a political connection.

[1] In the custody of the Corporation of Warwick, partly printed by H. A. Cronne and R. H. Hilton, 'The Beauchamp Household Book', *Univ. of Birmingham Hist. Journ.* 2 (1950), 208–18.

[2] M. Sharpe in T. F. Tout, *Chapters in Medieval Administrative History* (6 vols. (i and ii, 2nd edn.), Manchester, 1928–33), v. 356–7.

VI. SERVICE, MAINTENANCE, AND POLITICS

WHEN a captain set out for the war, he took with him a retinue, the size of which varied, as did the duration of his service, in accordance with the terms of his contract with the king. From the records of the central government as well as from one or two private accounts, it is often possible to discover the names, military rank, and wages of those who followed him. What cannot be so easily defined are the conditions on which they were recruited, since the number of sub-contracts, those between the captains and their men, now known to exist is miserably small. Originals and copies together, they amount to only a few hundreds, not as many all told as the men-at-arms who took part in one ordinary year's campaigning, far less than, for example, the fifteen hundred recorded to have accompanied the Duke of Lancaster as his personal contingent to France in 1373.[1] The great majority of them, as you know, are contracts for life. In this they differ from those between the king and his captains, which are usually for short periods, a year or less.

But it is questionable whether this contrast reflects a genuine difference. It would, to judge from other evidence, be quite wrong to *assume* that these retinues were manned predominantly by soldiers who had committed themselves to a life of service with one captain. The muster-lists of the English garrisons in France under Sir John Fastolf's command are full of the names of men whom he certainly did not fee in time of peace. Nor is his case in the least exceptional. Although some great lords, like John of Gaunt, may have adopted the practice of maintaining a large permanent body of retainers—there were something like two hundred at a time on the duke's[2] books—the private records of

[1] p 24 above.

[2] R. Somerville, *Duchy of Lancaster*, pp. 130–1; cf. N. B. Lewis, 'Indentures of Retinue with John of Gaunt, Duke of Lancaster, Enrolled in Chancery, 1367–1399', *Camden Miscellany*, xxii (C.S., 1964), 77–112; K. B. McFarlane, 'Bastard Feudalism', *B.I.H.R.* 20 (1943–5), 164.

others suggest that his example was in fact not widely followed. It may indeed have had some connection with his private designs upon the Castilian throne. Otherwise prodigality in the matter of retinues seems to have been confined to the competitive recruiting that accompanied civil war. A household account of Thomas, Earl of Lancaster, for the year 1313–14 records very high payments both for liveries and fees, but not all of these were necessarily for life.[1] In 1399 the same thing happened; between February and his usurpation in September Bolingbroke retained so many supporters that his receiver-general had to pay out more than £500 in life annuities[2] and had to buy nearly two hundred collars of his master's livery nearly all in silver and silver-gilt.[3] And once more after 1450 there was a marked revival in the number of life indentures, especially by the house of York and its partisans; the list of those 'belaste and faithfully promised' to serve William, Lord Hastings, during the reign of Edward IV, printed by Dugdale from a roll which was derived from the original indentures, is our latest example of a noble retinue to set beside Gaunt's.[4]

Otherwise the captains showed unusual moderation. Not even the fact that a life-retainer cost them nothing in time of war, when the king paid the wages and regards of those serving, seems to have encouraged the more hopeful spirits to over-liberal recruitment. The theory that the wars were prolonged by lords unable to face the prospect of having to honour contracts too light-heartedly entered into, though attractive, has no obvious justification. In Thomas of Woodstock's proposed Irish expeditionary force, there seems to have been only one life-retainer, though

---

[1] J. F. Baldwin, 'The Household Administration of Henry Lacy and Thomas of Lancaster', *E.H.R.* 42 (1927), 192, 198–9; J. R. Maddicott, *Thomas of Lancaster, 1307–1322* (Oxford, 1970), pp. 27–8, 40–66, now gives a definitive account of his retinue and its cost, concluding that at his maximum it had about fifty to fifty-five knights.

[2] DL 28/4/1 (receiver-general's account 2 Feb. 1399–2 Feb. 1400), f. 11.

[3] Ibid., f. 15ᵛ. Of 192 collars accounted for, 81 were in silver, 91 in silver-gilt, and the material of the remainder is unstated; in addition 27 crescents were distributed.

[4] Dugdale, *Baronage*, i. 583–4. For Hastings's retinue now see W. H. Dunham Jnr., 'Lord Hastings' Indentured Retainers 1461–83', *Trans. Connecticut Acad. of Arts and Sciences*, 39 (1955), 1–175.

he is known to have had a few others in his service both earlier and later.[1] A number of receiver-generals' and local ministers' accounts belonging to such well-known captains as Thomas and Richard, successive Earls of Warwick, Thomas of Lancaster, Duke of Clarence, John Mowbray, the Earl Marshal, and Ralph, Lord Cromwell, makes it clear that these at least were in no danger of over-burdening themselves with the payment of retaining fees between campaigns. For landowners to spend 'alle the good they have on men and lewery gownys' was William Paston's idea of rustic stupidity.[2] Most noblemen seem to have agreed with him. That the majority of surviving contracts gives the opposite impression may be because life indentures were the only ones to be carefully preserved. Those for shorter terms could have no interest for the parties once accounts had been settled; indeed it is possible that good parchment was rarely wasted on them. Whatever the solution, of the fact there is no doubt.

It is perhaps easier to explain why it was only desperate gamblers in times of civil disturbance who were tempted to promise more than they could comfortably perform. Their calculations were straightforward enough: if treason were successful, there would be no difficulty about paying; if it failed, then in any case all was lost. But *ordinarily* the consideration which governed the number of life-retainers a lord attracted may have been less the size of his military effort than the scale of his domestic living. However much they may have varied in detail, on one point the contracts were agreed: the life-retainer, as opposed to his short-term fellow, was bound to answer his employer's summons in *peace* as well as war; *that* was the order in which they were named; and peace meant peace and not private war or rebellion. Service in the king's army has usually been regarded, mistakenly it seems to me, as the *sole* purpose of the bond. I am inclined to doubt whether it was even the main purpose. There is a case for believing that this was rather to secure the attendance

---

[1] Sir Walter Clopton appears to have been the only life-retainer in the Irish force in so far as of him alone it is noted in the duke's treasurer for war's account (cf. p. 26 above) that he was in receipt of a life annuity, B.M. Add. Roll 40859 A, m. 2.

[2] *Paston Letters,* ii. 330.

of a sufficient following about the lord's person when he was
resident in England.[1] The life-retainer did not wait at home
drawing his fee until he was needed in war; he was a member, if
an irregular member, of his master's household, in addition to
those who were called, without any of the contempt now attached
to the phrase, menial servants; though in common with them he
was often spoken of as belonging to the *meinie*, from which the
word menial is derived, the crowd of liveried dependants with
which every great man was surrounded. And since, for example,
John of Gaunt's cook was retained by him for life and described
as an esquire it would obviously be unwise to draw a clear line
between one group and another.[2] They were not even sharply
distinguished by birth. For in accordance with a practice as old
as history, the households of the magnates were staffed, at least in
part, by those of gentle blood. As a seventeenth-century writer
could still complain: 'to serve noblemen in most unnoble offices, to
pull of their boots, brush their cloathes, waite at table with a
trencher in their hand, ride with a cloakbag behinde them, dine
and sup with footmen and groomes is the ordinary course of
gentlemen in England'.[3]

Unlike those who held actual offices in the household, the
retainer's attendance was intermittent. His duties resembled those
performed by the knights and esquires of the king's chamber; he
took his turn with others. But when the lord toured his estates,
went on pilgrimage or was summoned to court, Council, or
Parliament, he might call on his whole retinue to ride with him. If
they failed to appear, they risked losing their fee; as did Ralph
Brit, an esquire in the service of Sir Ivo Fitzwarin, early in Henry
IV's reign. He had been retained in peace and war on 4 February
1392; and in October 1402 when Sir Ivo called upon him to ride
with him from Dorset into Wiltshire, Brit pleaded infirmity and

[1] In his later lectures on livery and maintenance McFarlane came much more
definitely to the conclusion that the main purpose of life-retainers was service in
peace rather than in war. It is intended that these lectures shall be published in a
later volume.

[2] McFarlane, 'Bastard Feudalism', pp. 166 and n. 7, 167 n. 1.

[3] Henry Belasyce, 'An English Traveller's First Curiosity' (1657), *H.M.C. Rep.
Var. Coll.* ii. 204.

stayed at home; as a result the annual rent which he had been granted from the manor of Stourton Caundle was stopped.[1] That is why the lord had no need of any other sanction against a defaulting retainer; he paid for services rendered and not otherwise. His motive for having a retinue was once again largely display. A man's worship, his standing among his fellow noblemen, and his influence in his own country, were measured by the number and consequence of those who were enrolled in his *meinie*. Failure to answer his summons brought him into contempt. A large company was essential to save his face. In January 1471 it was said that the Duke of Suffolk 'might not come at London himself at þis time to his worship' because 'his servants [were] from him' in Suffolk for Christmas.[2]

Hence the lord's temptation to dilute the permanent membership of his household and retinue by something cheaper, namely by the grant of liveries and fees *pro tempore* instead of *pro vita* to any available neighbour or tenant. To do so, from Richard II's time onwards, was to offend against the law. Retainers, provided they were subject to life contracts, were like the other, regular, members of a lord's service, excluded from the prohibitions of the earlier statutes against liveries. No one, neither king nor commons, showed any disapproval of them. What all this legislation aimed to suppress was the casual recruitment of idle and potentially lawless hangers-on to the fringes of households already adequately staffed on traditional lines. It was made illegal for anyone below the rank of banneret to retain others and for anyone below the rank of esquire to be retained; while liveries were only to be worn in household and at the wars. But as long as the retinue was sufficiently aristocratic and of stable composition no harm was expected of it. Only with the act of 1468 was the attack mounted

---

[1] B.M. Add. Roll 74138 (record of an action of nouvel disseisin brought by Brit against Fitzwarin and others).

[2] *Stonor Letters*, ed. C. L. Kingsford (2 vols., C.S., 3rd ser., xxix–xxx, 1919), i. 117. (McFarlane noted in his copy that Kingsford's uneasiness in dating this letter 1471 (ibid., p. 116) in so far as 'it involves a reference to an otherwise unknown meeting of the Parliament of the Lancastrian Restoration' was unjustified because the reference to a letter under the Privy Seal indicates that the meeting concerned was one of a Council.)

against all retainers as such;[1] and this was strongly reinforced in 1504. But it was for giving liveries to those who were not of his household on Christmas Day 1413 that Sir Edmund Ferrers of Chartley was tried *coram rege* in June 1414. Though not a member of the House of Lords, he pleaded that he and his ancestors since the Conquest had been barons and that the statute did not apply to such; before judgement could be given, he obtained Henry V's pardon.[2] It is unlikely that the law was enforced for many years after 1422. An entry in Edmund Ferrers's accounts for 1423–5 suggests that he had given liveries to three of the Earl of Stafford's esquires.[3]

The distribution of fees and annuities by itself was not illegal; nor, in spite of a vague ordinance of 1316,[4] was there any limit to the size of a noble household. It early became the practice to convert the stewardships of groups of manors into what were virtually sinecures, the holder doing what work there was by deputy. In 1334 or 1335 the monks of Christ Church, Canterbury, believing that the judge Sir John Stonor was 'prudent, well-known and beloved amongst the great' offered him the steward-ship of their estates; but the invitation was declined.[5] By about the middle of the fifteenth century most stewardships were filled on this system. In Edward IV's reign the stewards of Anne, Dowager Duchess of Buckingham, included the Earl of Shrewsbury, William, Lord Hastings, and Sir Thomas Montgomery as well as

---

[1] In his 1966 lectures McFarlane argued that the 1468 statute was 'aimed at the retaining of non-residents, not at the life-retainer by indenture. There was lawful retaining and unlawful retaining.'

[2] G.E.C. v. 317. Cf. pp. 123–4 below.

[3] Longleat Mun. 66 (Edmund Ferrers's receiver-general's account 24 June 1423–26 Mar. 1425), m. 2. McFarlane later modified his views on the enforcement in this period of laws against livery. In lectures given in 1956 and 1966 he stated that 'It is difficult to be sure, but on the whole the balance of evidence is heavily in favour of the unfashionable view that during the years following 1399 the problem of livery was at least temporarily solved.' In 1966 he suggested that the fourteenth, rather than the fifteenth, may have been 'the century of unbridled livery'. Cf. pp. xxxii–xxxiii above.

[4] *Chronicles of the Reigns of Edward I and Edward II*, ed. W. Stubbs (2 vols., R.S., 1882–3), i. 238–9. This is a sumptuary ordinance and its chief concern to restrict extravagance.

[5] *Stonor Letters*, vol. i, p. ix.

her son, the Earl of Wiltshire.[1] Similarly in Henry VIII's reign the Earl of Northumberland was not above receiving £20 a year as the Duke of Buckingham's steward in the lordship of Holderness.[2] What a man who was known to have the king's ear could collect in this way is fully set out by Dugdale in the case of William Hastings, the friend and courtier of Edward IV.[3] But the servants of royal servants were worth feeing also. In July 1459 Fastolf refers in a letter to Ralph Alygh 'squyer wᵗ my lord Chauncellr' . . . whom I hafe graunted to hafe xxs a yer to be of my councell and supporter of my tenantes' yn Southwork to be wyth all a goune'.[4] It was in the same spirit that the fifth Percy, Earl of Northumberland, paid £10 a year to Mr. Heneage 'gentleman usher to my lord cardinal' and half that amount to master Page, Wolsey's chamberlain.[5]

Courtiers and their creatures were not the only men to attract these attentions. In 1448–9 Sir Humphrey Stafford of Grafton, a substantial west-midland knight, had a valor made of his lands; to it was added a list of the annual fees he enjoyed. From the Duke of Buckingham, his very distant kinsman, came 40 marks a year, from James Ormond, Earl of Wiltshire, and Cecily, Duchess

[1] B.M. Add. Roll 22644 (declaration of account of the receiver of Caurs Michaelmas 1472–Michaelmas 1473); John, Earl of Shrewsbury, paid £73. 6s. 8d. for his fee of 20 marks p.a. as steward of Caurs for 5½ years to Michaelmas 1472. B.M. Add. Roll 29608, m. 3 (part of a valor of the duchess's English possessions, except Tonbridge Castle, in the year ending Michaelmas 1473); Lord Hastings receiving £13. 6s. 8d. p.a. as steward of the lordship of Oakham and constable of the castle, Lord Wiltshire £3. 6s. 8d. for half a year as steward of Rothwell (Northants) (but his name is crossed out), Sir Thomas Montgomery £6. 13s. 4d. as steward in Essex. P.R.O. SC 6/1117/11 (the duchess's receiver-general's account Michaelmas 1463–Michaelmas 1464); m. 6, payment of 20 marks to William Hastings as his annual fee for the constableship and stewardship of Oakham, which the duchess had granted to him for life 25 Nov. 1461. Cf. McFarlane, 'The Wars of the Roses', p. 110, n. 6. In his 1966 lectures on livery and maintenance McFarlane stated that there was almost no sign in the Stafford accounts of sinecure appointments being employed as means of bribing royal officials, councillors or courtiers before the middle of the century but that a tendency to use them in this way was carried far after 1461.

[2] G.E.C. ix. 719; E 36/226, pp. 8, 117.

[3] Cf. p. 103 above, and n. 4.

[4] B.M. Add. MS. 39848, no. 49, abstracted *Paston Letters*, iii, no. 380.

[5] P.R.O. E 36/226, pp. 149, 151, 203.

of Warwick, 20 marks each, and smaller sums from five other lords. The clear value of his estates was £420; his regular fees added another £71.[1] His son and namesake, an esquire who succeeded him in 1450, was by 1451 on the books of the Earl of Wiltshire, Lords Sudeley and Beauchamp of Powick, as well as of six neighbouring ecclesiastics and he had the promise, or at least the hope, of fees from the Earl of Warwick and the Bishop of Worcester.[2] Nor were his receipts confined to fees; on 13 April 1455 he tipped a servant for bringing him Lord Sudeley's livery; but he was certainly neither retainer nor menial servant to that magnate.[3]

When a feed man died there was a scramble for his places, as happened on the death of William Marmion in 1474 described in a Stonor letter.[4] The same correspondence provides the best statement of a lord's attitude towards those who received his fees. Sir William Stonor in 1478 asked Lord Strange if he might become one of his feed men. The surly answer was 'as for my graunt of a fee, I wold ye thowght yf ye do me servyce, as the wrytinge is, I woll dele more largly with yow, but I woll not be ovirmastred with none of my feed men . . . of my voluntary [I] send yow xls. . . . Yf ye dele as ye owght [in the next half year] I wolbe your goode lord; and eke I dare better displese yow than ye me. . . . If ye cherish my tenants, I will cherish you.'[5] One gathers that Stonor was put on probation. Fees were not wasted on those who did nothing for them.

It is possible to obtain a very rough idea of the size of a lord's household from the number of meals served; but, for reasons not worth going into, this method of calculation cannot give accurate results. The only absolutely satisfactory evidence is derived from three closely related types of source, namely: the 'Kalendars' or lists of all servants residing in the household in a given year; secondly the 'check-' or 'checker-rolls' on which were inscribed

---

[1] B.M. Add. MS. 74168, mm. 1, 2; cf. McFarlane, 'The Wars of the Roses', p. 109 and n. 3.

[2] Ibid., p. 109, n. 4.

[3] B.M. Add. Roll 74174 (account of Humphrey Stafford's receiver and steward of his household Nov. 1454–Nov. 1455), m. 3.

[4] *Stonor Letters*, i. 140–1.   [5] Ibid. ii. 70.

the names of those entitled to draw wages; and thirdly the rolls of such as were issued with liveries. The last probably contain the names of persons not strictly menial; all types are extremely rare— I have found but five examples of the three together;[1] and it so happens by ill luck that only one comes from a representative baronial household. Nevertheless, we do learn something of value.

Of the two 'Kalendars' the earlier is that of the inner household of Richard, Earl of Warwick, mostly at Berkeley castle, for the year 30 September 1420 to 9 March 1421.[2] By 'inner' is meant that part of the household which did not accompany the lord to France; the picture it gives is therefore incomplete. Including the countess and her three daughters, six gentlewomen, one of them accompanied by a child, three women of the chamber, ten gentlemen, five yeomen, Rose the laundress, and twenty-six *garciones*, it numbered in all fifty-six. When the earl paid it a flying visit in March 1421 he was accompanied by six henchmen, nine grooms of the stable, and a retinue of over sixty persons; but these were not all normally resident in his household.[3] His arrival indeed may have been planned as a show of force; for Berkeley where his wife was then living was being illegally held by her against the rightful heir. It looks as if the regular Beauchamp household was well below a hundred. The other Kalendar is also that of an absentee at the wars: John Fastolf's for the year Michaelmas 1431–2.[4] It is headed by his wife Dame Milicent and two of his kinswomen; the gentlemen and women number five; there are twelve yeomen and nine grooms; a total of twenty-nine.

The single 'checker-roll' belonged to the household of Edward, Duke of Buckingham, and was drawn up after the marriage of his heir, Henry, Earl of Stafford, to Ursula Pole in 1519.[5] Attached to it is a set of ordinances for its members which bears out the

---

[1] When McFarlane wrote this he was apparently unaware of the existence of a livery roll of Elizabeth de Burgh, Lady of Clare, for 1343–4 (P.R.O. E 101/92/23) on which he later worked.

[2] Longleat Mun. Misc. IX, f. 4ʳ. (Cf. C. D. Ross, 'The Household Accounts of Elizabeth Berkeley, Countess of Warwick, 1420–1', *Trans. Bristol and Gloucs. Arch. Soc.* 70 (1951), 81–105.)

[3] Longleat Mun. Misc. IX, f. 4.

[4] Magdalen College, Fastolf Paper 8.   [5] Longleat Mun. 457.

duke's reputation for piety. The first clause asserts that since without the service of God 'no good governance in politic rule may be had', it is necessary for all servants to attend mass daily. Unfortunately no detailed list of names is given. Besides the family, there were nine gentlewomen and seventeen gentlemen, a chancellor, a dean, an almoner and a physician, yeomen, grooms, and pages, in all 148. The maintenance of this large establishment year by year is likely to have been a heavier financial burden than the quite frequent and lavish hospitality.

The livery roll of Edward Courtenay, Earl of Devon, for the year 1384–5 antedates not only the blindness which later incapacitated him but also the first thorough-going statute against liveries issued in the Parliament of January 1390.[1] While it may therefore be useless as a guide to the size of the household, it gives us a clearer impression of an affinity, the whole body of men dependent on a great lord, than does any other of these documents. Apart from the earl, five male Courtenays are listed. In addition, there are seven knights, drawn from such well-known families as Bonville, Prideaux, Camoys, and Malet; forty esquires among whom will be found John Hawley, the Dartmouth merchant, and men with such familiar west-country names as Ferrers, Clifford, Chalons, Chiseldon, and Champernoun; fifty-two yeomen, four minstrels, eight parsons, three damoiselles, and six pages. Among the esquires and yeomen were included many of the estate officials as well as a few women such as the nurse. Finally there are fourteen men-of-law, three of them the earl's stewards, the rest, including four sergeants, retained to plead his causes in the king's courts; of these Clopton, Hull, Wadham, and Hankford had distinguished legal careers. According to a valor of 1382–3, Devon's landed income was just short of £1,350 per annum;[2] but with the death of his grandmother in 1391, it may have reached £2,000. That he could afford to give liveries to 130 persons, even though many of these were household and estate servants, is not without interest.

[1] B.M. Add. Roll 64320.
[2] B.M. Add. Roll 64318. This valor is dated 6 Richard II and may be for either the year 1381–2 or that for 1382–3. The value seems to be a net one.

The other livery roll is that of the household (this limitation is clearly mentioned) which went with Margaret, Duchess of Clarence, to join her husband in Normandy in November 1419.[1] It thus suffers from the same disadvantage as the two Kalendars. The Duchess took with her nineteen knights, twenty-five esquires including ten priests, six ships-masters, forty-five yeomen, nineteen grooms, thirteen pages, eleven sumptermen in charge of the baggage-train, and four choristers, total 143. With the duke, already overseas, was his military retinue, but since he cannot have gone abroad wholly without personal attendants, this figure is unlikely to be complete. The Duke of York, when he went to dinner with the Earl of Warwick at Rouen on 5 April 1431, brought with him no less than four knights, twelve esquires, and fourteen yeomen.[2] Even a man of comparatively humble rank like Sir John Dinham in the 1380s regularly travelled about England with a chaplain, four esquires, three yeomen, and three pages.[3]

The unwisdom of keeping too large a household was a favourite theme when giving advice to young men. In 1480, for example, William Harleston of Denham in Suffolk wrote to his nephew on the death of the latter's wife:

for Goddes sake be ware now, for now ye may breke your howshold with your honour and worshchep, now after the decesse of my good lady your wiff, and stabill your howshold now sadely and wisely with a convenient feleshepp so as ye may kepe you withynne yowr lyveliode; for a wise man will cast afore what falle aftirwarde. . . . And of certain thynges I wold desire you and pray you in the name of God: that ye wolle not owyr-wisshe you, ner owyr-purches yow ner owyr-bild you. For these iij thynges wolle plucke a yongman ryth lowe. Ner medyll not with no gret materis in the lawe. . . . And, syr [continued this fifteenth-century Polonius], of on thyng at is tolde me, that ye do make a fayre newe garden. In the wiche I pray you for my sake to sette too

---

[1] Westminster Abbey Mun. 12163, f. 16ᵛ.

[2] Beauchamp Household Book (for which see p. 101 and n. 1 above), f. xiiᵛ.

[3] Wardour Castle Ministers' Accnt. 427 (account of the personal expenses of Sir John Dinham 17 Richard II), e.g. ff. 6, 6ᵛ. The numbers given in the text are typical, not constant.

herbis, the whihe ben Paciens [and] Tyme; And that theis too herbis be put in the potage that ye ete, so as ye may ete them dayly.[1]

The warnings were unnecessary; the young man proved well able to take care of himself. But the mention of a garden reminds me that I omitted from my list of objects on which money was spent the construction not only of gardens but of great parks involving enclosure, the destruction of villages, and the loss of much good agricultural land. These were matter for complaint.[2]

The keeping of scores of feed men and a large staff of household officers had other purposes than mere display. Worship, the loss of which was frequently described as a shame and a rebuke, had its practical side.[3] It enabled its possessor to help his friends and grieve his enemies. He offered to those who served him well that good lordship and protection which were necessary to their worldly advancement. Their active presence and support endowed him with the influence through which he could promote both their worship and his own. The association between them was one of mutual convenience and profit. The world, as every surviving collection of private letters shows, was full of patrons seeking clients and clients in need of patronage. The substantial men of every shire were much courted by those above and below them. Even the remotest degrees of kinship were kept in mind and taken advantage of; as one writer put it: 'it is reasonable [for] a gentil-man to know his pedegre and his possibilyte' and to be upset if a third-cousin acted with 'gret straungenese' towards him.[4] The approach might come from either side; it might be threatening or honeyed; or it might be conducted, to save loss of face, through

---

[1] *Stonor Letters*, ii. 98–9.

[2] For instances of the construction of such parks see J. Rous (Ross), *Historia Regum Angliae*, ed. T. Hearne, 2nd edn. (Oxford, 1745), pp. 121–6, cf. M. W. Beresford, *The Lost Villages of England* (1954), pp. 147–8, 168, 205, 210.

[3] e.g. Sir John Fastolf, contemplating the possibility of defeat in a law-suit, wrote: 'For in good feith I drede most the shame and the rebuke that we shulde hafe and the matere concernyng the warde went contrary ayenst your' entent & myne as god deffende' (B.M. Add. MS. 39848, no. 26); cf. *Stonor Letters*, i. 97: 'And myne owne Jane, I thanke God myne adversari of Devenshere hath no wurshyp . . . and he is shamyd and nonsuyd in the cort to his great shame' (Thomas Stonor to Jane Stonor, 1468).

[4] *Stonor Letters*, i. 136.

an intermediary. In 1469, for example, the Bourchier brothers used one of their dependents to sound Thomas Stonor. This is how he did it:

> For as much as I understonde by my lorde Fitzwareyn þat he hathe diverse thynges to doo with you for certein matiers touchyng bothe his *worship* and *profite*,[1] wher in ye maye greatly please and also put you in suertey to have in tyme to come, if you neded, right good lordship as well of my lorde of Essex, to whom I am moste bounde, as of other my lordes his brethern; for trouth, my lorde of Essex, and he [i.e. Fitzwarin] also, specyally desired me to write to you, thynkyng þat ye sholde be þe better willed for my sake, the which I wyll veryly trust ye will doo.[2]

And so with naïve worldly wisdom these busy letter-writers cover their crisp sheets of paper, one after another ladling butter, rolling logs, and scratching backs. If public duty was ever remembered, it came at any rate second to a man's over-riding duty to his family and friends. We are assured by Professor Cam that this society of jobbers and parasites was 'far removed indeed from the atmosphere of responsibility, loyalty, and faith which had characterised the relationship of lord and vassal in the earlier middle ages'.[3] But did it really make so much difference if the man a lord protected from justice was his vassal or if those who fought for him in a private quarrel had done him homage? I am afraid I fail to see why. Nor do I much believe in 'that peculiar virtue' of the lawful man 'whose oath was unquestioned and whose integrity was the safeguard in turn of Saxon judgement and Norman inquest'.[4] But it is obvious that those who wish to believe in a golden age when men's appetites were subdued by simple faith are well advised to seek it, along with Mr. Jolliffe, in the period before 1066, for which there are practically no records. It is odd that it is the very richness of their sources which has given the later middle ages a bad name. Yet there is no need to deceive ourselves; by modern standards medieval justice was always rough; and it is still matter for investigation whether it was rougher in one century

---

[1] McFarlane's italics.   [2] *Stonor Letters*, i. 103.

[3] H. M. Cam, 'The Decline and Fall of English Feudalism', *History*, new ser., 25 (1940–1), 225, reprinted in H. M. Cam, *Law Finders and Law Makers* (1962).

[4] J. E. A. Jolliffe, *The Constitutional History of Medieval England* (1937), p. 410.

than in another. Provided that every piece of evidence is not treated as proof of backsliding from an orderly past, there is no harm in asserting that English justice in the fourteenth and fifteenth centuries was capable of improvement, was in fact better for the strong than for the weak. The existence of large bands of feed men and menial servants of gentle birth, in many ways the more civilized counterparts of the household knights of the Norman period, though they were not often wholly landless, who wore their master's livery and were ready for a consideration to embrace his quarrels, was bound to make it difficult for the king's justices to enforce the law; and not less so when those justices were themselves in receipt of fees.

If there was a difference, it lay in the fact that by the time of Edward I disorder was obliged to assume subtler forms. It being no longer possible, at any rate most of the time, to settle a dispute out of court by open violence, it was necessary to have recourse to legal guile. Men in fact found it safer to pervert the law than to break it. Feuds that in an earlier century would have ended, if not begun, in bloodshed, were now pursued within the framework of justice—with no loss of zeal. Hence from the end of the thirteenth century the growth of a demand for legislation on such topics as maintenance, champerty, conspiracy, and embracery. But it is as well to remember that the offences were not necessarily as new as the remedies provided to deal with them.

Though vague general complaints were frequent, especially in the petitions to which legislation was the response, it is difficult, at least until after 1422, to find many actual examples of simple maintenance, by which I mean attempts to overawe the court by the presence of armed men. Even during the times of worst disorder under Edward II and Henry VI it seems to have been unusual. The truth is that all evidence is not of equal value. If history is written from the preambles to statutes, the denunciations of moralists and reformers, and the *ex parte* statements of those engaged in litigation, there is every chance that it will be a record of bloodshed and injustice. The reality was a great deal less sensational. Corruption and wire-pulling were commoner than force. The balance of interests in a shire was well known to its inhabitants and only a fool risked a clash with those in a position to carry the day. Hence the advice so often given to 'get you lordship'; before coming into the open, it was as well to make sure of adequate support. If the substantial men of the neighbourhood were favourably disposed, there was little to fear save a dishonest sheriff; and he was generally amenable to strong local opinion, or, failing that, to bribery. Above all the decencies had to be observed. When Protector York recommended his servant John Alington to the Sheriff of Norfolk and Suffolk in everything that he 'shal have ado or to poursue w'in youre office' he was careful to add, though not necessarily to mean: 'iustice not offended'.[1] Men conscious of their worth might easily be angered by an inopportune show of high-handedness: careful management was the secret of good lordship.

It was also necessary to know when to lie low. There were times when it was wiser to let a case go by default than to invite defeat. For thirteen years Fastolf, irascible and overbearing though he was towards those in his power, endured injustice at the hands of Tuddenham and Heydon without a remedy. Even when the tide turned, he was willing to compromise unless his honour was thought to be too deeply involved. In the end he left it to his council to decide whether 'the rygour or utmost off the lawe be shewed and doon unto hem till I be satisfyed of my costes and damages'.[2]

In late medieval letters and documents references will sometimes be found to the fact of a litigant's having 'informed' the jury about the merits of his case well before the actual trial. Odd—and indeed suspicious—as this may sound to modern ears, there was, as Professor Plucknett has pointed out, nothing necessarily illegal about such an action.[3] A medieval jury was supposed to know the facts of the case before it came into court; its members were not indifferent persons who based their verdict upon the evidence elicited during the trial; they were well-informed neighbours who arrived knowing the answer. If they were offered information by

---

[1] P.R.O. SC 1/51/95.   [2] B.M. Add. MS. 39848, no. 10.
[3] T. F. T. Plucknett, *A Concise History of the Common Law* (4th edn., 1948), pp. 123–4; cf. J. B. Thayer, *Preliminary Treatise on Evidence at the Common Law* (1898) p. 92.

one of the parties to an action, there was no harm in that. This may be the origin of a practice which does not appear to be quite so innocent. When it is found—as in my experience it generally is—that informing the jury costs money, the explanation is surely a bribe, the offence to which lawyers give the name embracery? The accounts of Fastolf's man-of-law, Thomas Playter, are full of such entries as these 'Item, to Clougth' and Forster to labour' the jury, for Clement Paston' a yens seyntlo vi^s viii^d'; 'Item delivered to Clougth' for to drynk with' the jurr' ayens Sentlo & to enfo^{r}me hem'.[1] And not only his; those of many other landowners provide similar evidence. Nor is it confined to the disorderly middle years of the fifteenth century. Here are two examples from the reign of Henry IV. In 1400 John, Lord Lovel, was involved in litigation about his estates in Northamptonshire; a receiver's account shows that he gave the sheriff in all £7, that the under-sheriff received 40s., and that another 40s. were distributed among the members of the jury.[2] Secondly when in 1411–12 Ralph Green went to law over his manor of Warminster in Wiltshire, he paid twelve jurors altogether 43s. 4d.[3]

As the payments to sheriffs prove, there was no need to wait until a jury was empanelled before taking action. Here the favourite word is 'labour' as in the following quotation from one of Fastolf's letters of April 1451: 'And ye w^t suche helpe must labour' effectuelly to the shiref for retornyng of suche panells as will sey for me in my right.'[4] On another occasion his plan was more complicated. In the first place the sheriff or his under-sheriff was to be entreated to delay the action; 'and if that will not be, to entreat him to make a good panel; if that will not be, to return an indifferent panel . . . if that will not be, to get a copy of the panel that he will return, and entreat as many of the inquest as ye can . . . that they will not appear; and those that appear not and

---

[1] Magdalen College, Fastolf Paper 71 (Thomas Playter's expenses 1459–60), m. 6, cf. ibid., m. 7 'Item to xii Jurro^{r}s which' passed a yens Seyntlo xls.'

[2] Magdalen College Misc. 315 (account of Lord Lovel's receiver in Northants., Leics., Staffs., Rutland, Bucks., and Oxon., Michaelmas 1399–Michaelmas 1400), m. 2.

[3] Longleat Mun. 9421 (account of Ralph Green's Warminster receiver 30 Sept. 1411–30 Sept. 1412), dorse.   [4] B.M. Add. MS. 39848, no. 18.

they be not seen in the town, they shall never lose money there for it.'[1] And corruption could be helped out by maintenance. In November 1454 Fastolf's clerk, Thomas House, wrote to John Paston the lawyer as follows:

> my maistyr is agreed, what reward ye geve the Shereff he holdeth hym content . . . so he woll ther upon returne the panell for the seyd ateynte; and thanne yef Jenney [another of Fastolf's counsel] wold meove my Lord of Norffolke that he wold be my good lord, amyttyng me for hese chapeleyn and Jhankyn Porter for hese servaunt, wheche is hese chek roll, it shuld cause the matere to have the redyer expedecyon, as well be the Shereff as be the gret jury.[2]

These calculations were often falsified, but that does not alter the fact that the evidence of corrupt practice is overwhelming. No wonder that men often preferred to settle their disputes out of court. Yet, even if at the best of times, juries and sheriffs were being bribed and—less certainly—intimidated, conditions in the 1450s *were* exceptional. A chronic weakness had been greatly magnified by thirty years of 'lack of governance'; it would be a mistake to spread the impressions so vividly conveyed by the correspondence of Fastolf and the Pastons over two centuries—or even one. Yet the later years of Henry VI's misrule are the main source from which historians have derived the evidence upon which the whole age is condemned. The reign of Henry V, short though it was and preoccupied by the conquest of a foreign throne, provides the contrast. Although, in expectation of his service in Normandy, Edmund Ferrers was leniently treated, his indictment gave fair warning that such breaches of the statutes against liveries would not be ignored.[3] Petty corruption is one of the most difficult offences to detect, and doubtless many cases similar to those I have mentioned occurred even under Henry V. But towards the end of the reign a prominent Oxfordshire esquire, Reginald Malyns, was put on trial because in July 1419 he bribed a jury with money, food, and drink to secure a favourable verdict.[4] Better evidence, perhaps, of the good order maintained in those years

---

[1] We have been unable to trace this.
[2] *Paston Letters*, iii. no. 268.   [3] Cf. p. 107 above.
[4] Longleat Mun. 30.

was the peaceful settlement of three great disputes in which some of the most powerful baronial families were involved. I have no time to go into details now, but between 1415 and 1420 the failure of the direct male line of the Fitzalans, the Berkeleys, and the Burnells gave rise to problems which a quarter of a century later would hardly have been solved without bloodshed. By 1421 all three had been satisfactorily compromised. One, it is true, the dispute over the succession to the Berkeley lands, broke out again during the minority of Henry VI, when the Earl of Warwick saw a chance of bettering the terms he had previously accepted; but even then it was for a time patched up by the good sense of the Council.[1] It says much for the self-restraint of the parties that no attempts were made to disturb the two other settlements. But when she died in 1435, one of the Fitzalan coheiresses, our old friend Joan, Lady Bergavenny, that second Jezabel, who had also profited from the failure of the Burnell line, left her grandsons in her will, along with her inheritance, £500 and 700 marks respectively 'to be dispent . . . about the defence of the lands' she was leaving them. The money was not needed.[2]

Naturally labour and good lordship was not confined to local affairs. If the head of an affinity was to serve his followers well, he had to have recourse to that greatest of all dispensers of patronage, the king. What took men to court was not merely their duty of attendance and council, but the need, if they were to prosper in their own designs, to have access to the royal ear. The king was in fact the good lord of all good lords; if he played his hand with reasonable skill, he could fill his affinity with all the greatest of his subjects; only an ill-advised ruler confined his patronage to the few, for that was to be guilty of the sin of favouritism. I am not suggesting that there were no politics save jobbery. Nor that they were exclusively the king's concern, though he alone was responsible for decision. It is clear that members of the nobility,

---

[1] For references to the Berkeley case, McFarlane, 'The Wars of the Roses', p. 106; for the Fitzalan case, G.E.C. i. 247–9, and E. R. Fairbanks, 'The Last Earl of Warenne and Surrey', *Yorks. Archaeological Journ.* 19 (1907), 193–264; for the Burnell case p. 67 above.

[2] *The Register of Henry Chichele*, ed. E. F. Jacob and H. C. Johnson (4 vols., Oxford, 1938–47), i. 536.

the chief of whom regarded themselves as the king's natural councillors, had often very definite, though rarely unanimous, views on policy; on war and peace, for example, the way of Spain versus the way of Flanders, on the tolerable limits to ecclesiastical privilege, on the regulation of wages, on taxation and even on the administration of the law; and in their attitude towards these matters I personally fail to see any line of possible cleavage between lords and commons; their common interests and sympathies were stronger than any conceivable causes of division between them. But the king governed. He took or rejected advice; he appointed servants to obey his orders. But even the greatest of his subjects were councillors, not aspirants to office. Use of the word 'party' to describe their groupings only obscures the real character of fourteenth-century political activity. Before he could obtain his taxes, an Edward III had to listen to complaint and promise redress. In many cases he sympathized with those who complained and was sincere in his attempts to make the law effective; sometimes he was not. But the real politics of the reign were not confined to the short if frequent parliaments; they were inherent rather in Edward's daily personal relations with his magnates. The king's service was profitable; his favour the only sure road to honour and success; men went to court and to the royal camp, not to express unacceptable views, but for what they could get. Under a ruler who knew his job they were amply rewarded. His lordship could scarcely be good without *largesse*.

The root trouble about most late-medieval constitutional history is its assumption that the interests of king and nobility were opposed, that conflict could not be avoided. This assumption seems to me false. The only thing that can be said for it is that conflicts sometimes occurred; that they did so was almost always the fault of the king; which is as much as to say that it depended how often the hereditary succession brought those unfit to rule to the throne. Edward II, Richard II, and Henry VI were the penalties that monarchy paid for its dependence upon the chances of heredity. It would be a mistake to judge the institution solely by its failures. The fact that neither Edward II nor Richard II could get on with their magnates and that Henry VI was totally incapable of government may be allowed to bulk too large, though the consequences were serious for them. In fact the area of possible conflict was extraordinarily small and any competent king had no difficulty in avoiding it. But for him some qualities were almost essential. He had to inspire his magnates with confidence and he had to know how to manage them with firmness or tact, just as, on a smaller scale, they managed those who were subject to them. It was difficult for him if he did not share their prejudices, interests, and pastimes. Above all he needed to be able to lead them in war. Occupied as they were with their own affairs, they had no wish to do his work for him; but they expected him to give them the opportunity to carve out their own careers under his leadership. His weakness did not give them cause to rejoice; lack of governance was a misfortune that brought them more trouble than advantage. If he happened to be a child they felt it their duty to shoulder responsibility and to try to maintain order until he came of age. As the ordinances drawn up from time to time during the long minority of Henry VI show, they knew their own weaknesses and made practical efforts to guard against them. That civil war broke out in the 1450s was less their fault than that of the king who failed them. There is no need to look for more deep-seated causes; the abuse of lordship and the prevalence of corruption were merely the signs that England lacked a ruler. It is worth remembering that her nobility was masterless for thirty years, with the certain prospect of twenty more like them, before self-restraint finally crumbled at St. Albans in 1455. Once that had happened, the restoration of the old community of interests between Crown and baronage which had characterized the reigns of Edward I, Edward III, and Henry V was difficult to achieve. Both Edward IV and Henry VII came near to doing it. Henry VIII for all his abilities was too suspicious—and his creatures played upon his suspicions—to be trusted. His murders were a confession of failure. Divide and rule may be a good maxim for tyrants and usurpers; but unite and rule is a better one for the law-abiding sovereign. Its neglect was to lead ultimately to the Glorious Revolution. It was the essence of late medieval government at its best.

The Stratification of the Nobility and Gentry in the Later Middle Ages[1]

B Y the mid fifteenth century English society was becoming more stratified *at the top* than it had been. Even 'gentleman' or *generosus* had since the beginning of the fifteenth century acquired a specialized meaning. A man so described belonged to the lowest stratum of the armigerous, below that of esquire, in its turn below that of knight.[2] These barriers against too easy social mobility had not existed a century before. If, as historians of the Tudor period often claim, such barriers are only raised when the privileged feel themselves in danger of being swamped by the mass of invaders, then their fear of too much social mobility must be back-dated to at least the reign of Edward III, after which it is increasingly betrayed. It can be seen in the sumptuary legislation, however ineffective that may have been in practice. It can be seen, too, in the growing emphasis on rules of social precedence: in the books of nurture or courtesy which survive from the reign of Richard II and proliferate in the fifteenth century, intended to provide guidance for those whose business it was to seat guests at feasts and other social occasions. From the Pope who 'hath no peer' down to the 'gentleman well-nurtured and of good manners' each had his place.[3] It can be seen again in the legislation regulating the giving of liveries which also dates from Richard II's reign. By the ordinance of 12 May 1390 issued in response to a petition in

---

[1] The views given in this passage from McFarlane's 1965 lectures differ from those expressed in the first of the Ford Lectures (pp. 6–9 above). Cf. also his 'The Wars of the Roses'; and 'The English Nobility in the Later Middle Ages' below, pp. 268–78.

[2] For a recent view on the stratification of the gentry see N. Denholm Young, *The Country Gentry in the Fourteenth Century* (Oxford, 1969). G. R. Sitwell, 'The English Gentleman', *The Ancestor*, I (1902), 58–103 is still valuable.

[3] p. 8, n. 2 above.

the previous Parliament, not only were churchmen forbidden to give their servants 'livery of company', that is liveries to be worn outside their households, but 'knights bachelor, esquires and others of less estate' were also deprived of that mark of rank.[1] In the January Parliament of 1393 the king ordered that liveries of cloth might only be *worn* by those of lower estate than esquire if they were menial and familiar residing continually in their lord's house and not beyond it.[2]

Most clearly of all, this stratification is visible in the development of ranks within the peerage and of the clear line of demarcation which separated peers from lesser breeds without the lords. In 1300 there was only one heritable *rank* in England, that of earl; by 1500 there were five. But in addition, within each rank an order of precedence, claimed and quarrelled over, based partly on date of creation and partly on special privilege conferred by the king, was rapidly growing up. The growth of a dividing line between the temporal and spiritual lords on the one hand and the rest of armigerous society on the other is hardly capable of exact dating. It is indeed *implicit* in the statutes dealing with liveries which confine the giving of livery of company to temporal lords as opposed to knights bachelor and others. But the term 'lord' is only negatively defined: he is something above a knight bachelor. How variously this could be interpreted was shown by a dispute in Henry V's reign. During 1413 Staffordshire was disturbed by a feud between the Ferrerses of Chartley and the Erdswicks of near-by Sandon. Both parties complained to the Leicester Parliament of April 1414.[3] Henry V interrupted his preparations for war long enough to accompany Chief Justice Harkford into the area to hear the indictments in person. Sir Edmund Ferrers of Chartley, whose ancestors had not received a personal summons to Parliament since 1311 (though before 1269 they were Earls of Derby), was presented for having on Christmas Day 1413 distributed to many persons, not of his household, liveries of green and white cloth. He appeared before the king for trial in June 1414. His defence that he and all his ancestors since the Conquest had held their lands as

[1] *Statutes of the Realm*, ii. 74–5.   [2] *Rot. Parl.* iii. 307ᵃ.

[3] G.E.C. v. 317–18.

barons by barony and that the statutes therefore did not apply to him was not accepted. Nor was it true, since Chartley was not a tenurial barony. If it had been true it would have been irrelevant. But Henry V did not wish to proceed to extremes and the case was adjourned. On Ferrers's undertaking to accompany the royal expedition to France he was pardoned. He found a better outlet for his lawlessness abroad, fighting at Harfleur, Agincourt, and all through the Norman campaigns from 1417 until Henry V's death. Neither the jurors nor the court regarded Ferrers as a temporal *lord* and his own view of his station was rejected. But it was still arguable. On the other hand, whatever doubts the courts might have about the meaning of temporal lord as used in a statute, its equivalence with a peer of Parliament was increasingly taken for granted. It will be found that as early as 1374 Chief Justice Belknap assumed that all who held by barony ought to come to Parliament as a baron.[1] As a matter of *fact* he was wrong; only those whom the king summoned could come, but it would not be long before the assumption that only those who were summoned were temporal lords ceased to be seriously questioned. Lords were peers and if they possessed no higher title they were barons. The *Paston Letters* provide many vivid examples of the popular recognition of this development. In 1454 Thomas Dennis was defamed 'of settyng up billes agayn lordis' and the context makes it clear that peers were meant.[2] In 1455 Henry Windsor was 'loth to write any thing of any Lord';[3] and John Paston claims that he was 'not usid to meddel with Lordes maters meche forther than me nedith'.[4] Ten years later he draws a sharp distinction between gentlemen on the one hand and lords on the other;[5] while in 1472 his son protests 'I was never yitt Lordys sworyn man; yit have I doone goode servyce and nott leffte any at hys most neede ner for feer.'[6] Perhaps the best example is found in an unprinted letter belonging to the 1450s from Thomas, Lord Scales, to Sir John Fastolf, since this distinguishes between the good lordship (i.e. patronage by a lord) of such a one as himself and 'the good master-

---

[1] G.E.C. iv. 689.   [2] *Paston Letters*, ii. 317.
[3] Ibid. iii. 45.   [4] Ibid. iii. 46.
[5] Ibid. iv. 165–6.   [6] Ibid. v. 163.

ship' of his correspondent, rich and influential though Fastolf was.[1] Finally in 1481 we find a Nottinghamshire esquire explaining why he had remained inactive in the face of a forcible entry by Francis, Lord Lovel: 'considering he is a lorde, I may not soo deale'.[2] Lords were no longer as other men. In the same period the heralds' visitations were similarly attempting to protect the armigerous gentry from invasion from below. In theory at any rate the stratification was complete.

[1] Magdalen College Mun., Hickling 104, abstracted *Paston Letters*, ii. 82.
[2] McFarlane, 'The Wars of the Roses', p. 108.

The Hungerford Family and the Hundred Years War[1]

THE ransom demanded and paid for Robert, Lord Moleyns, after his capture in 1453 was £6,000. This already considerable figure was swollen to more than £9,800 by a number of extras. The finding of nearly £10,000 was a source of some embarrassment to Moleyns and his kinsmen (who showed a strong sense of their family responsibility throughout) for many years after his release. It was raised by mortgaging both Moleyns and Hungerford estates. The investors were not so much professional financiers as neighbours and friends.[2] Had Robert Moleyns taken reasonable care or had reasonable luck, the mortgages would have been paid off without recourse to that last desperate remedy of the embarrassed landowner: the sale of some part of his estates. Margaret Hungerford's plan involved no raid on capital; only a temporary loss of income. What made a sale necessary was Moleyns's misplaced loyalty to the cause of Lancaster. The Hungerfords had been clients of the house of Lancaster before John of Gaunt succeeded to the dukedom. Their fortunes had been made, especially by Walter, Lord Hungerford the Treasurer, in Lancastrian service and Robert clung too long to the dynasty to which his ancestors owed so much. He followed Margaret of Anjou to Scotland in 1461, to be captured and executed three years later by Edward IV. Since he had succeeded his father in the unmortgaged parts of the Hungerford estates in 1459, these were forfeited by his attainder in 1461.[3] As a result his mother was

---

[1] This extract from the 1965 lectures supplements the account of the ransoming of Robert, Lord Moleyns, given in the second Ford lecture, pp. 29–30 above.

[2] References to the mortgages are to be found in the wills both of Robert, Lord Hungerford (d. 1459) and Margaret for which see p. 29, nn. 3, 4 above. Cf. *C.P.R. 1461–7*, pp. 283, 284.

[3] G.E.C. vi. 619–20.

obliged soon afterwards to sell at least two manors of her own inheritance in order to repay those creditors from whom she had borrowed her son's ransom money.[1] How much this hurt her is shown by the will she drew up in 1476, about eighteen months before her death, in which she begged *her* heirs to 'have none occasion to grugge for that I leve not to theyme so grete enheritaunce as I myght and wulde have done, yf fortune had not bene so sore agenste me'. For this she blamed neither folly nor excess nor indiscreet liberality, but 'misadventure that hath happend in this seasons of troubill-tyme late paste'.[2] And by that she meant political events in England, not the loss of the war with France. The financial burden of her son's ransom could be carried, heavy though it was. The attainders (for Moleyns's son and heir had met the same fate as his father in 1469) were by comparison shattering. Yet even there the effects were only temporary. Margaret, Lady Hungerford, made her will and died in the darkest hour of the family's fortunes and her gloom was justified —in 1476 and 1478. In Henry VII's reign the attainders were reversed and her descendants were to recover everything except the manors she had been forced to sell.[3] The loss of those manors was the permanent scar consequent upon Robert's capture at Castillon in 1453; and even that scar would have been invisible but for his adhesion to the wrong side—for the time being—in the Wars of the Roses. The Lancastrian Hungerfords were given a fresh start under Henry Tudor.

When Moleyns was taken prisoner he was almost certainly a newcomer to the French war. As far as *he* was concerned, therefore, the war was a dead loss: *he* had no gains to balance against his huge ransom. But if the fortunes of the Hungerford family as a whole are taken into account instead of those of its unluckiest member, the arithmetic would come out quite differently. Three other Hungerfords took part in the second half of the Hundred Years War: Moleyns's father, the second Lord Hungerford; his

---

[1] *H.M.C. Calendar of MSS. of the Dean and Chapter of Wells*, i (1907), 498, 499, 502.

[2] Colt Hoare, *Heytesbury Hundred*, pp. 101–2.

[3] G.E.C. vi. 622–3.

uncle, his father's elder brother Walter, and his grandfather Walter the first lord. Of these only one, Walter the uncle, was ever taken prisoner, at Patay in 1429; his ransom of £3,000 was paid during the next four years.[1] That completes the total of losses. Unfortunately it is not possible to cite any actual figures for the gains. But there is a good deal of imprecise evidence that these were large. In 1433, for example, Moleyns's father and grandfather were negotiating 'the finance, ransom and deliverance' of their prisoner, John of Vendôme, Vidame of Chartres.[2] Vendôme was of much higher birth and rank than any Hungerford and consequently good for a large ransom. And he was far from being the Hungerfords' only prize. The member of the family whose military career, sandwiched between his speakership of the Commons in 1414 and his peerage in 1426, was the most notable was Walter the first baron, 1378–1449; and the most active and remunerative part of that career fell within the reign of Henry V. At Agincourt or shortly afterwards he took at least eight prisoners valuable enough to be worth shipping home to England. For his services from the siege of Caen onwards he received a series of grants of lordships and castles in the conquered duchy, including the barony of Le Hommet in tail male.[3] A hundred years later the antiquary Leyland was told that Sir Walter Hungerford's rebuilding of his castle of Farleigh, carried out in the 1420s, was paid for by the proceeds of Agincourt.[4] On balance, therefore, the family would seem to have profited greatly from the war. And few English families were as unlucky as it with two oldest sons captured in two generations.

[1] J. H. Ramsay, *Lancaster and York* (2 vols., Oxford, 1892), i. 398; *Ordinances and Proceedings of the Privy Council*, ed. N. H. Nicholas (7 vols., 1834–7), iv. 149–50.

[2] *Foedera*, x. 537, 566, 574, 580.

[3] For Walter Hungerford's career and gains through war see J. S. Roskell, 'Three Wiltshire Speakers', *Wilts. Archaeolog. and Nat. Hist. Mag.* lvi (1955–6), 301–41.

[4] Leland, *Itinerary*, i. 138.

APPENDIX C

Aspects of Noble Finances[1]

W E know far more about incomes from land than we do about what may be called casual profits—for a terribly simple reason: the latter were normally paid direct into the lord's coffers or privy purse in charge of a confidential servant, usually called a cofferer. But, as far as I know, no cofferer's account survives from our period; the earliest known belonged to Edward Stafford, third Duke of Buckingham, and dates from the last years of Henry VII's reign.[2] The mistake we must not make is to assume that none ever existed before. Their existence is proved by mentions of them in accounts belonging to other officials which do survive. When, for example, expenditure exceeded revenue in one department of a lord's household and the receipts from their estates were insufficient to make the deficit good, it was usual to transfer the cash needed 'from the lord's coffers'. Into these coffers went most, sometimes all, casual revenue and all unspent income from the lord's estates. Once deposited there, it disappears from view. This was equally true of the king's coffers. This is brought home to us by a clerical error which occurred in the 1360s. By some mistake the money received for the ransom of King John of France reached the Exchequer; it was ordered to release it at once and to meddle no further with what was no business of its.[3] It would be called upon to pay the expenses of the war; it did not handle the profits. Thus, apart from his own prisoners, Edward III bought prisoners others had captured—the Exchequer paid the agreed price, but the ransoms received went into the royal coffers. As with the king, so with the nobility. You may find a receiver-general providing new shoes for the lord's prisoners—

[1] Extracted from the 1965 lectures.
[2] B.M. Add. Roll 40859^B (account of the treasurer of the duke's household, 31 Mar. 1503–31 Mar. 1504).
[3] Above, p. 38.

there were four drawing shoes in the household of Richard Beauchamp, Earl of Warwick in the winter of 1417–18—but he will have no hand in extracting their ransoms.[1] The most absurd example of this division of responsibility by which one official met all losses and another pocketed all gains arose out of the noble sport of gambling. The debts might fall on the receiver-general or the treasurer of the household, but there were never any winnings. Since a good many of the games were games of pure chance—dice for example—and played between social equals the lord must sometimes have won. Part of an account, probably a household account, belonging to Edmund, the last Mortimer Earl of March, survives for the six months between September 1413 and March 1414, for part of which time the earl was with Henry V and his brothers at Eltham during Oldcastle's rising. During that period he lost at play—at cards, tables, raffle, and chance, and betting on cock-fighting as well as several other games I do not recognize—over £157 on forty-five separate occasions. Possibly he won on the days he did not lose; we do not know.[2] The earl was in his twenty-third year and historians have probably been justified in reckoning him a lightweight (though it is an impression his accounts do not altogether support). Even so he cannot always have lost. £157 was by the way, the income of a pretty substantial knight; the earl could afford it.[3]

That other magnates had full coffers and opportunities for investment, though scarcely of the Earl of Arundel's scale, there is some fragmentary evidence. Arrest followed by forfeiture could in times of civil war bring such evidence into the possession of the Crown; sometimes it remained among the public records. Some survives for Edward II's reign, less for Richard II's, less still for the period of the Wars of the Roses. Unfortunately very little of

[1] B.M. Egerton Roll 8773 (Receiver-general's account, Michaelmas 1417– Michaelmas 1418), m. 5ᵛ.

[2] B.M. Egerton Roll 8746, mm. 1, 2, 3, 4, 5.

[3] In the original lecture there followed an account of the wealth of Richard, Earl of Arundel (d. 1376), as revealed by the inventory of his movables and by his testament, and of that of Ralph, Lord Cromwell, as revealed by his building activities and his executors' accounts. For these fortunes see pp. 49, 84, 94, 88–91 above.

it lays bare the whole story. The materials for the confiscations of the years 1386–8 are, as Miss Clarke found, extensive but disappointing. The 'Book of Forfeitures' concerned with the property of Robert de Vere and his fellow victims only reveals how generally the condemned men, their families and servants made away with their movable property and successfully concealed it from the victors.[1] If Edward IV's government was more successful than the Appellants the evidence has disappeared. Indeed, the only clear piece of evidence from either Richard II's reign or later is the valuation placed upon the cash and goods of Edward III's gold-digging mistress after their seizure in the autumn of 1377: £20,000 in addition to a number of outstanding loans and an extensive estate in land.[2] The records for Edward II's forfeitures are slightly more informative though very far from complete. As Dr. Fryde has shown, the elder Despenser, in spite of attempts to conceal it, had at least £3,000 in cash stored away in 1326 and his son nearly £6,000 deposited with the Italian banking houses of Bardi and Peruzzi two years earlier.[3] Considering their greedy acquisitiveness this hardly seems to justify Dr. Fryde's adjective: 'enormous'. Compared with the amounts revealed by Arundel's and Cromwell's papers, £10,000 after a good many years of power and royal favour appears almost moderate. The landed wealth of the two Despensers may not have been as great as Arundel's after 1361; it was a good deal greater than Cromwell's.[4] Evidently it would be unwise to assume that the size of a man's rent-roll gives the measure of his probable fortune. And we should be *prepared* to believe that, whatever was happening to the value of land, wealth derived from other sources was increasing, at any rate down to 1450.

We have seen traces that members of the landed nobility were

---

[1] M. V. Clarke, 'Forfeitures and Treason in 1388', *Fourteenth Century Studies* (Oxford, 1937), pp. 115–45.   [2] We have been unable to trace this.
[3] E. B. Fryde, 'The Deposits of Hugh Despenser the Younger with Italian Bankers', *Econ. H.R.*, 2nd ser., 3 (1950–1), 344–59.
[4] For the Despensers' lands see T. F. Tout, *The Place of Edward II in English History* (2nd edn., 1936), pp. 124–7, 138–40; J. C. Davies, 'The Despenser War in Glamorgan', *T.R.H.S.*, 3rd ser., 9 (1915), 21–64; Holmes, *Estates of the Higher Nobility*, pp. 8–9, 36–8.

in the habit of depositing sums with merchants, presumably as in Arundel's case for these to 'traffic with' to the lord's advantage. At the beginning of our period those who received such deposits were usually Italians: the Alberti, the Bardi, the Frescobaldi, and the Peruzzi. A few scattered references suggest that in Edward I's reign such practices were common. Isabel, Countess of Devon and Aumale,[1] and Henry Lacy, Earl of Lincoln,[2] are known to have had money in the hands of Florentine bankers. Though Italian firms continued to be employed for this purpose right into the fifteenth century, they were mostly used for exchange business, for the transmission of money to the Roman Curia or to ransom prisoners in French hands and more often to transfer the profits of war from Normandy to England. When, for example, Sir John Fastolf made use of an Italian banker to transfer large sums from Paris to London, he *invested* the money with native merchants.[3] The same preference was shown earlier by John of Gaunt.

Gaunt's cofferer's and executors' accounts unluckily are not preserved. However, his receiver-general was sometimes employed to deal with surplus cash temporarily in his hands. In this respect Gaunt's receiver-general's accounts are more informative than most. Unfortunately only four survive.[4] One for the year ending at Michaelmas 1377 and the other three from the 1390s. In 1376–7 Lancaster's receiver had no cash to spare and even the coffers may have been empty. This was because his wages of war and those of his retinue had fallen into arrears. During the year he received from the Exchequer £6,000 which had been outstanding since June 1371; even more may have been

---

[1] N. Denholm-Young, *Seignorial Administration in England* (Oxford, 1937), pp. 63–6.

[2] Fryde, 'The Deposits of Hugh Despenser the Younger . . .', p. 355; cf. J. F. Baldwin, 'The Household Administration of Henry Lacy and Thomas of Lancaster', *E.H.R.*, 43 (1927), 189, 195.

[3] McFarlane, 'The Investment of Sir John Fastolf's Profits of War', pp. 96, 97, 100.

[4] P.R.O. DL 28/3/1 (1376–7); 38/3/2 (1392–3); 28/3/5 (1396–7)—before its transfer to the P.R.O. in 1968 this account was among the documents deposited in Leeds Central Library by Sir Alvary Gascoigne and was there listed as G[ascoigne] C[ollection] DL 3. (These three are full accounts.) P.R.O. DL 28/32/21 is a certificate of account of the receiver-general for 1394–5.

owing for his great *chevauchée* of 1373–4. As we have already seen he had been borrowing from the Earl of Arundel in just this period.[1] In 1376 his receiver-general repaid loans of 1,000 marks from Arundel's younger son John as well as one of £100 from John Philipot.[2] On the other hand, when we come to the next account, that for the year ending 2 February 1393, the receiver-general was in funds. Not only had thousands of pounds come from Spain under the treaty by which Gaunt had renounced his claim to the Castilian throne, but Richard II's Exchequer was paying for the diplomatic and other employments of the duke, who was now also Duke of Aquitaine.[3] As a result it was the receiver-general's turn to lend. Loans by him amounting to more than £6,000 were recorded. About a third of this sum was to London merchants; most of the rest to members of the duke's own family, his son Henry, Earl of Derby, his brother Thomas of Woodstock, and his sister-in-law, the Duchess of York. Only two sums lent to Italian bankers are noted, £478. 12s. 1½d. in all, of which £278. 12s. 1½d. was to Walter Bardi, the bank's agent long resident in England.[4] In the next year but one, that ending

[1] Above, p. 90.

[2] P.R.O. DL 28/3/1, m. 4.

[3] The receipt of 6,000 florins of Aragon from Thomas Tutbury, treasurer of the duke's household, is recorded P.R.O. DL 28/3/2, f. 4ᵛ (they were worth between 2s. 1¼d. and 2s. 2½d. each, f. 1ᵛ). Since the payment of the Castilian subsidy was two years in arrears in 1393 (P. E. Russell, *The English Intervention in Spain and Portugal*, p. 538) this money presumably came from the £100,000 lump sum paid in accordance with the treaty of 1388 (ibid., pp. 506, 510–11), which had been paid over to Tutbury in the first instance (ibid., p. 511) and some or all of which had presumably remained in his charge, or else from the annual payments made up to 1391 (ibid., p. 536). Some or all of the 2,739 florins of Florence and ducats of Genoa, 12,189 *doblas* of Castile, 12,869 florins of Aragon, 5,413 francs and 858 old *écus* and nobles of Bordeaux with which the receiver-general was charged at the beginning of the financial year (ff. 1, 1ᵛ) probably also derived from the payments from Castile. (For the later history of the Castilian subsidy see Russell, op. cit., p. 540 n. 2, and S. Armitage Smith, *John of Gaunt*, p. 332 n. 1.) Payments from the royal Exchequer in the year totalled £4,653. 10s. 1½d., of which £1,046. 13s. 4d. was in repayment of a loan, ff. 3ᵛ, 4ʳ, 4ᵛ.

[4] For these loans see p. 92 and n. 3. The figure for the total sum lent is higher than that given in the Ford Lectures (p. 92 above) because of the inclusion of some or all of the sum recorded as *Prestita* made in 1392–3 (DL 28/3/2, f. 20ʳ–20ᵛ), by far the largest part of which was an advance of £1,333. 6s. 8d. to the Earl of Derby.

2 February 1395, the receiver-general's account shows that large sums of money from Castile were still arriving. There are, however, only two relatively small loans.[1] In the last account, for the year ending at Michaelmas 1397, there are references to existing loans which had amounted to about £2,000, including the £278. 12s. 1½d. to Walter Bardi, but new loans amounted to only £30.[2] To judge from the huge legacies in cash and kind contained in the will Lancaster drew up on 3 February 1399 his coffers were very far from empty.[3] Apart from Henry, Earl of Derby's Prussian crusades and the mixture of pilgrimage to Jerusalem and grand tour of European courts that followed the second, Lancaster's chief expense during the 1390s was in buying land with which to endow his son John Beaufort, made Marquess of Dorset in 1397, without reducing Bolingbroke's inheritance. In 1394–5 he had paid the childless Earl of Salisbury the sum of 5,000 marks for the reversion of two manors in Somerset.[4] The Dorset lands he bought must have cost at least as much again.

John of Gaunt's gross income from his estates as estimated by his auditors in the two years ending Michaelmas 1394 and 1395 was roughly £11,750.[5] These figures, by the way, differ from those printed by Sir Robert Somerville since his breaking down of the information contained in the valors needs some correction.[6] The net income, i.e. after subtracting the wages and fees of his local ministers, repairs, and other necessary expenses of administration was almost exactly £10,000; i.e. the net income is about

---

[1] P.R.O. DL 28/32/21 (certificates of receiver-general's accounts); summarized Armitage Smith, *John of Gaunt*, pp. 447–50. The loans were of £66. 13s. 4d. to Henry Hoghton and £200 to William Maghfeld and Thomas Graft, citizens of London.

[2] P.R.O. DL 28/3/5, ff. 3, 3ᵛ, 4ᵛ, 14ᵛ (in some cases it is unclear whether these were loans in more than a technical sense).

[3] Above, p. 88, n. 1. The total of the cash legacies was over £8,000, exclusive of those from the uncollected arrears of the Castilian subsidy and of rents. The executors had discretion to reduce legacies if funds were insufficient.

[4] Above, p. 55.

[5] This figure is derived from the valors for the years concerned, P.R.O. DL 29/11980–3; DL 29/11984–6.

[6] Somerville, *Duchy of Lancaster*, i. 91–4; for McFarlane's criticisms see his review, *E.H.R.* 70 (1955), 110–11.

five-sixths of the gross. If such an income exceeded that of any other lord—and it certainly did—it is doubtful whether its owner did more than 'live of his own'. To use the contemporary phrase for a man's landed income, it was his 'livelode' or livelihood. His savings, if any, had to be made from his casual (or, as his receiver-general called them, his foreign) receipts. Having deducted £3,000 for the annuities paid to his retainers, he had £7,000 at most for the expenses of his wardrobe and household, the subordinate households of his consort, his mistress, and his children by both, and the maintenance of his council, lawyers, and central financial servants. These absorbed most of his livelihood in time of peace.

APPENDIX D

The Continuity of Great Estates[1]

THERE was a marked contrast between the transitoriness of male lines and the continuity of so many of the great estates. Although the manors in the hands of the greater nobility rarely, if ever, came into the market, sale was not the only means by which they might be dispersed. The commonest as well as the most obvious reason was division between coheirs. If those coheirs all had descendants, as, for example, the three sisters of the last Clare Earl of Gloucester (killed at Bannockburn) did, the dispersal was permanent. Unless prevented by a tail male settlement, this was bound to happen to an inheritance sooner or later. Different kinds of entail for different parts of an inheritance might equally lead to their lasting separation, as happened to the Fitzalans' estates in 1415. John Fitzalan, the heir male and cousin of the dead Earl Thomas of Arundel, received the old Fitzalan patrimony settled in tail male, while the Warenne lands inherited from his mother by Earl Richard in 1347 were divided between Earl Thomas's three sisters since they had been settled in fee tail.[2] Provisions for younger sons, either for life (a common limitation) or in tail male, detached portions of the inheritance, sometimes for ever. This permanent curtailment did not in fact often happen largely because cadet lines died out quickly or became the main line or both. Younger sons with no more than a life tenancy were slow to find a wife and often died unmarried; when they married it was frequently to dowagers past child-bearing. Take a relatively prolific family like the de la Poles or the Courtenays. In every generation manors were set aside for younger sons (unless like William Courtenay they became ecclesiastics); in almost all cases these cadet branches failed to strike roots and the manors

[1] Extracted from the 1965 lectures.
[2] For the Fitzalan settlements see p. 119, n. 1 above.

returned to the head of the family. The Courtenays of Powder-ham, now Earls of Devon, were the only exception. Last term I mentioned the division of the Lovel estates under the will of William, Lord Lovel, in 1455 between his four surviving sons;[1] only two of them, including the eldest, had issue. Francis, first and last viscount, William's grandson, was soon in possession of more than three-quarters of the manors distributed in 1455; as the servant of Richard III his promising career was soon cut short by Henry VII.[2]

There was one form of dismemberment which, though frequent, was essentially not permanent: that necessitated by the obligation to endow a widow with dower. If she got a jointure in the whole property, as Margaret Marshal did in that of her husband John Seagrave in 1338 (and retained it until her death in 1399), then there was of course no dismemberment; the next generation simply had to wait for the whole inheritance.[3] But though such jointures were, as I said, not uncommon in the case of heiresses (it was the price of marrying one), the normal dower was no more than a third of the dead husband's lands. This might mean the detaching of that considerable portion of the estate for a long lifetime, though it would ultimately return. The sort of thing that was constantly happening may be illustrated by the matrimonial career of Agnes Bareford. She had three baronial or near-baronial husbands: John Argentine whose lands lay in Suffolk, Cambridgeshire, and Herts.; John Narford, a landowner almost wholly East Anglian; and lastly John Mautravers, head of an ancient Dorset family with manors confined to the south and west of England. From Argentine who died in 1318 his widow obtained dower-lands in Cambridgeshire and Herts.; Narford's death in 1329 left her in possession of several manors in Norfolk and Suffolk, all of which together with the Argentine dower passed into the hands of Lord Mautravers on their marriage which took place before February 1331. From that year until

---

[1] See 'The English Nobility in the Later Middle Ages', p. 277 below.

[2] G.E.C. viii. 223–5; G. Baker, *History and Antiquities of Northamptonshire*, (2 vols. 1822–41), i. 682–3.

[3] Above, p. 66.

Mautravers's death in 1364 portions of two heritages in the eastern counties were therefore administered—along with estates in Somerset, Dorset, Gloucestershire, and Wiltshire—from Lytchett Mautravers not far from Poole in Dorset. Dame Agnes then survived her third husband by another eleven years during which she was free to enjoy and administer lands in eight counties, the accumulated dowers of her three marriages. In 1375, torn apart from their temporary union by her death, these were redistributed among her three husbands' heirs. John Argentine's only son had waited from 1318 to 1375 for his share; for nearly sixty years his inheritance had been divided, two-thirds managed from Halesworth in Suffolk, the remainder first from Narford in Norfolk and then from Lytchett Mautravers in Dorset.[1] This was not an unusual story, only made slightly exceptional by Agnes's longevity. When we emphasize continuity it is necessary to remember that families sometimes had to bear coexistence with as many as three dowagers at once. Continuity had to be compatible with much temporary—and not so very temporary—dismemberment.

On the other hand, scattered properties in many counties could only be efficiently exploited by means of a strong and flexible central administration. If the inheritances of the Anglo-Norman lords had been compact baronies or counties confined to one area their government might have presented few difficulties and called for little in the way of a trained administrative personnel. Precisely because their estates lacked territorial solidarity, and had to be prepared for either temporary or permanent disruption, landowners had to develop an efficient system of centralized financial control. The local units, usually manors but in the case of the greatest magnates whole lordships, had to be detachable while leaving the central administration unaffected, yet ready to deal with them when they fell in. Take for example the estates of Richard Beauchamp, Earl of Warwick, at his death in 1439. The largest number of English manors were in the shires of

---

[1] Agnes's accumulation of lands by dower and jointure is set out in her inquisition post mortem, *C.I.P.M.* xiv, no. 180. For her successive husbands, see G.E.C. i. 197; viii. 584–5; ix, 170. Cf. A. Suckling, *History of . . . Suffolk* (2 vols., 1846–8), ii. 328–9.

Worcester and Warwick but there were others, some numerous and valuable, in twenty-three other English counties as well as four great lordships in the Welsh Marches including the greatest of all, Glamorgan. They are listed in Charles Ross's useful occasional paper published by the Dugdale Society.[1] By comparison the Bigod lands that were acquired along with the earldom of Norfolk by Edward I's son, Thomas of Brotherton, were peppered thickly in East Anglia round their castle of Framlingham. There were outliers and these increased with time as Mowbray lands in Yorkshire and the Isle of Axholme and Seagrave manors in the Midlands were joined to them by marriage. Although the Mowbray Dukes of Norfolk in the fifteenth century had widely scattered lands, the Bigod nucleus remained important. It corresponded to the ancient patrimony of the Beauchamps in the western Midlands.

Now the supervision of officials in charge of outliers was as difficult as it was bound to be costly. It had to be highly skilled and it had to be backed by detailed records. Your estate office and muniment room had to be efficiently run or others would encroach upon and despoil what you were too ignorant or too inefficient to protect. This continuity of the great estates is reflected in the continuity not only of the administrative methods adopted to govern them but also of the bureaucratic families that manned them. For there was no one model, least of all was that model the king's government at Westminster. Each of the administrations of which the records survive had its own peculiarities of structure; it had clearly grown to its own particular shape in response to its own needs rather than under outside stimulus or in imitation of others. Of course they had much in common: at manorial level, for example, there was nothing distinctive in any of them. The differences higher up show that their development had been as it were organic. There was no institute for the training of accountants; each was apprenticed to a particular service. Even though the men who ran these offices sometimes changed employers this does not seem to have led to much cross-fertilization. Like the king's officers they were

---

[1] C. D. Ross, *The Estates and Finances of Richard Beauchamp, Earl of Warwick*, Dugdale Soc., Occasional Papers, no. 12 (1956), pp. 20–2.

conservative in their methods. Things continued to be done in the way they always had been in that office. If they changed it was as a result of growth to meet new needs. Even at the end of the fifteenth century there was little uniformity, even in the names and duties of the higher officials. These private civil services were often large. They contained a high proportion of trained laymen, mostly lawyers, at the centre. Not only was their continuity preserved by the medieval preference for apprenticeship as a method of training, but also by a tendency in certain families for sons to follow fathers into the skilled service of the same lord. Most private civil services had a marked hereditary character. Generations of Hugfords[1] and Throckmortons[2] are found in the service of the Earls of Warwick, of Whitgreaves[3] in that of the Stafford Dukes of Buckingham. Hungerfords in the fourteenth century and Leventhorpes in the fifteenth succeeded one another in the employment of the Dukes of Lancaster.[4]

These two factors, continuity of administrative structure plus continuity of personnel, gave to the great estates—whether or not they passed from one family to another or continued to be held by the male line—the same sort of stable tradition and expertise that the royal governmental institutions gave the Crown. Since the king usually continued them in control when the estate was in his hands even if he drafted in an occasional auditor or surveyor, they were if anything better adapted to minorities and temporary forfeitures, because they were only concerned with the efficient management of an estate not with the government of a kingdom.

[1] Dugdale, *Warwickshire* (1730 edn.), i. 278–80; Wedgwood, *History of Parliament, Biographies 1439–1509*, pp. 478–80; Ross, *Estates and Finances of Richard Beauchamp*, p. 8.

[2] Dugdale, *Warwickshire* (1730 edn.), ii. 749–50; Wedgwood, *History of Parliament, Biographies 1439–1509*, pp. 851–3; Ross, *Estates and Finances of Richard Beauchamp*, p. 11 and n.; T. R. Nash, *Collections for the History of Worcestershire* (2 vols., 1781–2), i. 452; J. L. Kirby, 'The Rise of the Under Treasurer of the Exchequer', *E.H.R.* 72 (1957), 673; *D.N.B.* lvi. 330 (supplemented *B.I.H.R.* 24 (1951), 95).

[3] T. B. Pugh, *The Marcher Lordships of South Wales 1415–1536* (Cardiff, 1963), esp. pp. 17, 159, 299; Wedgwood, *History of Parliament, Biographies 1439–1509*, p. 941; Roskell, *Commons in the Parliament of 1422*, p. 236.

[4] Somerville, *Duchy of Lancaster*, i. (see index); P. W. Kerr, 'The Leventhorpes of Sawbridgeworth', *East Herts. Archaeolog. Trans.* 9, pt. ii, pp. 129–51; Roskell, *Commons in the Parliament of 1422*, pp. 196–7.

In saying this it is not my intention to subscribe to the recent tendency to regard the royal administration and in particular the Exchequer as hopelessly inadequate to its tasks. To say with Professor Galbraith that 'the Exchequer was already suffering from arterio-sclerosis when Richard FitzNeal wrote the *Dialogus* in the twelfth century' is to malign an admittedly slow but for that reason sure method of collecting revenue. It is possible that too much was sacrificed to making sure. But if Edward IV and Henry VII are to be given credit for introducing 'new, speedier and more flexible' methods in the management of the royal finances, it should be added that they were merely applying the methods which had been developed on the estates of their noble ancestors centuries before. It is no accident that when the royal finances are to some extent reformed it is precisely when a political revolution brought the members of a magnate civil service into the employment of the Crown. In 1399 the duchy of Lancaster was preserved intact and separate from other Crown lands. Until well after the death of Henry V it continued to be efficiently administered. In 1461 the officials of the Dukes of York, with traditions that can be traced back to the service of the Mortimer Earls of March and even to those of the Clare Earls of Gloucester, remained in charge of Edward IV's inheritance to which other estates were steadily added. Henry VII had no inheritance as he had no experience; with the help of his mother's servants, mostly like Sir Reynold Bray drawn from the service of the Stafford Dukes of Buckingham, he was gradually able to resume the practice of the house of York. It is doubtful whether a kingdom should be treated like a great estate and it is possible that preoccupation with the detailed work of running a very much enlarged territorial lordship, a sort of super-duchy, deflected kings from their real business: government. But that is not our point; our point is that in 1399, still more in 1461, and again after 1485 the normal methods employed by all great landowners, whatever the particular varieties of structure, were now being applied to the lands and household of the king.

2

Extinction and Recruitment[1]

WHILE there was a nobility of one sort in 1300, which included what was later called the gentry, and of another sort, much more circumscribed as well as graded, by about 1450, in the interval between those dates the term is incapable of precise definition. Nobility was ceasing almost imperceptibly to be applicable to the large mass of the armigerous; it had not yet been confined to the peerage; it was in process of transformation from one to the other. During this period the gentry did not so much rise as fall from the nobility, though others were rising to join the gentry.

As far as the higher ranks of the peerage were concerned some steps in that process of transformation can be dated.[2] Below the rank of viscount, however, conditions were much more fluid. Those whom the king saw fit to summon personally to his parliaments one year might be overlooked the next—unless they had been granted their rank by charter or patent. And before 1450 a barony by patent—a clearly hereditary honour—was still rare. In the fourteenth century the great majority of lords of Parliament were there because they had been summoned. Such a summons created no presumption that they or their descendants would be summoned again, let alone give them any *right* to be so summoned. At the same time there were scores of gentry families, members of which had in the past been summoned once or twice and then never again. Those summoned had no title to distinguish them from those who were not. The line was drawn slowly and even by 1400 it was still uncertain. During the next half-century most of the doubtful cases fell to one side or the other. It is impossible to be more precise.[3]

---

[1] Extracted from the 1965 lectures. [2] See pp. 122-5 above and p. 273 below.
[3] The most recent discussion of the development of the House of Lords is J. E. Powell and K. Wallis, *The House of Lords in the Middle Ages* (1968).

But although in 1400 there was no hard and fast line the area of uncertainty was no longer wide. For one thing the heads of certain families, usually families of long settlement upon their estates, to whom inherited wealth and ancient renown had given a consequence which was more than local, were *in fact* regularly summoned from generation to generation from the very beginning of our period. Their presence had no basis in theory or in hereditary right; it was merely fitting in the king's eyes that such men should be there; their position was one *de facto* rather than *de jure*. Many of them, indeed most who survived, were of course the recipients of those earldoms, etc., created by Edward III and his successors—the Staffords, the Nevills, and the Percies will serve as examples; their elevation secured their pre-eminence among the new peerage. Others remained to form the hard core of its lowest grade, the 'barons': for example the Cliffords, the Greys of Ruthin, the Rooses and the Willoughbies of Eresby who did not earn promotion to a higher rank until after 1450, if at all. By 1375 what we may call the 'occasional' or 'temporary' lord of Parliament was becoming a rarity. Newcomers, like the hard-core of early regulars, tended to stay for keeps, at least after 1400. That is, if they produced male issue.

Which, not surprisingly, many didn't. This brings us to the matter of survival. Only three comital families in 1400 had enjoyed their dignity for more than a century: Vere, Beauchamp, and Fitzalan. The rest of the earldoms in 1400, namely fourteen, were creations of the previous seventy-five years; well over half, ten out of the total of seventeen, of the last fifty years. As a group the earls in 1400 were mostly newcomers to their rank. And in this—you will have to take my word for it—1400 was no way exceptional. The higher ranks of the nobility rarely deserved the epithet 'old'. The turnover was always rapid, the eminence short-lived, the survivors invariably few.

But was this true of the nobility as a whole? Earls were peculiarly vulnerable, it may be thought, especially if they had inherited, as most had, a share of royal blood. In trying to provide a rough statistical answer we come up against a pair of difficulties. Since during half our period if not more, membership of the group, especially at its lower edge, was, to say the least, ill defined, whom are we to include? If we try to take a random sample from the three thousand or so armigerous families of 1300, we soon find ourselves unable to say with any confidence which of our sample had or had not male issue, since many of the three thousand were too obscure for their descendants to be traced. The only sample that is easily traceable is not random: it consists of those who at any time during our period received a personal writ of summons to Parliament.[1] They varied widely in wealth and importance; and even here there are a few who have defied the attempts of scholars, genealogists, and peerage-lawyers, to identify their remoter issue. Leaving aside doubtful cases, we are left with a pretty large sample of the nobility, including all of any real prominence. Though it is possible—and some would say probable —that the higher nobility inherited a greater predisposition to sterility than the population as a whole, they are unlikely to have differed markedly in this respect from lesser members of the same group. Unlikely, because the reason given for their comparative infertility is that they tended to marry heiresses and that heiresses were more likely to derive from enfeebled stocks. I am not a geneticist and would not care to hold that this theory is sound. All I can say is that some geneticists of standing accept it. The point that matters for us is that *if* that *was* the reason for the infertility of the higher nobility, it would apply hardly less to those families which later formed the gentry since their members also married heiresses, apparently as often. Whatever disadvantages our sample may possess, it is the best we have.

In 1300 there were 136 families whose head had by then received at least one personal writ of summons to Parliament from Edward I and whose issue can be traced. To these must be added the 221 families the heads of which received a similar writ during the course of the next two centuries. Total: 357. Of these only 61 survived in unbroken male descent[2] until 1500; the rest had either no descendants at all—a rare event—or the male succession

---

[1] The tables upon which the calculations which follow are based are printed as Appendix B below.

[2] For the sense in which 'unbroken male descent' is defined see pp. 172–3 below.

had been interrupted by the intervention of an heiress or of several coheiresses or even by a series of them. Most of these 61 survivors in 1500 came from fairly recently established families. Of the original 136 only 16 were still represented by a male in 1500; not all of these had achieved a peerage.

It was against the danger of leaving only female heirs according to the common-law rules of inheritance that landowners had been settling their estates on their heirs male since the middle of the fourteenth century. But tail male could work only if there were males. For this reason those who settled their lands in tail male needed an escape clause; it was therefore usual to provide that in the event of there being no males whatever left, the lands should then go to the settler's 'right heirs' as if there had been no entail. Thus in 1446 there were no Beauchamp descendants of the mid fourteenth-century Earl of Warwick in the male line left. His earldom and lands settled in tail male then passed first to the daughter and, then on her death in infancy, to the sister of the last earl. She brought them to her husband, the 'Kingmaker'.[1] Tail male might stave off the day all feared; it could not prevent it from ever coming; few English noble families were able to achieve anything like the record of the house of Capet. For most the adoption of a version of the Salic law only postponed for a generation or two the date of their extinction.

How well aware at least some contemporaries were of the high rate of male failure is illustrated by the action of an East Anglian knight in 1419. Sir Thomas Erpingham was an old servant of the house of Lancaster, having been retained as a knight bachelor by John of Gaunt in 1380. He accompanied Gaunt's heir Bolingbroke to Prussia in 1390, to Jerusalem in 1392, and into exile in Paris in 1398. His services were rewarded by the Garter soon after the usurpation. At the age of fifty-eight he commanded the English archers at Agincourt. Twice married, he had no issue. In 1419, nine years before his death, he gave a new east window to the church of the Austin Friars at Norwich. It was a large window, probably in the current perpendicular style, and he placed in it his

[1] G.E.C. xii, pt. ii. 384–5; Ross, *Estates and Finances of Richard Beauchamp*, p. 19 n. 2.

coat of arms and the name and arms of all those 'lords, barons, bannerets and knights who had died without issue male in Norfolk and Suffolk since the coronation of Edward III'. The window was long ago destroyed, but fortunately William Worcester, the first English antiquary, made a record of its contents half a century after it was set up. It commemorated the heads of 87 families. To these Worcester himself added another 29 knights and 25 esquires to bring the list down to 1461.[1] 141 East Anglian landowners, 116 of them baronial and knightly, were known to have perished without male issue since 1327. The impression we derived from our sample is independently confirmed.

The date 1419 might suggest another reflection. It is well before the outbreak of the Wars of the Roses, which are usually held responsible for the wholesale destruction of the old nobility; we have seen reason for thinking that it was mostly far from old; have their destructive effects also been exaggerated? An examination of our sample suggests that they have been. On the average during the period 1300–1500, a quarter of the families contained in it became extinct in the direct male line every twenty-five years; in fact just over 27 per cent, and this wastage is spread pretty evenly over the whole period. The figure was highest for the quarter-century 1400–25 and lowest for that between 1325 and 1350: 35 per cent as against 23½ per cent. That is to say that over a third of the families which before 1400 had produced members of the upper House failed in the male line in the first quarter of the

---

[1] Worcester's account of this window and his supplementary list are preserved in, and the figures in the text are derived from, Spelman's extracts from Worcester's lost *De Agri Norfolcensis familiis antiquis* in Norwich Public Library MS. 7197, ff. 304–6ᵛ. For this manuscript see McFarlane, 'William of Worcester. A Preliminary Survey', pp. 216–17. Francis Blomefield printed another account of the window which he took from 'an old parchment roll' in a hand of 'about the end of Henry VI' (*Norfolk*, iv (1806), 86–8). Possibly this roll was also Worcester's. The account of the window printed by Blomefield contains the inscription on it, part of which is quoted in translation in the text above. There are some differences between the two accounts of the actual window and great differences between the supplementary lists provided. In total the Spelman MS. mentions fifty-one names Blomefield does not, but Blomefield fourteen the Spelman MS. does not. The statement by T. John, 'Sir Thomas Erpingham, East Anglian Society and the Dynastic Revolution of 1399', *Norfolk Archaeology*, 35 (1970), 107 that this window was in St. Michael's, Conesford is based on a misreading of Blomefield.

fifteenth century. *Not* the third quarter but the first. In every generation of our period this happened on the average to one family in four. The Wars of the Roses do not deserve their lethal reputation. The percentages of failures in the male line for the last two quarters of the fifteenth century were in fact below the average: 25¼ per cent and 24⅔ per cent respectively. They were higher in every quarter of the fourteenth century except the second. The figures for those of the rank of earl and over tell the same story, but here the small numbers involved make statistical comparison unprofitable. In fact the number of such families failing in the quarter century 1450–75, that is to say the main civil war period, is below the average.

This is not after all so very surprising. There had been wars before, and civil wars too; in Edward II's reign and both before and after the usurpation of 1399. Throughout our period political miscalculation has a way of ending on the battlefield or the scaffold. That alone might be why so few comital families were able to last a century, why the extinction rate among the nobility as a whole maintained so high a level. Had there not been constant replacements there would hardly have been a nobility to fight for Lancaster and York.

A closer look, however, suggests that death in war or on the block was not so potent a cause of the failure of male heirs as one might think. Men married young and were often fathers of sons before they were old enough for knighthood. The fear of extinction and the fear of that lesser evil, a royal wardship during a minority, hurried parents into early marriages for their children. The need to produce an heir was no waiting matter. So, struck down at the beginning of their adult military lives, young noblemen often left male heirs to succeed them. They merely left fewer. Even in savage civil wars it was not usual to slaughter children—unless they were princes of the blood royal; and even then it was far from common. Hence the lasting notoriety engendered by the disappearance of Edward V and his brother. Edward, the Lancastrian Prince of Wales who lost his life at Tewkesbury in 1471, although under eighteen and not yet married (as a penniless refugee overseas he had not had much chance of finding a wife), was at least old enough to bear arms and to pay the penalty of defeat on the fields of battle. Still, for obvious reasons, the chief casualty of the civil wars was the royal house in its various branches, Lancaster, York, and Beaufort. It failed altogether in the male line with the execution of Warwick, an innocent victim if ever there was one, in 1499. But no child, since he was in his thirtieth year. He had not been allowed to marry.

By contrast the Wars of the Roses themselves brought very few *noble* families to a childless end.[1] In fact too many of them possessed royal blood through the female line for their systematic elimination to strike even Richard III or Henry VIII—to name the most bloodthirsty—as a feasible policy. And nothing short of total elimination would have been any use. What occurred was much more haphazard and *ad hoc*. Between 1450 and 1500, thirty-eight noble families (excluding the three royal houses above-named) failed in the male line, twelve by violence and twenty-six by natural causes. But of the twelve few can be counted as genuine casualties of civil war. Lord Scales, for example, who was lynched by the Thames watermen at Southwark in 1460, was an oldish man—born in the late 1390s—and died leaving an only daughter of at least twenty-four. Had he survived to die in his bed he would not have much improved his chances of an heir male. Similarly a far more important figure, the Kingmaker himself. When he fell at Barnet his wife was already forty-six and lived on for another twenty-one years. Their only children were daughters of marriageable age. War or no war, Warwick's chances of surviving male issue were hardly good. Warwick's uncle, William Nevill, Earl of Kent, left a wife aged fifty-seven at his death on campaign in 1463. To have outlasted her in order to marry again he would have had to live to over eighty. His only sons were bastards. Lord Wenlock was seventy and more and childless when he was killed at Tewkesbury. To describe these extinctions as the result of war rather than of natural infertility— their own or their wives'—is quite unjustified. The war may have had a small contributory influence; it was not principally to blame. Seven of the twelve had been married for many years and left no

[1] Cf. 'The Wars of the Roses', pp. 115–17.

sons. That leaves altogether five noble houses whose disappearance during the half-century can legitimately be ascribed to the effects of civil war and royal vengeance: Courtenay of Devon, Welles, Bonville, Hungerford, and Lisle (Talbot). Apart from the house of Courtenay which had given counts to Edessa and Latin emperors to Byzantium and that of Talbot of which Lisle was a cadet (the main line survived and still in fact survives), these were not particularly illustrious families; Courtenay and Welles alone had inherited ancient baronies, ones that could be dignified or vilified with the adjective 'feudal'. What is more the families of Courtenay, Welles, and Hungerford were not totally extinguished in the male line. Three unmarried Courtenays, brothers, perished in turn as a consequence of civil war at York (1461), Salisbury (1469), and Tewkesbury (1471), leaving sisters and coheirs, but in 1485 Henry VII conferred the earldom of Devon on their cousin Edward, the heir to their entailed estates. Similarly Lords Welles and Hungerford left collateral heirs male who eventually —under the Tudors—made good their claims to the title. Only Bonville and Lisle, both of recent origin, were genuinely extinct. To these could be added the doubtful case of Richmount Grey.[1] It is not an impressive list. This was briefly pointed out as long ago as 1872 in the first volume of the *Transactions of the Royal Historical Society* by a certain T. L. Kington Oliphant.[2] No one seems to have heeded what he said.

Before I turn to my next theme, the recruitment of new families to replace those who became extinct, there are one or two matters which need to be mentioned. You will remember that three families whose direct male line failed as a result of the Wars of the Roses were subsequently revived under the Tudors, when the male collaterals of the Courtenays, Welleses, and Hungerfords were restored to their lands and titles. It is worth emphasizing the fact of these restorations since it shows how little desire Henry VII and his son had to prevent such houses, in particular the ancient and

[1] In 1964 McFarlane also included the houses of Hoo and Wiltshire among those whose extinction was due to the Wars of the Roses, 'The Wars of the Roses', p. 117, n. 1.
[2] 'Was the Old English Aristocracy Destroyed by the Wars of the Roses?', *T.R.H.S.*, 1st ser., 1 (1872), 351–6.

royal-blooded Courtenays, from recovering from the effects of civil war. These families had after all suffered for their loyalty to the house of Lancaster—few had equalled their consistency—and that in itself was enough to commend them to the Lancastrian Tudors. Not that a Yorkist past was much more damning. It is too often and too easily assumed that the survivors of the dynastic conflicts had nothing to look forward to after 1485 but persecution and extermination at the hands of the final victors. Henry VII owed his throne to the active help of both Lancastrian and Yorkist families: most of them had indeed been in their time both Lancastrian and Yorkist and were now only too anxious to place their *de facto* loyalty at the last usurper's feet. And oddly enough Henry VII was neither ungrateful nor, until his health declined, unduly suspicious. Neither in war nor peace was violent extinction the inevitable lot of the pre-1485 nobility. A few much-publicized examples, in particular Suffolk and Buckingham, give a false impression. Even Henry VIII hardly deserves his reputation as an exterminator.

On the other hand, the list of those families who were the natural sufferers from infertility or poor health and the infant mortality which so often eliminated males, always harder to raise than their sisters, during the half-century 1450–1500, included the ducal houses of Holland (Exeter) and Mowbray (Norfolk), the more short-lived comital houses of Woodville (Rivers) and Tiptoft (Worcester), and such notable old 'baronial' stocks as Cromwell, Grey of Codnor, Willoughby of Eresby, and Strange of Knockin, the last male representatives of which all died in their beds, half of them in their early youth. If war assisted the process, it was not primarily responsible for the end result. In case anyone is inclined to think that it does not matter whether they died of disease rather than of wounds so long as they died *out*, it is necessary to remember that some of the most durable because fertile stocks were still there in 1500: Berkeley, Courtenay, de la Pole, Fitzalan, Nevill, Percy, Stafford, Talbot, and Vere, among them some of the oldest and most illustrious, as well as a great many others hardly less distinguished. The Plantagenets, recently so fertile in sons, had been wiped out. Not so the nobility they had created—

which had meanwhile intermarried freely with the many female descendants of Edward I. It is difficult in 1500 to find a single member of the higher nobility who was unable to number that king among his ancestors, often more than once.

With so high an average rate of failure in the male line, new creations and promotions failed, at least after 1350, to keep pace with the steady wastage. If earls were more numerous after 1350 than in 1300, this was not true of the nobility as a whole. Whereas there were about 3,000 heads of families whom Edward I could distrain to knighthood, their equivalent in 1500 were almost certainly less numerous. Confining ourselves to the 357 families whose heads were summoned by personal writ at least once—our sample for purposes of comparison as I explained last week—we find that between 1350 and 1500 there were exactly 200 failures in the male line and only 114 replacements. Of these about three-quarters were genuine new creations or summonses. The remaining quarter were either new families or cadets of old families, descended from those they replaced through a female. They had married their way into the higher nobility. Having inherited the estates they were summoned to Parliament by virtue of the territorial wealth and connection they had inherited. In the case of the earls more than three-quarters were genuinely new; less than a quarter descendants from the old through a female. Sixty-one new earldoms were created between 1350 and 1500; of these 49—or just over 80 per cent—were conferred as direct marks of royal favour rather than inherited through females.

Why were there so few representatives through a woman of houses extinct in the direct male line? Partly because of the absence of primogeniture among females. To represent an extinct male line one had to marry a sole heiress. Heiresses were often numerous; the estates might therefore be distributed among many new families, no one of which was rich enough to step into the dead man's shoes. Many ancient estates were simply dispersed; quite a number of earls left a plurality of coheiresses.

Another and more potent reason why new families did not inherit more often from old was that the daughters of the nobility did not so often as heretofore marry outside their class. In the earlier middle ages the king had disposed of the hands of heiresses, often using them as a means of rewarding a loyal or landless servant—as Henry II and Richard I made the fortune of William Marshal. Resistance to the disparagement of heiresses and evasion of the royal right of marriage by betrothing children in their cradles had by 1300 considerably weakened the king's position— and that of overlords generally. If the king wanted an heiress for one of his younger sons he was as a rule obliged to negotiate early with her father like any other suitor; and he could only negotiate successfully from strength: the heiresses, that is to say, were won by heirs or by those whose fathers had otherwise endowed them with great estates. A king's son needed an appanage before he was an eligible candidate. Only very rarely did an unbetrothed heiress fall to the king's unfettered disposal as did Eleanor and Mary Bohun in 1373 when their thirty-one-year-old father Humphrey, Earl of Hereford and Essex, died without male issue. They were quickly snapped up for cadets of the royal house, Thomas of Woodstock and Henry of Bolingbroke. Hence the tendency for two or more earldoms, often accompanied by other lesser lordships, to be united by marriage—so that, for example, Humphrey Stafford was able to describe himself in 1444 as 'the Right Mighty Prince Humphrey Earl of Buckingham, Hereford, Stafford, Northampton and Perche, Lord of Brecknock and Holderness';[1] later in the same year he was created duke. The longer a family survived in the male line the more likely it was to achieve such accumulations of inheritances; hence those great principalities in the hands of such families as the Nevills and the Staffords which have made the greater nobility of the fifteenth century a byword for excessive wealth and power. It was by such marriages that the houses of Lancaster and York became what Fortescue called 'over-mighty'. Royal cadets had an initial advantage in that race. Naturally wise fathers with only daughters to dispose of sought the hands of the rich for them in preference to the poor. The high extinction rate of the male lines merely con- centrated more of the available landed wealth in the hands of those male lines which had the luck to perpetuate themselves. But for

[1] Dugdale, *Baronage*, i. 165.

accidents this tendency to snowball would have gone even further than it did.

It was counteracted, for instance, by the freedom enjoyed by widows to choose their second and later husbands without any interference from their own families. The king's interest in the matter could usually be bought out by the payment of a comparatively negligible fee; to this had his former claim to marry widows of tenants-in-chief now dwindled. When a widow was also an heiress her male kinsmen could no longer legally prevent her from bestowing her hand on whom she would. And often she used her liberty with very little regard for the interests of her property or her kin, sometimes with a want of wisdom that even she may have lived to regret. Dowagers were fair game for adventurers with pretty faces. A notorious victim in the mid fifteenth century was Katherine Nevill, Duchess of Norfolk. Born in or before 1400 (her eldest son was born in 1415), she married in 1465 her fourth husband, a youth aged twenty. Sir John Woodville had recently become Edward IV's brother-in-law, but the Woodvilles were a large and needy brood, none too scrupulous in the means by which they gained advancement. Even hard-bitten contemporaries thought this union a shocking one: *maritagium diabolicum*[1] in the words of one chronicler. Katherine's enjoyment of her young husband was brief; but she survived his execution in 1469 by at least fourteen years.[2] Nevill ladies, most of them dowagers, were monstrous tough.

Another reason for dispersal rather than accumulation was the fact that women might *become* heiresses after marriage as a result of a series of unpredictable strokes of fortune, sometimes long after they had been given husbands on the assumption that their prospects were nil. Fathers might for one reason or another be unable or unwilling to raise the marriage portion in cash necessary to secure for a girl who was not yet an heiress a landowner of any great wealth or rank. If they had a large number of children, they might be compelled to sacrifice the interests of daughters to those of sons, only to discover too late that the daughters alone survived, married to nonentities who then inherited. Sooner or

[1] Above, p. 11.   [2] G.E.C. ix. 607.

later the head of a great noble family, however skilfully he played the political game, was likely to find himself, if not on the losing side, at least not on the winning side in the dynastic conflicts of the period. Temporarily threatened by, if not the actual victim of, attainder and forfeiture, he might be obliged from sheer lack of means and influence to marry his daughters or his sisters where he could—a form of disparagement not very different in its results from that suffered at the hands of earlier kings. Fortune changed and the ruined family emerged once more on top—only to see its lands and honours inherited by the fortunate upstart who had been willing to marry the portionless girl. Her male kinsmen dead, she had become an heiress.

Two such marriages, not so well known as they should be, deserve special mention since they made the fortune of one gentry family and mended that of an ancient one whose nobility had decayed. No better examples could be found of the unforeseeable consequences of a matrimonial gamble. The story begins with the exile of Thomas Mowbray, first Duke of Norfolk, by Richard II in 1398.[1] When Thomas died in Italy in September 1399 his enemy Hereford was putting the finishing touches to his arrangements for usurping Richard's throne. Norfolk's five surviving children—two sons and three daughters—were well under age, the eldest son being thirteen. This son's involvement in the Percy–Scrope rising of 1405 before he had recovered his inheritance completed the temporary ruin of the family. Later, under Henry V, his younger brother and heir, coming of age in 1413, was slowly able to rebuild its fortunes; in 1425 he recovered the dukedom. But meanwhile the sisters had had to find husbands without the advantage of ducal marriage portions and with the more positive drawbacks of being the daughters and sisters of a discredited murderer and an executed traitor. One did pretty well for herself by marrying the son and heir of the second de la Pole Earl of Suffolk, though he too was a member of an impoverished and discredited family which was also parvenu. She had no sons and her daughters died unmarried. Her sisters were luckier, at

[1] For what follows on the Mowbray family see G.E.C. ix. 601–12; ii. 132–4; v. 357–8.

least in their issue. Margaret, the elder, married a Suffolk neighbour, Sir Robert Howard, the modest fortunes of whose family
had been founded a century before by a royal judge. Isabel, the
younger, had two husbands: Sir Henry Ferrers of Groby, the heir
of an ancient but minor lordly house, and James Berkeley, one of
two rival claiments to the headship and depleted lands of another.
For some sixty years the consequences of these marriages did not
become apparent. The restored second Duke of Norfolk and his
son and grandson who in turn succeeded him in the dukedom,
died in 1432, 1461, and 1476 respectively. The last (fourth) duke
left an infant daughter Anne, the discovery of whose coffin has
recently been exciting the newspapers.[1] Anne Mowbray was a
great heiress and she was promptly married by Edward IV to his
younger son Richard, Duke of York, in 1478. She died, aged eight,
in 1481. The results of infertility and ill-health in the main Mowbray line instead of enriching a royal cadet now made the fortunes of the Howards and Berkeleys. The second, third, and
fourth Dukes of Norfolk had not died by violence but from
natural causes; each had had only a single child. When the sole
representative of the fourth generation, Anne Mowbray, perished,
to be quickly followed by her youthful widower, everything went
to the sons of Margaret Howard and Isobel Berkeley. In 1483
John Howard became Duke of Norfolk and Earl Marshal and
William Berkeley became Earl of Nottingham (another of the
Mowbray titles); in 1489 Henry VII raised the latter to a marquessate. Since I have spoken much of infertility, it is worth
recalling that the Howards and Berkeleys are with us still.
Though heiresses were becoming rarer in the fifteenth century,
thanks to tail male, it is still possible to find examples where
marriages brought accidental advantage. There was justice in the
case I have chosen for detailed treatment: the Mowbrays themselves had risen to prominence by one lucky marriage in the
mid fourteenth century.

These were windfalls. So too was the Kingmaker's acquisition
of the Beauchamp inheritance and earldom in 1449 since when he
married Anne Beauchamp she was not an heiress, but she was at

[1] e.g. *The Times* for 15, 16, 18, 19, 23, 25, 26 Jan.; 11, 19 Feb. 1965.

least not far off being one and the contingency may have been taken into account. In any case he was already heir to the earldom of Salisbury and in that respect typical of the bridegrooms heiresses were normally destined for. When the number of well-endowed heiresses was diminishing, thanks to the existence of settlements in tail male, the Nevills were particularly fortunate to pick up two of the best going in as many generations. The increasingly short supply is the main reason why replacements had got to be mostly the product of royal creation. The new men ennobled had therefore either to be rich already or had to be endowed by the king out of capital or income—out of royal capital or income, since endowment could take the form of a grant of land, that is capital, or the grant of an annuity either at the Exchequer or from some particular source such as the customs of a particular port or ports.

If creation also involved endowment one may well ask, why did the king wish to create new earls and other peers? If the members of the higher nobility were such obviously bad things, obstacles to good government, natural enemies to the royal authority, why didn't sensible kings let them die out? Why multiply a conspicuous evil, why create obstacles to one's own exercise of power? Was it just blind folly that led Edward III to reverse his grandfather's policy of limitation? To revive the lapsed earldom of Devon for Hugh Courtenay in 1335 and to create six new earldoms on a single day in March 1337? And five more by 1362? If not, then what were his reasons? And for summoning still more new men to his frequent parliaments? His reasons, it seems, were two: kinship and service, the two motives for patronage throughout the centuries.

Let us consider these two reasons in turn. The first, kinship or nepotism, need not detain us long. It is the reason for which Edward III in particular has been blamed, though all kings with sons and brothers and nephews acted as he did. Edward I, tight-fisted where others were concerned, here set his grandson an example of extravagant generosity. No English king was more lavish in the endowment of his kin; as a result he too has incurred the historian's censure. Edward III's provision for his four surviving younger sons, Lionel of Antwerp, John of Gaunt, Edmund of Langley, and Thomas of Woodstock, is commonly held to have been in large measure responsible for the Wars of the Roses, just as Henry III's and Edward I's affection for Edmund and Thomas of Lancaster has been blamed for the misfortunes of Edward II. This royal partiality for sons and brothers is condemned as short-sighted and in particular as against the best long-term interests of the monarchy. It was a case of putting family before crown. Whether it did or not, we must at least try to grasp the fact that it was inevitable, that it was due as much to a sense of what was right as to indiscriminate affection, and most of all that contemporary opinion would have been outraged by anything less generous. English historians are so much attached to the idea that primogeniture compelled the younger sons of the nobility to fend for themselves as commoners, thereby preventing the development in this country of a hereditary *noblesse*, a noble caste, that they have firmly closed their eyes to the fact that the men of the middle ages did not always subscribe to this notion.[1] But as far as the kings were concerned, though after 1216 primogeniture strictly governed the descent of the crown—it had not before—this did not mean that cadets should not have as good a provision as possible; and what was possible was a great deal. Henry II's delay in providing for his fourth son had earned the boy the satirical nickname of 'Lack-land' before the king's clumsy attempts to remedy matters involved him in trouble with his other offspring. From Richard of Cornwall to Henry Tudor of York, princes of the blood all received appanages, even the younger sons of younger sons like John Beaufort, Marquess of Dorset, Thomas Beaufort, Duke of Exeter, and Richard of Conesborough, Earl of Cambridge. The policy of Edward III was that of every king from Henry III to Henry VII except Richard III; for though Richard II and Henry VI had neither brothers nor younger sons, they consoled themselves by doing the same thing for their uterine half-brothers, the Hollands and the Tudors. For the more a king could do to exalt his family, the greater king he. So far was Henry VII from subscribing to the historians' view

[1] Cf. pp. 71–2 above.

that the Wars of the Roses were the outcome of an excessive endowment of royal cadets that he was only prevented by the death of Arthur, Prince of Wales, from founding and liberally endowing a new house of York in the person of *his* second surviving son. It was the Tudors' poverty in sons, not a change of policy, that deprived the rulers of the sixteenth century of the companionship of royal dukes. It is doubtful if Henry VIII would have welcomed congratulations on that score. Being deprived, like Henry I, of legitimate younger sons he did his best, like Henry I, for his bastard, Henry Fitzroy, Duke of Richmond. The failure of the royal line was seen as a greater misfortune than an excess of cadets; the danger of failure had at least been avoided before 1485; its spectre haunted Henry VIII and made him at times nearly mad.

But if there *were* cadets they had to be numbered among the leaders of the nobility; there was no other place for them. The blood royal, therefore, contributed its quota to the 'new' and highest ranks of the peerage—as did the other members of the royal consanguinity, the issue of the king's daughters, unless these last were found foreign husbands. Nor should the royal affinity be forgotten, those who were related to the king through his wife as distinct from blood relations. Of this affinity who rose to greatness through their kinship with queen consorts the Woodvilles and the Greys are the outstanding examples—until we come to the Bullens and the Seemers to remind us once again that the Tudors were in this matter if no other traditionalists. Addressed ceremonially as cousins, the magnates were very often cousins in deed. The relations between the sovereign and those above the rank of viscount had something of the quality of those which might be expected to exist between the head of the family and its members in a still largely patriarchal society. And such England still was in our period.

Though the tie of kinship with the ruler was responsible for some of the most important new creations of the later middle ages, service was the commoner reason for advancement and as far as the lower ranks of the peerage were concerned it was the sole reason. Take Edward III's creation of six earls on 16 March

1337 on the eve of the king's decision to invade France. They provide an interesting cross-section of Edward's new recruits to what was still the highest rank of the nobility. Firstly there was Henry of Grosmont, created Earl of Derby.[1] Henry was of the blood royal, the king's second cousin, the son and heir of the blind Earl of Lancaster. His promotion in his now useless father's lifetime was unexceptionable and was asked for by Parliament. So too was that of Hugh Audley, the husband of the second of the three coheiresses of the Clare Earls of Gloucester; both of her sisters were widows.[2] Her descent from Edward I, her inheritance and the service her husband had performed since the downfall of the Despensers justified the request of the prelates, nobles, and commons in Parliament that he should be created an earl. The eclipse of the Despensers—the younger Hugh had married the eldest sister—enabled Audley to be assigned the earldom of Gloucester. Henry of Grosmont and Hugh Audley could support the dignity,[3] the one thanks to his father, the other because of his wife's landed wealth. Their four companions, William Montagu (created Earl of Salisbury), William Bohun (created Earl of Northampton), William Clinton (created Earl of Huntingdon), and Robert Ufford (created Earl of Suffolk), were very differently placed. The chief thing they had in common was their prominent part in the palace revolution of 1330 which led to the capture and execution of Roger Mortimer, Earl of March, and the retirement of Queen Isabella. Montagu was the prime mover; Bohun, Clinton, and Ufford all took an active part. Of these Montagu and Ufford were the heirs of minor noble houses,[4] Bohun the younger son of an earl,[5] and Clinton the younger son of a man who had been a knight of the shire in the Parliament of 1301.[6] None possessed the landed income necessary to support the estate of earl

---

[1] K. Fowler, *The King's Lieutenant* (1969).

[2] G.E.C. vi. 715–19; iv. 44–5, 269–71.

[3] Henry was nevertheless granted 1,000 marks a year for his father's lifetime when he was created earl (*C.P.R. 1334–8*, pp. 400, 538).

[4] G.E.C. xi. 385–7; xii. pt. i. 429–30.

[5] G.E.C. ix. 664–6.

[6] G.E.C. vi. 648–9; iii. 313 and note *c*. For the Clinton family cf. also Dugdale, *Warwickshire* (1730 edn.), ii. 992–4, 1006–7, 1142–3.

and without that income the estate was insupportable. So in 1337 Edward III, with the largesse expected of a chivalrous master, supplied their needs: Montagu, Ufford, and Clinton were each granted 1,000 marks a year in land (or, until this could be found for them, in money); and Bohun, perhaps because his father had been an earl and his mother a daughter of Edward I, so that he might have been expected to be used to a higher standard of living than the others, £1,000 p.a. on similar terms.[1] They had done Edward a great service, but gratitude was not his only motive; another was to create about himself a group of men whose loyalty and competence had been tested and could be relied upon in his future undertakings as well. They served Edward III *hard* and faithfully both before and after 1337 until they died; and their sons after them if they had any; and not only in war and tournament, but in administration, counsel, and diplomacy. The record of the Montagus is particularly striking.[2] William Montagu's grandfather Simon had a long record of service in the armies of Edward I in Wales, Gascony, and Scotland. His father, Simon's heir, was steward of Edward II's household 1316–18 and then Seneschal of Gascony until his death in 1319. William himself began his career as a king's yeoman by 1325. His younger brother Edward was one of the king's household knights retained for life in 1337. His son and heir, the second earl, was one of the most active of royal captains and councillors from Crécy when he was eighteen until well on into the reign of Richard II. Another son John was steward of *that* king's household from 1381–7 and *his* son, the third earl, was one of Richard's closest intimates in the period of personal rule at the end of the reign. Anything less like the popular idea of baronial independence and opposition to the Crown could scarcely be imagined. The Montagus were royal

[1] For the money grants see G.E.C. as cited p. 159, nn. 2, 4, 5, and 6, above. All four were in tail male, but Bohun's was upon condition that if he came to the inheritance of the Earl of Hereford and Essex then the annuity paid to his heirs male was to be halved; similarly it was to be halved if and when this inheritance came to one of his heirs male.

[2] G.E.C. xi. 385–95; Holmes, *Estates of the Higher Nobility*, pp. 26–9; R. Douch, 'The Career, Lands, and Family of William Montagu, Earl of Salisbury', *B.I.H.R.* 24 (1951), 85–8.

servants first and last; they earned—and went on earning—their keep until the fourth and last earl, Thomas, was killed before Orleans in 1428; he had been one of Henry V's principal lieutenants in the conquest and government of his French possessions. Edward III's largesse paid ample dividends. It would be difficult to interpret it as extravagant or short-sighted, even though the first earl died in 1344. Since his creation in 1337 he had been constantly employed as admiral, Marshal of England, soldier, councillor, and ambassador. The records of the other earls of 1337 and their descendants (when they had any) were not markedly different. Henry of Grosmont, later first Duke of Lancaster, surpassed them all.

That servants should be ennobled for their loyalty and executive abilities was not remarkable. There had never been a time—no, not even before the reign of Henry I—when this had not been customary, indeed necessary. Even Edward I, though he made no new earls, rewarded his servants, particularly the ecclesiastics among them. What an examination of such a record as that of the Montagus brings home to us is that second *and later* generations of families thus advanced do not lapse into the growling and factious backwoodsmen who are still too often the popular—and even would-be scholarly—stereotypes of medieval earls. Successful kings had no loyaler and more hard-working servants in war and peace than the members of the higher nobility. Whether their nobility was old or recent they were expected to serve; moreover, they wanted to serve since service alone commanded not only the big rewards, but also that continuous access to royal patronage on which they and their dependants relied. If an earl was a stay-at-home, it will usually be found that he was blind like Henry of Grosmont's father or like Edward Courtenay, Earl of Devon, at the beginning of the fifteenth century, or an invalid like Humphrey, Earl of Hereford, from 1336 to 1361. Apart from these and similar rare exceptions, the higher nobility until late in the fifteenth century remained politically and *militarily* active in the king's service. I sometimes wonder whether historians of the Tudor period have not exaggerated the decline of the nobility in this respect. The victors of Flodden and Pinkie were after all dukes and

Henry VIII's army was no less aristocratic than Edward III's and Henry V's. The belief that in the later middle ages the noble soldier was being replaced by the professional soldier of fortune lacks reality: the noble still was a professional soldier.

On the other hand, it would be a great mistake to emphasize the nobility's military interests and duties at the expense of the administrative. If military service was the commonest form of lay service in our period, that was partly because it offered the chance of larger rewards for those engaging in it, both at the hands of a defeated enemy and at those of a warlike master, partly also because the nobility owed the king their service in arms so to speak *ex officio*. The earls stood out against receiving pay for fighting under Edward I's command; when they abandoned this expensive self-denial under Edward III, it did not mean that they had ceased to regard a place near to the king in war as theirs by right; but they no longer saw any reason for not receiving a share of whatever money was going; their tradition remained a martial one. Naturally not all of them possessed the capacities necessary for an independent command; their folly or inadequacy was often paid for by death. What is perhaps surprising is that so many of them proved more than adequate. Evidently Edward was as good a trainer of commanders as his grandfather—and as his great-grandson Henry V.

Of course none of these kings felt himself obliged to limit his choice of lieutenants to his councillors by birth, the earls. Military capacity was often discovered as it were in the ranks and promoted. Not that the ranks of men-at-arms consisted of the low-born; rather of the lesser gentry, particularly of younger sons, often from that home of small gentry, the Welsh border. A good many of Edward III's captains and still more of Henry V's started life as landless or near-landless adventurers; but still gently born, since they had been trained to bear arms. Successful though many of them were, few qualified for a summons to Council or Parliament by military service alone. As a rule the fighting man's highest reward, if he were a fighting man and nothing more, was the Garter; other qualifications were needed for admission to the higher grades of the nobility. Among the original twenty-five knights of Edward III's new order of chivalry—the majority of whom were and remained mere knights—there were such pure soldiers of fortune as Sir James Audley (bastard of a noble house), Sir Neal Loring, and Sir John Chandos; the first and last of those certainly accumulated sufficient wealth to support a peerage; and, had they lived, their close friendship with the Black Prince might well have secured them summonses. Chandos had indeed shown that he possessed those capacities to organize and to govern that a successful commander, as opposed to a brave fighting man, required. *Sagesse* was rated as highly as prowess and was necessary for the higher posts. On that count also Chandos's death was untimely. In the fifteenth century the death of John, Duke of Bedford, and the alienation of Richard, Duke of York, from the Lancastrian regime were to deprive many of Henry V's soldiers of fortune of the chance of entering the House of Lords. Sir John Fastolf and Sir Thomas Kiriell received Garters; the former at least had the *sagesse* and the landed wealth needed for a peerage; had he lived to see Edward IV crowned he might have received that reward.

We have seen how Edward III was prepared to endow the earls he created in 1337. Lesser servants, who proved successful fighting men, were summoned to his parliaments and provided with the means to maintain their estate. Men like Sir Reynold Cobham, Sir Thomas Dagworth, and Sir Thomas Breadstone had contributed greatly to Edward III's victories. Although they had had little time to display administrative talents at home, all three had held independent commands involving more than mere fighting in the field. Their elevation to the higher nobility cost their grateful prince the price of a baronial income. Cobham and Breadstone both received grants of 500 marks p.a. in fee tail.[1] Dagworth was given no less and was granted over £4,000 for capturing Charles of Blois;[2] having married the widow of one

---

[1] For Cobham *C.P.R. 1345–8*, pp. 250, 407. For Breadstone *C.P.R. 1340–43*, pp. 28, 422; *C.C.R. 1339–41*, pp. 511, 560; *C.P.R. 1343–45*, p. 517; *C.P.R. 1348–50*, pp. 272–3. According to John Smyth Breadstone's grant was still being received by his heirs at common law 'at this day, 1628'; John Smyth, *The Lives of the Berkeleys*, ed. J. Maclean (2 vols., Gloucester, 1883), i. 284.

[2] *C.P.R. 1348–50*, p. 146.

earl who was the sister of another, he did well for himself in other ways too.[1]

The versatility required of a royal servant if he were to prosper is the thing that must strike our age of specialists. Soldiers were ambassadors, household officials, commissioners, and councillors by turns. Even those whose profession was the law acted as many parts and fought in the royal armies as well. Such ennobled families as the Norwiches, the Bourchiers, the Scropes of Masham, and the Scropes of Bolton were founded by royal judges who served the three Edwards in many ways. The Bourchiers may be taken as a particularly notable case. Their name has a fine old Norman ring, but they owed their origin to a thirteenth-century bursar from Essex. John, the bursar's son, became a lawyer under Edward I and a justice of common pleas in 1321.[2] When he died in the winter of 1329–30 he had acquired an estate, partly by purchase and partly by marriage, at Halstead in his native county. His eldest son Robert was both lawyer and soldier, fighting at the head of his retinue at Cadsant in 1337 and at Crécy. From 1340 to 1341 he was the first layman to become Chancellor of England; thereafter until his death in 1349 he was councillor, ambassador, and a lord of Parliament. His descendants were most notable as fighting men until his grandson Sir William brought the family to the front rank by marrying a widow who was also an heiress. Their son Henry was Earl of Essex (cr. 1461) and treasurer of England 1455–6, 1461–2, and 1471–83; his brother Thomas was Archbishop of Canterbury from 1454 to 1486. The treasurership in the fifteenth century was no sinecure; the Treasurer's personal responsibility for the royal finances is evidenced by the records of the king's Council.[3]

The king's judges were his servants. And so too might be his money-lenders. That any of these last should enter the nobility

---

[1] He married Eleanor, Countess of Ormond, sister to William, Earl of Northampton (G.E.C. x. 118–19).

[2] For the Bourchier family see G.E.C. ii. 246–50; v. 137–8; and p. 45 above. The source of the account above of the thirteenth-century origins of the family has not been found. It may be that it derives in part from G.E.C. ii. 246 and has by compression become over-definite.

[3] Cf. p. 232, n. 1 below.

was, however, exceptional. The case of the de la Poles cannot be paralleled. Michael de la Pole, who received a personal summons in 1366 and an earldom in 1385, had been his father's active partner in his business as wool merchant and royal banker before he embarked upon a long and varied military career, to follow that by the chancellorship and the earldom of Suffolk before the crash came with impeachment in 1386. If he owed the earldom to Richard II's profligate inexperience, at least he had received a personal summons to Parliament from Edward III before that king had entered his dotage. Michael's father William and William's brother Richard had both been knighted for their financial services in the 1330s, a useful reminder that merchants and money-lenders could enter the order of chivalry under that most chivalrous king (from Edward III's reign onwards it was usual to knight London's most prominent citizens). The brothers de la Pole, like John Bourchier, sound aristocratic enough. They had in fact borrowed the name of an old Anglo-Norman family and the truth was much more plebeian. When they first appear in the records of Hull they were called Richard and William 'at the pool' because they lived on the quayside. Their father's name is unknown; their mother's husband was called John Rotten-herring. A century after William de la Pole's death the head of the family was a duke and the brother-in-law of the king. From fisherman to duke in five generations. Though exceptionally splendid, the rise of the de la Poles was only an outstanding example of something that usually only happened on a minor scale.[1]

The de Norwiches, for example, before they produced a chief baron of Edward II's Exchequer who was the father of a peer, had been townsmen of the city from which they took their name. Like the de la Poles they were ashamed of their origins and employed a genealogist to invent a more respectable ancestry. They provide the first known case, known to me at any rate, of a family which with the help of forged deeds fabricated a pedigree which went back to a fictitious companion of William the

[1] For the de la Pole family see p. 9 above.

Conquerer.[1] This was done in the mid fourteenth century; one does not have to wait until the Tudor period for bogus pretensions to ancient gentility. The Norwiches told an elaborate story of family misfortune to explain how the descendants of a Norman baron had been reduced to the position of tradesmen in a provincial city.

The Norwiches had a short run before their name was extinguished. John Norwich was summoned in 1360; his grandson and heir died without issue in 1373. By comparison with many families of urban origin they may even be regarded as unusually fortunate, because the extinction-rate of merchant lines was even higher than that of the nobility. Nothing was more exceptional about the de la Poles than their remarkable fertility and powers of survival. The infant mortality in the towns, above all in London, was very high indeed. Very few of the more successful merchant capitalists of that great generation of royal financiers to which the brothers de la Pole belonged had much luck in bringing up their children. Rich they may have been but they had no sons to build upon their riches and the lands they bought with them. Sir John Pulteney is a case in point.[2] A contemporary and fellow member of the syndicates in which Sir William de la Pole made his wealth, Pulteney was scarcely less successful in the 1330s and 40s than he. He was in his day certainly London's richest citizen, the builder of Penshurst castle and of an inn in the city which was later thought magnificent enough to serve as the town house of the Princes of Wales, and a heavy investor in manors in the home counties. Had not his only surviving son died in childhood the Pulteneys might have competed in the next generation with the prolific de la Poles. Merchants deprived of male heirs suffered the fate of transmitting their new wealth through their daughters to members of landed and often noble families. The first *earl*, I think, to marry a merchant's daughter was John Montagu, third Earl of Salisbury; his father-in-law, Adam Francis, had been Mayor of London in 1352–4; she was the widow of a London citizen also.[3]

---

[1] Bodleian Library MS. Top. gen. c 62 (a family cartulary of the mid fourteenth century, formerly Phillipps MS. 3796), ff. 3ᵛ–4.

[2] S. L. Thrupp, *The Merchant Class of Medieval London*, pp. 361–2.

[3] Ibid., p. 341.

I mentioned that Sir William de la Pole's generation was outstanding in its production of great merchant capitalists. This was due to Edward III's attempts to manipulate the wool trade to his own advantage. He may not have achieved his desired object, but he provided the conditions in which his humbler partners could make their fortunes, largely at his expense. To that extent the rise of de la Pole and Pulteney may be regarded as the result of service under the Crown. They did not owe their enrichment to ordinary trade, but to their services as royal agents—or rather to the opportunities that that position offered them. Though citizens and townsmen had prospered since the twelfth century and invested their profits in land, this was rarely if ever on a scale sufficiently great to enable them to buy many manors. It seems as if they were so anxious to become gentlemen that they could not wait to become noblemen. The citizen-knight who founds a family of country squires is common enough; the de la Poles are the exception that calls the rule to our notice.

APPENDIX A

Plague and the Nobility[1]

IT may be thought that one of the reasons for a high extinction rate among the nobility might have been the Black Death. If that pestilence in its first visitation alone accounted for something between a third and a half of the population, as is often alleged, then it and its successors may have contributed greatly to reduce the total number of armigerous families liable to knighthood during the fourteenth century. Since I have shirked the task of tracing the fortunes of these 3,000 or so families individually, I am perhaps in no very good position to say that plague was not, at any rate partly, responsible. All I can say is that the statistics I have collected lend no colour to the view that it was. In my sample the extinction-rate for male lines during the twenty-five years 1350–75 is slightly above the average, but only 28·4 per cent as against the average of 27 per cent; but for the quarter-century 1325–50 which included the Black Death of 1348–9 the figure is in fact unusually low: 23·4 per cent. In the case of earls the figure is once more high for the third quarter of the fourteenth century: 31·8 per cent though not as high as in the first quarter when it was 35·3 per cent; once again it was exceptionally low 23·8 per cent in the second quarter, that of the first plague; nor does a theory of delayed action commend itself since in the fourth quarter the percentage was again low in the case of the earls, 23·1 per cent; and in the case of the larger sample not particularly high: 28·7 per cent.[2]

---

[1] From the 1965 lectures.

[2] A table showing the extinction rate for earls, 1300–1500, is among McFarlane's papers. The figures, apart from those given above, are as follows: 1401–25, 29·6 per cent; 1426–50, 22·2 per cent; 1451–75, 24·3 per cent; 1476–1500, 38·2 per cent; the average being 28·5 per cent. They were probably arrived at as follows: (i) by defining extinction as was done with baronies (see pp. 172–3 below); (ii) thus counting extinction as having taken place at the death of the last male heir as defined for baronies, not at forfeiture or at absorption in the Crown, and pay-

These low percentages in the quarter-century ending 1350 suggest that the higher nobility somehow escaped the mortality that affected the population as a whole. To say that that was because they were better nourished is not very satisfactory since pneumonic plague is not discouraged by that; nor is bubonic—the form carried by the fleas of the black rat—known to be. The point is sufficiently interesting to be examined in slightly more detail. I have therefore taken those archbishops, bishops, earls, and 'barons' (receivers of personal writs) who attended Edward III's parliaments. The number summoned to different parliaments varied between 84 and 98 (the variations were mainly due to vacant bishoprics or minorities). Taking the decade 1338–47, i.e. the decade before the first visitation of the Black Death as a control, we find that on average $5\frac{1}{4}$ per cent died each year but that some years naturally saw more and some less than the average. In fact it fluctuated between 10·3 per cent in 1338 and 1·2 per cent in 1341 so that a peak of as much as 10 per cent could not be regarded as abnormal. In the decade 1348–57 the average was in fact less than in the previous decade: 4·4 per cent; but the peak of 13 per cent in 1349 can reasonably be attributed to the Black Death; on the other hand, 1348 the first year of the plague only produced a death-rate of 4·5 per cent—less than that of an average pre-plague year. The decade 1358–67 saw the average rise to 6·3 per cent and the peak year with 23·9 per cent coincides with the second visitation of 1361. The next decade 1368–77, which saw the third and fourth visitations of 1369 and 1375, saw

ing no attention to the terms on which the earldom had been granted, e.g. to its being in tail male; (iii) but also, when an earldom was granted to a younger son of an earl and that son or his issue succeeded to the elder earldom, counting the end of the younger earldom at the date of such succession; (iv) by excluding (*a*) grants of earldoms to heirs apparent of existing earls, (*b*) earldoms granted to foreigners (e.g. Huntingdon, cr. 1377, Bath, cr. 1486), (*c*) earldoms granted in exchange for existing earldoms (e.g. Huntingdon, cr. 1479), (*d*) foreign and Irish earldoms and counties, even when their holders were summoned as earls (e.g. Athol, Eu, Ormond; (v) by, when there is doubt of the date of creation of an earldom, taking the earliest date possible; (vi) by including dignities higher than that of earl when the recipient at the time of creation was not already an earl (e.g. York, cr. 1474). For his tables on the extinction of baronial families in general see Appendix B below.

an average death-rate of 4·8 per cent, i.e. not much above the pre-plague average, though once more the peaks of 11 per cent and 10·6 per cent respectively fell in the plague years. The conclusions suggested by these figures are:

(1) That 1361 was far and away the most serious visitation of the plague as far as the magnates were concerned.

(2) That 1348 was the least lethal of any, the figure being little different from those of the pre-plague years.

(3) That 1349, 1369, and 1375 only slightly exceeded the figure for the worst year in the decade before the Black Death (1338) and *could* be accounted for by ordinary fluctuations unconnected with the plague. On the other hand, these peaks coincided with visitations and almost certainly were caused by them to some degree.

(4) It is noticeable that the decade averages are kept low because in non-plague years the figures are markedly *low*, suggesting that the plague may have shortened the lives of the sickly and that the survivors were stronger than the average. For instance, after the figure 13 per cent for 1349, we have 1·1 per cent in both 1350 and 1351.

(5) That even assuming that every death in the plague years above the pre-plague average was caused by plague—an assumption which the high figure in 1338 makes questionable—we get the percentage of plague-deaths

$$\text{in 1349 } 7\tfrac{3}{4} \text{ per cent}$$
$$\text{in 1361 } 18\tfrac{2}{3} \text{ per cent}$$
$$\text{in 1369 } 5\tfrac{3}{4} \text{ per cent}$$
$$\text{in 1375 } 5\tfrac{1}{3} \text{ per cent.}$$

Though the figure in 1361 is high it is still well below a fifth, to be set against the traditional figure for the whole population of a third or a half. The other three visitations accounted only for much smaller fractions. It therefore becomes clear why the Black Death had so little, if any, influence on the extinction rates that I emphasized in an earlier lecture.[1]

[1] These findings are consistent with J. F. D. Shrewsbury, *A History of Bubonic Plague in the British Isles* (Cambridge, 1970), pp. 122–30, who believes that mor-

tality in 1349 did not exceed 5 per cent of the population and that the epidemic of 1361 was probably influenza which affected young adults particularly severely. Professor Shrewsbury's assessment of mortality in 1349 depends, however, upon his assumption that the pestilence was bubonic plague accompanied by typhus. This is vitiated by his failure even to consider the possibility of pneumonic plague which would have had a much higher morbidity rate and greater infectiousness, although its importance is stressed by L. F. Hirst, *The Conquest of Plague* (Oxford, 1953), pp. 30–3 and by recent demographic historians. McFarlane believed that it was extremely difficult to make any reasonable estimate of what fraction of the whole population perished in 1349, but he believed that the losses of its governing groups were much less than those of others. In 1958 he wrote, 'Of the seventeen English sees only two (Canterbury and Worcester) were deprived of their bishops and I have found no certain evidence that Bransford of Worcester's death was the result of plague. According to Professor Hamilton Thompson's findings, the same immunity seems to have been enjoyed by the principal cathedral clergy. Certainly in some cases diocesans wisely stayed in their remoter manor-houses until the worst was over—as did Zouche of York. But Zouche's suffragan who remained actively employed and Bishop Ginewell of Lincoln who himself moved about in his badly stricken diocese survived without mishap.... Of the twenty-five founder-knights of the recently established order of the Garter only one, Sir Hugh Courtenay, was cut off.'

The Rate of Extinction of Noble Families

TABLES I and II are based on the data provided by the *Complete Peerage* and relate to all the families recorded therein whose head at any time in or after 1295 received a writ of summons to an assembly recognized as a Parliament by the *Complete Peerage*. They thus include not only the whole of the higher nobility but also many families which did not receive personal writs of summons continuously. McFarlane regarded 'extinction' as having taken place for the purpose of these tables when the head of a family died either (i) leaving no known heirs—this was very rare—or (ii) leaving, according to the common law rules of inheritance for fee simple, only a female heir or heirs, or a male heir or heirs whose claim came through a woman. That is to say extinction is held to have taken place at the point at which, according to modern peerage law, a peerage held in fee simple becomes extinct, passes to a woman or to an heir whose claim comes through a woman, or falls into abeyance between female coheirs or their descendants. Thus a line is held, for the purposes of these tables, to have become extinct when, e.g. a peer died leaving only daughters, notwithstanding the existence of a collateral male heir in a direct male line from one of his prede- cessors, e.g. a nephew. That is to say that 'extinction' does not necessarily imply that *no* continuous male line of the family con- cerned survived. For example in the case of Ferrers of Chartley extinction is regarded as having taken place at the death of William Ferrers in 1450, leaving only a daughter, notwithstanding that his brother and three nephews outlived him.[1] In cases where a peer or his heir apparent died leaving only daughters and the title passed, by entail or otherwise, to his heir male, an extinction is re- garded as having taken place. Therefore the earldoms of Warwick,

---

[1] G.E.C. v. 320–1 and intervening table.

Suffolk, Arundel, and Devon, and the 'barony' of Berkeley are treated as having become extinct in 1369, 1412, 1412, 1471, and 1417 respectively and as having been re-created (and counting as new creations) in 1369, 1415, 1441, 1485, and 1417. On the other hand, the succession of a collateral male heir in a direct male line is not counted as an extinction provided he did not exclude females who should have succeeded according to the common law rules for fee simple. For example the Astley 'barony' is not counted as becoming extinct in 1325, when Nicholas Astley died childless, but *c.* 1430 when William Astley died leaving a daughter as his only child.[1] The account above of how the tables were constructed is based on deductions from McFarlane's working papers. Although many of these papers have been found his final list of noble houses has not. Some points of detail relating to the construction of the tables therefore remain obscure; but these are not of sufficient importance to have more than small statistical significance. The total of 136 families who had received personal writs of summons by 1300 excludes Argentine, Boteler of Warrington, and Pinkney.

I

1. In 1300 there were 102 'barons' who had been summoned to Parliament on 30 December 1299; and 34 others who had been summoned in or after 1295 or were the heirs male of the body of those so summoned. Total, 136.

Of these 36 were extinct by 1325 leaving 100

,,	21	,,	,,	1350	,,	79
,,	18	,,	,,	1375	,,	61
,,	14	,,	,,	1400	,,	47
,,	14	,,	,,	1425	,,	33
,,	8	,,	,,	1450	,,	25
,,	4	,,	,,	1475	,,	21
,,	5	,,	,,	1500	,,	16

surviving in 1500: 16

[1] G.E.C. i. 283–4.

2. New summonses 1300–24: 60

Of these 15 were extinct by 1325 leaving 45

,,	11	,,	,,	1350	,,	34
,,	12	,,	,,	1375	,,	22
,,	8	,,	,,	1400	,,	14
,,	7	,,	,,	1425	,,	7
,,	1	was	,,	1450	,,	6
,,	2	were	,,	1475	,,	4
,,	0	,,	,,	1500	,,	4

surviving in 1500: 4

3. New summonses 1325–49: 47

Of these 13 were extinct by 1350 leaving 34

,,	15	,,	,,	1375	,,	19
,,	5	,,	,,	1400	,,	14
,,	4	,,	,,	1425	,,	10
,,	4	,,	,,	1450	,,	6
,,	2	,,	,,	1475	,,	4
,,	0	,,	,,	1500	,,	4

surviving in 1500: 4

4. New creations 1350–74: 29

Of these 5 were extinct by 1375 leaving 24

,,	9	,,	,,	1400	,,	15
,,	4	,,	,,	1425	,,	11
,,	3	,,	,,	1450	,,	8
,,	2	,,	,,	1475	,,	6
,,	2	,,	,,	1500	,,	4

surviving in 1500: 4

5. New creations 1375–99: 17

Of these 5 were extinct by 1400 leaving 12

,,	6	,,	,,	1425	,,	6
,,	3	,,	,,	1450	,,	3
,,	1	was	,,	1475	,,	2
,,	1	,,	,,	1500	,,	1

surviving in 1500: 1

6. New creations 1400–24: 11

Of these 5 were extinct by 1425 leaving 6

,,	4	,,	,,	1450	,,	2
,,	0	,,	,,	1475	,,	2
,,	0	,,	,,	1500	,,	2

surviving in 1500: 2

7. New creations 1425–49: 25

Of these 2 were extinct by 1450 leaving 23

,,	9	,,	,,	1475	,,	14
,,	3	,,	,,	1500	,,	11

surviving in 1500: 11

8. New creations 1450–74: 22

Of these 4 were extinct by 1475 leaving 18

,,	7	,,	,,	1500	,,	11

surviving in 1500: 11

9. New creations 1475–99: 10

Of these 2 were extinct by 1500 leaving 8

surviving in 1500: 8

II

1. Total on 1 Jan. 1300   136⎱ 196—51 extinctions = 145
         new 1300–24   60⎰ 26·02 per cent

2. Total on 1 Jan. 1325   145⎱ 192—45 extinctions = 147
         new 1325–49   47⎰ 23·44 per cent

3. Total on 1 Jan. 1350   147⎱ 176—50 extinctions = 126
         new 1350–74   29⎰ 28·41 per cent

4. Total on 1 Jan. 1375   126⎱ 143—41 extinctions = 102
         new 1375–99   17⎰ 28·67 per cent

5. Total on 1 Jan. 1400   102⎱ 113—40 extinctions = 73
         new 1400–24   11⎰ 35·4 per cent

6. Total on 1 Jan. 1425   73⎱ 98—25 extinctions = 73
         new 1425–49   25⎰ 25·51 per cent

7. Total on 1 Jan. 1450   73 ⎱ 95—24 extinctions = 71
   new 1450–74   22 ⎰   25·26 per cent

8. Total on 1 Jan. 1475   71 ⎱ 81—20 extinctions = 61
   new 1475–99   10 ⎰   24·69 per cent

Average: 27·17 per cent

3

The Wars of the Roses and the Financial Position of the Higher Nobility[1]

WHEN in 1399 the Duke of Lancaster became King of England the only fortune of the order of magnitude of John of Gaunt's ceased to remain in private hands. Together with about £2,000 p.a. gross or £1,650 net from the inheritance of Henry Boling-broke's wife Mary Bohun, it continued under the first two Lancastrian kings to ensure that they at least, to borrow Fortescue's phrase, could never be the poorest lords in their land.[2] How then are we to regard Fortescue's other and even better-known phrase about the king's over-mighty subjects? We happen to know from surviving records the estimated value of the estates of the three largest landowners in the reign of Henry VI: Richard, Duke of York, Humphrey, Duke of Buckingham, and Richard Beau-champ, Earl of Warwick—in that order. In York's case there were Irish lands also, but it seems unlikely that they brought in very much. All three had also possessed lordships in France, and Buck-ingham in 1448–9 reckoned that his Norman county of Perche was worth 800 marks in peace.[3] It passed into French hands just as this estimate was being made. The English and Welsh lands of the Duke of York were worth nearly £7,000 a year gross;[4] those

---

[1] From the 1965 lectures. Some of the same ground is covered in 'The Wars of the Roses'.

[2] J. Fortescue, *The Governance of England*, ed. C. Plummer (Oxford, 1885), p. 118.

[3] Longleat Mun. 6410, m. 21.

[4] In his lectures of June 1966 McFarlane stated: 'No complete valor survives for Richard, Duke of York, but in view of the disagreements between Messrs. Ross and Pugh on the one hand (C. D. Ross and T. B. Pugh, 'The English Baronage and the Income Tax of 1436', *B.I.H.R.* 26 (1953), 14) and Dr. J. T. Rosenthal on the other ('The Estates and Finances of Richard, Duke of York', *Studies in Medieval and Renaissance History*, ii (Lincoln, Nebraska, 1965), 122–37, and

of Buckingham were worth £6,300 gross[1] and those of the Beauchamp Earls of Warwick £5,900 gross.[2] Allowing a sixth for expenses, etc., this gives *maximum* net figures of £5,800, £5,250, and £4,900 respectively. It is necessary to emphasize the word *maximum* since the ministers' accounts (as opposed to the auditors' valors) suggest that by 1490 landowners were having difficulty in collecting rents and that arrears were mounting even on those best administered. We must leave the causes of this for later discussion; it is by no means clear that all such arrears proved desperate debts and had to be finally written off; the evidence suggests a wide variety between one estate and another.[3] But if for the moment we assume that the maximum was attained, then these so-called over-mighty subjects were not a new species, unknown before the reign of Henry VI. As we have seen John of Gaunt had been worth almost as much as any two of them. Since he was the king's uncle perhaps he does not qualify, though it is a little difficult to see why, since the possession of royal blood is generally regarded as a source of further danger to the occupant of the throne. For the same reason we might also have to rule out Edward II's two half-brothers Thomas of Brotherton and Edmund of Woodstock who, though never quite as well endowed as their father had intended them to be, in one case surpassed and in the other came not far behind Henry VI's Earl of Warwick. Thomas of Lancaster? He surely qualified. Indeed the advocates of the over-mighty-subject theory of royal weakness

'Fifteenth Century Baronial Incomes and Richard, Duke of York', *B.I.H.R.* 38 (1964), 233–40) it may be worth saying that my own calculations agree with those of Messrs. Ross and Pugh: namely that the total income was over £5,000 from his English and Welsh lands . . . Mr. Rosenthal's method of reckoning is wrong.' McFarlane had transcribed the relevant materials in the P.R.O., B.M. Egerton Rolls and Additional Charters, and at Westminster Abbey and Longleat. The figure of £5,800 net should be regarded as a preliminary estimate and as a maximum.

[1] For the sources on which this figure is presumably based see pp. 205–6 below.

[2] After 1435; for the sources on which this figure is presumably based see pp. 197–9 below.

[3] For efforts to collect arrears see pp. 51–3 above and pp. 213–27 below; for the problem in general R. R. Davies, 'Baronial Accounts, Incomes and Arrears in the Later Middle Ages', *Econ. H.R.*, 2nd ser., 2 (1968), 211–29.

would be content here to point to the disastrous consequences of Lancaster's excessive territorial power. The only weakness in their argument is that the dog it was that died after Borough-bridge. But if Thomas of Lancaster then also his brother Henry and his nephew, Henry's son Henry of Grosmont, first Duke of Lancaster. In 1330–1 a valor of the elder Henry suggests that his net landed income was of the order of £6,000.[1] Though no valors and indeed no full accounts survive for Henry of Grosmont's estates after his father's death they must have approached John of Gaunt's in annual value.[2] Nor must we forget Richard, Earl of Arundel.[3] The existence of two such noblemen as Duke Henry and Earl Richard should, on the over-mighty-subject theory, have been the undoing of Edward III. Instead they were lions under his throne as Henry Lacy, Earl of Lincoln, had been under Edward I's. At times both Edward I and Edward III were hard put to it to find the money they needed for the policies they desired to pursue. 1450 was different from 1350 and 1300 not because over-mighty subjects now threatened the stability of government but because Henry VI was not Edward III or Edward I. It is only under-mighty kings who have over-mighty subjects.

If the opposing magnates in the 1450s were not, as Fortescue believed, men whose wealth dwarfed that of the king, then, it has been suggested, they were men facing an economic crisis them-selves.[4] Impoverished by falling rents on this side of the Channel as well as by the consequences of military failure in France, the members of a formerly affluent and spendthrift class sought to avoid total ruin by turning upon one another. Starved of the rich diet they had been brought up to expect and had once enjoyed they took to cannibalism in an attempt to keep alive. The civil war on this view was the work of desperate and irresponsible

---

[1] P.R.O. DL 40/1/11, ff. 43, 48ᵛ, cf. ff. 49–53; Somerville, *Duchy of Lancaster*, i. 84–5.

[2] Fowler, *The King's Lieutenant*, pp. 225–6, estimates Henry of Grosmont's gross income from his English and Welsh possessions at over £8,380.

[3] Above, pp. 88–91.

[4] e.g. M. M. Postan, 'Some Social Consequences of the Hundred Years' War', pp. 11–12.

men. In believing that the causes were economic Fortescue was right; where he went wrong was in mistaking want for affluence. Henry VI may have been the poorest lord in his land, but his nobles faced bankruptcy also. This theory—for it was little more —has proved too attractive to receive cool scrutiny. If Fortescue's simple explanation won't do, why not stand Fortescue on his head? To that question the short answer is that it does not work either. Fortescue was wrong because, as we saw, the magnates of 1450 commanded no greater material resources than their *like* a century before. The suggested explanation to replace his runs into equal trouble in the face of the same evidence. The financial records and the past histories of the families most prominent at the outbreak of the Wars of the Roses show no catastrophic decline in *total* revenue in the second quarter of the fifteenth century. On the other hand, those heads of great families who through the accidents of inheritance or earlier treason were less well off either temporarily or permanently than their recent forebears were precisely those whose part in the civil wars was moderately or wholly inconspicuous. The Mowbray Dukes of Norfolk and the Earls of Arundel and of Westmorland are cases in point. The Mowbrays were just recovering from the effects of treason and forfeiture at the beginning of the century when a long-lived dowager with three subsequent husbands detached a considerable fraction of the inheritance from the second duke's death in 1432 until her own more than half a century later.[1] The Fitzalan estates had been divided in 1415 as the result of earlier entails with different remainders.[2] The second Earl of Westmorland had been partially disinherited in 1425 in favour of the children of his grandfather's second marriage.[3] If these men were desperate they concealed it with remarkable success. Neither Arundel nor Westmorland sought to make good their losses by vigorous partisanship in the wars; they merely lived quietly through them. And considering their kinship with the house of York the lukewarmness of the third and fourth Dukes of Norfolk was conspicuous and at times inglorious to a degree unusual even in civil war.

---

[1] Katherine, Duchess of Norfolk, was still living in 1483; G.E.C. ix. 607.
[2] Above, p. 119, n. 1.   [4] Above, p. 67, n. 2.

On the other hand, very few of the *principals* on either side in the struggle were not in receipt of larger incomes from land than their own fathers', still more than their grandfathers'. In a good many instances it is easy to demonstrate that those who led the opposing armies were drawing larger incomes from land than they themselves had enjoyed when first they inherited their estates. This is true even when we allow for the loss of lands and offices granted them in Normandy, Maine, and Anjou by Henry V and Bedford, and, to a more liberal extent than their accounts allow, for difficulties and delays in collecting rents, and for failures such as Miss Carus-Wilson has noticed to make the most of what they had.[1] Incidentally if the Duke of York was deriving so little financial advantage from the expanding cloth industry on his land near Stroud it does not sound as if he felt particularly hard pressed— —but we will have to consider the evidence of seignorial rack-renting and the like later.

Nor did it make very much difference whether the contestants were 'new men' or the representatives of old-established noble families. If they were new men the case needs no arguing; to be prospering is what being a 'new man' means. These were to be found, at first at least, mostly among the courtiers of Henry VI, men who had achieved prominence as followers of Cardinal Beaufort and then Suffolk in the king's household in the 1430s and later in the Council. It was during these years that Suffolk himself restored the shaken fortunes of his house. The de la Poles had suffered considerable losses both of goods and estates as the result of the downfall and flight of the first earl, Michael. When William succeeded as fourth earl in 1415 he was one of the poorest of the earls. By 1450, raised first to a marquessate and then a dukedom, he was undoubtedly rich; how rich unfortunately we do not know. The war, marriage to an heiress, and the royal favour all contributed, particularly the last. On the Duke of Gloucester's death in 1447 the earldom of Pembroke with its palatine lordship passed into Suffolk's hands.[2] He had more than repaired the family's fortunes;

[1] E. M. Carus-Wilson, 'Evidence of Industrial Growth on some Fifteenth Century Manors', *Econ. H.R.*, 2nd ser., 12 (1959–60), 190–205, esp. 196–7.
[2] G.E.C. x. 397.

and he was planning further gains when his impeachment and death cut short his schemes. He was the patron and political ally of many new men who came to the fore in the decade before 1450:

Sir Ralph Boteler, created Lord Sudeley 1441; died 1473. He was the builder of Sudeley castle, Gloucestershire, which Edward IV coveted.[1]

Sir John Beauchamp, created Lord Beauchamp of Powick 1447; died 1475.[2]

The brothers Roger and James Fiennes, the builders of Hurstmonceux and Knole respectively; James was created Lord Saye and Sele 1447 and lynched 1450.[3]

Sir John Stourton, created Lord Stourton 1448; died 1462; builder of Stourton castle.[4]

These and many lesser clients of Suffolk were the hated favourites whom popular ballads lampooned and against whom the Commons clamoured. No one could plausibly suggest that such men were the victims of straitened means on the eve of civil war. Their new-got wealth was the reason for their unpopularity, the cause of violence in others. Nor must it be assumed that there were no 'new men' among those opposed to them. To interpret the civil war in terms of Lancastrian haves and Yorkist have-nots once more is too simple to be true. Some Yorkists were renegades from the court like Ralph, Lord Cromwell, the Treasurer from 1433 to 1443 whose quarrel with Suffolk is obscure in origin. By 1449 he was Suffolk's enemy and York's councillor. Warwick was to maintain that he was responsible for the outbreak of hostilities in 1455. To call Cromwell a 'new man' may seem to stretch the term too far, since he was the third baron of his line. But when he inherited in 1417 his patrimony was modest. What he made of it, enough for an earl and more than some earls had, we have already seen.[5]

Cromwell's accession to the enemies of the courtiers was exceptional. The majority of the self-made members of the opposition owed their wealth to success in the French war and

---

[1] G.E.C. xii, pt.1419–21.   [2] G.E.C. ii. 46–7; Dugdale, *Baronage*, i. 249–50.
[3] G.E.C. xi. 479–81; Dugdale, *Baronage*, ii. 245–6.
[4] G.E.C. xii, pt. i. 301–2.   [5] Above, pp. 49, 84, 94.

looked to York as their natural leader.[1] Their court had been the court over the water, their baronies French ones conferred by Bedford rather than English ones conferred by Henry VI on Suffolk's advice. Most of them had been in the war as young men under the king's father or his uncles Clarence and Exeter (Thomas Beaufort). All were councillors of the Duke of Bedford and afterwards of Richard of York. They formed a compact group of friends as well as political allies. That the loss of Maine and then Normandy had deprived them of continuing sources of profit may explain their hostility to Suffolk; but to suppose them ruined is quite unjustified. William Worcester, who belonged to their circle and was secretary to the most famous of them, is our chief informant about the scale of their land-purchases, their building, and their household spending. In one case accounts have survived to confirm his testimony. Since I have summarized these in print there is no need to describe the progress of Sir John Fastolf from an esquire worth £46 a year to a baron of France, a banneret, and a great landowner in England with a rent-roll of over £1,450 per annum clear.[2] He died in 1459; had he lived he would almost certainly have been summoned as a peer to the first Yorkist Parliament in 1461; he had ample means to support the dignity but no son to take his place.

Most of these other old soldiers of fortune, like Fastolf, did not live to see and profit from the Yorkist victory. They were senior in age to the new men of the court. That Cromwell was of their generation and had fought alongside them in his youth *may* explain his joining them. Most, like Fastolf, died without surviving male issue. Sir Andrew Ogard, a noble but penniless Dane, was naturalized and settled in England.[3] Worcester tells us that his French lands and offices had been worth £1,000 sterling a year. Like Fastolf he had taken care to invest his profits in English lands.

---

[1] Cf. McFarlane, 'A Business Partnership in War and Administration, 1421–45', pp. 299–300; 'The Investment of Sir John Fastolf's Profits of War', pp. 106–7; and cf. C. T. Allmand, 'The Lancastrian Land Settlement in Normandy 1417–50', *Econ. H.R.*, 2nd ser., 21 (1968), 478–9.

[2] McFarlane, 'The Investment of Sir John Fastolf's Profits of War'.

[3] Wedgwood, *History of Parliament, Biographies 1439–1509*, s.n., has a 'full but not wholly accurate' [K. B. McF.] account of Ogard.

Having bought the castle of New Buckenham and other lands in Norfolk for 2,000 marks or more, he paid £1,000 for the manor of Emneth near Wisbech and spent another 2,000 marks on rebuilding the manor house there. The manor of Rye near Ware in Hertfordshire cost him £1,100 and the house he built there 4,000 marks. This house, the scene of a seventeenth-century plot, has not wholly disappeared. Worcester also tells us that Ogard's chapel with its four priests and twelve or sixteen clerks and choristers cost him £100 a year and that he had 7,000 marks in the coffers of one of his friends.[1] Across the Lea water-meadows within sight of the Rye House another of York's councillors was building himself Hunsdon House; this was Sir William Oldhall. His wardrober told Worcester that it had cost him just over 7,000 marks. It became a royal residence under Henry VIII.[2]

So much for new men, some courtiers, some soldiers, some like Cromwell and Beauchamp of Powick both in turn. The old families, who provided leaders to every faction, to some extent shared their good fortune both as soldiers and/or courtiers, but they were also the passive beneficiaries of the accumulation that attended male survival. Any noble stock, provided it protected itself against the worst consequences of political miscalculation *and* succeeded in producing a male heir in every generation, was almost bound to add effortlessly to the number of its acres. It might be temporarily embarrassed by an excessive number of surviving dowagers or even by an excessive number of surviving children. Capture in war and the payment of one or more heavy ransoms could be as damaging as political eclipse; fortunately for them the heads of few prominent magnate families were taken in war and some of those that were died in captivity before the ransom was paid. Most of the earls emerged without serious damage from the political conflicts and plots of the period 1386–1415. The three richest lords in 1455 were the heirs of men condemned as traitors during that earlier series of crises. York's father, Richard,

---

[1] *Itineraries*, ed. Harvey, pp. 46, 47 n. 1, 48.

[2] Ibid., pp. 48, 50; *V.C.H. Hertfordshire*, ed. W. Page, iii (1912), 324–5; cf. C. E. Johnston, 'Sir William Oldhall', *E.H.R.* 25 (1910), 715–22; J. S. Roskell, 'Sir William Oldhall, Speaker in the Parliament of 1450–1', *Nottingham Mediaev. Stud.* 5 (1961), 87–112.

Earl of Cambridge, was executed for his part in the abortive plot to depose Henry V in 1415. And York's uncle Edward the second duke was twice in danger of a similar fate for conspiring against Henry IV. Humphrey, Duke of Buckingham, was the grandson and heir of Thomas of Woodstock murdered at Calais by Richard II's orders in 1397 and attainted in that year's Parliament. Richard Nevill, Earl of Warwick, owed both earldom and lands to his marriage with the granddaughter and heir of Thomas Beauchamp, attainted also in 1397 but spared death by Richard II because he grovelled and begged for mercy. Families which were on a losing side during the Wars of the Roses might be deprived of all their lands by acts of attainder. Even so these acts were frequently reversed—either by clemency or by the turn of fortune. A change of dynasty led to the repeal of previous acts of vengeance. Executed traitors could not be restored to life, but their heirs could be reinstated in their possessions. Amnesty was usually seen to be the wisest course for a ruler anxious to retain the throne he had won by battle. So absolute disaster was avoided by all but a minority —a tiny minority—of those families able to survive. To survive, despite temporary set-backs, was to accumulate. Heirs might not always marry heiresses, but their wives or their mothers often belatedly became heiresses by the good fortune of others' mortality. No better illustrations of this process could be found— and certainly none better documented—than are provided by the Dukes of York and Buckingham and the Earls of Warwick. Let us look at them a bit more closely.

The rise—and growing wealth—of the house of York is too well known to need more than a reference. Richard, Duke of York's father was not only an executed traitor but a younger son for whom little or no provision had been made. His earldom of Cambridge was what would now be called a courtesy title, lent him by his brother. He was supported by a small annuity from Richard II, until his second marriage enabled him to enjoy his wife's dower from a previous husband. Since his heir was the son of his first marriage the future Duke of York had no claim on the dowager and all Cambridge's property was forfeit. It was Edward, Duke of York's death without issue at Agincourt a few months later which turned his six-year-old nephew from being a penniless orphan into the prospective lord of a great estate. Had Cambridge's treason followed his brother's death that estate would ᵢave been forfeit also. By outliving Cambridge's execution York greatly benefited Cambridge's son. But it was the death ot Richard of York's maternal uncle, Edmund Mortimer, Earl of March and Ulster, also without issue, in 1425 that much more than doubled the inheritance and made the young duke when he came of age in 1432 the richest landowner in Henry VI's kingdom.[1] With the memory of his father's fate and with so much more to lose, it is not surprising that York hesitated long before giving his supporters the order to fight after 1450. But it is important to remember that he was not only the culmination of a series of marriages which multiplied the lines of descent from former kings (the Mortimers were descended from Edward III through Lionel of Clarence, but also through the Clares from Edward I) but also the heir to the lands of many families, not only York but Mortimer, Clare, Burgh, Geneville, Braose, and Marshal united in his possession for the first time. None of his ancestors save the kings among them had been so well provided for as he.

It is possible to trace the progress in enrichment of the Staffords and Beauchamps more accurately thanks to the unusual quantity of their surviving muniments. And it is worth doing since it shows how the process of accumulation offset any decline in manorial profits. The fallacy of the proposition that falling rents meant a poorer family is clearly demonstrated. If you have more manors, that will compensate you for the fact that the yield of each is less. That is not to argue that declining manorial profits were a matter of indifference to the landowner. On the contrary, as we shall see, he usually increased pressure on his ministers and tenants in an effort to limit the extent of the decline. The point is that he still had more revenue to spend. He might not be mightier than past lords of families now extinct, but he was mightier than his father.[2]

[1] Above, p. 177.

[2] The account of the families of Beauchamp and Stafford which followed this passage in the original lecture has been printed separately below, pp. 187–212.

4

The Beauchamps and the Staffords[1]

LET us start with the Beauchamps since they had 'arrived' before the beginning of our period: they had been Earls of Warwick since 1268 and although they achieved a dukedom in 1445 this was little more than a year before the extinction of the male line. Since the greater part of the accumulation was carried, together with the earldom, by Anne Beauchamp to her husband Richard Nevill, who until his father's death in 1460 had little or nothing of his own, the Beauchamp records tell us what the Kingmaker enjoyed in the 1450s. As I said earlier the Nevill muniments have not survived. Those of the Beauchamps are only full from the 1390s onwards, but then they are particularly rich and varied: there are at least ten receiver-general's accounts, two valors, and a couple of household day-books as well as a good many subsidiary documents.[2] And even for the earlier period for which no accounts survive a huge private cartulary[3] and a set of unusually detailed wills for eleven members of the family, including all its heads from 1269 to 1439,[4] help to make up for their absence. Finally it

[1] From the 1965 Lectures. See above, p. 186, n. 2.

[2] Parts of the Beauchamp archives are preserved at Longleat, and in the British Museum, the Public Record Office, Warwick castle, and the Town Clerk's Office, Warwick; transcripts of a considerable number of documents are in the Dugdale MSS. in the Bodleian Library; some documents, which McFarlane did not, apparently, use are in the Worcestershire County R.O. (R. H. Hilton, 'Building Accounts of Elmley Castle, Worcestershire, 1345–6', *Univ. of Birmingham Hist. Journ.* 10 (1965–6), 78–87), in the Birmingham Reference Library and at Shakespeare's birthplace, Stratford-upon-Avon (*Ministers Accounts of the Warwickshire Estates of the Duke of Clarence 1479–80*, ed. R. H. Hilton (Dugdale Soc., 1952), pp. xviii–xix).

[3] B.M. Add. MS. 28024.

[4] The members of the family whose wills have survived are as follows: William (d. 1268), abstracted *Testamenta Vetusta*, i. 50–1, *Register of Bishop Godfrey Giffard*, ed. J. W. Willis Bund (Worcs. Historical Society, 2 vols., 1902), i. 7–9; Earl

was a family of great achievement, if not of consistent ability: at least one male in each generation had a successful career which improved the fortunes of the house. It is badly served, mainly by Round of all scholars, in the *D.N.B.*

Let me rapidly enumerate the generations of Beauchamps with which we are concerned.[1] The family's importance had been greatly enhanced in the thirteenth century by the marriage of William Beauchamp of Elmley, Worcestershire, with Isabel, sister and heir of William Mauduit, Earl of Warwick, which earl died without issue in 1268. The Beauchamps had been hereditary sheriffs of Worcestershire since Norman times; and Isabel Mauduit was the heiress not only of her own respectable official family—her great-great-grandfather had been chamberlain of Henry I's Exchequer—but also through her mother of the twelfth-century Beaumont Earls of Warwick. Her mother's marriage and her own were the making of the Beauchamps. Her son and heir William, the first earl of his family, died in 1298; thenceforward the earldom descended from father to son without a break until the male line failed in 1446. To William succeeded Guy in 1298; he died in 1315. He was followed by Thomas, third earl, who died in 1369 and he by Thomas, fourth earl, who died in 1401. To him succeeded the last and greatest warrior-statesman of his house, Richard, fifth earl. He died in 1439 leaving a son and heir, Henry, whom his godfather Henry VI made a duke at the age of twenty in 1445. He died in 1446.

William (d. 1298), abstracted *Test. Vet.* i. 52, cf. *Register of Bishop Godfrey Giffard*, ii. 498; Earl Guy (d. 1315), abstracted *Test. Vet.* i. 53–4; Earl Thomas (d. 1369), Lambeth Reg. Whittlesey, f. 110, abstracted *Test. Vet.* i. 79–80; Earl Thomas (d. 1401), Lambeth Reg. Arundel, i. ff. 170ᵛ–80, abstracted *Test. Vet.* i. 153–5; Earl Richard (d. 1439), Prerog. Court of Cant., Reg. Rous, ff. 147–8ᵛ (146–7ᵛ), abstracted *Test. Vet.* i. 231–3; Guy (d. 1359), eldest son of Earl Thomas, Lambeth, Reg. Islip, f. 160, abstracted *Test. Vet.* i. 63–4; Catherine (d. 1369), wife of Earl Thomas (d. 1369), abstracted *Test. Vet.* i. 78; Margaret (d. 1407), wife of Earl Thomas (d. 1401), Lambeth, Reg. Arundel, i, ff. 232ᵛ–5, abstracted *Test. Vet.* i. 169; Isabel (d. 1439), second wife of Earl Richard, *Fifty Earliest English Wills* (E.E.T.S., 1882), pp. 116–19, abstracted *Test. Vet.* i. 239–40; William Beauchamp, Lord Abergavenny (d. 1411), Lambeth Reg. Arundel, ii, ff. 155ᵛ–6ᵛ, abstracted *Test. Vet.* i. 171–2; Joan, Lady Abergavenny (d. 1435), *Test. Vet.* i. 224–31. Abstracts of all these wills are also to be found in Dugdale, *Baronage*, i. 227–47.

[1] For the details which follow, G.E.C. xii, pt. ii. 368–84.

Between 1268 and 1446 the Beauchamps had twice suffered set-backs, though these were soon made good. They occurred, as might be expected, in the two times of troubles through which the earls lived. It was almost impossible for anyone to trim his course successfully through the period 1307–30; it was equally difficult in the period 1386–1408. Some partial and at least temporary shipwreck was inevitable. The full force of the political disturbances of Edward II's reign was broken by the minority of Thomas, the third earl. Since he was aged one and a half when his father died in 1315 he was at least passive until the first years of Edward III; to some extent a passive victim, but at least he did nothing to make things worse. His father Earl Guy who drafted the Ordinances and murdered Piers Gaveston had been the ablest of Edward I's lieutenants in the Scottish war. Despite his responsibility for the favourite's death Guy had obtained from Edward II a particularly valuable concession, that his executors should farm his lands at the Exchequer in the event of a minority following his death. This would have secured continuity of administration and avoided damage at the hands of royal officials; and if the farm was, as it usually was, less than the lands could be made to produce, it could also be profitable. This grant the king confirmed to the executors soon after Guy's death.[1] It was characteristic of Edward's maddening unreliability that he was nevertheless prevailed upon in 1317 to grant the wardship of lands and heir to the elder Despenser. For some unknown reason these were transferred next year to the man who was soon to be the Despensers' enemy, Roger Mortimer of Wigmore.[2] As a result Thomas found himself married to Mortimer's daughter Katherine. He was still too young to be involved in his father-in-law's fall and execution in 1330. He emerged from his minority in time to join Edward III, who was two years his senior, in the Scottish war. His estates, if exploited by his guardians, soon recovered.

The second set-back was more serious and was to overshadow with failure the last years of Thomas's son and namesake, the fourth earl. Down to 1396 the Appellant of 1388 was left in peace.

[1] Conway Davies, *The Baronial Opposition to Edward II*, p. 480.
[2] G.E.C. xii, pt. ii. 372, n. *g*; Holmes, *Estates of the Higher Nobility*, p. 13, n. 2.

The first sign of trouble from Richard II was Warwick's defeat by his old associate Nottingham, now high in the king's favour, in a lawsuit over the lordship of Gower. On 1 June 1397 he was ordered to hand over Swansea castle and the lordship to Nottingham;[1] on 12 July he was arrested in London. His confession, condemnation, and forfeiture followed in the September Parliament. Only by grovelling did he save himself from death. He is said to have been ill treated in captivity by his gaoler William Scrope, Earl of Wiltshire.[2] Released by Henry of Lancaster and restored (though not to Gower) he was too discredited and perhaps too broken to start afresh. His death in the spring of 1401 opened the way for the brilliant achievement of his nineteen-year-old son.

Few families had managed to live through those periods of political turmoil with so little loss. For successful service under the Lancastrians it was no disadvantage to have been disgraced in 1397. Nor was Edward III likely to be unsympathetic towards those who had suffered at the hands of Despenser and Mortimer. The Beauchamps, by luck rather than by design, emerged from all crises ready to enjoy the favour of the ultimate victors. If they were ever on the wrong side it turned out to have been at the right times. The lordship of Gower was their only serious loss.

During the century and three-quarters of their span the six earls in fact added fairly steadily to their wealth. Accumulation was assisted in their case by the absence of that common cause of dispersal: younger sons. Only one earl, the third, had a large family of sons: five are known. For once it seemed safe and expedient to destine the fourth William for the Church. But when he was at Oxford and already possessed of a benefice or two including a canonry at Sarum (he was the first peer known to receive a university education) two of his elder brothers and also the youngest died without male issue.[3] His father quietly turned him into a soldier. As such he proved a benefactor to his house. For when the Beauchamps *had* younger sons—as they did too seldom for safety—these cadet lines died off conveniently to add their

[1] Cf. pp. 194, 199 below.   [2] G.E.C. xii, pt. ii. 377.

[3] A. B. Emden, *Biographical Register of the University of Oxford to A.D. 1500* (3 vols., Oxford, 1957–9), i. 138–9; G.E.C. xii, pt. ii. 374, n. *h*, cf. p. 235 below.

earnings to the store of the elder line. Thomas, the third earl, had a brother John, born in the year of their father's death, 1315. He had a short but distinguished military career, which included service at Sluys and the office of royal standard-bearer at Crécy. This earned him a Garter, a peerage, and the captaincy of Calais before he died unmarried in 1360.[1] William Beauchamp, the undergraduate canon of Salisbury, unlike his uncle John, was liberally provided for under his father's will. Manors worth 400 marks p.a. were detached from his elder brother's inheritance and settled upon him in tail male, a capital loss of more than £5,000.[2] Since the clear value of the Beauchamp estates at that time was not more than £2,000 a year, this meant the loss of about a sixth as long as William Beauchamp had male descendants.[3] Once again this Beauchamp proved himself a great warrior—he was the

[1] G.E.C. ii. 50–1.

[2] Holmes, *Estates of the Higher Nobility*, p. 49 and n. 3.

[3] It is not known how McFarlane arrived at this estimate of the value of the Beauchamp estates on the eve of the third earl's death in 1369. He may have worked back from the accounts of the receivers-general; he transcribed these accounts and checked their arithmetic. The earliest (SC 6/1123/5) is for a period which begins 30 Sept. 1395 and seems to end in Jan. 1396; it accounts for income from nearly all the fourth earl's lands; the total receipt is £1,531 exclusive of arrears, borrowings, and 'Foreign Receipts'. The next (B.M. Egerton Roll 8796) is for the year Michaelmas 1396–Michaelmas 1397, but the income it accounts for (£1,309 exclusive of arrears, borrowings, and 'Foreign Receipts') includes almost nothing received before Jan. 1397 nor after July, when the earl was arrested. In 1409–10, the first year in which a full year's income from these estates is accounted for, the receipt exceeds £2,300 (B.M. Egerton Roll 8772); accounts for 1402–4 point to a similar figure, again excluding arrears, etc. (B.M. Egerton Rolls 8770, 8771), cf. pp. 197–8 below. Even in the fullest of these accounts the monetary receipt is not the whole of the yield of the estates. A. Goodwin argues from the valuations put on the Beauchamp estates after the fourth earl's arrest in 1397 that his 'annual income, minus customary manorial expenses, would have been over £2,900' exclusive of Gower; *The Loyal Conspiracy* (1971), p. 142. (Mr. Goodwin's book came to hand too late for full use to be made of it in annotating the present lecture.) The evidence from 1395 to 1410 makes an estimate of not more than £2,000 for 1369, before the settlement of lands on William Beauchamp, appear surprisingly low. In the Ford Lectures McFarlane himself seems to have had a figure of £3,200 in mind as earl Thomas's income in the 1360s; see p. 73 above. (Thanks are due to Dr. E. S. Stone for his help with this footnote.)

fourth member of his family to be elected to the order of the Garter—was Captain of Calais, married an heiress, and added greatly to his landed wealth by receiving the marcher lordship of Abergavenny and a number of English manors under the will of a maternal kinsman.[1] These were not entailed but came to him in fee simple. In 1396 he settled them on himself and his wife jointly and their issue male; failing male issue they were to pass to his brother, the Earl of Warwick, and his heirs.[2] He died in 1411 leaving but one son, Richard, whom Henry V made Earl of Worcester for his services in France in 1421. Next year Richard died leaving no son. His mother's death in 1435 resulted in the addition of Abergavenny and other manors to the patrimony of the Earls of Warwick as well as the return of the portion detached in 1369. The conquests of the Beauchamp younger sons merely contributed to the inheritance of the head of their house; nothing was permanently alienated.

As we have seen it was by means of two marriages that the Beauchamps reached the front rank of the nobility in the thirteenth century. In the fifteenth century two more marriages greatly enlarged their fortune and prepared the way for their short-lived dukedom. By comparison the fourteenth century brought them no well-endowed brides. The first earl had married one of four coheiresses of the very minor baronial house of FitzGeoffrey. His son Earl Guy married the wealthy heiress of the Tonies, but her heir was her son by a previous husband; the earl merely enjoyed her inheritance from their marriage in 1310 until his death five years later. The next two generations of earls were even less advantaged by their marriages. Earl Thomas I's wife Katherine Mortimer had no portion; Earl Thomas II received one of unknown amount—it is unlikely to have been large—when he married a Ferrers of Groby. It was the fifth Earl Richard who made up for the omissions of his father and grandfather by marrying two heiresses, one of them very wealthy. But the disadvantage of doing that was that you could not easily transmit the proceeds

[1] G.E.C. i. 24–6; Dugdale, *Baronage*, i. 238–40. For his succession to Abergavenny and other Hastings lands see pp. 74–6 above.

[2] Ross, *Estates and Finances of Richard Beauchamp*, p. 6, n. 2.

to a single heir. His first wife Elizabeth, the only child of Thomas, Lord Berkeley, and the heiress of the minor baronial house of Lisle, had two disadvantages: her father's lands were settled on the heir male and so she had no valid claim to them (though that did not prevent her from holding on to some of them); and secondly she presented her husband with three daughters and no son.[1] The only service she could perform after that was to die and leave the way clear for someone more obliging—which she did towards the end of 1422. The second countess was the sole heir to the much more wealthy house of Despenser and a dowager countess into the bargain with an only daughter by her previous husband. Provided she bore Warwick a son, the succession to the Despenser lands was assured. When therefore she gave birth to a son Henry, the future duke, in 1425, the prospects for the Beauchamps seemed bright. It was the duke's only sister who carried their mother's as well as their father's inheritances to the Kingmaker. Their half-sisters had to be content with the Lisle and Berkeley manors of Earl Richard's first wife.[2]

Those who start with the preconception that the medieval nobility was essentially factious would do well to consider the record of the house of Beauchamp. Between 1268 and 1446 there were seven earls, and three cadets raised to the peerage. Of this total of ten only two, the second and the fourth earls, could possibly deserve the adjective: the Ordainer and the Appellant. The one served Edward I loyally as well as ably, the other's appearance as an Appellant in 1387 had been preceded by thirty years of strenuous service in the armies of Edward III and Richard II's minority. Is it a coincidence that the only evidences of disloyalty in 178 years coincided with Edward II's incompetence and Richard II's waywardness? If the adjective factious must be used at all it would be better applied to the conduct of the two kings than to that of their critics. Under other rulers the Beauchamps were active and rightly trusted supporters of their masters.

---

[1] G.E.C. viii. 53–5; xii, pt. ii. 381; for the Beauchamps and the Berkeley inheritance see p. 119, n. 1 above.

[2] G.E.C. xii, pt. ii. 384–5; viii. 54–5; Ross, *Estates and Finances of Richard Beauchamp*, p. 19.

And as such they received their rewards. To recite the list of offices, lands, and cash payments granted them would be tedious. Let me pick out some of the most important. The first earl, whose death in 1298 puts him strictly outside our period, had served Edward I well in Wales and in Scotland until 1296 without much return from that somewhat stingy master. It may have been in consideration of these services that his heir Earl Guy received lands in Scotland valued at 1,000 marks p.a. on the morrow of Falkirk where he had fought beside Edward himself.[1] Lands in Scotland, alas, proved as unattainable as castles in Spain. Guy was luckier when in February 1307 he was granted the lordship of Barnard Castle and its dependent manors in county Durham forfeited by the Balliols.[2] This north-country estate, far separated from the Beauchamp manors and castles in the west Midlands, was retained and exploited by his descendants. It became a great cattle ranch partly for the market and partly for the earl's household. In the fifteenth century bullocks from Barnard Castle were driven periodically to provision Elmley and Warwick castles, the earl's suburban house at Walthamstow, and his favourite Thames-side manor at Caversham. His *instaurator* or stockman at Barnard Castle was one of his most active officials.[3]

Of Earl Thomas I's grants from Edward III the most important were the office of Marshal of England which he held from 1344 until his death in 1369,[4] 1,000 marks p.a. for life in 1347,[5] and the lordship of Gower in 1356 on the eve of his departure on the expedition which ended at Poitiers that September.[6] Richard, the fifth earl, was Captain of Calais from 1414 to 1425 and in 1419 was granted the county of Aumale in Normandy.[7] From 1437 until his death he was the king's lieutenant in France. There were few—very few—military expeditions between that against the

---

[1] G.E.C. xii, pt. ii. 370 and note *f.*   [2] Ibid. 371.

[3] There are references to cattle coming from Barnard Castle in the receiver-general's account for 1417–18 (B.M. Egerton Roll 8773, mm. 2d, 3d, 8).

[4] G.E.C. xii, pt. ii. 373.

[5] *C.P.R. 1348–50*, p. 145; the grant was in return for his service with 100 men at arms in accordance with the terms of an indenture made between him and the king.

[6] G.E.C. xii, pt. ii. 373, n. *l.*

[7] G.E.C. xii, pt. ii. 380; ibid. i. 358 and Appendix J.

Welsh in 1277 and Gloucester's foray into Flanders in 1436 in which an Earl of Warwick was not prominent—at Maes Madog (in command), Dunbar, Falkirk, the sieges of Carlaverock, Stirling, Berwick, Tournai, and Vannes, Crécy, Calais, Espagnols-sur-Mer, Poitiers, Shrewsbury, Harfleur, etc., etc. What this meant in terms of wages, booty, and ransoms we have little means of knowing, though an occasional glimpse is provided by our sources. At Poitiers Earl Thomas rounded up the Archbishop of Sens in what seems to have been the rout following the battle. 'You might see', wrote an eye-witness, 'many an archer, many a knight, many an esquire running in all directions to take prisoners.' The archbishop paid the earl £8,000 for his liberty. Warwick seems to have been most lucky with the clerical non-combatants, since he also won three-quarters of another prelate, the bishop of Le Mans, the actual captor of whom, an esquire, disposed of his share to Edward III for £1,000.[1]

The best evidence of the increasing wealth of the fourteenth-century Beauchamps is their expenditure. Both Earl Guy and his son Thomas I were increasing the area of their estates by purchase. The Beauchamp Cartulary shows both of them engaged in the same policy as the Berkeleys and the Bohuns in the early fourteenth century, that of buying up small parcels of land adjacent to or within manors they already owned in Worcestershire, Warwickshire, and Buckinghamshire.[2] In the case of the Beauchamps this policy was continued under the next two earls into the fifteenth century. Earl Thomas II for example was buying up a shop and tenements in the borough of Warwick in 1396–7.[3] Nor were their purchases confined to these small acquisitions. In the middle years of Edward III's reign Earl Thomas I was able to buy a number of whole manors, one in 1345 and three, all in Cheshire,

---

[1] Above, p. 30.
[2] For purchases by the Bohuns and Berkeleys: Holmes, *Estates of the Higher Nobility*, pp. 113–14, and Smyth, *Lives of the Berkeleys*, i. 325–31, 370–1; ii. 13.
[3] B.M. Egerton Roll 8769, m. 2d. A shop opposite St. Peter's church had been bought for £3 from Thomas Stanley and tenements in West St. from Peter Lyndrapere for £6. 13s. 4d. Cf. *Calendar of Inquisitions Miscellaneous 1392–7*, no. 305 for other, it seems extensive, acquisitions in Warwick.

in 1351.[1] Even when the Appellant earl had no right to be particularly prosperous, in 1397 when he was arrested, he had recently put through the purchase of the Norfolk manor of Panceworth for 1,400 marks and was trying to buy out a rival claimant to Gower with the offer of £6,000.[2]

The increasing money at Edward III's marshal's disposal is indicated by the growing scale of the provision he was able to make for his numerous daughters. In 1344, having no cash to spare, he made an enfeoffment of lands to trustees to raise some £2,700 to provide portions for his four eldest daughters—in descending amounts. The eldest, Elizabeth, was to have £1,200, Maud and Philippa 1,000 marks each, and Katherine a mere £200.[3] Yet in 1353 when he actually contracted to give Philippa in marriage to the Earl of Stafford's heir, instead of 1,000 marks he offered £2,000, exactly three times as much.[4] Crécy and Calais had intervened.

Once more building provides evidence of cash to spare. In the fourteenth century Thomas II was, it seems, the great builder. At the time of his arrest he had not long completed the rebuilding of Warwick castle and of the great collegiate church of St. Mary's in which the Beauchamps were buried. In the financial year 1393–4 the north-east tower of the castle accounted for almost £400.[5] And again William Worcester provides evidence of Earl Richard's activities as a builder: the south tower of Warwick castle, a large stable there at a cost of 500 marks, Elmley, Hanslope, and Henley castles rebuilt as well as a number of manor houses, park lodges, and chapels.[6] Worcester's list, as the earl's accounts show, was by no means exhaustive.[7] But then, these accounts show how well he could afford them.

---

[1] *Warwickshire Feet of Fines*, iii (1345–1509), ed. L. Drucker (Dugdale Soc., xviii, 1943), no. 1972; Dugdale *Warwickshire* (1730 edn.), i. 494; *Black Prince's Register*, iii. 40.

[2] B.M. Egerton Roll 8769, m. 2d records the payment for Panceworth.

[3] B.M. Add. MS. 28024 (Beauchamp Cartulary), f. 15–15ᵛ; *C.P.R. 1343–5*, pp. 517–18.   [4] Above, p. 86.

[5] Bodleian Library, Dugdale MS. 13, p. 481. This extract must be the source of Dugdale's statements in *Warwickshire* (1730 edn.), i. 401, 427; cf. *V.C.H. Warwickshire*, viii (1969), 456.   [6] *Itineraries*, ed. Harvey, pp. 218, 220.

[7] The most important building-work not mentioned by Worcester appears to

The evidence for the finances of Earl Richard is probably better than that for those of any other contemporary English magnate.[1] Although its fragmentary nature imposes caution, which must be increased by the knowledge that the accounting procedures used by the earl's servants became badly confused during the reign of Henry V,[2] it leaves no doubt that he was very much richer at the end than at the beginning of his life. His inheritance from his father probably brought him an income of some £2,000–£2,500 or more a year, once the death of the Dowager Countess Margaret in 1407 had ensured him control of the whole.[3] The De Lisle inheritance of his first wife, Elizabeth

have been that at the earl's 'vetus hospicium' in London (presumably the house in what was later called Warwick Lane, off Newgate, J. Stow, *Survey of London*, ed. C. L. Kingsford (2 vols., Oxford, 1908), i. 343; ii. 351) on which just over £500 was spent 1418–21 (Longleat Mun. 6416, dorse mm. 7–8).

[1] The paragraph that follows replaces one on the same subject in the original lecture. On examining McFarlane's working papers it was concluded that the summary description which he gave in the lecture did not take account of some of the conclusions that he had drawn in analyses of some of the documents and that this was probably by oversight. The present paragraph, which should not be regarded as providing more than broad indications, has been written in the light of his working papers and of a limited analysis of the relevant documents. The summary account of the growth of Richard's income on p. 200 has also been modified. The description of Earl Richard's finances by Dr. Ross, *Estates and Finances of Richard Beauchamp*, though useful, is reduced in value by his not having taken note of the important accounts preserved in the British Museum. Cf. also C. D. Ross, 'The Household Accounts of Elizabeth Berkeley, Countess of Warwick', *Trans. Bristol and Gloucs. Arch. Soc.* 70 (1951), 81–108, and R. H. Hilton, ed., *Ministers Accounts of the Warwickshire Estates of the Duke of Clarence* (Dugdale Soc. 21, 1952), pp. ix–xxx.

[2] Ross, *Estates and Finances of Richard Beauchamp*, pp. 17–18.

[3] If the value of the original Beauchamp inheritance is calculated from the valuation of the relevant estates in an incomplete valor of *c.* 1430–1 (SC 12/18/45), filling the gaps by using a valor of 1446–7 (E 368/220 rot. 108ᵛ–121ᵛ; made for the Warwick lands in the custody of the Duke of Suffolk, and, in the circumstances, not free from suspicion) and filling such gaps as then remain by taking the sums accounted for from the estates concerned by the earl's receiver-general in his account for 1420–1 (Longleat Mun. 6414), a net income of about £2,450 is indicated. (Reaching a 'net' figure by deducting from the gross values in the valors the wages of minor officials, repairs, etc., but not annuities and more extensive building works.) The surviving receiver-general's accounts show an income of £2,200 to £2,400 from these lands being accounted for. Thus that of the earl's receiver-general for 1402–3 (B.M. Egerton Roll 8770) accounts for an income from land of approximately £1,400 at a time when much of the estate was in the

Berkeley, was worth between £550 and £600 a year net; it was joined to his after the death of her father in 1417 and after her death in 1422 he retained, by the custom known as 'the courtesy of England', possession of it for life.[1] He also obtained possession of some of the Berkeley inheritance to which she was heir general, though the heir male ultimately gained most of it.[2] £100 a year is an absolute (and rather implausibly low) minimum for the value of the Berkeley lands of which he won life tenure.[3] His second countess, Isabel Despenser, whom he married in 1423, brought with her a richer inheritance still.[4] Although its value is uncertain it was probably worth something of the order of £1,250, or perhaps

hands of the dowager Countess Margaret; and her receiver-general's account for 1403–4 (B.M. Egerton Roll 8771) accounts for approximately £950 from the Beauchamp lands of her dower and jointure. After these lands had returned to the earl, the earl's receiver-general accounted in both 1409–10 and in 1417–18 for approximately £2,400 from land (B.M. Egerton Rolls 8772 and 8773). In the receiver-general's account for 1420–1 the income accounted for from the original Beauchamp lands (a certain number of Lisle estates also make their appearance in this account) is approximately £2,200. Cf. p. 191 above. In his 1954 lectures on 'English Seigneurial Administration and its Records' McFarlane emphasized the impossibility of drawing a 'full balance-sheet' of the earl's income, even for the unusually well-documented year 1420–1, in the absence of the accounts of his cofferer and his treasurer-of-war (who may have been the same person).

[1] A value of the Lisle lands can be obtained from a valor of before 1437 (SC 12/18/42 dorse) which indicates a 'net' value of about £570 for the estates valued and it does not contain quite all the Lisle lands.

[2] For Beauchamp and the Berkeley inheritance see p. 119 above and Ross, *Estates and Finances of Richard Beauchamp*, p. 12.

[3] The minimum value suggested for the Berkeley lands the earl gained is based on the valuations for those valued in the Lisle valor SC 12/18/42 recto. A certain amount of Berkeley property also appears in the valor of 1432–3. In addition further Berkeley estates were held temporarily, cf. Ross, 'The Household Accounts of Elizabeth Berkeley', p. 101.

[4] The value of the Despenser lands is hard to calculate. A very crude indication of their value is that when the Countess of Northumberland ultimately received assignment of her dower as a Despenser dowager it was supposed to be worth £500 a year (Ross, *Estates and Finances of Richard Beauchamp*, p. 6, n. 1). The Despenser estates surveyed in the valor of *c.* 1430–1 were worth approximately £325 net; further lands surveyed in a valor of 1444–5 (E 368/220, rot. 98–102) were worth approximately £315 net. None of these lands was among those assigned as the Countess of Northumberland's dower and there are a considerable number of further estates for which no figures have been found. Cf. C. D. Ross and T. B. Pugh, 'Some Materials for the Study of Baronial Incomes in the Fifteenth Century', *Econ. H.R.*, 2nd ser., 6 (1953), 188.

more. By 1430 his landed income was almost certainly over, and probably well over, £4,000 a year. An extract from a valor of 1432–3 puts the (almost certainly gross) income of his estates at £5,471, which would suggest a net value of about £4,500.[1] Finally, the death of Joan, the widow of Sir William Beauchamp, in 1435 meant the addition of the 400 marks p.a. of the Beauchamp inheritance settled under the third earl's will plus the lordship of Abergavenny which Sir William had granted in reversion to the earls. A not very reliable valuation made after the earl's death makes the lordship worth just over £300 a year, net.[2] Hence the earl's landed income was probably about £4,900 net at his death in 1439. Of this the £550 of the Lisle inheritance did not descend to his son but to the daughters of his first wife.[3] In addition the Kingmaker, when his wife inherited in 1449, had to provide a pension of £500 to a Despenser dowager, now Countess of Northumberland, who survived the reign of Henry VI.[4] So Richard Nevill as Earl of Warwick in the 1450s was poorer than his father-in-law by more than £1,000 p.a. He had a landed income of £3,900 clear at most.

The fluctuations should now be clear. At the beginning of our period the Beauchamp earls were of modest landed wealth. Indeed only the Vere Earl of Oxford was poorer and he could scarcely support the rank. The grant of Barnard Castle improved Earl Guy's fortunes. Whatever its value in 1307 it was producing over £220 p.a. in 1420.[5] Then in 1356 came the lordship of Gower worth rather more than £300 p.a. Purchases and a life annuity of 1,000 marks p.a. at the Exchequer 1347–69 raised the fortunes of the family to their first peak. Earl Thomas I's death produced a new trough: the stopping of the 1,000 marks p.a. and

---

[1] Ross, *Estates and Finances of Richard Beauchamp*, p. 18 and n. 3. The 'net' given is arrived at by using McFarlane's (avowedly very rough) rule of thumb that the net value (as defined p. 197 n. 3 above) is likely to be of the order of five-sixths of the gross.

[2] E 368/220, rot. 122ᵛ (Communia Recorda, Hilary Term) (valor of the Beauchamp lands in Wales 1444–5). The figure given is that for gross income less the fees of local officials.

[3] Above, p. 193.

[4] Ross, *Estates and Finances of Richard Beauchamp*, p. 6, n. 1.

[5] Longleat Mun. 6416, m. 13 (£221. 10s. 1d.).

the detachment of 400 marks for Sir William. However, Earl Thomas II received his share of the £20,000 voted to the Appellants in the Merciless Parliament.[1] This was not meant to be a reward but a contribution towards the armies that fought off Vere's Cheshire men at Radcot Bridge. Still it seems generous and may have put Earl Thomas II in funds. Then came the loss of Gower in 1397 and a dowager from 1401–7 to reduce the earl's landed income to *c.* £1,400 p.a clear.[2] From 1407 to 1417, when Earl Richard's father-in-law's death meant the addition of the Lisle lands, it rose to *c.* £2,000–£2,500 clear; from 1417–23 to *c.* £2,500–£3,000, from 1423 to over £4,000 and from 1435 to something approaching £5,000.[3] Earl Richard had of course many other sources of income including a retaining fee of 250 marks p.a. in 1411 for life from the Prince of Wales and what he gained as Captain of Calais, councillor, Henry VI's tutor, and finally as his lieutenant in France.[4] Some idea of what was left over after his generous spending and building is brought home to us by the provisions of his will drawn up two years before his death.[5] Once more there is the evidence of many legacies of gold and silver plate and household stuff and a plentiful supply of gifts to pious uses. One in particular, must be mentioned: he told his executors to cause to be made 'four images of gold, each of them of the weight of twenty pounds of gold, to be made after my similitude with my arms holding an anchor between the hands'. These were to be distributed to four of the most fashionable shrines in England. If the pounds were troy weight the materials alone before casting would have cost £1,200. As 'heriot' to our lady he gave her gold statue to the church of St. Mary's, Warwick, where his body was to be. His memorial chapel with its effigy of copper gilt and its weepers remains the most splendid reminder of the scale of

[1] *Rot. Parl.* iii. 245; F. Devon, *Issues of the Exchequer* (1837), pp. 239–40.

[2] For the Countess Margaret's dower, *C.C.R. 1405–9*, pp. 182–6.

[3] It should be emphasized that no claim to precision can be made for these figures. They can only indicate orders of magnitude and demonstrate how much the earl's wealth increased as he grew older.

[4] P.R.O. E 101/69/338; Ross, *Estates and Finances of Richard Beauchamp*, p. 14, n. 3.

[5] Above, p. 187, n. 4.

his spending. When in 1434 he betrothed his heir Henry to Cecily Nevill and his fourth daughter to Cecily's eldest brother Richard, heir to the earldom of Salisbury, the balance was so uneven that the Earl of Salisbury had to throw in 4,700 marks as a make-weight.[1] This was the largest marriage portion known to me in England before the sixteenth century; yet it, plus the heir to the earldom of Salisbury, was needed to obtain the hand of the Beauchamp heir. Falling rents and 'narrowing horizons'[2] (to borrow Professor Postan's phrase) had not affected the house of Beauchamp. Two deaths were to make the Nevills a present of this good fortune.

The Staffords were even luckier than the Beauchamps at least at first. Their nobility was ancient but their landed wealth even more modest than that of the first Beauchamp Earl of Warwick. The barony of Stafford which gave them their surname and was the nucleus of their territorial wealth had been inherited from its Domesday tenant and was held by them—barring minorities, dower rights, and temporary forfeitures—in the direct male line from 1193 to 1637. Their rise was due to the usual combination of service and marriage and the additions to their *estate* were made, also as usual, by marriage rather than grant or purchase. Service brought them the surplus wealth to spend more and more royally.[3]

The Robert Stafford who died in or shortly before 1261 had married a coheir of Corbet of Caus from which his successors derived their Shropshire lordship. But at the beginning of the fourteenth century they had nothing worth mentioning outside the western midlands and there were overshadowed by other families. The true founder of their greatness was Ralph, born 1301, succeeded 1323, created earl in 1351 and died 1372—another of those founding fathers whose manhood coincided with the reign of Edward III. And once again it was his assistance in the overthrow of Mortimer that earned him the gratitude of the

[1] See p. 87, n. 3 above.

[2] M. M. Postan, 'Some Social Consequences of the Hundred Years War', *Econ. H.R.*, 1st ser., 12 (1942), 3.

[3] For, in particular, genealogical details of the Stafford family G.E.C. xii, pt. i. 171–82; ibid. ii. 388–91.

young king. He was one of the most active and daring of the English captains in Scotland and France and like so many others with whom we have been dealing he was a founder-member of the order of the Garter. In 1348 he was retained for life for a fee of 600 marks, raised to 1,000 marks in 1353.[1] Still, he owed most to his successful abduction of a great heiress; the royal favour merely protected him from the possible consequences. This was in 1336 when he and his friends carried off Margaret, the only child of Hugh Audley by Margaret one of the three coheiresses of the Clare Earls of Gloucester.[2] In 1337 Audley was himself made Earl of Gloucester. In 1347 his death brought everything to the Staffords and endowed Ralph with the patrimony sufficient for an earl. In 1351 he was created Earl of Stafford. The Audley share of the Clare inheritance began the conversion of the Staffords from lords in one comparatively limited region into lords with nation-wide interests and responsibilities. It included the marcher lordship of Newport in South Wales, the almost equally valuable lordship of Tonbridge with manors in Kent and Surrey as well as scattered estates, like the huge manor of Thornbury in south Gloucester-shire, from Essex to Cornwall. Its value gross was about £2,000 a year, perhaps more.[3] What his military employments brought him we cannot tell, but for his service between April and December 1352 as the king's lieutenant in Gascony he drew £6,100.[4] And in 1348 he had begun to build castles at Stafford and at Madeley, Gloucestershire.[5] Nor was he a mere fighting man. He was steward of the household from 1341 to 1345. His younger brother Richard, after a successful career in the administration of the Black Prince and in his armies, established a lesser baronial family by his marriage to a Camville heiress. Earl Ralph's military

---

[1] *C.P.R. 1348–50*, p. 183; *C.C.R. 1349–54*, p. 556. The first grant required him to serve the king with sixty men-at-arms, when required, and not to be in the retinue of any other than the king; the second raised the number of men-at-arms to a hundred.   [2] G.E.C. xii, pt. i. 177, n. *a.*

[3] Holmes, *Estates of the Higher Nobility*, pp. 36–7.

[4] See above, p. 25 and n. 1.

[4] *C.P.R. 1348–50*, p. 13, licence to crenellate at Stafford and Madeley, 6 Feb. 1348; L. F. Salzman, *Building in England*, pp. 438–9, indenture for the construction of the castle at Stafford, 13 Jan. 1348 (from the Bagot Collection, Stafford MSS. now in the Staffordshire R.O.).

career lasted into his sixty-ninth year. His immediate successors were of less account. He had had two sons, the elder of which Ralph made as great a marriage as his father before his early death in 1347. His wife was Maud the elder daughter of the first Duke of Lancaster. Had he lived and had issue he would have divided the duchy of Lancaster with his brother-in-law John of Gaunt. Earl Ralph's remaining son and heir Hugh, another Garter and companion of the Black Prince, was one of the councillors of Richard II's minority. In the history of his family he is chiefly notable as the father of five sons by the Philippa Beauchamp whose marriage portion has already been mentioned. The eldest Ralph was killed unmarried by Richard II's half-brother in Yorkshire in 1385. Anger and grief killed the father on pilgrimage at Rhodes the following year. Three of the four remaining sons were in rapid succession Earls of Stafford between 1386 and 1403. The fifth son Hugh, having married the Bourchier heiress, was Lord Bourchier from 1410 until his childless death in 1420. Since the second and third sons as well as the first and fifth died without issue and the fourth had an only son, despite Earl Hugh's fertility the Stafford line came near to failure when Earl Edmund was killed fighting for Lancaster at Shrewsbury in 1403. It was his son Humphrey, born in 1402 and killed, also fighting for Lancaster, at Northampton in 1460, who as the sixth earl was created Duke of Buckingham in 1444. His promotion was the consequence of his father's marriage. Once again a girl had *become* a great heiress *after* the wedding.

This is a particularly interesting case. Earl Hugh before his departure to the Aegean had entrusted his estates to feoffees.[1] No wardship of the lands therefore followed his death though his heir Earl Thomas was either seventeen or eighteen. On the

---

[1] He enfeoffed most of his lands to feoffees on 7 Aug. 1382, Staffordshire R.O. D (W) 1721/1/2, no. 31; D (W) 1721/1/1, f. 45, 45ᵛ, cf. *C.P.R. 1385–9*, pp. 364–5. His will made on 15 Apr. 1385 before his departure for the Mediterranean, sealed instructions to his feoffees of the same date, and two subsequent codicils contain large cash legacies but say nothing of the disposal of his lands. The will and codicils are in Lambeth Reg. Courtenay, f. 220, 220ᵛ and are inaccurately abstracted, *Testamenta Vetusta*, i, pp. 118–20; the separate instructions to the feoffees are in Staffordshire R.O. D (W) 1721/1/2, no. 33 and D (W) 1721/1/1, ff. 45ᵛ–47ᵛ.

other hand, Earl Thomas was unmarried. His elder brother's being killed near the royal presence had much angered King Richard, who on 24 November 1389 retained Thomas for life. On the same day the king granted him the custody of his inheritance and reduced the sum he was to pay for his own marriage from 3,000 marks to 2,000 marks.[1] Earl Thomas used his liberty to marry Anne, the daughter of the king's chief enemy, Thomas of Woodstock. This marriage had taken place before September 1391 when Earl Thomas accompanied his father-in-law into Prussia. He died on 4 July 1392, having, it seems, consummated his marriage but without issue. Anne his widow was the eldest of the three daughters of the Duke of Gloucester who also had a son Humphrey. His next brother William died unmarried and aged twenty in 1395, having never been invested with the earldom; Edmund, aged seventeen, succeeded. Before 28 June 1398 he had married his brother Thomas's widow without a royal licence, since on that day he obtained a pardon for so doing.[2] Meanwhile the Duke of Gloucester had been murdered at Calais early in September 1397. His son and heir was sixteen years old. The Duchess of Gloucester and her youngest daughter Isabel took the veil after the duke's death. Then three more deaths made Anne sole heiress to her father's and mother's lands. Humphrey, the young Duke of Gloucester, and his mother died in the autumn of 1399, his sister Joan a year later. Earl Edmund of Stafford added Bohun and Gloucester estates to what he already had. A valor of 1400–1 put the annual value of his lands at £3,100 gross and £2,400 net.[3] His death in 1403 temporarily broke up this accumulation, most of it going to his widow. She had (1) her inheritance, (2) her dower as the widow of Earl Thomas, (3) her dower as the widow of Earl Edmund.

Until her grandmother, the last Bohun Countess of Hereford, died in 1419 her *inheritance* was burdened by dower, but as twice a Stafford widow she enjoyed five-ninths of that inheritance.

---

[1] *C.P.R. 1388–92*, p. 160.   [2] *C.P.R. 1396–9*, p. 376, cf. p. 384.
[3] Staffordshire R.O. (Stafford Collection, Stafford family) D 641/2/6. For details see T. B. Pugh, *The Marcher Lordships of South Wales 1415–1536* (Cardiff, 1963), p. 149, n. 2.

By 1405 she took all she had to a third husband, a Bourchier cadet
with no property of his own. This Sir William Bourchier having
distinguished himself in France was created Count of Eu in 1419
and died in 1420. By him the Countess Anne had four sons and at
least one daughter. Surviving all husbands she lived on until 1438.
A valor of her English lands made in 1435–6 gives a gross total
£2,200, net £1,900.[1] It excluded Holderness, which was worth
about £800 gross and £700 net.[2] Taking the valuations of the
Welsh lands from her son's valor of 1441–2, it looks as if another
£1,350 gross and £1,100 net would have to be added for these.[3]
Therefore her son was kept out of lands worth £4,350 gross or
£3,700 p.a. net. In 1441–2 he had £6,000 p.a. gross and £5,000
net.[4] So from attaining his majority in 1423 until he was thirty-
six in 1438 his income from land was of the order of £1,650 gross
or £1,300 net. At nineteen in 1421 he had begun the military
career which was to end on the battlefield thirty-nine years later.
Long before this in about 1408 his marriage had been bought
from Henry IV by Ralph Nevill, Earl of Westmorland.[5] His wife
was Westmorland's tenth daughter, Anne Nevill. His services to
Henry V and VI were variously rewarded. In 1431 he was granted
the county of Perche in Normandy. He was Captain of Calais
from 1442 to 1451 and Warden of the Cinque Ports from 1450
to 1460. In 1437 he acquired the castle of Maxstoke, Warwicks.,

[1] P.R.O. SC 11/816. The total charge is £2,186. 15s. 10¾d. The (rounded) net
figure given in the text was probably arrived at by deducting the reprises stated
for repairs (£164. 4s. 2½d.), fees (£48. 12s. 4d.), and wages (£79. 16s. 6d.), but
not that for annuities (£128. 13s. 4d.).

[2] C. D. Ross and T. B. Pugh, 'The English Baronage and the Income Tax of
1436', *B.I.H.R.* 26 (1953), 5 and n. 3; Staffordshire R.O. D 641/1/2/17, mm. 19–22.

[3] Staffordshire R.O. D 641/1/2/17, mm. 16–19. The figures given are for the
lordship of Newport, and for Brecon, Hay, Huntingdon, and Talgarth. They are
derived from the total charge for the lordships concerned including the judicial
revenues, with the manorial reprises deducted, but not those (annuities, certain
repairs, etc.) which fell on the receiver. For the accounting system and for the
relationship between the charges in the valor and the actual income see Pugh, *The
Marcher Lordships*, pp. 145–83.

[4] Staffordshire R.O. D 641/1/2/17. The gross figure is the sum of charges
exclusive of all reprises, the net was reached by deducting all manorial reprises but
not those incurred by receivers (e.g. for annuities). Certain adjustments were
made for Holderness, the valor for which was constructed on a somewhat different
basis from the rest.   [5] Ross, 'The Yorkshire Baronage 1399–1435', ff. 46–7.

by exchange[1] and in 1447 he was granted the manor and castle of Penshurst and other lands in Kent.[2] So well had he managed his property that by 1447–8 it was worth £6,500 gross and £5,500 net.[3] Thereafter it may have slightly diminished in value to the figures I gave in an earlier lecture.[4]

Duke Humphrey had a large family. Of these children Humphrey his heir had predeceased him from plague in 1457. His second son Henry married Lady Margaret, the mother of Henry VII, and died without issue in 1471. His third son John married the heiress of the Greens of Drayton and being a zealous Yorkist was made Earl of Wiltshire in early 1470. Neither of these received much in the way of parental provision. If the Staffords suffered it was from minorities not younger sons. Minorities rendered intensely damaging by long-lived dowagers. Duke Humphrey's heir was his grandson Henry aged five in 1460. Duke Humphrey's widow, a sprightly matron of over sixty, carried her dower lands and her mature charms about 1467 into the arms of a rising Yorkist servant, Walter Blount, Lord Mountjoy. He died in 1474, she in 1480. From 1460 to 1473 many of the rest of the Stafford estates were in the custody of a series of Yorkist lords at beneficial farms. There is evidence that their values did not fall—indeed some rose—during this period, but for the second time in the fifteenth century (the first had been 1403–23) others than the Staffords enjoyed the benefit.[5] In 1473 the second duke, Henry, obtained the custody.[5] In 1466 he had been married to Queen Elizabeth Woodville's sister, Katherine. Therefore no marriage portion. And it was not until his grand-

---

[1] *V.C.H. Warwickshire*, iv, ed. L. F. Salzman (1947), 139.

[2] *C.P.R. 1446–52*, pp. 45, 67.

[3] These figures are derived from the valor for all his estates of 1447–8, Longleat Mun. 6410. The gross figure is the total of all charges for the lands in England and Wales (£6,452. 5s. 3½d.). McFarlane probably arrived at the net figure by adding to the total of values after all reprises given in the valor (£5,047. 0s. 10½d.) the value of most of the annuities which had been deducted in the valor to produce its net values. Cf. Pugh, *The Marcher Lordships*, pp. 176–8.

[4] Above, p. 178; for the reduction in the duke's income after 1450 cf. Pugh, *The Marcher Lordships*, pp. 176–80.

[5] Pugh, *The Marcher Lordships*, pp. 179–80, 240; *C.P.R. 1476–85*, pp. 422–3, 439–40, 496, 514, 525.   [6] *C.P.R. 1467–77*, p. 367.

mother's death in 1480 that he got possession of all his patrimony. Meanwhile the death of the last descendant of Henry IV's first wife Mary Bohun, i.e. Henry VI, gave him a claim to her half of the Bohun inheritance since he represented Mary Bohun's sister Eleanor the wife of Thomas of Woodstock. As long as Edward IV lived there was no sign of this claim being satisfied. It was part of the price Richard III was prepared to pay for Henry's support in 1483.[1] Only *part* since Duke Henry was made the virtual ruler of Wales for life in May 1483.[2] Nevertheless, in October he joined the plot to make Henry Tudor king. On the day of his execution 2 November 1483, the whole of his estates were seized into the king's hands. His widow as a Woodville got a mere 200 marks p.a. the following year.[3] All this was reversed in 1485. Once more a minority and a long-lived dowager burdened the patrimony. The Duchess Katherine married Henry VII's uncle Jasper, Duke of Bedford, and received nearly half her son's inheritance.[4] When Bedford died she married again in 1496. Her death the following year was followed in 1498 by the end of Duke Edward's minority.[5] He found his estates in some disorder.[6] Between 1498 and the end of Henry VII's reign he was, despite his ancient blood, that thoroughly Tudor and 'modern' thing, a rack-renting, improving landlord. He will provide us with much evidence of harsh seigneurial exploitation in a later lecture.[7] As long as he enjoyed the royal favour all went well with him. This, despite a little trouble with Henry VIII over his claim to the hereditary office of Constable in 1514,[8] lasted until the rise of Wolsey. He was still

---

[1] On 13 July 1483 Buckingham was granted the rents and profits of the lands concerned (valued at £1,084 annually) and was promised that at the next parliament an act would be passed to give him ownership notwithstanding the act of attainder against Henry VI. In the event Buckingham rebelled before such an act could be passed. (Dugdale, *Baronage*, i. 168–9; J. H. Ramsay, *Lancaster and York*, ii. 502–3.)

[2] For grants of office in Wales and elsewhere see Pugh, *The Marcher Lordships*, p. 240, n. 2.   [3] *C.P.R. 1476–85*, p. 436.

[4] Pugh, *The Marcher Lordships*, p. 241 and n. 5.

[5] For a sketch of Edward, Duke of Buckingham's career see now D. Mathew, *The Courtiers of Henry VIII* (1970), esp. pp. 54–64.

[6] Pugh, *The Marcher Lordships*, pp. 239–75.

[7] Above, pp. 51–2; below, pp. 223–6.

[8] J. H. Round, *Peerage and Pedigree* (2 vols., 1910), i. 147–66 and *The King's*

described as high in the king's favour as late as 1518.[1] But there are signs that for all his careful management he was beginning to get into debt.[2] He had received the marriage of the Earl of Westmorland for one of his daughters early in the new reign.[3] His brother Henry had been made Earl of Wiltshire in 1510; in about 1503 at the age of twenty-four or so he had married a dowager marchioness, who was also an heiress, some twenty years older than himself.[4] Down to 1513 at any rate the Staffords were as prosperous and as favoured as ever. It was Wolsey's monopoly of the royal patronage as well as of the royal power that caused Buckingham's ruin.

The evidence of Edward, Duke of Buckingham's prosperity— or, as Tudor apologists prefer to call it, his senseless extravagance —can be found in his household accounts and in those of his cofferer, which also bear witness to the duke's personal interest in every detail of his economy. On 6 January 1508, the feast of the Epiphany, he entertained 519 persons to dinner and 400 for supper. For this he is held up to reprobation by Professor Mackie.[5]

Serjeants (1911), 43, 78, 80. Documents relating to this claim are transcribed in Staffordshire R.O. D (W) 1721/1/1 ('Registrum factum memorandum de rebus diversis per Edouardum dominum Staffordum' (1568)), pp. 133–52.

[1] A. F. Pollard in *D.N.B.*, s.n.

[2] The series of Buckingham's 'creditor rolls', some written in his own hand, begins with that for sums owed up to 31 May 1518 (B.M. Egerton Roll 14 B XXXV A 2). It records debts totalling £1,922. 3s. 4d., by far the largest (£1,322. 3s. 4d.) being to the king. By 10 Jan. 1519 that proportion of his debts which was payable by the following Christmas amounted to £2,422. 10s. 10d. (A 5). An undated list of debts (A 7) indicates that by early 1519 he owed some money payable at a later date than the following Christmas, and if, as is likely, but not certain, this list dates from before 24 June 1519 this longer-term debt by then amounted to over £4,000. On the other hand, a list of debts owing to him, probably of after 16 Feb. 1519 (A 1) amounts to over £2,000. In and after 1519 his indebtedness seems to have risen fast. In 1520 he owed over £10,000 (A 9). The accounts cited above are partly printed in *Letters and Papers . . . Henry VIII*, vol. iii, pt. i, no. 1285 (5), where other information on his debts is also to be found.

[3] He was granted the earl's wardship and marriage on 9 July 1510; Westmorland married Buckingham's second daughter Catherine before June 1520, apparently having been originally intended for her elder sister, Elizabeth, who in fact married the Duke of Norfolk (G.E.C. xii, pt. ii. 553, 554 and n. *l*).

[4] He married Cicely, widow of Thomas Grey, Marquess of Dorset, heiress of Lord Harington (G.E.C. xii, pt. ii. 739).

[5] Above, p. 4.

Yet the cost of this 'tremendous' party was a trifle more than £13. Epiphany, before the rise of the Victorian Christmas, was the great winter feast. For a man with an income of more than £6,000 a year gross to spend a mere 20 marks on entertainment on that day was no evidence of extravagance, still less improvidence. But Buckingham's accounts do show him spending freely as his ancestors had done and at first without embarrassing his estate. In those days of his prosperity he rebuilt his manor-house at Blechingley in Surrey with an early example of that sixteenth-century amenity of the rich, a long gallery for winter exercise.[1] And before his fall he had begun the huge and sumptuous palace at Thornbury in Gloucestershire which stands today much as he left it unfinished. In it the crenellations, turreting, and machicolations of military architecture survive only as romantic adjuncts of nobility. The great glazed oriels on the external walls prove how indefensible Thornbury castle was intended to be.[2] In the one building season 1513–14 the cost was £825.[3] What brought all this to a standstill was Henry VIII's demand that he should spend, without recompense, on a scale that even his fortune could not maintain. In 1519 he had to entertain the king with lavish magnificence at his castle of Penshurst.[4] The following year he was compelled to throw away all he had in the junketings of the Cloth of Gold in Picardy.[5] Tudor historians, quick to damn the old

[1] For a description of the house at Blechingley 'properly and newly builded' see *Letters and Papers . . . Henry VIII*, vol. iii, pt. i, p. 508. The gallery is mentioned, ibid., p. 492. A fragment of Blechingley Place still stands, I. Nairn and N. Pevsner, *Surrey* (Harmondsworth, 1962), p. 98.

[2] G. Webb, *Architecture in Britain: the Middle Ages* (Harmondsworth, 1956), pp. 202–4, 205–6; W. Douglas Simpson, '"Bastard Feudalism" and the later Castles', *Antiquaries Journ.* 26 (1946), 165–70; Dr. Simpson rated the military significance of Thornbury more highly than McFarlane did (see esp. p. 170, n. 1) as does Professor L. Stone, *The Crisis of the Aristocracy, 1558–1641* (Oxford, 1965), pp. 201, 203, 217, 253–4. Henry VIII's surveyors regarded Tonbridge castle (Kent), as 'the strongest fortress, and most like unto a castle of any other that the Duke had in England or in Wales', *Letters and Papers . . . Henry VIII*, vol. iii, pt. i, p. 508.

[3] Longleat Mun. 6415, m. 7 (account of the receiver for the counties of Glos., Somerset, Hants, and Wilts., 5–6 Henry VIII).

[4] *Letters and Papers . . . Henry VIII*, vol. iii, pt. i, no. 412.

[5] His wardrobe expenditure for the year ending 30 Sept. 1520 was £4,490 (B.M. Royal Roll 14 B XXXV C, roll 4). In the previous two years it had been

nobility, have in consequence described him as an empty-headed spendthrift. In fact it is his economies that should impress them. But, called upon by the king to spend for the honour of the kingdom and to impress the French—and not rewarded for what he did for his master's greater glory, he was being forced—with what a struggle his accounts bear witness—into the hands of gulls and money-lenders.[1] He was also being forced to squeeze his tenants and ministers more and more ruthlessly to maintain his revenues at a high level.[2] They were to form the nether grindstone upon which Wolsey broke him. He lost the loyalty of the servants who bore witness against him at his trial.

By 1520 he was facing ruin. So he sold two manors to the rising banker and merchant Sir Thomas Kitson for £2,340[3] and at about the same time he parted with another valuable estate to the rich parvenu courtier Sir William Compton.[4] Altogether land of a capital value of more than £4,500 was alienated on the eve of his arrest and execution for treasons he had not committed.[5] He had merely wished to rid the king and kingdom of an upstart and

£2,664 and £2,558 (B.M. Royal Roll 14 B XXXV C, rolls 2 and 3). His indebtedness increased very rapidly in 1519 and 1520, see p. 208, n. 2 above. For the Field of Cloth of Gold see J. G. Russell, *The Field of Cloth of Gold* (1969), esp. pp. 49–51, 191. For other reasons for Buckingham's financial embarrassment and for his financial position in general, see Pugh, *The Marcher Lordships*, pp. 241–61, and B. J. Harris, 'Landlords and Tenants in England in the Later Middle Ages: the Buckingham Estates', *Past and Present*, 43 (1963), 146–50.

[1] Cf. p. 208 above.

[2] Below, pp. 223–6.

[3] J. Gage, *The Histories and Antiquities of Suffolk. Thingoe Hundred* (1838), pp. 180–3; J. Gage, *The History and Antiquities of Hengrave* (1822), pp. 102–6; *Statutes of the Realm*, iii. 273–6. The purchase price was paid in May and June 1520 (*Letters and Papers . . . Henry VIII*, vol. iii, pt. i, p. 503). The manors concerned were Hengrave (Suffolk) and Colston Bassett (Notts.), and were warranted by the duke to be worth £115 clear.

[4] *Statutes of the Realm*, iii. 271. The purchase price of £1,640 was paid in May 1520 (*Letters and Papers . . . Henry VIII*, vol. iii, pt. i, p. 503). The manors concerned were Tysoe, Much Walford, Little Walford, and Whatcote (War.). Their clear value, according to the valor of 13 Henry VIII (E 36/181), for which see p. 211, n. 3 below, was £78. 16s. 2d., ff. 1, 3.

[5] Besides the estates mentioned above an estate at Ratcliffe-on-Soar (Notts.) of an annual value of £23. 4s. 2d. clear (E 36/181, f. 4) was sold to Sir William Sacheverel for 850 marks (*Statutes of the Realm*, iii. 277) and property in Southwark of an annual value of £4 was sold to the Duke of Suffolk (E 36/181, f. 4).

greedy favourite. Wished—not even tried, however feebly. He and the other members of his order 'durst not break their minds together'.[1] They knew they were powerless. And, besides, the last thing they wished was a renewal of civil war. Even if they had, they would have found, as Buckingham clearly realized when he set out in obedience to a summons to the death he knew awaited him, that no one would have supported them. Buckingham did not fight even for his life. Mr. Christopher Hill's remark that he was powerful 'because he had many feudal dependants who would fight for him' completely misses the point. They would not fight and he knew it.[2] He himself chose death with dignity rather than even a show of resistance. When Henry VIII's auditors came to value his estates, they arrived at the figure of £6,050 p.a. gross.[3] Financial difficulties may have embarrassed him and forced him to borrow and to rack-rent his tenantry, but they were not due either to any secular decline in land values or to his own

[1] 'The said Duke (sc. Buckingham) said, that he would suffer till that he might see a more convenient time, and that it would do well enough if the noblemen durst break their minds together, but some of them mistrusteth, and feareth to break their minds to other, and that marreth all' (Confession and Deposition of the Duke's chancellor, Robert Gilbert, *Letters and Papers . . . Henry VIII*, vol. iii, pt. i, p. cxxx, cf. McFarlane, 'The Wars of the Roses', p. 118, n. 1).

[2] We have been unable to trace this reference; it may well come from a book review. Professor L. Stone takes a similar view to Dr. Hill's, regarding Buckingham as 'the last great border magnate . . . a man of towering strength the like of which was never to be seen again', *The Crisis of the Aristocracy*, pp. 253–4. But cf. Pugh, *The Marcher Lordships*, pp. 260–1, where it is shown that the duke lost much revenue from his Welsh estates because lack of a royal licence prevented his taking the large escort which he needed if he was to go to Wales to extract the money.

[3] This figure comes from the valor of 13 Henry VIII (E 36/181, summarized S.P. 1/22, ff. 85–88, cf. *Letters and Papers . . . Henry VIII*, vol. iii, pt. i, no. 1288 (1 and 2)). The gross value is given as £6,045. 7s. 1¾d., the clear value as £4,905. 15s. 5¼d. This valor can give only a general account of Buckingham's potential income. It includes the estates alienated before his death (see p. 210, above) and others which he had exchanged with Lord Berners, the value of both together being £276. 12s. 2d. clear. It does not appear to take account of all the difficulties in collecting revenues, especially on the Welsh estates (cf. n. 2 above) but on the other hand there may have been sources of revenue excluded from this valor. Harris, 'Landlords and Tenants in England in the Later Middle Ages: the Buckingham Estates', p. 146, puts the duke's net income at £5,061. 18s., but does not say for what year.

incompetence as an improver. His lands were worth more than £120,000 at his fall.[1]

The fluctuations of fortune that dogged both Beauchamps and Staffords were, we can see, caused largely by factors that had nothing to do with either agricultural prosperity and slump or managerial competence. They were the result in the first place of such inescapable accidents as mortality and survival: the minorities of heirs, the toughness of widows, the births and deaths of children. Until 1521 the Staffords endured and outlived all political dangers as the Beauchamps had those of the first and last quarters of the fourteenth century. The first Duke of Buckingham was a Lancastrian to his death, the second a Yorkist until Richard III split his brother's supporters, the third a member of the Tudor family circle, the stepson of Jasper Tudor, the ward of Lady Margaret and himself the son of a Beaufort mother. They courted whichever dynasty was in power, until it fell or looked like falling. The second duke mistimed his conversion to the cause of Tudor; a wiser man would have waited, but it was important not to wait too long. Trimming is a dangerous game and involves men in going to court here while they write letters to the king over the water with what secrecy they can. Duke Henry was found out and paid the penalty. Duke Edward was guilty of no disloyal *action*; what little he may have said was aimed at the butcher's cur from Ipswich and Wolsey had spies in his household quick to report and distort his lightest word. It would have been better for him if he had held his tongue in his own house. But do not let us talk of him as the hidebound representative of feudal reaction. The Staffords and the Beauchamps like many of the statesmen and nobles of the late seventeenth century, faced by a similar dynastic problem, were less factious backwoodsmen than watchful trimmers conscious of how much they had to lose; and also of how much they had to gain from stable government and authoritative kingship. In this as in so much else they were typical of their order.

[1] This is, of course, a rough estimate, valuing them at twenty years' purchase; as Hengrave and Colston Basset were valued when sold to Kitson; J. Gage, *Thingoe Hundred*, pp. 180–1.

5

Landlord versus Minister and Tenant[1]

In this lecture I wish to consider some evidence of attempts by landlords to maintain or increase revenue by putting pressure via their ministers upon those who owed them rents, services, or suit of court. The phrase 'via their ministers' may mean one of two things: either that the ministers were the skilled and willing instruments of extortion or that they were themselves subjected to harsh measures for their failure to pay over what was expected of them. There are examples of both activities.

That there is no such evidence before the middle of the fourteenth century must not be misinterpreted. It *may* be true that before that date the landowners had little difficulty in collecting rents or exacting services and that our evidence is the product of a crisis caused by the Black Death and was gathering momentum in the years between 1348 and the Revolt of 1381. On the other hand so little evidence of any sort survives, particularly for the activities of lords' central administrations, from before 1348 that even if seigneurial pressure had been intense we should scarcely be aware of it. The development of the valor as a statement of what local ministers *ought* to produce suggests that this was already a matter of concern. And such valors were at least as old as the very first years of Edward III's reign as the surviving examples for the estates of the elder Henry of Lancaster and Elizabeth de Burgh, the Lady of Clare, prove.[2] Their purpose *may* not have been so

[1] For subsequent work on the subjects dealt with in this lecture (which was one of the 1965 series) see R. R. Davies, 'Baronial Accounts, Incomes and Arrears in the Later Middle Ages', *Econ. H.R.*, 2nd ser., 21 (1968), 211–29; C. Dyer, 'A Redistribution of Incomes in Fifteenth Century England', *Past and Present*, 39 (1968), 11–33; Harris, 'Landlords and Tenants in England in the Later Middle Ages: the Buckingham Estates', 146–50.

[2] Davies, 'Baronial Accounts, Incomes and Arrears in the Later Middle Ages', pp. 215–16.

much to extract the most possible from the lands and their tenants as to keep a check on the venality or slackness of local officials, a sort of annual inquest of ministers. For with widely scattered estates as well as other calls on their time, the great lords were just as exposed as the kings to the corrupt practices of their officials. It was one of the main duties of their central staff of auditors and receivers to keep a watch on the possible misdeeds of those distant from the lord's eye whose local loyalties might be stronger than those that should have bound them to his interests.

In 1925 Miss Levett argued that one source of trouble in the fourteenth century was the emergence of the baronial council. Such a body, composed in the main of lawyers and financial experts, introduced, Miss Levett believed, a strong professional element hitherto wanting into estate management and forced the manorial court to change from a model of fair dealing into an instrument of oppression: it now functioned under vigilant supervision.[1] The subsequent discovery that baronial councils were less novel than Miss Levett claimed—indeed could often be traced as far back as the twelfth century—has tended to discredit the view that their activities were the cause of manorial unrest.[2] But if there was unrest it was almost certain to run into conflict with a group of central officials whose business it was, as it probably always had been, to watch over the lord's interests and to keep both tenants and officials up to the mark. The councils were not new, the resistance and evasion they had to deal with may have been. It would not be surprising if this caused a redoubling of conciliar activity: the result rather than the original cause of the unrest which their responsive pressure could only intensify. To that extent they were a secondary cause of unrest, attempts at repression begetting more resentment. The primary causes, it seems to me, were more psychological than economic, a loss of contentment with things as they had always been and the growth of a critical and angry mood which was less due to the worsening

[1] A. D. Levett, 'Baronial Councils and their Relation to Manorial Courts', *Studies in Manorial History* (Oxford, 1938), pp. 21–40.

[2] N. Denholm Young, *Seigneurial Administration in England*, pp. 25–6; F. M. Stenton, *The First Century of English Feudalism* (2nd edn., Oxford, 1961), pp. 74–5.

lot of the rural poor than to a developing consciousness that it was, as it had always been, unjust. But we are not so much concerned with the causes of discontent as with the ways in which lords, acting on the best available professional advice, attempted to minimize its impact on their landed revenues.

Before we turn to actual examples, two or three general points need to be made:

1. Though the baronial council may have been the policy-making body as well as that to which all important matters were referred by the lord, it did not assume that degree of detailed and local supervision that Miss Levett allowed it—at least on those estates for which we have plentiful evidence. Special officials, who may or may not have been councillors, called surveyors or 'approvers' (i.e. improvers), were appointed from the mid-fourteenth century onwards to supervise and tighten up the management of a lordship or group of estates. Alternatively a small group of men called 'commissioners', as it were a committee of high officials and councillors, generally including an auditor, the chief steward, or the receiver-general, were sent to investigate and report on ways and means of increasing revenue and preventing peculation and inefficiency. These tours by commissioners at first *ad hoc* (for example if there were spectacular difficulties in getting in revenue) could, and in some estates did, become regular —additional to the chief steward's annual or triennial tours. Like the king's Council—and perhaps even earlier—the lord's council tended to proliferate.

2. Economic historians have been more interested in the so-called peasantry and their relations to their lord and to his methods of husbandry than in other classes of tenants, including those who held by knight service. But some landowners at least were as keen as the Tudors in their search for 'concealed' lands and in their determination to exploit their feudal as opposed to their manorial lordship. Hunting a ward was almost as good a sport as pursuing a villein and might be quite as profitable.[1]

---

[1] The incomplete nature of the surviving records prevents accurate estimation of the importance of these revenues, but it is clear that great lords continued to find their feudal rights remunerative. Such revenues probably fluctuated a great

3. Thirdly there was the effect on estate management of the widespread and rapid abandonment of demesne husbandry in favour of leasing either the demesne or the whole manor to a farmer. That this change was due to the rise in wages and the shortage of tenants in villeinage as the immediate consequences of the depopulation and displacement caused by the Black Death is reasonably clear. The trouble was that it could not be carried far enough—as yet. The depopulation and displacement had not usually been complete enough to make enclosure possible. The manor was structurally too tough an institution for its disappearance to be a practicable short-term solution. It was left to a slow, a very slow, death and was to hinder agricultural improvement in large areas of the country for centuries. But leased demesnes or manors reduced the number and variety of the landowner's labours and thereby the duties required of his staff of ministers. The result was less a reduction in the number of officials than a tendency for them to be retained as honorary office-holders or sinecurists. These posts were tenable not by skilled working lawyers and the like but by gentry and even fellow noblemen. The Earl of Northumberland was Buckingham's steward in the honour of Holderness in Henry VIII's reign.[1] William Hastings the rising courtier in the 1460s was steward to numbers of the peerage.[2] The survival of manors and the officials they had

deal; thus the Earl of Warwick's receiver-general's account for 1409–10 (B.M. Egerton Roll 8772) records (m. 8) an income of £166. 1s. 9d. from the feodary, of which £133. 6s. 8d. had been paid by Sir Humphrey Stafford for the wardship and marriage of William Botiler; the only comparable revenue (at least the only one recorded on the receiver-general's account) in 1417–18 was £4. 4s. 4d., from the Elmley feodary (Egerton Roll 8773, m. 3). In 1420–1 the receiver-general received £75 from the feodary (Longleat Mun. 6416, m. 15). Similarly, the Earl of Northumberland's cofferer's account for 1514–26 (E 36/226) records a fluctuating income from the feodaries of Lincolnshire, Yorkshire, and Cumberland, varying from less than £20 to over £100, e.g. pp. 7, 51, 82, 98, 115, 141, 172, 201, 233, 283. The potential income from feudal sources could sometimes be very large. An account of money owed 'de exitibus feodorum' to Thomas of Brotherton, Earl of Norfolk, records £520. 4s. due from reliefs, etc., in Norfolk and Suffolk (B.M. Egerton Roll 8761).

 [1] Above, p. 108.
 [2] During Edward IV's reign he was granted stewardships by the Duke of Norfolk, the Duchess of Buckingham, Lord Lovell, Lord Bergavenny, the Earl of

formerly needed conceals how much the economy of a great estate
had been simplified by the end of the fifteenth century. To call
the nobleman a *rentier* is to misuse the term which properly means
an investor in government stock. But he was certainly a rent-
enjoyer rather than a husbandman on a grand scale. To some
extent—we should dearly like to know how much—this completed his alienation from those who inhabited and worked the
soil of which he was lord. He took money and did little else. If
he were eliminated, the gentry who collected his sinecures and
leased his manors would be quick to snap up a share of his rents.
But perhaps they always had been; by 1500 it is easier to watch it
being done since the records are fuller.

But there is no doubt that these records reveal how justified
was the unpopularity of most of the great landowners. The
smaller fry are less well documented, but it is unlikely that they
incurred and deserved less odium. The odd thing is that historians
should condemn in them what they praise in the king. If poverty
justified the Crown's exactions it should justify the measures
taken by the nobility in the later middle ages. It is better to re-
strain one's itch to condemn altogether and be content to record.

Now for some examples—in roughly chronological order.
First the fourteenth century. One of the problems that naturally
caused concern to tenants-in-chief was the practice (which they
employed themselves) of conveying one's lands to feoffees in
order to deprive one's lord of his feudal incidents. On 26 January
1362 the Black Prince ordered an inquiry into the case of his
late tenant in Hunstanton, Norfolk, Hamon Lestrange, member
of a widely scattered noble family. Lestrange had enfeoffed the
manor to uses, but on his death the prince's steward had seized
the wardship. The feoffees appealed to the prince's council. The
steward was therefore ordered to ascertain by inquisition or
examination 'whether Hamon by charter enfeoffed the petitioners
. . ., whether seizin thereof was thereupon delivered to them and
whether he made [sc. a legal] release to them', in order to find a

Warwick, the Duke of Clarence, Sir Walter Griffith, the Abbots of Welbeck,
Chester, and Merevale, and the Bishops of Exeter and of Coventry and Lichfield
(Dugdale, *Baronage*, i. 580–3).

flaw in the conveyance.[1] If the answer was that there was no flaw, the steward was to report 'for what reasons and on what conditions and to certify the prince's council of Westminster thereof and of all other circumstances affecting the preservation of the prince's right in this behalf as soon as possible'. By 15 April the facts had been reported. The 'information taken by the steward' had been considered by the lawyers 'and others' of the prince's council, 'who are of the opinion that for anything contained therein the prince has no reasonable cause to meddle'.[2] During 1362 and 1363 other similar cases were exercising the council's attention.[3] The only loophole, apart from the omission of some legal step in the conveyance, was the suspicion of the incompetence of the feoffor to create a use. Sir Matthew Folville in 1362 was found to be of sound mind when he granted two manors in Leicestershire to feoffees.[4] In an earlier case it was decided to take precautionary steps on the report of Sir John Wingfield the chief steward 'perceiving William de Praers, an old man and infirm, whose memory is not so good as it was and who holds of the prince in chief, to be purposing to alienate his lands by collusion in order to bar the prince of the wardship and marriage of his heirs'. 'Four days before the alienation would have been made', the lands were seized by the prince's officers. But second thoughts caused the council to doubt the legality of the seizure and orders were given to take advice 'as to what can lawfully be done to save the prince's estate, since the prince is not advised whether the seizure in question can have been rightly made'.[5]

This same problem—loss of wardship through a use—is referred to also in John of Gaunt's register. The manor of Horsington, Lincolnshire, was found to be beyond his control in 1372 because of an enfeoffment by its tenant, Sir William Bealsby.[6] A letter sent on 1 December 1374 to sixteen stewards and feodaries in Gaunt's duchy ordering them to make a return of the wardships and marriage that ought to fall to the duke, for his council's information, is evidence of general anxiety on this score.[7] The

[1] *Black Prince's Register*, iv. 411–12.   [2] Ibid. 432.   [3] Ibid. 417–18, 437.
[4] Ibid. 453.   [5] Ibid. iii. 177.
[6] *John of Gaunt's Register, 1371–5*, ed. S. Armitage Smith, ii, no. 1004.
[7] Ibid. no. 1584.

king, protected by the need for a royal licence to alienate (even to feoffees) land held in chief, suffered less than the magnates (unless by negligence) from the growing popularity of the use. It considerably reduced the *feudal,* i.e. casual, revenues of the greater landowners.

The desire to maintain the yield of his lands encouraged the lord—or his advisers—to listen to informations laid by third parties, often from interested motives, and to appoint commissions to investigate. On 30 October 1351 the Black Prince sent an order by advice of his council to his justice and chamberlain of Chester telling them that 'inasmuch as Rees ap Roppert has shown before the prince and his council that, if he had sufficient warrant, he could profit the prince in several things and in divers ways' [as in escheated lands withheld in the palatine county] . . . to cause the said Rees to have a commission enabling him to do the said things for the next two years, to wit, to assess the said lands and make all the profit he can thereof, taking for his trouble a sixth part of all such profits'.[1] Although a mass of informations was produced by the plausible Rees, the experiment of giving him a free hand was disastrous. By 28 July 1354 he had been removed from the office of the prince's 'approver' and an inquiry was ordered into his misdeeds, because 'he has not at all kept his promise', but on the contrary had ensured that lands were withdrawn from the prince and his right thereto concealed.[2]

Though there are a number of examples of information laid by individuals on the Black Prince's estates as well as widespread evidence of the vigilance of those officials who wished to improve his revenue, his *Registers* contain no example of the appointment of a board of special commissioners with a general duty to examine and report. But more than one such commission can be found in the records of his brother Lancaster. On 14 July 1373, for example, four men, including two knights, were charged to inquire, survey, and amend any defaults they might find within the duke's honour of Tutbury 'so that we suffer neither loss nor damage in that matter'.[3] In 1381 the Peasants' Revolt had dislocated Gaunt's

[1] *Black Prince's Register,* iii. 45–6.   [2] Ibid. 174.
[3] *John of Gaunt's Register, 1371–5,* ed. S. Armitage Smith, ii, no. 1735.

administration in his East Anglian estates and done considerable damage to his property. On 10 December 1381 he appointed a commission of three to investigate, to deal with the miscreants in Norfolk, bond and free, and to exact compensation.[1] Commissions reported to the council. And it became customary for the auditors also to explain any decline in the estimated value of particular manors. Dr. Holmes has printed one such report for 1388.[2]

Other lords, instead of appointing special commissions, were content with leaving investigation and correction to their chief steward. By the 1460s chief stewards were often sinecurists leaving their work to deputies.[3] Not so in the fourteenth century. One of the most valuable survivals is a long roll recording the tour of the chief steward of Hugh, Earl of Stafford, between May and July 1386.[4] The official was Sir Nicholas Stafford, the lord's (probably illegitimate) kinsman and in those summer months he travelled widely from Gloucestershire to Leicestershire and Essex to Shropshire. The proceedings, at his tourn as it was called, resembled an episcopal visitation. Tale-bearing was encouraged, tenants complained of the misdeeds of officials, debts of long standing were inquired into, debtors were made to produce sureties for speedy payment, officials in arrears were brought to book and threatened with court proceedings and arrest.

To suggest that these efforts were wholly effective would not be justified on the evidence. They prove anxiety rather than its relief. The same may be allowed in the case of dilatory or defaulting rent-collectors. There is more evidence of the disease than of its cure. The signs of effort are clear; the disease was not neglected. And there are at least some signs that the worst difficulties were over on the more efficiently managed estates by the end of the fourteenth century. The arrears of rent were disappearing from the accounts. The first great period of readjustment to new conditions was over. Except where Owain Glendwr's followers were active, the early years of the fifteenth century saw recovery and something like the outward signs of prosperity that had been

---

[1] *John of Gaunt's Register, 1379-83*, ed. E. C. Lodge and R. Somerville, ii, no. 1109. [2] Holmes, *Estates of the Higher Nobility*, pp. 126-8. [3] Above, p. 216. [4] Staffordshire R.O. D 641 1/2/3.

lacking earlier. That meant no slackening of vigilance. On the duchy of Lancaster under Henry IV and V where recovery is particularly marked there were two general commissions into defaults and concealments affecting three and five counties respectively in 1411 and 1412.[1] Henry V's ordinances for the financial management of his private duchy show a determination to exploit its resources to the full.

Some landowners were less successful, usually because temporary forfeiture or a minority leading to a wardship had caused disruption and/or neglect. The Mowbrays in Henry IV's reign were particularly unfortunate and when Earl John recovered the inheritance in 1413 it was both wasted and encumbered.[2] In order to raise money to equip his retinue for France in 1415 he had to borrow 1,000 marks from the Earl of Arundel[3] and to have resort to a practice which became increasingly common later in the century: claiming prosperous townsmen as runaway villeins and extracting money for them for their blackmail manumission. A citizen of Norwich 'belonging to the manor of Forncett' paid £20 and so did an alleged *nativus* of Chacombe, Northants.[4]

Another estate that appears to have been embarrassed was that of Elizabeth Bourchier who was the sole heiress of Bartholomew, Lord Bourchier, in 1409. Her first husband, Hugh Stafford, died in 1420. Soon after she married Sir Lewis Robsart, K.G., standard-bearer to Henry V. Hugh Stafford's long absence in France seems to have caused a breakdown in the efficiency of his wife's inheritance. Her second husband was only intermittently at home but when there he took drastic action before he in turn got killed in the war in November 1431. Of the records of this two interesting documents survive. The first, a roll made in December 1424, makeþ mencyon' what moneye S' Richard Fitz Nichole late resceyuo* wᵗ my lord Bourghchier in Essex' haþ resceyved of the arrerages that

---

[1] Somerville, *Duchy of Lancaster*, i. 174–5, cf. 175, n. 1.

[2] It was encumbered by two dowagers, the earl's mother, the Duchess Elizabeth (d. 8 July 1425) and his sister-in-law, the Countess Constance, d. 12 or 14 Nov. 1437 (G.E.C. ix. 604, 605).

[3] Berkeley Castle Mun., General Series, General and Personal Accounts 20 Ed. 1–21 Ed. 4 (no numbers). (Account of the earl's receiver-general, Michaelmas 1414–Michaelmas 1415), m. 8.   [4] Ibid., m. 8.

were owyng' . . . what moneye he haþ paid þerof to my lord and to his use and what moneye is yit owyng and to whiche persones my lord haþ yone' da [. . .¹]due, . . .¹] whiche schulde ben sued be writ as yt was seþyn apoynted be fore my lord and his conseyll at Westminstr' and tytled in my lordes detarye be Roger Appulton his auditour.²

This is divided into sections. The first is of debts paid, mostly arrears of rent, £98. 6s. 0d.

The second is of debts unpaid dating from Hugh Stafford's time, £123. 18s. 10¾d. These are 'apoynted be the auditour for to pᵣsue be writ'.

The third consisting of arrears of farms 'to pursue by writ', £105. 8s. 10½d.

The fourth, £150. 12s. is of respited debts—i.e. those of persons who had been assigned future days of payment 'by my lord's grant'.

Among those granted under surety time to pay off their debts was one John Elde. He owed £11. 7s. 10d. to be paid at Whitsun 1425. The other surviving document is a petition from him to his lord 'sutyme' yowr ffermer' at Stanford Revers and at all tymys yowr seruant' who had been heavily surcharged on his account.³ All the details are set out in this plea for mercy, including the nine days he was imprisoned by his lord in the Marshalsea:

þe wyche coste þe seyd John Elde in dyuerse costages iii li, & ell' he scholde haue be gyued lyke a theff', and þe vylenye þt he hadde he wolde nawȝt have hadde for xx li. . . . Also þe same John Elde was sewyd by my lord by wryt . . . Also þe same John Elde . . . & othyr' personys haue ryde for' to sewe to my lord and to my lady for' theze materys þe sume' of vii c mylys and mor' . . . in costes to John' Elde xls. and mor'.

Yet in 1431 Elde was still begging to be discharged.

Debtaries or lists of debts become increasingly common in mid-century. There is a particularly fine one belonging to Sir John Fastolf made shortly before his death in 1459.⁴ The king's courts

---

¹ Illegible in the MS.   ² Longleat Mun. 352.
³ Longleat Mun. 235. Cf. p. 49 above.
⁴ Magdalen College, Oxford, Fastolf Paper 62.

and the threat and actuality of imprisonment were being constantly used to wring arrears from his manorial officials. The roll contains over sixty such cases and his correspondence both printed and unprinted has evidence of many more. Even his receiver-general was not exempt from his lord's severity. Beside John Elde's petition can be set another from Nicholas Bocking to Fastolf's executors: 'These ben the hurtes, greuaunces and losses whiche that Nicholas Bokkyng ayenst conscience & good ffeithe hathe hederto borne & suffred in the service of my maistre Fastolf the tyme that he was his generall receivour.'[1] Some twenty clauses follow.

The accounts of Humphrey, Duke of Buckingham, reveal the same tensions developing at much the same period, from 1440 onwards—the same gaoling of ministers as a preliminary to their finding sureties for payment, the same arrears of unpaid rent. But lest this should be thought to be evidence of purely economic factors at work, it should be mentioned that those who failed to pay their rent were not thriving or struggling peasants but members of the duke's own class. The arrears in the Staffordshire receivership at Michaelmas 1458 were £208. Of this more than half was rent owed for the manor of Drayton Basset by no less a kulak than Richard Nevill, Earl of Warwick: £108. 16s. 0d., while £41. 6s. 8d. was owing by another land *owner* for rent, Sir Roger Aston.[2] The rest of the arrears consisted mostly of petty cash in the hands of numerous local ministers, some of whom were dead before they could account. A closer look at these accounts suggests less economic recession than the obstinate determination not to pay on the part of those who could. Buckingham with reason hesitated to try gaoling the Earl of Warwick.

Finally something briefly about the third duke's methods. Here there are two important surviving books which show how his councillors tried to maintain his receipts. The first is entitled 'A booke of informations geven by diverse by [*sic*] my lordes graces officers of diverse his lordeships', the contents of which belong to various dates between November 1515 and January

---

[1] Magdalen College, Oxford, Fastolf Paper 98.
[2] Staffordshire R.O. D 641/1/2/62, roll 13.

1518.[1] The duke's tenants in Hatfield forest accuse his keepers of poaching and of deceiving his commissioners about the sale of timber (many entries are concerned with this question of silviculture, an important source of casual receipts); the farmer of 'Desnynges', Suffolk 'ys not meete to contynewe in the same farme for his lyght behaiuyoᵣ makyng estrepe [sc. estreat] and wast in my lordes woddes, suffryng the howsis of the farme to fall into grete ruyn';[2] the wardship of Henry, son and heir of Thomas Trussell, the whole value of whose lands is 80 marks 'or thereaboute' has not been claimed;[3] John Littley of Rokeby 'hath by his bill supplicatory informed my lordes grace that he woull shewe unto his grace and his counsell' when his grace shall comaund' hym certen' grete injuries and wronges concelid to the disheritaunce of my seid lord in the lordeship' of Rokeby' and the supplication is annexed.[4] The sheriffs, under-sheriffs, escheators and other the king's officers have entered the duke's franchise at Petersfield and have executed and served writs upon divers of the inhabitants 'contrary to suche grauntes and liberties as hath byn' used there tyme owte of mynde';[5] many suitors in the lord's courts who have failed to put in an appearance are reported as well as those who have otherwise evaded the obligations of tenure; encroachments on the lord's lands, negligence by the lord's bailiffs, illegal enclosure—notably by Edmund Thame, the Cotswold clothier and wool merchant in the duke's lordship of Rendcomb[6]—and concealed bondmen worth squeezing are all brought to Buckingham's notice, his *personal* notice since marginal references are made to 'my lord's pleasure' on a number of points.

The other book consists of reports made to the duke by his receiver-general John Pickering clerk about fines, concealed lands, and other matters during the year 1517–18.[7] Here are some extracts:

Item Spyllysberry is content to pay hys offer of xvii li. for the mylles

[1] Staffordshire R.O. D (W) 1721/1/6, cf. pp. 51–2 above.

[2] f. 6ᵛ (the manuscript is unfoliated; the foliation used here counts the first folio of the 'book of informations' as f. 1.) Desning was a manor in Gazeley (perhaps also in Denham) par., Risbridge Hu., W. Suff. *Ex inf.* Mr. Norman Scarfe.

[3] f. 7.   [4] ff. 7ᵛ–8.   [5] ff. 8–8ᵛ.   [6] ff. 16–16ᵛ.

[7] Westminster Abbey Mun. 5470 (cf. pp. 51–2 above).

and ther is none wyll offer soo muche by 4 li. nor stand to no reparation' as he wyll.[1]

Item I have seesed your bondman' John Dyx of Padbury and takyn' suerty for hys body and gooddes by obligation' in forty li. . . . and also a invitory of hys goodes as herre after doythe apere' [followed by the inventory—worth just over £18] item he offerthe for hys lyberte lii s. iiij d.[2]

Item John' Plaisted offerr' vii li. for fine of Policote, but he wyll pay no mony to he have your grace's indent[r] sealled; and also he haythe occupyed iiij cotages of your grace's wi[t]ow[t] auctorite thys xix ȝeerr' and above; and soo I have warned hyme owt of them wi[t]ow[t] he wyll fine for them.[3]

Another bondman William Evett pays £4 for his liberty:

Item this Wylȝam haythe on' sonne called John' and he schall mary a ryche wyddew as it is sayd, and ther for I dyd not melle w[t] hymme to that he be mared.[4]

Item John Hardyng' your wodward says he wyll make your grace thys ȝerr' in the hy frythe of underwod xx li.; he selse every acr' for xx s.[5]

Item ass tuchyng your wod sold to Thomas Copyldyke by m' chancelar and m' Cade it was sold farr w[t]in the price, for he payd no more for it but lx li. and he haythe made of the barke lxvi li. and for ii[c.] and xl okes sold to my lord of Norfolke xxiiij li. and for tymber sold to Bryanne Tuke x li. and ther is wodde fallyn' thys ȝerr' and standyng now to the valew of xxvi li. xiii s. iiii d. by syde all the fyrwod he sold and the wod for tymber to dyverse oder men.[6]

Item your tenauntes of Hatfeldbrodeoke [sc. Hatfield Broadoak] in no wyes wyll condescent to the in clos' of the foreste, for thay say that it was never inclosed nor thay wyll not assent to no clos'.[7]

There is much about the encroachments and other misdeeds in Essex of the Lady Barrington, in Suffolk of the President and Fellows of Queens' College, Cambridge.[8] There is rather an ugly squabble over the wardship of an heiress with 'master Beddyll, Tresȝoar' with my lord Kardenall''; a tenant has gone mad and

---

[1] f. 3[v]. [2] ff. 3[v], 4. [3] f. 4.
[4] f. 5. [5] f. 12[v]. [6] f. xv.
[7] f. xv[v]. [8] ff. xv[v], xvi, xvi[v], 32.

must be got rid of; a steward is old and must be replaced; every-where are franchises needing to be maintained, for example rights of wreck along the Norfolk coast.[1]

Here lastly is a good example of espionage:

Norfolk: Couper natiuus: Item I was at Norweche on Trinite Sonday all the day and I lay at Couper's howse your bondman' wheche was goyn' to Sayncte James in Gales [i.e. Santiago] xv days or that I come ther, and soo with as gret policy as in me was I dydde prively inquere what substance he is off, and be my estemacion' summe parte of hys stuffe by me seyn' he ys worthe ccc marke or a bove. For he haythe xxxvi gudde beddes in hys howse and hys plate is worthe xl or l li. and hys howse is vera well stuffed with all maner of necessariis that longges to a coke, with gret ledes and fattes for bruyng' of bere and aylle. He utters more and is better custommed then two of the beste of hys nyburres and kepythe a schoppe of cokery and a taverne of wyne ... and for be cause that he was not at home I mayd no besynes nor no man' knew, sir, wherfor I come; for yffe he hadde beyn at home I wold and dyd intend to have browyght hyme' to your grace and to have seased all' hys gudes and to have tayn' severty for theyme'.[2]

By the beginning of the sixteenth century the practice of entrusting the exaction of fines and other casualties to regular itinerant commissioners, to the work of whom both Buckingham's books refer, sometimes makes it difficult to obtain an adequate idea of income from the accounts of receivers-general. Casualties collected by special ministers were frequently paid straight into the lord's coffers. Already early in the fifteenth century wool-sales on the estates of Lords Cromwell and Hungerford which formed an important item in their economy had been taken out of the hands of their receivers and went to swell their private reserves. The accounts of the Earl of Northumberland's cofferer 1514–26 show how active his commissioners were and how much their circuits brought in.[3] The fear of falling revenue caused landowners, unable to alter fixed rents, to concentrate on the exploitation of those rights, whether 'feudal' or otherwise, which

[1] ff. xvi^v, xvii, 20, 34; (for Queens' College cf. Stafford R.O. D (W) 1721/1/6, 'book of informations', f. 5).

[2] f. 34.

[3] P.R.O. E 36/226.

offered the best field for their efforts. One thing is certain—that however extravagant they may have been as landowners they were no more negligent than their ancestors. They were abreast if not indeed ahead of their reforming kings. As far as the nobility was concerned 'improvement' was the watchword as much at the end as at the beginning of our period.

6

The Education of the Nobility in Later Medieval England[1]

SINCE this paper was planned the need for it has been summarily denied by a pair of scholars whose authority it is dangerous to question. '*No one*', we are assured by Messrs. Richardson and Sayles, would suggest that a layman in public employment in the fifteenth century, in the age of Littleton and Fortescue, of Humphrey duke of Gloucester, of Caxton and Pynson, was to be presumed illiterate. *No one* would make that presumption of the fourteenth century, the age of Chaucer and Gower, of the lay chancellors of Edward III and Richard II, the age when all the judges on the bench were laymen.[2]

By 'no one', they mean everyone but themselves. It is a well-known gambit, but I hope they will allow me to join them. No one, I agree, *ought* to suggest anything of the kind. Nevertheless, such suggestions are often made; and it was precisely for that reason that it seemed to be desirable to review the scattered evidence, some familiar and some not, bearing on that section of the laity to which my title refers, most of it 'in public employment' (strange phrase!), the only representative of which to be so much as named in Messrs. Richardson and Sayles's list is the surely rather untypical Duke Humphrey.

For it is a long-lived and widely held opinion, supported indeed by some not quite negligible contemporary testimony, that the old nobility at the end of the middle ages—that is to say about 1500—was not merely illiterate, but apt to look upon the study of letters as a degrading occupation fit only for the baser born.[3]

---

[1] A paper read to the Anglo-American Historical Conference of July 1963.

[2] H. G. Richardson and G. O. Sayles, *The Governance of Mediaeval England* (Edinburgh, 1963), p. 289.

[3] For a recent statement of the traditional view see Professor J. H. Hexter's

It is usual to cite John Skelton and Richard Pace in favour of this proposition, which, perhaps for that reason, is most readily accepted today by scholars whose field of study has been limited to the Tudor period. But not by them alone. In the standard modern edition of the *Paston Letters* it is argued that while most of the gentry, male and female, could write a letter, however stilted and diffuse, the nobility was as a rule incapable of achieving even that degree of self-expression; and Gairdner's judgement has been repeated and even surpassed in severity by Kingsford and Mr. H. S. Bennett.[1] It was a medievalist who wrote that 'in the middle ages the members of the ruling class were in general men of arrested intellectual development, who looked to those below them in the social scale for the intelligence necessary to order and govern society'.[2] It was another who maintained that the distinction between the person of the king and his office was one 'too deep for the conservative baronage'.[3] Too *deep*, you notice; Tout cannot conceive that it may have been objectionable to them on other grounds. That the fault was one of nurture rather than of nature is presumably implied in the phrase '*arrested intellectual development*'. Whatever their innate capacities, these men lacked the advantages of education and so had taken the easier way of delegating their responsibilities to others.

Now it is precisely this thesis that seems to me incredible. Unless it can be supported by a reasonable amount of unambiguous evidence it is surely unworthy of serious consideration. For if it is being suggested that 'the ruling class' was in fact no such thing but rather a collection of figureheads under whose shadow and in whose name others performed the duties most of its members were too idle or too stupid to do themselves, then there can be no doubt where the burden of proof falls. We are

lively essay, 'The Education of the Aristocracy in the Renaissance', in his *Reappraisals in History* (1961), pp. 46–9. For once his salutary scepticism deserted him.

[1] *Paston Letters*, i. 318–19; C. L. Kingsford, *English Historical Literature in the Fifteenth Century* (Oxford, 1913), p. 195; Bennett, *The Pastons and their England*, pp. 116–17.

[2] V. H. Galbraith, 'A New Life of Richard II', *History*, new ser., 26 (1942), 227.

[3] T. F. Tout, *The Place of Edward II in English History*, 2nd edn., p. 130.

entitled to believe that those who appeared to function did so until the contrary is proved. For the appearance cannot be questioned. Anyone who is familiar with the public and private archives of the fourteenth and fifteenth centuries must know that the responsibilities of lordship were apparently little less arduous for an earl than for a king, that many of them were shared by earls and king, and that the penalties for their neglect by those concerned were similar. If a king was a man of business whose inadequacies as such were likely to be visited with the fate of Edward II, so too were the magnates. Their business was twofold: to administer and improve the resources they had inherited or acquired; and to assist the king—with profit to themselves—in the *negotia regni*. The evidence would suggest that they were fully occupied.

Take first the management of a great estate. The records produced by any of the larger landed families of those two centuries may have been modest by comparison with the rolls and files found necessary for the transactions of the king's affairs, but the fragments that time has spared are impressive enough. Even the richest of the surviving collections has preserved but a minute fraction of what once existed. It is not my contention that this mass of accounts, deeds, bills, and warrants was read, let alone written, by the landowner whose property and expenditure they concerned. As far as I know even the most fanatical admirer of Henry VII would not claim that that industrious king read and approved of every record that his officials wrote; if he had, he would have been neglecting a king's real work: government. It was possible to do less than Henry VII and still be a successful king. So with the administration of a great estate. If it was left to be run without supervision by the lord's ministers, it would soon be run in their interests rather than his. Many of the records that survive assume that decisions were made by him, some of the most interesting are written as if for his eye; it is by his orders embodied in letters missive or in warrants under his seal or signet that the actions they describe were carried out. Is the explanation to be that all this is meaningless verbiage: that he was in fact incapable of the acts with which he is credited, that the points on which his opinion was sought and given were in fact decided by others, that, as a general rule (exceptions of course allowed), great estates were managed—unlike the kingdom—exclusively by their officials? Anyone who wishes to believe that will not only have to find supporting evidence but also to explain away much with which it conflicts. That these records were unintelligible to those in whose interests they were compiled is not a self-evident truth, though no doubt it accords with some popular notions of a medieval baron.

As a hypothesis it has one other disadvantage: it makes the amount of reliance that otherwise capable kings placed upon the service of such men very hard to account for. It would, I suppose, be possible to imagine the magnates in Parliament, and even those summoned to more select meetings of the king's Council, as scarcely able to grasp the details of the often complex business discussed. A group of men chosen, at any rate in part, by the accident of birth, was bound to include its due proportion of idlers and incompetents, but there would be some statistical improbability in the theory that the due proportion in this case was always equal to the total number, especially as in any generation there were new recruits, chosen, at any rate sometimes, because the king had a high opinion of their abilities. Still, even allowing for the possibility that the *average* magnate was not bright, there still remains the fact that a good many were required to do more than listen and assent, that they formed *part* of the royal administration itself. And not merely when that administration was mobilized for war, though anyone familiar with the paper-work involved in the mustering, financing, and equipping of the expeditionary forces of the Hundred Years War might be forgiven for wondering whether military commands could really be entrusted to the illiterate. But if such speculations can be dismissed, there still remain those members of the nobility who filled —and to judge from the length of their tenure filled adequately— such offices as the stewardship of the royal household and the treasurership of the Exchequer. As Messrs. Richardson and Sayles observe with reference to the twelfth-century justiciarship 'on general grounds it is impossible to believe that an administrative office which was served indifferently by ecclesiastics and lay-men, could be filled successfully by an illiterate'. Can it be doubted? It can. For Mr. Geoffrey Elton 'the treasurership [in the fifteenth century] became a magnate office, held for prestige reasons rather than for the purpose of doing the work, as any list of treasurers will show'.[1] The argument, which appears to be circular, will not commend itself to those who have had cause to study the official (and unofficial) activities of such baronial Treasurers as Lords Roos, Furnival, Hungerford, and Cromwell. Nor does it seem likely that Michael de la Pole, first Earl of Suffolk, whom his critics thought more at home in the counting-house than on the battlefield (though he had had a long military career), treated the chancellorship as a sinecure—since he was impeached for the advantages he was held to have derived from it. Should it be urged that Chancellors had only to take the great seal out of a bag from time to time and could therefore be illiterate without coming to any harm, there remains the office of king's Chamber-lain held from Edward II's reign at least by a succession of laymen, generally of lordly rank, one of whose duties from the 1370s onwards if not before, involved an ability to write. There exist from the first years of Richard II's reign—and they do not cease with his minority—a series of direct warrants from the king endorsed and signed by his Chamberlain. The earliest antedates the first surviving sign-manual warrant of a king.[2] The Chamber-lain was besides the head of that department of the royal household in which the literate laity who were active in the diplomatic business of the kingdom were to be found well before the middle of the fourteenth century. A good many of these knights of the king's Chamber lived like Guy Brian and John Beauchamp of Holt to enter the ranks of the baronage. Are we to suppose that the man who presided over such a talented and influential group was himself without administrative gifts and experience? In the first half of the fifteenth century, at least four baronial Treasurers

[1] G. R. Elton, *Tudor Revolution in Government* (Cambridge, 1953), p. 22 n. It is far from clear why Henry Bourchier, Earl of Essex, strikes Mr. Elton as a possible exception to his rule.

[2] H. C. Maxwell-Lyte, *Historical Notes on the Use of the Great Seal of England* (1926), pp. 145, 152.

had previously held the chamberlainship; others had been stewards of the king's household and keepers of his wardrobe. The sinecure character of the medieval administration was remarkably well developed if the occupants of all these offices were illiterate non-functioning prestige-seekers. Fortunately there are ample grounds in the surviving minutes of the king's Council and even in the Rolls of Parliament for doubting such unsupported assumptions of baronial thickheadedness and incapacity for work.

The truth is that the aristocracy *was* in the main one of service, that it was entered by service, and that acceptable service was the cause of promotion within it. The service might be military but it was rarely exclusively so; that was more likely to earn a man the Garter than a place in Council or Parliament. The higher rewards went to those who were also men of business. Consider, for example, the employments of John Tiptoft, father of the first Earl of Worcester. Cadet of an ancient baronial family he passed from membership of the household of Bolingbroke as Earl of Derby into the king's Chamber after 1399. He was Speaker in the Long Parliament of 1406, treasurer of the royal household from 1406 to 1408, and Treasurer of the Exchequer from 1408 to 1410. Under Henry V he was the councillor most frequently chosen to carry out his master's secret negotiations with foreign courts and in the intervals served as Seneschal of Gascony and Treasurer of Normandy. The minority of Henry VI saw him an active member of the government, a peer, and from 1426 to 1432 steward of the king's household. Until his death in 1443 he continued to serve the interests of the dynasty with which his own advancement was linked. The Lancastrian Council was rarely without several elder statesmen of John Tiptoft's kidney and they were no less common in the fourteenth century. Their expert labours earned them their appropriate rewards. We have therefore some excuse for our incredulity.

But, it will be objected, men such as Tiptoft were the founders of new families; what may be true of them does not necessarily apply to those heads of well-established comital and baronial houses with origins as different as they were remote. How about the Warennes, the Beauchamps, and the Fitzalans, the Ordainers of 1311, the protesters of 1341, the Appellants of 1388? It is characteristic of the shallowness with which this question is approached that those who opposed the king are assumed in general to have been not only wrong-headed but also stupid. 'As far as the rank and file goes both the barons who won the Great Charter and their grandsons who laid low the power of the crown in the Mad Parliament', wrote Tout, 'were every whit as *stupid* and as greedy, as *narrow* and as self-seeking, as were the mass of the lords ordainers.'[1] A loophole lies in the qualification; exceptions are cautiously allowed. One such must surely have been Guy Beauchamp, Earl of Warwick. Yet (to quote Tout once more) 'all that we can say in [his] favour is that the wise old earl of Lincoln'—it is a comfort to know that there was an occasional wise old earl!—'had so high an opinion of him that he advised his son-in-law, earl Thomas, to be directed by his counsels. The chroniclers also claim for him a knowledge of literature seldom found in the higher nobility of his age. This aspect of Guy of Warwick, combined with his treachery, reminds us of the culti-vated aristocratic ruffians of the Renascence.'[2]

It is worth following Tout here to his sources. That Warwick's degree of education was unusual is perhaps implied; what is not implied is that some knowledge of literature was 'seldom found in the higher nobility of his age'. That is Tout's gloss. What the chroniclers say is that Earl Guy was 'vir sapiens et probus', 'homo discretus et bene literatus, per quem totum regnum Anglie sapientia prefulgebat'.[3] Oddly enough Tout cites, but does not quote, another chronicler, the author of the *Vita Edwardi Secundi*, who in his lament for Warwick's death in 1315 remarks that it was 'by his advice and skill [that] the ordinances were drawn up'.[4]

[1] Tout, *Place of Edward II in English History*, p. 21.

[2] Ibid., p. 16.

[3] Ibid., citing *Chronicon de Lanercost*, ed. J. Stevenson (Maitland Club, 1839), ii. 216 and *Annales Londonienses* in *Chronicles of the reigns of Edward I and Edward II*, ed. W. Stubbs (R.S.), i. 236.

[4] *Vita Edwardi Secundi*, ed. N. Denholm-Young (1957), pp. 62–4. The whole passage is worth quoting: 'Sed comes Warewyke si in vivis fuisset, [fuisset] tota patria pro eo: consilio eius [et] ingenio ordinationes prodierunt, et ceteri comites eo audito multa fecerunt; in prudentia et consilio non habuit similem.'

Warwick was *bene literatus*. What does this phrase mean? In the case of fourteenth-century bishops like Robert Stretton, John Buckingham, and William Wickham, the charge of illiteracy clearly referred to their lack of a university degree. No one would suggest that Buckingham and Wickham who were civil servants of considerable experience were unable to read and write.[1] In fact we have a specimen of Wickham's hand which could reasonably be described as practised.[2] Must we therefore assume that Warwick had attended the schools at Oxford? I think not; but even in his case *literatus* can hardly have meant less than that he was well grounded in Latin grammar. Similarly when William Zouche, Archbishop of York, described his young kinsman Anketil Mallory as *armiger literatus* he was describing an abnormal degree of accomplishment, not literacy in our sense.[3] The Beauchamps of the fourteenth century provide other examples of an interest in higher education. One of Earl Guy's grandsons bequeathed forty-two books to the family abbey of Bordesley.[4] Another, exchanging his gown for a coat of mail, offers us our first documented example of a university-trained member of the lay nobility: Sir William Beauchamp, Lord Bergavenny.[5] It is not unfair to add that his education did not visibly differentiate him from his fellow peers; his will, which may well have been holograph, is among the earliest to be written in that very unacademic language, English.[6]

William Beauchamp's will and that of his elder brother Guy, the one 1408 the other 1359, indicate one possible line of inquiry: what light does this type of source shed on the literary tastes and capacities of their noble testators? In fact neither of the Beauchamp wills contains anything but the barest mention of books.[7] But

[1] T. F. Tout, *Chapters in the Administrative History of Medieval England*, iii. 254–5; J. R. L. Highfield, 'The Promotion of William of Wickham to the see of Winchester', *Journal of Ecclesiastical History*, 4 (1953), 37–54.

[2] Above, p. 45, n. 5.   [3] *Testamenta Eboracensia*, i. 56.

[4] H. S. Todd, *Illustrations of Chaucer and Gower* (1810), pp. 161–2, cf. p. 188, n. 4 above for the wills of the Beauchamp family.

[5] *A Biographical Register of the University of Oxford to A.D. 1500*, ed. A. B. Emden, i. 138–9. He was at the University in 1358 and still in 1361. Cf. p. 190 above.

[6] Lambeth lib., Reg. Arundel, vol. ii, 155ᵛ–156ᵛ.

[7] Lord Bergavenny left his wife 'the best messe boke' (ibid., f. 156ʳ).

those of other noblemen and women of the fourteenth century frequently do. Most of the books named are obviously valued as heirlooms, for their illumination and their fine bindings. It would be dangerous to assume that their possessors were inevitably great readers, but they are at least lovingly described. Take for example the testament of Eleanor Bohun, Duchess of Gloucester, dated 9 August 1399. To her only son and heir Humphrey she left four books in French and a psalter 'well and richly illuminated with the gold clasps enamelled with white swans and the arms' of her father; to her daughter Anne, Countess of Stafford, were to go 'a beautifully illuminated Golden Legend in French' and 'a book with the psalter, primer and other devotions, with two gold clasps enamelled with my arms which book I have much used'; to her other daughter Isabel (who was to become a minoress) she left two psalters, one glossed, the lives of the fathers, St. Gregory's pastorals, a book of decretals, a book of history, and a Bible in two volumes with two gold clasps enamelled with the arms of France all in French.[1] Similarly a collection of missals in fine bindings was bequeathed by Richard, Earl of Arundel, to his numerous children in the will he executed on 5 December 1375.[2] There is a good deal of evidence to show that these named and obviously valuable books did not exhaust the testator's library. Sometimes there is a brief reference to all his French books (Roger de la Warr, 1368),[3] to all her French and Latin books (Lady Say, 1369)[4] or to all his books of romances (Sir William Trussell, 1389).[5] So more than a century later the inventory of the goods of John de

---

[1] Lambeth lib., Reg. Arundel, vol. i, ff. 163^r–164^r. Another member of the Bohun family, Elizabeth, Countess of Northampton, had an interesting collection of psalters and other mass-books in 1356 (ibid., Reg. Langham, ff. 122^r–122^v).

[2] Ibid., Reg. Sudbury, ff. 92^v–95^v. See also his youngest son John's will (ibid., ff. 102^r–102^v) made four years later on 26 Nov. 1379.

[3] Ibid., Reg. Langham, f. 116^v. [4] *Testamenta Vetusta*, i. 83.

[5] Lambeth lib., Reg. Sudbury, f. 104^v. (Two other testaments among McFarlane's transcripts are relevant. Prerog. Court of Cant., Reg. Rous, f. 17, Margaret Courtenay, Countess of Devon, 28 Jan. 1390/1, 'a ma fille Luttrell . . . mon livre appelle Tristram', 'a ma fille Dangayne mes deux primers et un livre appelle Artur de Britaigne', 'Anneys Chambernon . . . un livre de medycynys et de marchasye et un aultre livre appelle vyces et vertues et un livre appelle merlyn'. Ibid., ff. 50^v–51^r, Isabel, Duchess of York, 6 Dec. 1392, to her son Edward two books 'marchart et launcelot', to her daughter Constance la Despenser 'mes deux petit primers',

Vere, Earl of Oxford, made after his death in 1513, while item-
izing the numerous mass-books that furnished his chapel refers
laconically to 'a Chest full of frenshe and englisshe bokes'.[1] It is
such inventories, unfortunately rare, that show up the inadequacy
of testaments as exhaustive evidence of their makers' libraries.
Most surviving inventories were those of traitors condemned to
forfeiture, Sir Simon Burley, Thomas of Woodstock, Henry,
Lord Scrope of Masham.[2] All three had large collections of books,
Gloucester at least eighty-three and Scrope no less. Scrope's will,
it so happens, is unusually full of bequests of books and it is
evident that neither it nor his inventory contains a complete list
of his possessions.[3] These chance survivals are likely to suggest a
very unlikely correlation between crime, in particular treason,
and literacy; Gloucester and Scrope read too much; such men
were dangerous. So very few inventories of the goods of the law-
abiding have been preserved. One made for Leo, Lord Welles, in
1430 mentions only twelve books, half of them mass-books.[4]
That of John Holland, Duke of Exeter, though full of other
splendours, contains nothing but the half-dozen volumes that
furnished his chapel.[5] Sir John Fastolf's stock amounted to about
twenty-five and we know that his inventory overlooked some.[6]
Much the most attractive collection known to me belonged to a
mere Speaker of the House of Commons, Sir Thomas Charleton,
who died in 1465: 'an engelische booke calde Giles de regimeie
principum, . . . an engelysche boke the whiche was called Troles

'al counte de Huntyngdon . . . mes deux bibles', to Sir Lewys Clifford 'mon livre
de vicez et vertuz'.)

[1] *Archaeologia*, 2nd ser., 16 (1914–15), 342.

[2] M. V. Clarke, *Fourteenth Century Studies*, pp. 120–2; *Archaeological Journal*, 54
(1897), 300–3; *Archaeologia*, 2nd ser., 70 (1918–20), 82–3 and 93–4.

[3] The testament is printed in *Foedera*, ix. 272–80. It is dated 3 June 1415.

[4] Lincoln Record Office, Ancaster Deposit, X/A/1. (I owe my knowledge of
this inventory to a transcript kindly sent me by Mrs. A. E. B. Owen.) (The others
were 'j liber vocatus apocalypes gallice scriptus, j lucidarium [ditto], j liber de
natura bestium, j quaterna anglice scripta de proverbiis, j rotulus vocatus le Brut,
liber vocatus pilgrimage vita humana'.)

[5] Westminster Abbey Muniments 6643 (incomplete). It was made after
Exeter's death on 5 Aug. 1447.

[6] *H.M.C., 8th Report*, p. 268; *Paston Letters*, iii. 188; *Studies Presented to Sir Hilary
Jenkinson*, pp. 205–6 and 215–16.

... a booke w^t prycked songe ... j of perse plowman, a nod^r of Caunt^{r}bury tales', two breviaries and two old mass-books.[1] The library of a man of evident discrimination.

To judge from Henry Scrope's detailed enumeration of the books he wished to leave his friends, he was no bibliophile owner of an unread library. *If* he and others like him were that and no more, the chances are that the fashion had been set by someone whose bookish tastes were genuine. At least it can hardly be argued that as a class noblemen found anything incompatible in the possession of books as well as armour; both were treasured. But Scrope's fondness for reading in the intervals of war and diplomacy and the cares of government (he was both a knight of the Garter and an ex-Treasurer of the Exchequer) cannot be proved. All that can be safely maintained on the basis of these wills and inventories is that those who could read had pastures at hand for the browsing. We may also note how expensive these fine books might be; in 1374 Edmund, Earl of March, paid 50 marks for a Bible 'pro camera sua'.[2]

As we have seen *literatus* in the fourteenth century probably had more than one meaning. Applied to an ecclesiastic, it meant that he was a graduate, one who had letters after his name; to a layman, perhaps no more than that he had been well grounded in Latin grammar. Similarly today 'literate' may mean able to read or able to read and write. A governing class could at a pinch manage by being literate in the first of these senses; second-degree literacy, given the secretarial help its members could command, might well have been thought by them supererogatory. We know that the king could write;[3] have we any evidence that his magnates also could? The answer is that we have, man for man just about as much.

In the first place there are those endorsements by the king's Chamberlains to which I referred earlier. These as a rule did not involve more than a sentence and a signature; but we have no more

---

[1] Westm. Abbey Muns. 6625 and 6630. (I have conflated items from two overlapping inventories.)

[2] B.M., Egerton Roll 8727, m. 2.

[3] V. H. Galbraith, 'The Literacy of the Medieval English Kings', *Proc. Brit. Acad.* 21 (1935), 201–38.

than that from the hand of any king before the fifteenth century. The ever-available secretaries made such labour superfluous. Even the gentry used them. The belief that they wrote their own letters is based mainly on the roughness of the handwriting and the eccentricities of the spelling. The true explanation is that they employed less highly trained secretaries than their betters. It can even be shown that Agnes Paston when obliged to write for herself had a more elegant and trained hand than had the servants she normally dictated to.[1] The only safe rule is to assume that letters, memoranda, and other documents were the work of professional scribes of some sort unless there is definite evidence to the contrary. The best evidence is the signatory's actual statement that he is using his own hand, though it would be absurd to suppose that whenever a man wrote a letter himself he invariably said so. In any case the formularies from which we derive our knowledge of many of the private letters of those times quite often cut out the dating clause in which such a statement was commonly made. No doubt a number of specimens of holograph writing will have been excluded by this test, but in trying to measure the literacy of a class it is advisable to err on the side of caution. What is left is good enough for our purpose.

For there were occasions when a secretary was not at hand or could not be trusted. The second case was perhaps the less common since in the days of private messengers it was as well not to commit the most confidential matters to writing at all. Still on occasion men wrote their secrets to one another with their own hands. Thus Richard, Earl of Arundel, in a letter which survives for us in a copy asked his brother the Archbishop of York 'to take great care of a letter written by my hand which I send you by the bearer of these'.[2] The enclosure is now lost; the

---

[1] *Paston Letters*, ii. 45: 'Wretyn at Paston in hast, the Wednesday next after *Deus qui errantibus* for defaute of a good secretarye, yowres, Agn. Paston.' The original is now Brit. Mus., Add. MS. 43,488, f. 4. For the question of the Pastons' handwriting in general see N. Davis, 'The Text of Margaret Paston's Letters', *Medium Ævum*, 18 (1949), 12–28, and the same author's 'A Scribal Problem in the Paston Letters', *English and Germanic Studies*, 4 (1951–2), 31–64.

[2] *Anglo-Norman Letters and Petitions*, ed. D. Legge (Anglo-Norman Text Soc., no. 3, 1941), pp. 76–8.

date was 1394 or 1395. Similarly the Earl of Kent's confession of treasonable correspondence in 1330, while implicating one William of Dereham 'clerk of his letters', admitted that one letter was in the hand of his wife.[1] The sceptical are therefore allowed to think that the son of Edward I was illiterate but only at the price of acknowledging that the Countess Margaret of the baronial house of Wake was well able to use a pen. The earl's execution cannot have encouraged others to commit their treasonable thoughts to paper. A like caution was unnecessary in the case of wills; they could be confidential and securely locked away. There were other reasons, with which we are still familiar, why a man should have preferred to leave the drafting to an expert. Nevertheless, a number of wills have survived in registered copies which were written by the testators themselves. Henry Percy, Earl of Northumberland, for example, wrote quite a long and complicated one in 1485.[2] William, Duke of Suffolk, with little time to spare, composed a shorter one on the eve of the Parliament that impeached him in January 1450.[3] But such technical displays were rare. Were it not for the survival of the original of Simon de Montfort's will, beautifully written by his eldest son Henry, one would be inclined to assume that no magnate before the fifteenth century would have attempted it.[4] Lesser men may have had greater professional competence or audacity.[5] Nor must it be forgotten that copies of wills in episcopal registers are comparatively scarce before the last quarter of the fourteenth century. The remarks of two testators are worth quoting for the light they throw on the problem of language. The first is that of Sir John

[1] 'Et dit . . . qe la une lettre fut escripte de la meyn sa femme' [*Adae Murimuth Continuatio Chronicarum*, ed. E. M. Thompson (R.S.), p. 255].

[2] *Testamenta Eboracensia*, iii. 304–10.

[3] *North Country Wills* (Surtees Soc., vol. cxvi (1908)), pp. 50–1. It is dated 17 Jan. Suffolk was committed to the Tower on the 28th, a week after he had faced his critics in Parliament (*Rot. Parl.* (Record Com.) v. 176–7).

[4] Above, p. 45.

[5] I have noted the following: Sir Nicholas Loraine 1375 (Lambeth lib. Reg. Sudbury, f. 88ʳ, a mere sentence of attestation at the end); Sir Bartholomew Bacon, 1389 (Norwich District Probate Registry, Reg. Harsyk, ff. 148ᵛ–149ʳ); Sir William Mowbray, 1391 (*Test. Ebor.* i. 158–61); Sir Giles Daubeney, 1444 (ibid., ii. 110–14); Sir Alexander Nevill, 1453 (ibid., 207–8).

Cavendish, the Chief Justice who was lynched in the Peasants' Revolt. He made his last will on 1 April 1381.

He begins in Latin, and after a sentence or two comes this: 'Et quia lingua gallica amicis meis et eciam michi plus est cognita et magis communis et nota quam lingua latina, totum residuum testamenti mei predicti in linguam gallicam scribere feci ut a dictis amicis meis facilius inteligatur.'[1]

A little over half a century later, another testator, this time a woman, begins her testament as follows: 'In Dei nomine Amen. I Anne countesse of Stafford, Bokingh[am], Her[e]ford and Northampton and lady of Breknoc of hool and avisid mynde ordeyne and make my testament in Englisshe tonge for my most profit, redyng and understandyng, in ʒis wise.'[2]

There remains the case of the magnate whom circumstances forced to write his own letters. In 1374 the warlike John, Lord Bourchier, allowed himself to be captured in Brittany without his secretary. Needing to inform his wife and arrange his ransom he wrote two letters home with his own hand. They are preserved among a miscellaneous deposit of Bourchier papers at Longleat and show that he had no difficulty in expressing himself lucidly and in a good clerkly script.[3] If examples of noble handwriting (apart from signatures) are rare, it was because like the busy men of today the busy men of the fourteenth century preferred to dictate.

So far I have said nothing about noble authors, partly because they are mostly well enough known and partly because, I suppose, one can be a poet and still be illiterate. But we have already discovered that one poet, Suffolk, wrote his own will.[4] Another, John Montagu, the third Earl of Salisbury, Richard II's Lollard friend, has, as far as I know, left us nothing, neither penmanship nor poetry; we are merely aware that his verses favourably

---

[1] Norwich Dist. Probate Registry, Reg. Heydon, f. 190ʳ.

[2] *Register of Henry Chichele*, ed. E. F. Jacob, ii. 596, op. cit.

[3] Longleat Mun. 396 and 400; cf. p. 45 above.

[4] For Suffolk's poetry see H. N. MacCracken, 'An English Friend of Charles of Orleans', *Publications of the Modern Languages Association of America*, 26 (1911), 141–80. T. Basin, *Histoire de Charles VII et Louis XI*, ed. J. Quicherat (Soc. de l'Hist. de Paris, 1855), i. 189, describes him as 'in litteris satis competente institutus'.

impressed a good judge, namely Christine de Pisan.[1] And it was in the households of English noblemen that two royal prisoners wrote the poetry which we can still read, Charles of Orleans and James I of Scotland. Then there were the translators, Edward, second Duke of York,[2] Sir Richard Roos, Stephen Scrope, John Tiptoft, Earl of Worcester,[3] and Anthony Woodville, Earl Rivers.[4] In what other century has the peerage been so active in literature? Yet the total number of lay magnates rarely exceeded sixty. That still leaves the most remarkable literary achievement of them all: the *Livre de Seyntz Médicines*, the devotional treatise which Henry of Grosmont, Duke of Lancaster, wrote between two of his many campaigns in France. Its recovery and publication have added a third dimension to our otherwise somewhat thin knowledge of the intellectual capacity of that warrior class.[5]

Such then are some of the vestiges of education, the traces left by it in the records of their adult lives. There remain the questions: what education did they in fact receive, when and where? Do their private archives not supply any of the answers we need? Some of them are, after all, voluminous enough. There are the great accumulations of Lancaster (both families), Stafford, and Beauchamp; there are the lesser but still considerable collections belonging to Clare, Mortimer, Mowbray, Courtenay, Vere, Cromwell, and Hungerford. Have these nothing to say about the education of the young lords and ladies of the family? Very little, since most of the accounts are devoted to other things. Children

[1] Wylie, *History of England under Henry IV*, i. 100, n. 2.

[2] *c.* 1406 Edward, Duke of York, translated a popular French hunting manual and added some chapters of his own to produce *The Master of Game*, ed. W. A. and F. Baillie-Grohman (1904).

[3] R. J. Mitchell, 'The Translations of John Tiptoft', *Modern Language Notes*, 61 (1926).

[4] The works of Roos, Scrope, and Woodville are listed in H. S. Bennett, *Chaucer and the Fifteenth Century* (Oxford, 1947), pp. 297, 300.

[5] Ed. E. J. Arnould (Anglo-Norman Texts, no. 2), Oxford, 1940. See also the editor's *Henry of Lancaster and his 'Livre de Seintes Médicines'* (Paris, 1948) and W. A. Pantin, *The English Church in the Fourteenth Century* (Cambridge, 1955), pp. 231–3. A 'liber gallicus de Duce Lancastrie' bequeathed by Mary, Lady Roos, to Isabel Percy (*Test. Ebor.* i. 200) was probably a copy of this treatise. One of the two surviving manuscripts was given by Thomas, the Baron of Carew, to Humphrey, Duke of Gloucester.

appear only rarely, and then all too often—like the younger Beauforts in the accounts of their stepfather Thomas, Duke of Clarence—are disposed of by the payment of a lump sum.[1] The itemized bills of their subsidiary households or the wardrobe accounts of their parents or guardians, which may have had more details, are some of the least common records to be preserved. Those that do exist are not necessarily for the most useful dates. Only two, those of Henry Bolingbroke, Earl of Derby, and of Katherine Stafford, widow of the second de la Pole Earl of Suffolk, go some way to meet our requirements. And produce interestingly different answers.

The six surviving children of Bolingbroke by Mary Bohun, four boys and two girls, seem to have been educated, as we should say, privately, either in their own homes or in those of their father's relations, friends, and servants. Something, often much, can be found about their doings and whereabouts in every year from 1391 until their father's usurpation eight years later, the names of their nurses, of Mary Hervy their 'mistress', of the young Humphrey's tutors, Thomas Epston or Epirston in 1397 when the pupil was seven years of age, Thomas Rothwell at Easter 1399.[2] Humphrey, Blanche, and Philippa were often at Eaton Tregose with their father's Chamberlain, Sir Hugh Waterton—who twenty years before had been in charge of Derby's own upbringing;[3] John is found in the household of Margaret Marshal, Duchess of Norfolk, at Framlingham;[4] Henry with his grandfather, John of Gaunt.[5] Three entries give us some

[1] Westm. Abbey Mun. 12163. The account covers the years 6–9 Henry V, from 1418 until Clarence's burial. I am grateful to Professor J. S. Roskell for lending me his transcript. On f. 13ᵛ £173. 6s. 8d. p.a. is paid to the duchess 'pro expensis domini Comitis Somersete & domini Thome fratris sui'. No details of how this sum was spent are given.

[2] The relevant accounts are P.R.O., DL 28/1/3–6 and 9–10, DL 28/3/–4, DL 28/4/1, and DL 41/10/43/6 and 10. For Mary Hervy 'Magistrissa Juuenum Do minorum', 10 Dec. 1393 see DL 28/1/4, f. 2ʳ; 'maistresse a noz enfantz' (DL 41/10/43/10, etc.). For Epston see DL 28/1/9, f. 20ᵛ. He celebrated his first Mass in Humphrey's presence at Eaton Tregose in 1398 (DL 28/1/6, f. 47ʳ). For Thomas Rothwell 'informanti predictum Humfridum' Easter Term 1399 see DL 28/4/1, f. 13ᵛ. [3] In 1376–7 (DL 28/3/1, m. 5ʳ).

[4] DL 28/1/9, f. 15 (Aug. 1397); DL 28/1/6, ff. 7ᵛ, 8ʳ, and 26ᵛ (Christmas 1397). [5] DL 28/1/9, f. 14ᵛ.

idea of what they were being taught. In the autumn of 1395, when he was eight years old, a purchase was made for the future Henry V: seven books of Latin grammar in one volume.[1] Then on 13 February 1397 20*d*. were paid at London 'pro ij libris de ABC pro iuvenibus dominabus erudiendis emptis', when Blanche was nearly five and her sister Philippa not yet three.[2] Finally, in February 1398, a Donet or elementary Latin grammar was bought for John, then aged just over seven and a half.[3]

Three of those children were to grow up to be notable book-collectors and patrons of learning, yet no one can reasonably argue that between 1395 and 1398 they were being educated above their station because their father already planned to seize the throne. It is no accident that the first king of England who has left us clear evidence of his literacy, since he could write in English, French, and Latin and even quote a useful civil law maxim—*Necessitas non habet legem*—was a baronial usurper.[4] He evidently believed in education; the winning of the Crown gave his children unusual opportunities of indulging their literary tastes. Duke Humphrey's enthusiasm for books is well known; at least two of his brothers shared it. A list of some 160 books belonging to Henry V is preserved and contains besides poetry and romances, historical, legal, and devotional works in Latin and French.[5] John of Bedford bought more than 800 books during his time as Regent of France.[6] It is all the more surprising that Richard II's deposition is usually represented—both on and off the stage—as that of a man of cultivated tastes by a ruthless man of action.

The family of the Dowager Countess of Suffolk comes clearly

[1] DL 28/1/5, f. 32; DL 28/1/6, f. 39 records the purchase of cords for a zither for him.

[2] DL 28/1/6, f. 39ʳ.

[3] DL 28/4/1.

[4] H. C. Maxwell Lyte, *The Great Seal* (1926), p. 130.

[5] This reference was not supplied in McFarlane's manuscript and the editors have been unable to trace it. P.R.O. E 101/335/71 is a list of 110 volumes in Henry V's possession which he had captured at Meaux in 1422 (printed K. B. McFarlane, *Lancastrian Kings and Lollard Knights* (Oxford, 1972), pp. 233–8) but it does not correspond to the description in the text above.

[6] Wylie, *History of England under Henry IV*, iv. 135; he bought 843 books from the French king's library.

before us for only one year, that beginning at Michaelmas 1416,
a year after she had lost husband and eldest son at Harfleur and
Agincourt. It then consisted of two younger sons Thomas and
Alexander (William, the new earl, had already left home), a
daughter Philippa, and two granddaughters Elizabeth and Isabel.
Thomas was at Oxford under his 'magister et tutor' Mr. Thomas
Rowebury; he was going into the Church and Richard Clifford,
Bishop of London, was providing for his education.[1] There is no
suggestion that Alexander also intended to become a clerk; it was
as a knight that he was slain at Jargeau in 1429. At Michaelmas
1416 he was at school with a married master, William Bury, at
Ipswich, returning to his grandmother at Wingfield at the holidays.[2] On 20 September 1417 he set out with an esquire and other
attendants 'ad scolatizandum' at Cambridge.[3] Philippa his sister
and her maid stayed with the Benedictine prioress at Bungay
throughout the year with occasional visits to Wingfield; nothing
is said about the way her time was spent.[3] Of the grandchildren
Isabel was aged between one and two and was boarded out with a
nurse at Fressingfield.[3] Her sister aged five began the year in the
charge of Christine Fastolf a nun at Bungay, but on 10 May 1417
she was moved to the house of Poor Clares at Bruisyard. Although
not yet six years old she then began her education, since 6s. 8d.
was given by her grandmother 'uni Fratri ibidem vocato le
President pro labore suo circa erudicionem dicte Elizabeth'.[3]
Lives were short in the fifteenth century (by 1422 both Isabel and
Elizabeth were dead);[4] no time could be wasted. In both the
families of which we have any detailed knowledge schooling
began early.

That Alexander de la Pole was not the only East Anglian
nobleman to be educated at a local school is proved by the
epitaph formerly on the tomb of Thomas, the second Howard
Duke of Norfolk. Born in 1443 'the seid Duke was in hys yong
age, ofter he had been a sufficient season at the gramer schole,
hencheman to Kyng Edward the iiij'.[5] Some fragmentary accounts

[1] B.M. Egerton Roll 8776, mm. 3, 4, 5.
[2] Ibid., m. 5; he was at Wingfield on 13 July.   [3] Ibid., m. 5.
[4] G.E.C. xii, pt. i, 442 n. *e*.   [5] Above, p. 42.

of a very much earlier date suggest that the practice was not new. In 1325 William Roach of Roche castle in far-away Pembrokeshire was paying John 'le scolmaister' of Haverford' 10s. a quarter 'pro salario suo'.[1]

I have said, I hope, enough to establish a reasonable case; but for fear that it may be thought that the late-medieval nobility was crammed in childhood and unhealthily studious in later life, let me end by referring you to the personal accounts of Edmund, the last Mortimer Earl of March. In the six months between September 1413 and March 1414 he lost in play—at cards, tables, raffle and chance, and cock-fighting as well as several other games I do not recognize—over £157 on forty-five separate occasions. How much he won during that period we do not know, for he pocketed his winnings but expected his treasurer to make good his losses. Only Lent seems to have brought this riot of gambling to a halt. There are also some suspiciously generous payments to a certain Alice at Poplar and some other signs of a fondness for low as well as high company.[2] He also played the harp, rather a lot to judge from the number of new harpstrings he needed. March was in his twenty-third year and historians seem to have been justified in reckoning him a lightweight. But from another of his accounts to the first half of 1415 it appears that he either gambled less or was a great deal luckier since he only lost 7s. 2d. at play. Instead he spent £20 on two missals, £12 on a breviary, and 8d. for a roll of seven psalms. Even at the height of the earlier gambling bout he could spare a pound for 'a book', though we are not told its name.[3] All the same he must have saved Henry V's court, where he spent at least part of his time, from being too straight-laced.

That some members of the late-medieval nobility wrote poetry and books of devotion does not of course mean that the class was wholly made up of cultivated and accomplished intellectuals. No doubt others preferred hunting to translating Cicero—or

[1] Longleat Mun. 3444.

[2] B.M. Egerton Roll 8746, mm. 1–5 (m. 2 15 Oct., 20s. to Alice; m. 3 18 Nov. 6s. 8d.).

[3] B.M. Egerton Roll 8747, m. 1, 28 Jan., 20 Feb., 23 Feb.; ibid. 8746, m. 2, 25 Oct. (10 Nov. 'pro uno ymagio sancti georgii xii li').

gaming, which even then seems to have been a favourite occupation of the peerage. But at least some were less unsophisticated. In any case such things were the relaxations of men whose positions—and tastes—imposed on them busy and varied lives. Those who distinguished themselves as book-collectors and patrons of literature and scholarship were among the most active of their class. Anyone less given to retirement from the traffic of this world than Henry of Grosmont it would be difficult to imagine. Both Salisbury and Suffolk were ambitious and hard working—if unsuccessful—politicians. There is no need to labour the point that these noble authors were deeply involved in the public life of their time. That was their main preoccupation and they brought to it minds that were far from untrained.[1]

[1] This paragraph is taken from a lecture of Nov. 1962.

7

Had Edward I a 'Policy' towards the Earls? [1]

THE stock of other medieval kings may rise or fall; that of Edward I remains firm and—despite some nagging doubts about 1297 and after—conspicuously high. Here Messrs. Richardson and Sayles agree with Stubbs. [2] Faced by so unlikely a coincidence of opinion the *advocatus diaboli* might well be reduced to silence and canonization seem inevitable. The king's contemporaries, however, were not so nearly of one mind. Thus the author of *Fleta* parted company absolutely from the *Song of Lewes*. This had described the noble Edward as treacherous and inconstant as well as leonine: 'when he is cornered he promises anything you like, but once he has escaped he goes back on his word. ... The ... lying by which he gains his end he calls prudence; ... whatever he wants he holds to be lawful and thinks that there are no legal bounds to his power.' [3] Instead of this compound of masterfulness and lack of scruple, *Fleta* preferred to see only the qualities of a merciful and impartial judge who governed his people 'with a never-failing righteousness' hardly short of divine. [4]

Both writers were of course prejudiced, the enemy as well as the flatterer. Do they cancel each other out? Or can the forebodings of 1264 be reconciled with the unqualified laudation of the early 1290s? It could, I suppose, be argued that Edward in maturity overcame the faults of his hot youth and achieved righteousness by a process of self-discipline. And if his behaviour in the decade that began in 1297 hardly bears this out, it could still be plausibly

[1] First published in *History*, 50 (1965), 145–59.
[2] Richardson and Sayles, *Governance of Mediaeval England*, i. 266: 'we need not doubt that Edward wished to rule well, after his fashion, all the subjects committed to his charge'. See also ibid. 393.
[3] *The Song of Lewes*, ed. C. L. Kingsford (Oxford, 1890), ll. 417–84.
[4] *Fleta*, ed. H. G. Richardson and G. O. Sayles (Selden Soc., 1955), ii. 1–2.

maintained that only when worn out by his exertions and harassed by the number and toughness of his problems did the ageing king lapse back into the high-handedness and faithlessness which had disfigured his youth. There can be little doubt that most historians would think even this compromise unduly hard on a great and sorely-tried ruler. *Fleta*, it would be said, was more or less right. The testimony of the *Song of Lewes*, even if sound when it was written, was that of a very short-sighted prophet.

If recently I have been compelled to ask myself whether the *Song* was perhaps a more reliable guide to an understanding of Edward I's outlook and methods than *Fleta's* more usually quoted panegyric, it was not because I wished to think any less well of him than, say, Sir Maurice Powicke. It was because I found it difficult to account for what happened to a number of comital families during his reign on the assumption that the king's intentions were honourable and could be made to accord with ordinary notions of justice and right as these were then understood. If such things occurred under the Lord Edward could he have been quite the man we have been taught to admire? The evidence for the events to which I refer is mostly quite accessible and, if only in a general way, well enough known. But because it has been approached from the king's side and usually with a desire to interpret it in his favour, it has not been fairly weighed since Tout took a preliminary look at it some seventy years ago. His paper, 'The Earldoms under Edward I', was a useful beginning.[1] Since 1894 much new evidence has been published and the subject badly needs to be considered afresh.

Between 1154 and 1265 the number of earls in England had steadily dwindled from some twenty-three to less than a dozen.[2] This was partly because marriage and the failure of direct heirs male sometimes brought two earldoms into the hands of one man: as when Lincoln was united with Chester in 1217, Gloucester with Hertford in 1225, and Essex with Hereford in 1236. Partly too because some earldoms were deliberately withheld from their

---

[1] *T.R.H.S.*, new ser., 8 (1894), 129–55.
[2] Ibid. See also G.E.C., esp. iv. 666 ff.; [R.] G. Ellis, *Earldoms in Fee* (1963), although not wholly to be relied upon, brings together much useful information.

lawful heirs or suppressed by royal acts which may have fallen within the strict bounds of law but were all the same manifestly inequitable. Thus was William de Forz in 1237 denied the earldom of Chester to which he had an unimpeachable hereditary claim, so that Henry III could annex it for the ultimate benefit of his own eldest son. Edward I owed his valuable palatinate to an act of royal injustice.[1] If in some of the transactions I am about to mention he strayed, *pace Fleta*, from the path of righteousness, he was no innovator in this form of wrong-doing, though that hardly rendered his conduct more tolerable to his victims. His admirers would think it the faintest possible praise to claim that the model here was his father.

Two reasons for the decline in the number of earls have been mentioned. A third may be rejected. Earldoms are often described somewhat vaguely as 'lapsing', 'escheating', or just 'becoming extinct'. These phrases seem to show as much ignorance of the vital statistics of the medieval English nobility as of the laws governing inheritance. The twenty-three earldoms in existence in 1154 were held to have been granted in fee—which meant that, failing the grantee's issue, his earldom like his lands could be inherited by his collaterals and their descendants, and that there were few if any limits to the remoteness of the common ancestor who established the kinship. Though one would scarcely think it to judge from the frequency with which escheats are alleged to have happened, landowners in the twelfth and thirteenth centuries rarely if ever died totally without heirs. Without issue, yes, often enough; but without any blood relations, virtually never. And the longer the Conqueror's followers were established in England the wider the network of their blood-ties spread. An escheat, that is to say, could not occur naturally; it had to be engineered. So it was by forfeiture and not for lack of heirs that, for example, Simon de Montfort's earldom of Leicester passed through the king's hands *en route* for those of Edmund of Lancaster after Evesham. In fact extinction by forfeiture was also extremely rare.

---

[1] R. Stewart Brown, 'The End of the Norman Earldom of Chester', *E.H.R.*, 35 (1920), 26–54; Powicke, *King Henry III and the Lord Edward*, i. 142 and ii. 788–9.

The Montforts were its sole victims in the Barons' Wars of Henry III's reign.

The only 'natural' way an earldom in fee could lapse was as the result of a plurality of coheirs; because while the family's lands were divisible—equally—between the coheirs, the earldom was not, and if the coheirs were sufficiently numerous no one of them might inherit enough land to support comital rank. It was probably for this reason that the earldom of Winchester disappeared in 1264,[1] and that there was no Earl of Pembroke for half a century after the death of the last of the great William Marshal's five childless sons. For Winchester the extinction was final, but Pembroke came slowly back to life for the benefit of the husband of one of Marshal's daughters' daughters.[2] Since heiresses, when married as the law required without disparagement, often married men of substance, their children or their more remote descendants were not uncommonly landed enough to support, and therefore to claim, and sometimes to receive, the rank. Where this was concerned primogeniture worked to some degree even among females.[3] An earldom's death from natural causes was therefore unusual. The heirs of the Quincy Earls of Winchester had exceptionally bad luck.

When such extinctions happened it was as a rule because it suited the king to murder an earldom or at least to refrain from

[1] An additional reason was that the eldest coheir was the mother of Robert Ferrers, Earl of Derby (G.E.C., xii, pt. ii. 753), for whose disinheritance see pp. 254–6 below.

[2] The notion that Edward I had not 'ventured to summon' William de Valence to Parliament as Earl of Pembroke before 1295 (G.E.C., x, App. L, 127) is a strange one. Henry III may not have 'ventured' though even that is doubtful; his son was made of braver stuff.

[3] The obvious exceptions were Sussex (Arundel) after 1243 and Pembroke after 1245. In each case the earldom and its lands had been acquired by marriage rather than by grant and it was the original patrimony of the family which was inherited by the eldest coheir, the Aubigny castle and manor of Buckenham by the Tattershalls of Tattershall (ibid. i. 239, n. (b)), the marshalcy by the Bigod Earls of Norfolk (ibid. ix. 590, n. (a)). Here, therefore, the *droit d'ainesse* was a disadvantage. Nevertheless, the decision to revive the earldom for the benefit of the issue of the junior coheirs to whom in one case the lordship, castle, and manor of Arundel, in the other the palatine county of Pembroke had descended, may have been sufficiently open to question to explain the ensuing long delays, until 1289 for Arundel, until 1295 for Pembroke.

the steps necessary to keep it alive. It was in the second half of the thirteenth century that royal behaviour—it would be premature to call it policy—increasingly led to this result. And since after 1154 the merest handful of new earldoms was created—and these mostly for cadet males of the royal house like Richard of Cornwall and Edmund of Lancaster—replacements failed to make up for the wastage. If there were fewer earls in 1307 than in 1154 this result had been achieved less by the accidents of birth and mortality than by royal acts of commission and omission which may or may not have amounted to a deliberate plan. The question, our question, is how far Edward I played a conscious game to that end. Had he a policy which aimed at restricting earldoms as opportunity arose to the blood royal?

Tout thought that the answer was yes: 'Edward I', he wrote 'pursued the policy of filling the great fiefs with members of the royal house and concentrating them in a few hands.'[1] But although this judgement is unequivocal and, to my mind, hard to traverse, it still leaves open the question whether the policy was adopted by Edward in his capacity as parent or as ruler. The king may not have been aware of the distinction; we must be. Was it merely a 'family settlement' or a scheme of government? To this question our most recent commentator returns a puzzling series of answers. 'Edward,' Powicke observes, 'apart from a watchful eye on Gilbert of Gloucester, does not seem to have pursued any political policy in his dealings with the baronage.' So far so good. But then his 'acquisitions were part of a general practice of land-jobbing. . . . Except in their complexity, they did not differ from the transactions of any pushing freeman in a rural manor.'[2] This ignores another respect in which they were exceptional: their size. Is there no point at which a difference in scale amounts to a difference of quality? Nor was it merely a matter of size or complexity. A king was endowed with powers that were peculiar to his crown; and when it came to litigation he was judge in his own case. The

---

[1] *The Earldoms under Edward I*, p. 140. Yet it is difficult to agree that this was the policy 'which Edward III was afterwards to carry out more systematically in his famous family settlement', ibid.

[2] F. M. Powicke, *Thirteenth Century, 1216–1307* (Oxford, 1953), pp. 518–19.

attempt to equate the kingdom of England with any 'rural manor'—the adjective is of course purely emotive—is too much like a piece of confident sleight of hand by a practised conjurer. Hey presto! and the Lord Edward's questionable activities as a land-jobber sink into insignificance, the fashionable pastime of his age and class, indeed of all freemen.

The same point is made rather differently, though no less adroitly, elsewhere. 'The king', wrote Powicke in *King Henry III and the Lord Edward*, 'took a hand as a landowner with capital to spare rather than as king.' The history of this 'remarkable series of transactions, whose significance has not yet been fully realized, ... might be described as studies in the fluidity of the land market'. The king thought of 'honours, wardship and marriage as everybody else thought of them—not as gross material things, but as the facts of social life subjected to the law and custom of the realm'.[1] We are at liberty to make what we can of that delphic utterance. All it says to me is that its author is reluctant to look the 'facts of social life', gross material things as they indeed were, calmly in the face; to do so might damage his fond image of a great king under whose leadership the community of the realm was all too briefly attained.

* * *

Others than the earls were involved in the 'remarkable series of transactions' to which Powicke refers. But some eight comital families—that is to say well over half their total number—found themselves obliged to submit, to a greater or less degree, to a course of slimming which left them actually or potentially worse off than it found them: Ferrers, Forz, Clare, Redvers, Lacy, Longsword, Bigod, and Bohun. It is a formidable list. The transactions were often complex, clandestine and prolonged, and all but the formal instruments by which they were ratified have generally been lost. Nevertheless, most of their stages can be traced in outline and at least the consequences they seemed to have been meant to achieve are reasonably clear. The details, though often illuminating, need not be elaborated here. Only a few of

[1] p. 704.

their more significant features can be touched on before we turn to consider how far they offer a solution to the problem of Edward's immediate aims and help to define his general attitude towards the greater baronage. In any case the genealogical evidence can and must be reduced to its barest bones.

Our first example is the best known. In his *Duchy of Lancaster* Sir Robert Somerville has lucidly analysed the sequence of events by which Robert Ferrers, Earl of Derby, notwithstanding the terms of the Dictum of Kenilworth, was in 1269 persuaded under duress to make over his great and ancient patrimony and with it his earldom to Henry III's younger son Edmund.[1] Kidnapped with the active connivance of the Lord Edward, by that date in any case the effective ruler of his father's kingdom, Ferrers was obliged to set his seal to a document whereby his lands were to be forfeited if he did not produce the impossible sum of £50,000 to ransom them within two months. Of course he defaulted and they were seized to become thenceforward a treasured part of the possessions of the house of Lancaster. In vain both Robert Ferrers and his son for the next thirty years petitioned King Edward for redress. The son, after joining the earls in 1297, went so far as to play into his despoiler's hands by an appeal to the Pope, an act of rashness that put him at the king's mercy.[2] Edmund of Lancaster retained what he had extorted with his brother's help from the captive earl. His descendant today still holds Tutbury. How naked Edward's partiality has left his modern admirers is demonstrated by Powicke's feeble attempt to extenuate it by putting the blame on Ferrers's 'lack of public spirit' as well as his 'lack of common sense', as if these defects excluded a rebel from the amnesty promised at Kenilworth.[3]

The truth is that Earl Robert had made a political miscalculation—as many another did during that time of troubles—but he

[1] Somerville, *Duchy of Lancaster*, i. 3–10, 16, and 19–20.

[2] For John Ferrers's prominence in 1297 see *Chronicles of Walter of Guisborough*, ed. H. Rothwell (C.S., 1957), p. 312, and *Registrum Roberti Winchelsey*, ed. R. Graham (Canterbury and York Soc., 2 vols., 1952–6), i. 204 and 206–8.

[3] Powicke, *Henry III*, ii. 523–6; though the story is instanced as 'a precious revelation of the legal trickery possible in his time' and vividly retold, Edward's share in these lawless happenings is passed over in silence.

was not punished in accordance with the law or by the judgement of his peers. He was illegally imprisoned by a fellow earl who was the king's son and compelled to sign away his birthright. He was the victim of Edmund's lawless greed and Edward's willingness to be his brother's accomplice in the act and his maintainer afterwards. The persistence with which he denied Earl Robert and his heir redress from 1269 to 1301 makes it difficult to regard Edward's part in this affair as a youthful escapade. The only evidence of immaturity lies in the crude high-handedness of the means. He assisted in the kidnapping of no more earls; in future less conspicuously illegal methods were to be employed—to achieve similar results.

The mandate which in 1301 forbade John Ferrers from prosecuting his case at the papal court was not his last injustice at the king's hands. This has attracted less notice from scholars, though since it involved the royal courts it is in some ways the most notable. How vindictively the English Justinian pursued the house of Ferrers for not accepting disinheritance in a Christian spirit was publicly displayed in 1307. At the Carlisle Parliament in that year a petition from John Ferrers accused Walter Langton the Treasurer of collusive maintenance in the king's court.[1] The merits of the original suit are difficult to decide and fortunately do not affect the issue. At Carlisle the king appointed the Earl of Lincoln to hear and determine the case. From the start Langton adopted an insolent policy of obstruction. Coming before the court in person he declared his inability to reply to the charges because Edward had ordered him to deal with the business of Parliament and this deprived him of time for other things, especially as he had been given insufficient notice to appear. There was point in Ferrers's retort that at least he had found time to be present. Obliged to answer Langton formally denied the accusation and both parties then elected to abide the verdict of a jury. Ferrers was well-counselled to point out that juries were empanelled by sheriffs and that sheriffs were subject to pressure from a treasurer before whom it was their duty to account. The court evidently did not regard

[1] *Select Cases in the Court of King's Bench under Edward I*, ed. G. O. Sayles (Selden Soc., 1939), vol. iii, pp. lvi–lvii and 175–8; *Rot. Parl.*, i. 191b.

the insinuation as frivolous since it ordered that the jurors should be specially chosen by the coroners of Northamptonshire. Notwithstanding these precautions Ferrers's suit was vain. On the first occasion that the jury was sworn the court was informed by privy seal that the king needed Langton near him and requested an adjournment. Then a month later when the case again came up for hearing a bill under the great seal arrived reciting that Langton stood in disfavour of many people because of his *im*partiality; as the king did not wish him to be vexed he granted him a pardon 'by special grace . . . even if the same bishop has acquired for himself the aforesaid manors and advowsons [i.e. those in dispute] in contravention of the said provision [Stat. Westm. II, c. 49] as is alleged against him, for the king is unwilling that the same bishop should henceforth be in any way inconvenienced or troubled . . . since punishment of this kind belongs to that king and to no other'. So Langton was acquitted and John Ferrers deprived of all redress. Well might men in 1307 recall the words of the *Song of Lewes*; in the very last year of his life Edward I was still inclined to prefer his own wishes to his own laws. The house of Ferrers had no reason to think of him as a lover of justice or a protector of the weak.

The circumstances leading to the seizure of the lands of the house of Forz after the death of Aveline, Countess of Aumale, in 1274 have attracted little notice.[1] Yet if anything they were still more to Edward's discredit, since unlike Robert Ferrers neither Aveline nor her heirs could be accused of any acts that had not been long pardoned or condoned. She was the childless child-wife of Edmund of Lancaster and her premature death robbed the king's brother of the enjoyment of all that she might have brought him. This time Edward bent the law to his own rather than to Edmund's advantage. It is usually stated that Aveline's death was followed by a simple escheat for lack of heirs.[2] The truth is that Aveline had heirs in plenty, albeit distant, among the numerous

[1] For what follows see A. Beanlands, 'The Claim of John de Eshton', *Miscellanea VII*, Thoresby Soc., xxiv (1919), 227–44, and *Early Yorkshire Charters*, vii (1949), ed. C. T. Clay, 23–7 and 222–8.

[2] e.g. Powicke, *Henry III*, ii. 710, and Tout, 'The Earldoms under Edward I', pp. 131 and 141.

descendants of her ancestor Stephen, Count of Aumale, who died about 1127.[1] Though innocent of any offence against the king they were cheated of their lawful inheritance by a trick. Edward, reluctant to surrender so valuable a prize, supported a bogus claimant with a forged pedigree, secured his recognition by a befuddled or intimidated jury and then bought him out of the lands he had obtained by false pretences for a minute fraction of their true value. John Eshton's willingness to accept £100 a year in tail in exchange for the great Aumale inheritance proves that he too was aware that the jury had been misled.[2] This highly successful operation was carried through between 1276 and 1281 when the king was middle-aged; there was no question here of rash youth or hard senility. Aveline's principal heir, Philip Wivelsby, accepted defeat and is heard of no more; he lacked the means to fight. But some Lucy cousins continued to press their well-founded claim to the lordship of Skipton until far into the reign of Edward II. Unlike Wivelsby they were already rich and influential enough in their own right to be troublesome. Edward I was deaf to their suit, but his more soft-hearted and improvident son bought them off in 1323 with the castle and honour of Cockermouth. The rich land of Holderness as well as much else were firmly and illegally denied to the lineal descendants of the ancient lords of Aumale. Skipton was granted to the Cliffords in 1310.

The next to be subjected to pressure was the mother of Aveline, Isabel de Redvers the Dowager of Aumale and in her own right Countess of Devon and Lady of Wight. Left a widow in 1260 she had lived to see her five children predecease her before they were out of their teens. By striking at once while the widowed countess was still freshly mourning the death of her last child, Edward, it has been suggested, hoped to cajole her into selling the reversion of her whole inheritance for 20,000 marks. The price was considerably below the market value. The countess agreed provisionally

[1] Failing Philip Wivelsby (see below), these seem in 1274 to have been the four sisters of Peter Bruce (ob. 1272). All were married, the eldest to Sir Walter Fauconberg, and were to leave issue. For Agnes Fauconberg see G.E.C., v. 268–9.

[2] In this I venture to disagree with Sir Charles Clay, op. cit., p. 25, n. 4. Eshton's behaviour would have been idiotic if he really believed himself to be the heir.

in January 1276 (fourteen months after Aveline's death) and gave a receipt for part of the purchase price. Nevertheless, the scheme fell through, perhaps because when she got over her grief the bargain did not seem good enough for her. Her heir presumptive Hugh Courtenay of Okehampton may also have protested effectively against his disinheritance.[1] Edward raised the matter again more than once, but it was not until Isabel was actually dying that she consented to part with the reversions of the lordship of the Isle of Wight and of the three manors of Honiton, Lambeth, and Christchurch to the king for 6,000 marks. Less than twenty-four hours before her death, when she was lying in her manor of Stockwell, the king's emissaries, including our old friend Walter Langton, hurried to her bedside, drafted a charter in her name and, it was alleged when the proceedings later came under challenge, obtained her free consent to its terms. This was on 9 November 1293; she died before another day had dawned. Meanwhile her cousin Hugh Courtenay had also died and it was his son and namesake who was now her lawful heir. Since he was a minor of seventeen years whose person and lands were in the king's wardship, he was incapable of causing trouble at the time of this critical transfer. On 11 November, with suspicious promptness, the royal Treasury paid the 6,000 marks to Isabel's executors. Their receipt, wrongly dated 4 November (perhaps because it had been prepared in readiness), only survives in a copy.[2] When all the circumstances are considered, I am afraid that I cannot share the confidence expressed by Mr. Denholm-Young and echoed by Powicke that nothing about this deathbed conveyance was amiss.[3] Naturally when Hugh Courtenay inherited the residue of Isabel's lands in 1297—he does not seem to have been a beneficiary under her will—he was not

[1] The facts are not in dispute. The interpretation here adopted is Powicke's (*Henry III*, pp. 707–9).

[2] *Red Book of the Exchequer*, ed. H. Hall (R.S., 1896), iii. 1022, where it follows the record of Hugh Courtenay the younger's subsequent proceedings.

[3] N. Denholm-Young, 'Edward I and the Sale of the Isle of Wight', *E.H.R.*, 44 (1929), 433–8; Powicke, *Henry III*, pp. 710–11 and n. The latter's comment ('After all Hugh de Courtenay did not do so badly') is characteristic of his indulgence towards Edward I's foibles.

convinced either and went on vainly urging his claim to the lost island and the three manors from 1298 until long after Edward I's death. But whatever he—and we—might suspect, he had only the thinnest case at law and indeed even had to wait until 1335 before a juster ruler allowed him Isabel's earldom. Nor did he feel that he could pin a charge of either undue pressure or straight forgery upon the king and those who claimed to have witnessed the Stockwell agreement. We may allow ourselves more freedom. If Edward's was a legal action, which I for one doubt, it was an unfriendly, perhaps an impolitic, one; and Isabel's was scarcely a friendlier one. By a matter of hours Hugh Courtenay had been deprived, if not cheated, of his reasonable expectations, by the will of an old woman in the article of death who may well not have known what was happening. For Edward this *coup* had been possible because Isabel had no surviving descendants to prevent her from yielding to the king's urgent offers. At best she had been willing to deprive someone who was only a collateral heir, and a fairly remote one at that—Hugh was her second cousin once removed—of at least a part, a very valuable part, of the inheritance when it was made worth her while. If so she consented to a very bad bargain.[1]

The collateral heir presumptive was to be the chosen victim of Edward I's calculations in the case of each of the five other earldoms on which he revealed that he had designs. Three of his covenants are familiar enough though too little attention has been paid to their details and to some of their common features. I refer of course to the Clare 'entail' of 1290, the Bigod 'entail' of April 1302, and the Bohun 'entail' of the following November. All that we need concern ourselves with here are those clauses which may offer some pointers to the king's ultimate objectives, if he had any.

Now the fact that two of these three settlements coincided with the marriage of the earl in question to one of Edward's daughters

[1] Our only source of evidence is the testimony of the king's witnesses (and servants) put up to resist Hugh's claim in 1298. If Isabel in fact did often say that Hugh was so remote a kinsman that she could have freely married him she was mistaken on a point familiar enough to members of her class. There is no reason for thinking that she ever said anything of the sort.

has given rise to the theory that their purpose was to secure earldoms for his grandsons yet unborn. To fix one's gaze on what
might, always provided that there were grandsons, happen a
generation later, when Edward was likely to be safe in his grave,
is to overlook the more immediate advantages that the king may
have had in view. After all, if he were only thinking so far ahead,
a scheme which conferred on two great comital families the
additional distinction of royal descent was hardly likely to be
counted an unmixed blessing to the Angevin line. And potentially
more than royal descent. In 1290 Edward had lost his wife and
three of his four sons. Only Edward of Carnarvon and one childless daughter stood before Gloucester's bride, Joan of Acre, in the
succession to the crown as this was laid down in solemn council a
month before the marriage.[1]

The fact that Edward settled the descent of his kingdom on his
daughters in preference to his brother in the spring of 1290 is
unlikely to have been fortuitous. It may have been the bait that
finally induced Gilbert of Clare to accept an apparently portionless
royal lady as his second wife. He was more than old enough to
have been her father, forty-seven to her eighteen, so that the
union may have had other attractions for him. What did the
marriage-settlement secure for her? A jointure in all her husband's
lands instead of the usual dower-third, which meant that she
would enjoy them for life if, as seemed probable, she long survived him. More important, his children by a previous wife were
disinherited in favour of those Joan might bear him. And finally,
if the marriage proved childless, twenty-five manors worth 2,000
marks per annum were to be detached from the Clare inheritance
as an outright present in perpetuity to Joan, her heirs and assigns in
fee simple. Gloucester, that is to say, ran the risk of impoverish-
ing the house of Clare after his death unless he left surviving
issue by this late second union.[2] His gamble was successful. Before
he died five years later his wife had given birth to a son and three
healthy daughters. But if it were a gamble for him, Joan was

---

[1] *Foedera* (Record edn.), i, pt. ii. 742; Powicke, *Henry III*, pp. 733 and 788–90.
[2] *Calendar of Charter Rolls*, ii. 350–1; C.F.R., i. 274–5. For the daughters of the
earl's first marriage see G.E.C., v. 707, n. (j).

bound, provided she did not predecease him, to win either way. She would possess the whole Clare inheritance until her death and whatever happened her issue were bound to enjoy all or a considerable fraction of it, whether they were the earl's offspring or another's. And so it turned out, except that she infuriated her father by sharing her good fortune with a penniless young man of her own choice in a second marriage-bed. The chief beneficiary of the settlement of 1290 was Ralph Monthermer, Earl of Gloucester *jure uxoris* as long as Joan lived.

This may explain why her younger sister Elizabeth was allowed less freedom when she was married to Humphrey, Earl of Hereford and Essex, in 1302. Her husband surrendered all his estates, his two earldoms, and the office of Constable to his royal father-in-law and received them back entailed upon himself and his wife jointly with remainder to the heirs of his body whether by her or another. If Elizabeth survived him without issue and followed her sister's lead by plunging into a *mésalliance* she would not be able to dispose freely of any part of the Bohun inheritance. That pleasure Edward reserved for himself. On her death the constableship and all the lands in south-east England that had belonged to her husband's earldom of Essex were to pass into the possession of the king and his heirs quit of the heirs of Bohun.[1] Hereford unlike Gloucester was only six years his wife's senior and she predeceased him after mothering ten surviving children in less than fourteen years. It is not clear what Humphrey hoped to gain from his marriage in return for the risk of depriving his brother and heir presumptive of half their enormous patrimony. On the other hand, it is evident that the king provided handsomely and inexpensively for a daughter and had an outside chance, if the bridegroom died or the marriage proved sterile—things that often happened—of a valuable windfall for himself. The king's main purpose in making such arrangeentms may have been to endow his daughters well at little or no cost to himself, but he was obviously also thinking how he and his children might benefit at the expense of his sons-in-law's brothers, cousins and other

---

[1] *Cal. Charter Rolls*, iii. 33; *C.P.R., 1301–1307*, p. 96; *C.F.R.*, i. 458–9. See also Holmes, *Estates of the Higher Nobility*, pp. 19–20.

collateral kinsmen. Neither Clare nor Bohun obliged him by dying childless. That is precisely what Bigod did and was intended to do.

Roger Bigod, Earl of Norfolk, was sixty years old and, though twice married, without issue when in the spring of 1302 he surrendered all his lands, his earldom, and his Marshal's office to the king and received them back entailed upon the heirs of his body. Should he die childless all were to revert to the Crown. To encourage him to pauperize an ancient and illustrious comital family, Edward granted him, for life only, additional lands worth £1,000 a year.[1] According to the chronicler Walter of Guisborough there was another inducement. Having to raise an army to withstand the king over the confirmation of the charters in 1297 he had borrowed money from his only brother, a well-beneficed ecclesiastic. By 1302 he was being dunned for the money. It proved useless for him to point out that his creditor need have no anxiety: when Earl Roger died his brother would inherit everything. The Revd. John Bigod was an impatient and choleric man. He answered that he did not care to wait; what he wanted was the payment of what he was owed. It was, says Guisborough, to spite him that the earl came to terms with the king.[2] To maintain, as Powicke does, that he therefore acted 'with the consent of his brother and heir' is to distort the whole story. In any case John Bigod, a celibate, was the next-of-kin only in a temporary sense. The ultimate heir was their cousin, Sir John Bigod of Stockton and Settrington, whose descendants (still prominent in the sixteenth century) would but for the surrender of 1302 have enjoyed the earldom and its lands, valued at £4,000 per annum, before many years had passed. It was at their expense that Edward I acquired another great appanage for his own issue.[3]

---

[1] *Cal. Charter Rolls*, iii. 25–6; *C.C.R.*, *1296–1302*, pp. 528–9 and 581; *C.P.R.*, *1301–1307*, pp. 29–31, 223, and 261; *Foedera* (Record edn.), i, pt. ii. 140.

[2] *Chronicle*, ed. Rothwell, p. 352.

[3] Settrington was their consolation-prize (*C.P.R.*, *1301–1307*, p. 30). They were also granted free warren on their demesnes there and elsewhere by Edward I on 10 July 1302 (*Cal. Charter Rolls*, iii. 25; see also ibid. 34). For some of the family's later history see A. G. Dickens, *Lollards and Protestants in the Diocese of York, 1509–1558* (1959), pp. 53 ff.

The Lacy earldom of Lincoln and the Longsword earldom of Salisbury had been united in 1268 by the marriage of Henry Lacy with Margaret, heiress of Longsword. Of their children only one, Alice, was still living in 1292 when she was betrothed to the king's nephew, Thomas of Lancaster. The marriage was celebrated in the autumn of 1294. On 28 October, immediately after the wedding, the bride's parents surrendered the greater part of their two inheritances to the king and were regranted only a life interest in them. Part was settled in tail upon Thomas and his wife Alice, part on Thomas's father, Edmund of Lancaster, in fee simple and part on the same Edmund in tail. This meant that if Alice Lacy had no children, the Lacy and Longsword estates would never revert to her lawful heirs. The descendants of the king's brother or, failing them, the king and his descendants would enjoy them though these had neither Lacy nor Longsword ancestry. It is again difficult to understand why Earl Henry and the Countess Margaret were willing to be parties to this arrangement, though perhaps it was not too high a price to pay for so advantageous a match for their only child. Once more the collateral heirs to their two earldoms were cut off from their legitimate expectations.[1] And this time, as events turned out, the settlements of 1294 alone barred their inheritance. For Alice Lacy, outliving three husbands, died childless in 1348. Her heirs had no right to her estates. The house of Lancaster instead continued in possession of Bolingbroke, Pontefract, Halton, Clitheroe, and her many other lordships and scattered manors.[2] The entails of 1294, like Bigod's of 1302, eventually brought advantage only to the king's kin.

★   ★   ★

And it is surely hard to avoid the conclusion that that was Edward I's primary object. By the settlements that accompanied their marriages, his daughters Joan and Elizabeth were secured in life occupation, should their husbands die before them, of the

---

[1] *Cal. Charter Rolls*, ii. 427 and 455–6; Somerville, *Duchy of Lancaster*, pp. 18–23, 26–7, and 33–5; Ellis, *Earldoms in Fee*, pp. 161–2.

[2] I have not complicated the story by any reference here to the vicissitudes of these properties as a result of Alice's desertion of her husband and Thomas's execution, since all came right for Henry of Grosmont in the end.

lands of two of the richest and most powerful families in the
kingdom—at no cost to their father. If their unions were childless
and they survived their husbands, the families with which they
had been allied were to be deprived for ever of a considerable
fraction of their landed wealth for the benefit of the king and
his offspring. The Lacies and the Longswords took an even greater
risk—the loss of nearly the whole of both inheritances to Edmund
of Lancaster's issue (or failing it the king's)—if their heiress
Alice did not present her husband with a child. And Edmund of
Lancaster's issue had already been endowed in princely fashion
at the expense of Montfort and Ferrers.

But Edward I did not seek advantage only for his own and his
brother's children; he also enriched himself: the great lordships of
Holderness and Skipton, the Isle of Wight, the many manors of
the Bigods clustering thickly in East Anglia remained in his
hands. His eldest son had been more than adequately provided
for during the king's lifetime with Chester and the principality
of Wales. It is likely that Edward was also intent on accumulating
a reserve to meet probable calls in favour of his younger sons.
As we have seen, all but one of the boys borne to him by his first
wife Eleanor died in infancy, but the king's earlier dealings with
Isabel de Redvers and the acquisition of the Forz inheritance in
the 1270s were almost certainly prompted by the prospective
needs of his then rapidly growing family. His second marriage in
1299 with Margaret of France imposed on him specific commit-
ments towards her future issue. He soon had three children by her,
Thomas of Brotherton, Edmund of Woodstock, and a short-
lived Eleanor. It was in discharge of his undertakings to his
brother-in-law Philip IV of France that on 31 August 1306 he
bound himself and his heir to assign lands worth 10,000 marks a
year to Thomas, lands worth 7,000 marks a year to Edmund, and
to give Eleanor a portion of 10,000 marks and a *trousseau* valued
at 5,000 marks.[1] The Bigod inheritance, which had just fallen in
and was estimated to produce 6,000 marks per annum, was to
form the nucleus of Thomas's share.

The size of these proposed endowments gives us the measure of

---

[1] *C.P.R.*, *1301–1307*, p. 460; ibid. *1307–1313*, p. 272; *Cal. Charter Rolls*, iv. 2–5.

Edward's intention to raise his sons and their descendants, as he had raised his brother, in landed wealth and therefore territorial power above the level of even the greatest comital families. The Bigod Earls of Norfolk had held one of the richest earldoms in England, but their many castles and revenues were insufficient for the king's second son; he was to have two-thirds as much again.[1] The lavish generosity—mostly at other people's expense—which had concentrated the possessions of three earldoms in the hands of Edmund of Lancaster and five in those of his son was to be repeated in favour of the royal cadets of the next generation; there is every reason to suppose that brides like Aveline de Forz and Alice Lacy would have been found for Thomas of Brotherton and Edmund of Woodstock had their father survived long enough to give them in marriage. Edward II not only partly dishonoured the pledge made to his half-brothers in 1306 but chose to be more generous to Piers Gaveston and the Despensers than to his own flesh and blood. The earldom of Cornwall which he conferred on Gaveston was another of his father's acquisitions, though not one that had had to be engineered. It is often said that Edmund of Cornwall's earldom escheated to the Crown in 1300 for lack of heirs;[2] in fact Edward I was his cousin's heir, so that Cornwall came to him by inheritance rather than by escheat, as the inquisitions confirm.[3] It and the lands of Forz and Bigod would have been enough for Queen Margaret's sons. It was characteristic of Edward II's disregard of his father's wishes that it was immediately squandered on the worthless Piers.

Edward I's concern for the aggrandizement of his kin was so consistently displayed that it perhaps earns the right to be called a policy. Yet even though its pursuit inevitably affected the relations between the Crown and the greater baronage in more ways than one, both positively and negatively, it does not of necessity follow that the king willed the later consequences of his acts. By 1307 most of the existing earldoms were held by his near

---

[1] The two earldoms united in the ownership of the house of Clare were together worth over £6,000 p.a. (Holmes, *Estates of the Higher Nobility*, p. 36).

[2] e.g. Tout, 'The Earldoms under Edward I', p. 139.

[3] *C.I.P.M.*, iii. no. 604.

kinsmen. That does not mean that Edward need have believed that it was in the interests of the monarchy that the earls should be closely related to their sovereign; or that he saw either advantage or disadvantage in such an event. It seems to me more likely that he did not care; and I should be prepared to argue that he was right not to care. To conclude that 'the family settlement of Edward I explains the reign of Edward II' is to take no account of the major factor: the character of Edward II himself.[1] Clumsily worded though the judgement may be, Powicke's claim that Edward I 'does not seem to have pursued any political policy in his dealings with the baronage' is almost certainly right. The king was merely seeking to do the best he could for the family of which he was the head, and failing that for himself.

On the other hand, there can be little doubt that Powicke has allowed himself to play down the unscrupulousness with which Edward pursued his dynastic aims—and still more the justice of the resentment aroused by some of the uglier strokes by which he gained his ends. The king, as the author of *Fleta* would have been the first to agree, was not only a maker of laws but also the maintainer of the rights of the weak. It was his primary duty to do justice and to see that justice was done. If 'any pushing freeman in a rural manor' used force or fraud to gain an advantage over a neighbour, he might find himself brought to answer in the king's court. Edward, we know, did not keep within the bounds of his own law and there was no one to bring him to do justice to those whom he had wronged. How much this wilful abuse of his power contributed to the strains and stresses of his last years it is hard to say. It must, however, contribute to the historian's assessment of his greatness as a king.

The comital families were his principal targets, mainly no doubt because theirs were the most desirable prizes. Is there any ground for believing that he disliked earldoms as such or wished to confine them to members of the royal house? Well, there is the fact that he created no new earldoms for the heads of the rising

---

[1] Tout, 'The Earldoms under Edward I', pp. 154–5. Tout's later work on the reign of Edward II gives ground for thinking that he would have revised the early view quoted here.

families who served him. It is another count against him that lifelong and devoted service was too often inadequately rewarded. His lordship was exacting rather than 'good'. There is also the fact that he omitted to recognize Hugh Courtenay as Earl of Devon and the less certain but probable fact that he was unwilling to allow his own father's half-brother William de Valence the earldom of Pembroke, the palatine county of which William had acquired by marriage. Against this must be set the acceptance of the Beauchamp heir as Earl of Warwick in 1268 and of the Fitzalan heir as Earl of Arundel in or soon after 1289. In both cases it was passive acceptance rather than active initiative.[1] If the evidence is to that extent indecisive, on balance it does appear that Edward shared the reluctance of his four immediate predecessors to make a new earldom or to go far out of his way to preserve an old one—except for princes of the blood royal. From the death of Stephen to the accession of Edward III no serious attempt was made to replenish from below the thinning ranks of the earls. Even the prodigal Edward II here showed some restraint—Piers Gaveston, the elder Despenser, and Andrew Hartley were the main beneficiaries—though the change of practice can be traced to his reign. Whether from conscious policy or sheer inertia Edward I's attitude hardly betrays enthusiasm to increase the number of his natural companions. The truth is that he showed no great belief in the virtues of largesse; hence some of his popularity with bourgeois historians—until they discovered the makeshift nature of his financial devices. No Gladstone he! Since a not too discriminating largesse was politic as well as gentlemanly, it is perhaps not difficult to understand why Edward III and his successors acted differently. Edward I preferred masterfulness to the arts of political management. In that sense he belonged less to the future than to the past.

[1] As was his willingness to recognize his daughter Joan's second husband as Earl of Gloucester.

8

The English Nobility in the Later Middle Ages[1]

THAT the period between the accession of Edward I and the death of Henry VII was a significant one in the history of the English nobility few would wish to deny. Often no doubt assent is given for the wrong reasons, the chief and most popular being that its end saw the old, the 'feudal', nobility destroy itself by its excesses to make way for something new and less prone to disrupt the kingdom: the Tudor 'nobility of service'. It would be hard to invent a more misleading summary. The period could with greater truth be described as one in which a nobility of a type peculiar to England, having little in common with the French *noblesse* and German *Adel*, first came into existence and established itself in that position of dominance in English society which it was to retain and exploit for several centuries to come. The essential changes had already occurred by 1485; they had hardly begun in 1300. In the reign of Edward I a dozen earls, the dwindling survivors of a seemingly obsolescent baronage, shared their nobility with an undifferentiated mass of some three thousand landowners, each of whose holdings were said to be worth £20 a year or over.[2] By the beginning of the sixteenth century a small and graded upper class of 'lords' numbering between fifty and sixty had emerged in possession of rank and privileges which

[1] A paper read to the 12th International Historical Congress at Vienna and badly printed, 12ᵉ *Congrès International des Sciences Historiques*, i. *Grands Thèmes* (1965), pp. 337–45.

[2] N. Denholm-Young, *Collected Papers on Mediaeval Subjects* (Oxford, 1946), pp. 56–67. The tax-gatherers of 1436 found 2,250 (H. L. Gray, 'Incomes from Land in England in 1436', *E.H.R.*, 49 (1934), 607–39). Allowing for successful evasion it does not seem that the number of persons owning at least twenty librates of land had markedly decreased by that date.

marked them off from lesser men. The interval had been occupied by the gradual processes of exclusion, definition, and stratification.

In these processes 'feudal' notions wielded no decisive influence. The peerage, to which the enjoyment of nobility was ultimately restricted, did not derive in unbroken descent as a body from the *maiores barones* of Magna Carta. As individuals some of its number did and others did not. The baronial relief, twenty times that owed by the tenant of a knight's fee, bestowed on those who paid it no right to a place in the new hierarchy above their knightly fellows. One has only to set the lists compiled by Dr. Sanders beside the surviving names of those summoned to parliaments and councils to realize how little even Edward I felt obliged or disposed to limit his choice to members of this 'honorial baronage'.[1] His immediate successors were no less unhampered. Landed wealth, however acquired and of whomsoever held, and a capacity to serve provided the main grounds for selection. Had it not been for a revived use of the term 'baron' to describe anyone who belonged to the lowest rank of the peerage there would have been less temptation to identify him with his tenurial name-sake. The resulting confusion has bedevilled the study of origins ever since.[2]

The possession of a certain amount of landed wealth—though that amount was never defined—remained throughout our period a necessary qualification for a personal writ of summons from the king. Without it no man, however illustrious his ancestry, would long continue to receive one. The degree of ease with which land was transferable and any changes in the rules governing its descent were therefore bound to affect the composition and size of the emergent peerage. In late thirteenth-century England alienation *inter vivos* was in practice unrestricted, provided the tenement was not held in chief. Where the king was the immediate lord a royal licence was advisable and might have to be bought. On the other

---

[1] I. J. Sanders, *English Baronies, a Study of their Origin and Descent, 1086–1327* (Oxford, 1960); *Reports touching the Dignity of a Peer*, iii. 36–172.

[2] A further minor source of confusion derives from the fact that the heads of the families of Stafford (of Stafford), Greystoke, and Hilton (or Helton) were from early times distinguished by the title of 'baron' (G.E.C., vi. 188; vii. 19; xii, pt. i. 172–3). No 'feudal barony' of Helton seems to be recorded.

hand, a fief could not be left to another by will. The heir or heirs had a legal right to whatever the ancestor held on the day when he was alive and dead. With minor exceptions the law governing the inheritance of a fief was simple and unambiguous: primogeniture among males, equal shares between females, a son always preferred to a daughter, a daughter to a brother or other collateral. For the fief to retain its coherence it was thus essential that its proprietor, if not childless, should have at least one son or, failing sons, not more than one daughter. Those were difficult conditions to fulfil.

But not only the integrity of the fief was at stake. Even if that were not endangered by a plurality of daughters, lack of male issue still involved the passage of the inheritance out of the family's possession in consequence of an only daughter's marriage. Nor were these remote perils. In every twenty-five-year period throughout the fourteenth and fifteenth centuries, for example, a quarter of the noblest families in the kingdom were on average faced by the sad prospect of losing their inheritances to others because their heirs were women.[1] It is not surprising that means were sought to enable those threatened to avoid such a disaster. A device suitable to their purpose was ready to hand in the conditional gift. If a man surrendered his fief either to the king, to his immediate lord, or to a group of his friends he could receive it back on terms different from those governing ordinary inheritance. He exchanged, as we should say, a 'fee simple' for an 'estate tail'.

Estates tail could be of several kinds and were certainly not invented for a single reason. They had, or came to have, one characteristic in common: they were inalienable, their tenancy being for life only. This brought with it one great compensating advantage, namely that all land held by a conditional gift was exempt, as that in fee simple was not, from forfeiture for treason.[2]

---

[1] The data for this calculation are derived from the fates of those families one or more of whose members received a writ of summons at any time between 1301 and 1500 (G.E.C. *passim*). See the tables above, pp. 173–6. (The average for comital families was nearer 30 per cent in every quarter century; cf. p. 168 and n. 2 above.)

[2] Owners were deprived of this benefit by the acts of attainder passed in the

There is little justification for supposing that estates tail were designed to meet this particular need, often as they were to benefit the families of traitors both in the fourteenth century and in the fifteenth.

Many early examples of this procedure did no more than confine the inheritance of the fief to the issue of the landowner on whose behalf the settlement was made. Such an estate is said to have been held in 'fee tail'. Its effect here was merely to annihilate the rights of all collaterals to inherit if and when the issue became extinct. Whether that was its sole purpose is less certain. It undoubtedly was the main one in the case of those estates in fee tail created for Edward I's sons-in-law, brother, and nephews. But when in 1290 Simon Montagu surrendered his lands to the king and received them back entailed on the issue, male or female, of his sons William and Simon, it is more difficult to guess the motive for his action.[1] Clearly it was not to avoid the possibility of inheritance by a female—a possibility which was realized in 1428 when Alice Montagu carried her ancestor's entailed lands to her Nevill husband in the lifetime of her paternal uncle.[2]

The variety of estates tail which became increasingly popular during the fourteenth century either excluded women from the power to inherit altogether or postponed their admissibility until all lineal male descendants were extinct. This was an estate in 'tail male', the instrument creating it being often referred to without qualification as an 'entail'. An early example of such a limited entail was that licensed in 1321 by which the inheritance of Maud Burnell was settled upon herself and her second husband jointly and thereafter upon their male issue, with remainder to her right heirs, namely her eldest son by a previous marriage or his

second half of our period, but many of these were repealed. [Professor J. G. Bellamy in *The Law of Treason in England in the Later Middle Ages* (Cambridge, 1970), pp. 115, 191–5, 236, has shown that, while this exemption from forfeiture was 'the normal common law doctrine' under Edward III and was also followed by the Lords Appellant, Richard II in 1397 made traitors' lands held in fee tail forfeit and his successors often seized such lands as forfeited by rebellion, provided the rebels 'had not come under the common law by appearance in court or by outlawry'. Cf. p. 269, n. 3 above. J. P. C., J. C.]

[1] *Calendar of Charter Rolls*, ii. 346.
[2] C.F.R. xv. 262–3; G.E.C., xi. 395 and App., 127–30.

descendants.[1] The Beauchamp entails of the mid-century gave the heir male preference over any female.[2] Those of the contemporary Fitzalan Earl of Arundel were a mixture of tail male and fee tail with the result that his inheritances had to be divided between his granddaughters and his great-grandson in 1415.[3] By the 1360s so much concern for the interests of females was old-fashioned. The preference for the heir male was hardening into habit. This left deep marks upon the subsequent fortunes of the greater land-owning families and helped to shape the mould in which the English nobility in its still unformed, almost liquid, condition was to set firm.

The consequences were soon visible upon the members of the oldest species of the genus, the earls.[4] In 1272 all the existing earldoms were earldoms 'in fee'.[5] Their descent, that is to say, was the same as that of land held in fee simple except that they were impartible. They could be surrendered to the king and by his permission they could be transferred to another along with the lands which constituted their endowment.[6] Edward I's reign saw at least three (Norfolk, Hereford, and Essex) and probably three more (Gloucester, Hertford, and Lincoln) converted by surrender from fee to fee tail to the detriment of collateral heirs.[7] Other

---

[1] See above, p. 67, n. 1.

[2] Holmes, *Estates of the Higher Nobility*, pp. 48–9 and the authorities there cited.

[3] Ibid., pp. 50–1. The entries cited by Dr. Holmes from *C.P.R. 1364–1367*, pp. 198, 237–8, and 239 are evidently imperfectly calendared and do not distinguish between fee tail and tail male. A clearer picture is given in *C.F.R.*, xiv. 162–7. The granddaughter shared a large part of the former Warenne lands.

[4] McFarlane wrote a, so far unpublished, paper on 'The Descent of English Earldoms in the Fourteenth Century'. It is hoped to publish it shortly. Cf. also 'Had Edward I a "Policy" towards the Earls?', above, pp. 248–67.

[5] But no specific grant of the earldoms of Lancaster and Leicester seems to have been made to Henry III's younger son Edmund. That they were regarded as earldoms in fee is highly probable.

[6] The earldom of Lincoln had been so transferred in 1230–2 (G.E.C. vii. 675–9). Between 1369 and 1375 John Hastings, Earl of Pembroke, hoped to arrange such a transfer if he died without issue. It looks as if he had obtained Edward III's encouragement, but the birth of his son postponed the matter until 1389 by which time Edward III was dead and Richard II unfavourable (*C.P.R. 1367–1370*, p. 223; *Catalogue of Ancient Deeds*, iii, nos. A 4874 and 4888–90; *C.C.R. 1374–1377*, pp. 286–8).

[7] The second trio are only doubtful because the estates were surrendered but

surrenders and regrants extinguished the ancient earldoms in fee of Oxford, Warwick, Arundel, and Surrey before the end of the fourteenth century. In each case the regrant limited the descent to heirs male.[1] But without such a limitation the earldom of Warwick had already passed to a younger son in preference to the daughter of a dead eldest son in 1369. This was because Thomas Beauchamp, the earl from 1330 to 1369, had settled his lands on his male issue; the descent of the lands governed the descent of the earldom.[2]

The same tendency to prefer the heir male and to interpret this in the narrow sense of lineal male issue can be seen in the terms of new creations. The last time that an earldom in fee was created was at the coronation of Richard II. Thenceforward, save for special remainders, new earls were granted their status in tail male.[3] And when it pleased kings to invent other grades such as dukedoms (1337), marquessates (1385), baronies by patent (1387), and viscounties (1440), creations in fee accorded so little with the outlook and practice of the times that nothing wider than tail male was thought suitable. To attribute those limitations exclusively to 'the crown's objection to the existence of dignities held in fee' is to mistake for royal policy what was by then the prejudice of a class, a prejudice which kings naturally shared.[4] As more and more of the great landowners settled their inheritances in tail male, it was only reasonable that dignity and estates should descend together. There was no doubt which exercised the stronger pull. The growth of tail male, reinforced anon by even stricter forms of settlement, was an essential stage in the evolution of a body of

not the earldom *eo nomine*. Contemporaries could hardly have conceived of an earldom divorced from the inheritance.

[1] G.E.C. x. 234 and App. E; *Rot. Parl.* iii. 435–6.

[2] The fact that it was to do so again in 1446 and 1449–50, in these cases in defiance of the terms of the regrant to heirs male only in 1399, weakens the force of the argument that the granddaughter was passed over because she was a nun (G.E.C. xii, pt. ii. 375, n. *c*). Her profession was more a consequence than a cause of her exclusion from the earldom. The notion of a landless countess was to contemporaries absurd.

[3] The question whether Edward III's creations were in fee, fee tail, or tail male (ibid. iv, App. 4 and x, App. k) must be left to be treated on another occasion.

[4] Ibid. iv. 679.

hereditary peers. The tradition that there was no primogeniture among females made their exclusion save in the last resort desirable. The fact that they could be more easily victimized by overlords and husbands, still more the fact that they placed the inheritance at the disposal of other men when there might still be males of the family alive to enjoy it, caused heiresses to be as far as possible eliminated. By 1509 the higher grades of the peerage were occupied by noblemen whose rank was theirs only in tail male. The last earldom in fee had disappeared.[1]

In addition to the barons created since 1387 by patent there remained those known to lawyers and so to historians anachronistically as holders of 'baronies by writ', who by the second half of the fifteenth century had gone far to establishing for themselves a claim to a hereditary summons. These were in most cases —for new ones were still being brought into existence—the descendants of men whom earlier kings had summoned with no intention of creating a heritable dignity. But whatever the intention a number had from the start been treated as hereditary in practice. It would be easy to put together a longish list of those families where heads, irrespective of wisdom and experience, were regularly summoned when adult from 1300 onwards. The criterion on which they were selected was, as we have seen, not tenure but consequence, based primarily upon territorial importance but allowing something for an ancestor's renown or ancient settlement.[2] These formed the nucleus about which less permanent elements clustered. But they did not retain their position nor transmit it to their issue if for any reason they parted with much of their land. Intermediate between the earls and the lesser knights they provided recruits according to their fortunes to the ranks above and below them. Many fell by the way early, their patrimonies dispersed by a plurality of daughters before steps had been taken to defend them from that evil. Intermarriage enriched some and further reduced the total number. Writs of summons to

---

[1] A possible exception is that of Buckingham (1377), swallowed up and possibly absorbed in a dukedom created in tail male.

[2] Since the heirs to an undivided 'feudal barony' were unlikely to be poor, they were naturally prominent among those regularly summoned, but the coincidence was very far from exact.

'new men' failed to keep up with the wastage. By the time 'barons by writ' became a recognized group they were not numerous.[1] Since for most of the survivors the existence of an entail now kept the inheritance together and made alienation hazardous they had achieved a stability which earned for them a presumptive right to be summoned. What had its origin in landed wealth and consequence ended in prescription. When that had happened the identity of peerage and nobility was complete. By the second half of the fifteenth century the lords were sharply distinguished from those without the fold. Nobility had parted company with gentility, the quality with which those rejected were still permitted to be endowed.

The gentry, that is to say, did not so much rise (though some did) during the later middle ages as fall from the nobility which their antecessors had enjoyed in common with all landowners from a great earl to the lord of an estate worth £20 a year. They were now distinct from and socially inferior to those who were peers of Parliament, some of whom were nevertheless poorer than some of them. By the Yorkist period lords are being referred to more and more often as a superior category of person by knights, esquires, and gentlemen sometimes of ancient family.[2] Their appellations and the modes in which they were to be addressed multiplied, became increasingly elaborate and exposed the servility of those who did not share their privileges. Men now were expected to know their place. In 1300 there had been no place for them to know. Not that old usages died out all at once. Well into the seventeenth century it was customary and courteous to attribute nobility to landed and armigerous families of ancient settlement and sometimes to those who had fabricated a claim to it. But the reality in such cases had been draining out of the word for something over two centuries. A knight may have been noble by courtesy but he was not a nobleman.

It remains for me to refer briefly to a matter so far only touched on: the recruitment of new members to the ranks of the evolving

---

[1] I ignore as unhistorical those baronies later held to have been 'dormant' or 'in abeyance'.

[2] Cf. Appendix A to the Ford Lectures, pp. 122–5 above.

peerage. As long as heiresses were numerous marriage with one could earn any man a writ of summons. Even in the fifteenth century the hand of a great heiress was still the shortest cut to fortune, but such prizes were few and getting fewer. In any case they rarely fell to poor men. Daughters, with expectations or without, were married by their families—and sometimes by the king—to members of their own class. Only as widows did they sometimes please themselves and raise a second, third, or even fourth husband from the dust. Otherwise the chief means of entry throughout our period was undoubtedly service. Not only, or even primarily, military service. That was more likely to be rewarded by election to the order of the Garter than by the issue of a writ of summons to Parliament. The 'peerage creations' of even so martial a king as Edward III were earned by counsel and by diplomatic and administrative service rather than by prowess in war alone. In the later middle ages an increasing amount of the business of government was performed by lords, some of ancient family, some of new. If the Tudor nobility was one of service so was that which preceded it, recruited by service and earning promotion to the higher grades by continued service, peaceful at least as much as warlike.

Inevitably prominent among the novices were the cadets of already established families since they started from a position of vantage. This was not their only source of opportunity. It is often said that the law of primogeniture made the development of a *noblesse* impossible in England because it drove younger sons into the ranks of the inferior gentry, into the professions, and even into trade. At times before and after this may have been true; in the later middle ages it was scarcely so. Indeed for a while it almost seemed as if the primogenitary law was doomed to lose its hold altogether on the descent of land. The truth was that there was a powerful undertow in its favour though some surface currents flowed the opposite way. Not long after 1300—it may have been just before—a means had been found of bequeathing land by will. A man transferred his estates to trustees (they were called 'feoffees') who took possession of them to his use as long as he lived and obeyed his instructions for their disposal after his death. His wishes were embodied in a last will. Since he no longer held them at death his heir at law could not claim them. They could be diverted to the heir's brothers, half-brothers, or even to those who were not his kin at all. The result was a marked improvement in the prospects of younger sons. There were few who received no share in their father's lands. Without wishing totally to disinherit his heir a landowner felt at liberty to distribute his tenements among his sons in varying proportions. Head and heart helped to write his last will. Thus Sir John Larchdeacon (whose father had been summoned to Parliament 1321–4) divided his lands into eight equal parts in 1365 and settled a part on each of eight of his sons in tail male.[1] His action ensured that none of his descendants again received a summons. Similarly in 1455 William, Lord Lovel made provision for each of his three younger sons on a scale not far short of the inheritance destined for his heir.[2] By these and similar means the children of second marriages could be favoured at the expense of the first-born, or a near kinsman on the mother's side preferred to a more distant heir to the patrimony. A remarkable example of this last occurred in 1389 when William Beauchamp, a younger brother of the Earl of Warwick, received the lordship of Abergavenny on the failure of the main line of Hastings. But for the existence of a will the heir would have been Lord Grey of Ruthin.[3]

The consequences of this new freedom to bequeath land were just beginning to make themselves widely felt—by the increase, for example, in the number of well-endowed younger sons such as the Beauforts, the Nevills, and the Bourchiers—when the pull in favour of primogeniture reasserted itself. Not many families

[1] J. Maclean, *Parochial and Family History of the Deanery of Trigg Minor, Cornwall* (3 vols., 1868–79), iii. 256; G.E.C. i. 186–8. A ninth brother who was a clerk received no share unless all his brothers died without male issue.

[2] *Lincoln Diocesan Documents*, pp. 70–87. This liberality did not too seriously undermine the wealth of the eldest son since Lord Lovel was very rich. He had inherited the Burnell lands in 1420 and had married one of the two coheirs of Deincourt and Grey of Rotherfield at about the same time (above, p. 67, n. 1; G.E.C. viii. 222). His grandmother Maud, Lady Lovel, had also brought into the family a Holland inheritance (*C.P.M.* xiii, no. 263; *C.F.R.* viii. 24).

[3] *C.C.R. 1374–7*, pp. 286–96; G.E.C. i. 24. [Cf. pp. 74–6 above and contrast p. 75, n. 4. J. P. C., J. C.]

were fertile or healthy enough to produce several cadet branches that endured. Entailed land could not be safely diverted from the heir, and more and more lands had been entailed, often under earlier wills. Landowners had only just tasted liberty when they began to lose it. Their heirs found allies in another quarter also: in their prospective fathers-in-law. These were alarmed lest they should give their daughters in marriage to those who were afterwards partially if not wholly disinherited. A girl's marriage portion was a useful bargaining counter. It not only enabled provision to be inserted in the marriage contract for the immediate settlement of a jointure in land upon the bride and bridegroom by the latter's father but could be used to extract from him a promise that he would not alienate any part of his inheritance thereafter.[1] By 1500 primogeniture, having outlasted two centuries of confusion, was once more securely enthroned. The time was gone when a father could devise any large part of his lands away from his heir, could sacrifice the interests of an eldest son to the blandishments of a second wife and her children, could do what he liked with his own. Some freedom remained to some but not much and not to many. Thus it came about that, in Maitland's words, 'our primogenitary law . . . obliterated class distinctions' by forcing younger sons to earn their own living. But this only happened towards the end of our period and not before a noble caste had seemed likely to emerge.

[1] An early example belongs to the year 1349 (*Catalogue of Ancient Deeds*, iv, no. A 8768); cf. p. 81 above.

An Early Paper on Crown and Parliament in the Later Middle Ages[1]

1. *Introduction: the Collapse of the Stubbsian 'Framework'*

IN opening any general discussion of English constitutional history in the later middle ages, it is usual—at least at Oxford—to begin by paying tribute to the memory of Bishop Stubbs. The reason for this is obvious, though as far as I can see not particularly creditable. It is that we have failed to do what it is the duty of every generation of historians to do, namely to rewrite the broad outlines of our subject in the light of those specialized studies which are our prime concern. To all intents and purposes the attempt to interpret the period as a whole, to give it a simple and intelligible structure begins—and has ended—with Stubbs. When he undertook the task, many of the materials had long existed in print, some had only recently been made available by publication in the Rolls Series. Stubbs imposed order. It goes without saying that the order which he imposed owed much to his preconceptions about human nature and human progress, both those which he shared with others of his time and those which were personal to himself. That does not matter. The important thing is that he produced an interpretation, a generalized view, which though not acceptable in every detail even to his contemporaries, provided them with something which their minds could grasp easily and retain firmly, something which made order out of chaos. In recent years it has begun to lose its hold; it has been found wanting at too many points. Yet the studies which have revealed its

[1] A paper delivered to the Stubbs Society, 9 November 1938. (This paper is printed here partly for its intrinsic value in making important points the weight of which still does not seem everywhere to be fully recognized but more particularly because of its historiographical interest in showing the point to which McFarlane's views had evolved by 1938. Cf. p. xviii above. It should be regarded as a *pièce d'occasion*, which its author would not have thought of printing.)

ramshackle character have been for the most part narrow and specialist; they have discredited it without putting anything coherent in its place. This failure to substitute anything for it *as a whole* has produced utter confusion. There is no current view. The Stubbsian framework—Lancastrian constitutionalism triumphing after nearly a century of endeavour in 1399, breaking down under the strain of practice, and giving way in its turn to the autocracy of York and Tudor—this framework has collapsed. But it has been replaced by anarchy. The third volume of the *Constitutional History* still remains without a modern rival. Yet the need is clear. Those whose business it is must set to to produce a new order, an advance on Stubbs perhaps but not more durable, something in short which will perform for a new generation the function that his has done for two or three. But first of all the anarchy must be surveyed to see if it contains any materials which can be used in building a new order. It is this preliminary work which I propose to start tonight.

II. *Two common fallacies*

At the start of this inquiry it is necessary to deal with two misconceptions that are bound to produce havoc if allowed to luxuriate in our minds. They are very common misconceptions. The first is the belief that it is possible and desirable to write the history of institutions apart from the men who worked them. Institutions sometimes seem to have a life of their own, but this is only an appearance. They are born, develop, change, and decay by human agencies. Their life is the life of the men who make them. Constitutional history is concerned with men. That is to say that it is not something distinct from political history; it *is* political history and the attempt to isolate it is vain, though the consequences may be far reaching. It is not, it should be said, an attempt of which Stubbs was guilty. He had too much common sense. But others, especially Professor H. L. Gray and his followers, have not been so careful.

The other misconception is perhaps more widespread. It is the habit of assuming a simplicity of behaviour and of motive in medieval politicians that is wholly unwarranted by our knowledge. It is, as a French historian has politely pointed out, the prevailing vice of English medievalists. This want of psychological penetration is especially noticeable in Stubbs, though he is by no means the only offender. There is scarcely a page of the *Constitutional History* which does not contain examples of his shrewdness and of the balance of his judgement, but these are rarely exercised in his treatment of character and motive. It is surprising—or perhaps it is not—that a bishop should display so slight a knowledge of his fellow men. Those who have written since his time are little better. Their pages are peopled by lay figures. The chief difficulty—and probably their excuse—is that for much of the medieval period the evidence for motive is almost wholly wanting. Men have to be judged from their actions alone. Compared with the Tudor period with its wealth of political correspondence and state papers, the later middle ages are nearly barren. But it is a mistake to suppose therefore that motives were less complex and characters more consistent. To do so is to submit to the tyranny of one's materials. It is doubtful, to say the least, whether human nature has changed at all between the fourteenth century and the twentieth. Success in politics demanded then much the same qualities as it does now, powers of persuasion, a sense of an audience, good nerves, a willingness to compromise, and a habit of application to business. To assume otherwise is a large and unjustified assumption. A man like Edmund of Langley, in spite of rank and wealth, cut precious little ice in the Council of Richard II precisely because he was devoid of such qualities. His nephew, Henry of Bolingbroke, had them in abundance and so was able to seize and keep a throne. It is a great but a growing mistake to picture the medieval baronage as if the House of Lords was something like the prefects' room of a public school. There is no excuse for our adult condescension. As a matter of fact there is plenty of evidence to the contrary though it happens to have been for the most part neglected. Take for example the diplomatic correspondence of the Lancastrians. One has only to read a state paper on foreign policy by Henry V—there are some in his own hand—to realize that one is dealing with a master. Subtlety did not come in with the Renaissance.

If, therefore, we are going to understand the constitutional developments of the later middle ages, we must never forget that we are dealing with men and with men with characters as difficult to analyse as our own.

III. *The 'New Monarchy'*

While much of the Stubbsian 'framework' (as I call it) has crumbled, one large fragment has survived. It is still widely held that the monarchy after 1461—or possibly after 1485—was something different in kind and not merely in degree from the medieval kingship which it replaced. Even those who would attach no definite date to the change are yet convinced that the political structure of which Edward IV was the architect and which the first two Tudors brought to completion contained original features hitherto unthought of. This view is summed up in the catchphrase: the New Monarchy. It is not a phrase used I believe anywhere—at least not in his *Constitutional History*—by Bishop Stubbs; it was in fact invented by his friend and contemporary, John Richard Green. But if Stubbs avoided the label, he described and popularized the thing. In one place he calls it 'that recovered strength of the monarchical principle, which in England as on the Continent, marked the opening of a new era'. Elsewhere he contrasts the 'unconstitutional arbitrary and sanguinary' rule of the Yorkists with the experimental constitutionalism of the Lancastrians. Now it seems to me that there is practically no foundation whatever for this view of a New Monarchy after 1461 and that an obstinate belief in it is one of the chief stumbling-blocks to an understanding of the period. Few if any now believe in the Lancastrian Constitutional Experiment; the more we know of the Lancastrians the more absurd it becomes. Why then cling to its sequel the New Monarchy? Possibly because its advocates feel that there must be something to justify the distinction between the middle ages and the modern world. The Renaissance upon which reliance used to be placed has hardly stood the strain; it has been pushed too far back into the middle ages. The truth is that the conception of the Renaissance as a dividing line between medieval and modern is an unscientific anachronism and should be discarded forthwith. Similarly with the New Monarchy. The only New Monarchy that England ever had came in with William the Conquerer.

I suppose that it is still necessary to justify this scepticism. What then are the supposed characteristics of this New Monarchy?

Well, first of all, I take it, the desire and the ability to liquidate that bogy of the textbooks—the 'overmighty subject'. Warwick the kingmaker was, we are often told, the last of the barons. The old feudal nobility was practically wiped out in the Wars of the Roses. There were no more 'overmighty subjects'. Well, what about the Duke of Northumberland in the reign of Edward VI and Elizabeth's Duke of Norfolk? They too tried their hands at queenmaking. The truth of the matter seems to be that both before and after 1461 weak kings were unable to cope with the problem and that strong kings—and queens—were. The nuisance of the overmighty subject was in fact a feature of the rule of weaklings and vanished with the accession of those who had the personal authority to deal with it. When the Percies tried to assume the role of kingmakers to Henry IV they were eliminated. To Edward III, Henry V, and Henry VIII the problem did not exist; to Edward II, Richard II, and Henry VI, it was insoluble. And a royal uncle was just as much a danger to Edward V or Edward VI as he was to the minors who preceded them. To talk as if only Yorkists and Tudors knew how to solve the problem of the overmighty subject is to enlarge the short period of quite abnormal anarchy which was the reason and the excuse for Yorkist usurpation to cover the whole of the fourteenth and fifteenth centuries. To take the measure of the abuse which this involves it is only necessary to cast the mind back across the reign of Henry VI to that of his father Henry V. At no time probably did the practical authority of the Crown, not merely over the baronage but over all classes, stand higher than it did during those nine years. Henry IV was a usurper and he had a usurper's problems. But after all he succeeded in kicking down most of those on whose shoulders he had climbed to the throne. It only took his son a couple of years to dispose finally of the residue of disaffection and rebellion; for the rest of his brief reign his royal will was enforced without challenge. Has anyone a single candidate to suggest for the post of 'overmighty subject' in the reign of Henry V? No, of course not. This talk of the overmighty subject as if it were a chronic disease does less than justice to the vigour of the later medieval kingship. Examples taken from the forty years of virtual minority after 1422 only emphasize the importance of having a king. In Henry VI second childhood succeeded first without the usual interval and under him the medieval kingship was in abeyance.

A second characteristic of the New Monarchy was, it is said, its reliance upon the service of lesser men. To a medievalist this seems so odd that it is necessary to quote J. R. Tanner as evidence that it is a view held by careful and scholarly historians. In Tanner's *Tudor Constitutional Documents*[1] one reads of Henry VII's wisdom in employing churchmen like Morton, Fox, and Warham and laymen like Bray and Lovel and Empson and Dudley and Poynings. But what pray is there new about that? Nothing, except perhaps that it was not a prominent feature of the government of that other New Monarch, Edward IV. But to suggest that it was the normal procedure of a medieval king to govern entirely—or even partly—by the aid of the feudal nobility betrays a quite extraordinary blindness to the facts. To recite a catalogue of churchmen and laymen of the official class upon whom devolved most of the day-to-day government of the Lancastrian period alone would tax your patience by its length. The Council of Henry IV, until his breakdown in health made other arrangements necessary, was except on formal occasions a body of such trusted servants. Indeed one often hears it made a reproach against the Lancastrians that they were not strong enough to compel the baronage to attend the Council regularly. One can't have it both ways! As a matter of fact that new Lancastrian nobility of which we hear so little was like the new Tudor nobility of which we hear so much, composed of the official class, the Hungerfords, the Tiptofts, the Cromwells, the Bardolfs, the Sudeleys, and the Says. In the same way the bench of bishops was stocked with promoted civil servants still active in the affairs of state; men like

[1] 2nd edn. (Cambridge, 1930), p. 4.

Bowet and Chichele, Kemp, Stafford, and Moleyns. As if the civil servant bishop were a Tudor novelty!

Ah, but the New Monarchs levied forced loans, exacted benevolences, and improved the assessment and collection of direct taxation. Far be it from me to suggest that Henry VII's economies and fiscal reforms were not important and valuable. But if economy and reform are made the test of the New Monarchy then Henry VII was the only New Monarch before Elizabeth. Neither Edward IV nor Henry VIII have the slightest claim on those grounds to the title. If the use, on the other hand, of 'new and exquisite means of getting of good' is the hallmark, then the argument for making 1461 the dividing line is a weak one. For not only did Richard II take forced loans, but so did the Lancastrians. It was from them that the Yorkists inherited the practice. It is a subject upon which much laborious work still remains to be done, but the chroniclers tell us that Henry V's forced loans of 1416 and 1421 especially excited indignation, while that of 1460 contributed to the popularity of the Yorkist invasion. Benevolences are perhaps a different matter. An early example, Richard II's *Plaisance* was one of the things which cost him his throne, but under Henry V the Receipt Rolls record the making of *Dona* which though rare must not be entirely overlooked. In any case it is difficult to see that it made much difference to the victim whether he made a gift outright or a loan which the government had not the means of repaying. So much for exactions which had not the sanction of Parliament. Few people will surely claim that arbitrary taxation was either an important or continuous feature of Yorkist and Tudor England. Occasional and sporadic levies will be found on both sides of 1461. With regard to parliamentary taxation the answer is much the same. The problem which faced both Lancastrians and Tudors alike was the difficulty of procuring an assessment which would achieve a substantial yield, an assessment that is to say which affects those who could best afford to pay. The ordinary one-tenth and one-fifteenth was collected on an antiquated and inequitable assessment, that of 1334. It was difficult to upset a traditional assessment, easier to try a new kind of tax. Various experiments were tried. In the opinion of Professor

Tait—and none could be more judicious—the tax of 1404 (1s. in the £1 on incomes from land together with a tax on chattels for those who had no land) was more equitable in its distribution than any before the reign of Charles II, except for one or at the most two of the time of Henry VII. And the Lancastrians have also the Land Tax of 1411 and the Income Tax of 1436 to their credit. The Yorkists, it should be remembered, twice attempted something of the same sort, but both attempts broke down. Edward IV was in fact unable to continue Lancastrian policy and had to fall back on the unreformed tenths and fifteenths. This is I admit a somewhat sketchy treatment of a complicated subject, but taken all in all finance does not provide a sure basis for the view that I am questioning. Far from there being a difference in kind, there is not even an unmistakable difference in degree between the new and the old monarchies.

It is sometimes said that Yorkists and Tudors made much less use of Parliament than their predecessors had done, that there were fewer parliaments after 1461 than before. The latter fact is undoubtedly true but the deduction is based on a statistical fallacy. There were twenty-two parliaments between the accession of Henry IV and the death of Henry V; twenty-two parliaments in twenty-three years. There were only seven parliaments in the twenty-two years of Edward IV's reign (excluding Henry VI's Parliament of 1470–1) and again only seven in the twenty-four years of Henry VII's reign. The figures are striking but misleading. I haven't counted them, but I doubt very much if there were as many as twenty-two parliaments in the sixty-four years of Queen Victoria's reign, but that doesn't prove that the Lancastrians made more use of Parliament than Queen Victoria. For as we all know parliaments sat longer in the nineteenth century. What we don't always remember is that they sat longer in the second half of the fifteenth century than in the first. Instead of dissolving them the king prorogued them and recalled them repeatedly for further sessions. The Parliament of 1472, for example, had seven sessions and was not dissolved until 1475. The practice had begun before 1461; the Parliament of 1445–6 had four sessions and the Long Parliament of 1406 three. But though not a Yorkist innovation, it was a practice which they extended and it is one which it has been customary to overlook.

Is it necessary to labour the point any further? I do not think so. The concept of the New Monarchy must be abandoned. To abandon it will not detract from the merits of Henry VII. The keynote of his reign is renovation not innovation. He saved money; he kept the peace; he made old laws work. But he is a medieval king and to think otherwise is to do a disservice to his qualities. And a disservice also to Henry IV and still more to Henry V. In the capable hands of the latter the medieval kingship betrayed no signs of weakness. He achieved his aims by methods upon which his ablest successors were unable to improve. There was little indeed that he could have learnt from them. Nor was his rule more noteworthy than theirs for that excessive respect for inconvenient constitutional forms with which his dynasty has sometimes been erroneously credited. On the contrary his inclinations were despotic and his practice not markedly different from that of Edward III on the one hand, that of Edward IV on the other. For example take the way in which he dealt with a budding Wolsey. In his treatment of Bishop Beaufort he showed Henry VIII's strength without his ingratitude. Beaufort accepted a cardinal's hat at the hands of Martin V without waiting for the royal permission. Henry not only killed the project but in order to get his way was prepared to strip his uncle not only of his new honour and the legateship for life which accompanied it, but also of his bishopric and all his worldly goods. It was only when the bishop made humble submission and a loan of more than £17,000 that the bishopric and the goods were allowed to him. In the same way Henry V's treatment of the alien priories established a precedent for the dissolution of the monasteries. His military ambitions should not blind us to the significance of his short but brilliantly versatile career.

iv. *The Place of the Commons in Parliament. Had they a will of their own?*

So much for the Crown. To launch an attack on the one generally accepted view may not seem at first sight to have been particularly constructive. But if the medieval kingship is to be properly appreciated, it must be freed from the slur to which the forty years of virtual minority under Henry VI has quite unnecessarily exposed it. That it stood up to such a test for so long without breaking is surely a proof of its vitality. *Those* forty years released at length forces which were usually under control. The truth is that without a strong king the medieval polity wouldn't work indefinitely. Under a strong king and for shorter periods even under a weak one, discontent and criticism found more peaceful channels. Which brings me to Parliament. Here are many problems and little agreement among historians. Of the many points with which one might deal I shall choose one, since it is the one about which disagreement is most violent. This is the part played by the Commons in Parliament.

To Stubbs this seemed a simple question. The captions in his history make his position clear: 'The commons [in 1401] seize their opportunity', 'the commons force their demands on the king'. To him the vigorous independence of the lower House does not admit of doubt. 'Never before and never again for more than two hundred years', he asserted, 'were the commons so strong as they were under Henry IV.' In dealing with the previous period, Tout is perhaps more cautious but hardly less explicit. In the Good Parliament of 1376, he says, John of Gaunt was 'afraid of the commons'. When he wrote that, he was aware that he was committing himself to an opinion which would be challenged. For some time previously the reaction to Stubbs had set in. As far as I know the first place in which it appeared in print was in an essay Professor Neale contributed in *Tudor Studies* and published in 1924.[1] After reviewing the evidence from 1376 to 1406, Neale suggests that 'we need no longer conclude that the real test of strength in parliament was between the king and the commons. In all likelihood it was between the king and the lords.' It is not perhaps remarkable that this suggestion should have come from a Tudor historian who was anxious that the prologue should not usurp the place of the play. But it has nevertheless profoundly impressed a number of medievalists who are prepared to go a

[1] Ed. R. W. Seton-Watson (London, 1924), pp. 257–77.

good deal further than Neale and to see 'the commons as the spokesmen of the Lords rather than the initiators of an independent policy'. A recent paper by Mr. H. G. Richardson puts this view with his usual ingenuity and unwillingness to compromise. 'The answer seems to be that the strength of the commons in parliament was not their own but the lords'.'[1] Now it cannot be denied that there is some basis for this opinion. But it may be doubted whether it takes account of all the evidence or even that it interprets what it does take account of correctly. I fancy that Tout is nearer the truth and that further inquiry will tend to enforce his conclusions.

Admittedly Stubbs went much too far. His idea that the Lancastrians actually encouraged the Commons by taking them into a sort of partnership with the government clearly will not do. Henry IV's inclinations were all the other way and even Stubbs cannot make much of a case for regarding Cardinal Beaufort as the repository of the Lancastrian tradition of constitutionalism. It was a fatal mistake thus to misread the character of this dynasty of usurpers. It was also unfortunate that he should have picked on Sir Arnold Savage, Speaker in 1401 and January 1404, as the embodiment of the spirit of Commons' independence. For the demonstration that Savage was a loyal servant of Henry IV and a member of his Council has tended to smother the true significance of his outspokenness. But the real flaw in Stubbs's case lies in his failure to consider the social fabric of which Lords and Commons were a part. He didn't ask himself sufficiently firmly, who were the Commons? An investigation of that question would have brought the answer that most of the knights—no one can maintain that the burgesses had the same importance—were the dependants, retainers, or servants of the lords. When therefore Richardson says: 'To assert that the knights should have been able to provide an independent opposition to the lords appears, in regard to the circumstances of the time, to be little short of fantastic' one's first instinct is to agree. But it would be as well to look further.

No one but a fool would deny that the territorial power of the

---

[1] 'John of Gaunt and the Parliamentary Representation of Lancashire', *Bulletin of the John Rylands Library*, xxii (1938).

nobility was the supreme factor in later medieval society. Nor
that it was much more extensive than the feudal relationship of
lord and man would imply. Bastard feudalism as it is called had
no such fixed frontiers. Like the society in which it flourished it
was much more fluid. The real link in this society is not the bond
between overlord and tenant but that between patron and client.
It should be observed, by the way, that this bond is not indis-
soluble; its continuance is dependent upon the parties giving
mutual satisfaction. The most obvious expression of this relationship was the agreement by which a man became another's retainer, but this is only the most formal of a number of such
contracts. There can be no doubt that this practice enormously
increased the potential size of a magnate's influence. But only if he
was able to offer his clients sufficient in return. Men would flock
to the service of those who appeared to be able to promote their
careers and shunned those who it seemed could not. It was the
duty of a 'good lord' to find jobs for his servants and for his
servants' relations, to present them with opportunities for gain
and the acquisition of power and position for themselves, to
maintain their quarrels in the king's courts, to protect them against
their rivals, and to reward their service in a score of different ways.
It was in fact an acquisitive and competitive society like any
other. Those who desired to better themselves could only do so by
attaching themselves to those who could best serve their interests.
Patronage and service were the essence of contemporary society.

To realize this must profoundly modify one's conception of the
nature of Parliament. The more the biographies of M.P.s are
studied the more obvious it becomes that these men were not
stalwart independents but men with affiliations which perhaps
might not unfairly be compared with those which link many
M.P.s today to their Trade Unions. When for example it is found
that Peter de la Mare, the Speaker in 1376, was the Earl of March's
steward and that his successor, Thomas Hungerford, held the
same sort of position in the service of John of Gaunt; and when
still more it is found that these are in no sense isolated cases but
examples of a general rule, then there seems scarcely anything
more to say. The evidence produced by Richardson for saying

that John of Gaunt nominated the knights of the shire for his palatinate of Lancaster carries the argument a stage further. Not only were the members the dependents of the lords; they were members because they had been elected by their lords' influence. It might be argued that Lancaster was exceptional. But this is by no means the only instance known. As the fifteenth century advances and the sources become more plentiful there is clear evidence of the influence exerted both at county and borough elections by the magnates. In 1450 the Dukes of York and Norfolk met together to decide who should be returned for East Anglia. And the Paston Letters provide several other references to the commonness of this practice. The creation of a number of pocket boroughs after the middle of the century points in the same direction. In short if any answer is to be made to Richardson it can only be done after a frank admission of the truth of the facts. One cannot deny that most M.P.s belonged to what the eighteenth century called a 'connection' and that elections were not wholly free.

Nevertheless, I believe that a case—and a strong case—against Richardson exists.

In the first place it is impossible to dispose entirely of the chronicle evidence. Mr. Richardson tries to do so by pointing out that the chroniclers 'rarely give such details as would enable us to fit an incident into the framework of the official record, which must necessarily be our primary authority'. That is true but Mr. Richardson goes too far when he calls the evidence of the Rolls of Parliament 'unimpeachable'. To take that view comes easily perhaps to a distinguished civil servant, but there is a growing body of opinion for the view that the Rolls of Parliament are far from the dispassionate record they seem to be. The considerations put forward recently for regarding the Rolls version of the revolution of 1399 as a calculated misrepresentation of the facts will take a good deal of answering. The Rolls give the royal side of the picture. So little did the Commons trust the clerks who drew them up that in 1406 after a stormy session they exacted from the king permission for six of their number to be present when the Rolls were engrossed. Again at the beginning of Henry V's reign the

House complained that the statutes promulgated by the king in response to its petitions sometimes differed materially from what was sought. At any rate there is sufficient evidence for disposing of the view that where chronicles and Rolls disagree the fault cannot lie with the Rolls. And the chroniclers are convinced that the members of the lower House were not mere ciphers. When they praise them it is for making a stand as they did against John of Gaunt in the Good Parliament; the Speaker, Malvern tells us, was a popular hero whose deeds were celebrated in many contemporary ballads now unfortunately lost. When the chroniclers condemn them it is because the *knights* were 'pussillanimés' and 'aberrantes a vero'. The story of the Good Parliament is well known, that of the Long Parliament of 1406 has only recently been more completely brought to light. The account given by Thomas Walsingham seems to put the matter beyond a doubt. For three sessions the Commons criticized the royal administration and withheld the grant of taxation for which they had been summoned.

During this time they obtained several important concessions including the parliamentary audit of the king's accounts. It is open to anyone to believe that all this activity was due to the promptings of their masters in the Lords. But that can scarcely be claimed for the final episode as described in the St. Albans Chronicle. The king had made it clear that Parliament would not again be adjourned; it would remain in session until the tax was granted. At length after the first all-night sitting on record in the early hours of 22 December—when Christmas was upon them—the Commons yielded. But they attached an important condition to their grant, that the lords who had been nominated to serve on the Council and who were to have control of the administration until Parliament met again were to bind themselves to refund out of their own pockets any part of the tax which should be misappropriated. In the event these lords not unnaturally joined the king in an angry rejection of this startling proposal, and the Commons were abashed into withdrawing it, but then only on terms. This incident shows that not only could the parliamentary knights take an independent line but their distrust of the king could be extended to include the lords. They were capable of formulating a scheme which would have made the lords responsible for their financial shortcomings. Stubbs did not know of this incident but he was surely not far wrong in describing this Parliament as 'an exponent of the most advanced principles of medieval constitutional life in England'. Unfortunately such chronicle evidence is scanty, but if we read the Rolls of Parliament in its light it becomes probable that incidents like this were far from rare during the late fourteenth and early fifteenth centuries. Even if they were rare, they cannot be got rid of by allegations of malice against the chroniclers. These latter were often ignorant of parliamentary procedure and relied upon hearsay for the most part, but that they had honest ground for their belief that the Commons were an independent influence in Parliament seems clear. It is not the sort of thing they would make up if it were not true. Mr. Richardson's line is that it was unthinkable and fantastic. Well, the answer is that there were contemporaries who thought it.

How then are we to reconcile the social background with this independence? It can be done, I think, along the lines suggested by a remark of Mr. Richardson himself. 'The knights of the shire were', he writes, 'for the most part, self-respecting country gentlemen, of considerable administrative experience, and with a standard of honour which would not permit them to be made mere tools of faction.' It is for these reasons that one cannot believe that they would ever remain for long, if they ever were, mere tools of any sort. To show that one M.P. was the steward of one lord, that another owed his advancement to the influence of a second lord, and that another was the retainer of a third does not prove that these men never used their own judgement and were willing to be used passively by their leaders. To assert this is to misunderstand and to falsify the character of late medieval society. Gratitude or the hope of further favours might make a knight unwilling to oppose his benefactor's interests, might make him anxious to go as far as he could in support of his policies, but they did not make him a slave. These were 'connections' in the eighteenth-century sense, not parties in the modern sense; these groups were loose, unhardened as yet by any organization; they could clearly dissolve, not merely because a magnate couldn't find pasture enough for his clients, but because they didn't agree with the line he was taking. Must we believe that when Bushey and Green and Bagot changed sides between 1388 and 1397 that they had simply been bought by Richard II? The dissolution of the clientele of the Lords Appellants after 1388 is proof that whatever ties bound them to their masters, these were not unbreakable. And it seems unreasonable without further proof to assume that such desertions were entirely venal. Many probably were, but public opinion may have had something to do with it. At least it is a point worth considering. The relationship between a lord and his dependants was a reciprocal one. As we have seen, it was not necessarily a permanent one. He is not likely to have been able to force them to uphold a policy against their interests any more than they were likely to oppose his. They were brought together by the desire for mutual help. It seems to me that the clients are likely to have influenced the policy of their lords as much as he could influence theirs. So that when Parliament is found advocating measures which have as their object the salvation of the taxpayers' pocket it is more reasonable to suppose that the policy was that of the taxpayers. And if that is so then it is the policy of the Commons rather than the Lords, since the latter did not bear their share of direct taxation. It is striking how much of the opposition in Parliament is inspired by taxpayers' grievances and how many of the limitations on the Crown proposed had no other object but the achievement of economy. In this the burgesses were as much involved as the knights. In 1429 for example we have actual proof of their activity in the archives of the corporation of King's Lynn. The representatives of the borough in Parliament informed the corporation that 'the citizens of London, York, Bristol, Hull and other towns proposed to labour the knights for a restriction of the subsidy'. The merchant class, we know from Hanseatic reports, was very active in lobbying the Commons in their interests all through the period. And however difficult the incident may be to interpret, there can be no question that in 1407 the Commons made a great fuss because they thought that the Lords were attempting to interfere with their right to initiate taxation. It was this right which gave the Commons the whip hand in Parliament, that prompted their demand for the *de jure* recognition of their *de facto* right to redress of grievances before supply in 1401, and which made them in fact the House whose wishes had to be gratified by an impoverished government. Mr. Richardson asks us to believe that in these circumstances they remained and were, it seems, content to remain the passive instruments of their betters in the other House.

If any further proof were needed of the improbability of such a view, it is to be found in the personnel of the Commons and its record of service. Mr. Richardson produces some statistics to show that the number of knights who sat in two consecutive parliaments in the reign of Richard II was rarely more than twenty and often as few as ten or twelve. This may seem to support the contention that they were as a body inexperienced and therefore capable of being led. But to take even two or three consecutive parliaments is not enough; nor is it enough to produce statistics for a whole series of parliaments. The only safe method is to consider the record of each man. If this is done a very different picture is composed. M.P.s were not merely well-to-do gentlemen of considerable administrative experience; many of them were also persons of considerable parliamentary experience too. Of the seven parliaments which sat between 1376 and 1380 (including both years) Sir John Botiller of Warrington sat in all but one. He was knight of the shire for Lancashire in all ten times. Robert Urswyk sat as M.P. for Lancashire in thirteen Parliaments between 1379 and 1401, Nicholas Haryngton for five between 1372 and 1402, and Robert Pilkington for six between 1363 and 1384. All these for Lancashire. In the next century between 1432 and 1460, we have the returns of only fourteen parliaments; during that period eleven persons represented the county (two seats) and only two were unconnected either by marriage or by interest with the allied families of Stanley and Harrington. The heads of these two families sat for the county in ten and six parliaments respectively. These records are by no means unusual. The same is only slightly less common among the burgesses. William Graa (Gray) was returned fourteen times and his son Thomas at least twelve times for the city of York in the late fourteenth century. And the representatives of the larger towns were often merchant princes who are not likely to have been any less capable than the knights of making use of their opportunities and their experience. Thomas Graa of York had been mayor of the city and served as ambassador to Prussia. Men like John Northampton, Nicholas Brembre, John Philipot, and Richard Whittington who represented the city of London under Richard II and Henry IV were financiers whose influence with the government was throughout this period considerable. Such men as these and such parliamentary old stagers as I have mentioned—and I could mention scores more—cannot have sat together and debated the king's needs and the shortcomings of his government without developing some opinions of their own and even perhaps the outlines of a common policy. To think the contrary is surely—to adopt Mr. Richardson's own word—fantastic.

The truth of the matter seems to be that the support of the Commons was as necessary to the Lords as that of the Lords was to the Commons. It was an alliance to which each party contributed its share. It was based no doubt largely on common interests and common aspirations. But in the struggle with the Crown it was the Commons who were called upon to bear the brunt, because it was their duty to petition, to impeach, and to grant taxation. It is an alliance as old at least as Simon de Montfort, that is to say as old as Parliament itself.

It should have become clear during the course of these remarks that what is needed is a more detailed study than we have at present of English society in the age of bastard feudalism. Political influence was so much bound up with territorial influence and with the geographical distribution of the great families that it is only by undertaking a large number of local surveys that a just understanding of political history can be obtained. What above all is required is complete biographies of all those who sat in Parliament, an enormous and difficult task since much of the material is unprinted and for other purposes often not worth printing. It is necessary to be able to study the representation of one particular district over a longish period as well as that of the whole country in one Parliament. When these data are available it will be possible to do for the fourteenth and fifteenth centuries what Professor Namier is doing for the reign of George III. For the ages, you will have noticed, have politically much in common. It is fortunate that this work has begun. We already have an excellent survey of the representation of Lancashire from 1377 to 1460 by Mr. John Roskell[1] to which I am indebted for one or two of my illustrations just now. The same writer is now engaged upon an intensive examination of the Parliament of 1422. Meanwhile the vast co-operative publication inspired by Colonel Wedgwood is wasting a great deal of labour and money in showing how the job should not be done. The first effect of all this new material will probably be to render generalization difficult, if not impossible for a time. But as it is sorted and arranged the outlines of a new framework will become clear. In that framework I shall expect to find room for a less feeble kingship and a more enterprising House of Commons than it is fashionable at present to assume.

[1] *Knights of the Shire for Lancashire 1377–1460*, Chetham Soc., N.S., vol. 96.

BIBLIOGRAPHICAL INDEX

This includes all printed works cited, except those given on page xli; abbreviated titles have been used; titles of separately published items are in italics.

GENERAL INDEX

Abergavenny, or Bergavenny, lords, *see* Beauchamp, William and Richard; lordship of, *see* Bergavenny

Accounts, magnates', 25–6, 197–8; treasurer of wars, 26; cofferers', importance of, 129, 132, 197 n. 3, 215 n. 1, 226; centralized system, 138–40; accountants' training, 139–40; influence on royal administration, 141; confusion of Beauchamp's *c.* 1420, 197

Acre, Joan of, Edward I's daughter, her marriages, 260–1

Agincourt, battle of, 32, 124, 185

Airmyn, William, paymaster, 24

Alington, John, servant to York, 116

Alygh, Ralph, squire to the Lord Chancellor, 108

Ampthill, Beds., castle, 23, 94

Antwerp, Lionel of, 157

Archdeacon, Sir John, divides his estates, 71

Archer, Sir Simon, 6

Argentine, John, 137; his son, 138

Arrears, of rent, increasing by 1490, 178; alleged consequences of, 179; offset by accumulation of land, 186; in fourteenth century, 220; pursuit of, 221–3

Arundel, earls of, *see* Fitzalan

— Thomas, provision to Ely, 90

Astley, Nicholas, baron, 173

— William d., *c.* 1430, 173

Aston, Sir Roger, arrears owed by, 223

Audley, Hugh, earl of Gloucester, creation of, 159

— Sir James, 163

Aumale, Stephen, count of, d. 1127, 257

— Aveline, countess of, d. 1274, child-wife of Edmund Crouchback, 256; her heirs, 257 and n. 1

— Isabel de Redvers, dowager of, *see* Forz, Isabella de

Bacon, Sir Bartholomew, will of, 240 n. 5

Bankers, Italian, deposits with, 131–2, 134

Bareford, Agnes, her husbands, 137–8; *see* Argentine, Mautravers, Narford

Barnard Castle, cattle ranch at, 194; value of estate, 199

Baronies, difference between tenurial and peerage, 269; by writ, 274–5; 'dormant', 275 n. 1

Basset, Ralph, lord, of Drayton, receives ransom, 31, 76; loan by, 92

Bastards, 69; of magnates, 71; Gaunt's, 84; William Nevill's, 148; James Audley, 163; 220

Batsford, Thomas, London merchant, 90

Baugé, battle of, 31, 32

Bealsby, Sir William, enfeoffment to use by, 218

Beauchamp, earls of Warwick, family of, 79, 93, 186, 267; archives of, 187 and n. 2; wills of, 187 and n. 4; account of, 188–201; relationships with crown, 193, 212; rewards, 194; military service, 195; fortunes of, 199–201

— William, 1st earl, d. 1298, 188, 192, 194

— Guy, 2nd earl, d. 1315, 188–9; marriage of, 192; grants to, 194, 199; education of, 234–5

— Thomas, 3rd earl, d. 1369; his prisoners at Poitiers, 30, 195; settles his estates, 72–3; minority of, 189; his younger sons, 190–2; his income, 191; grants to, 194; purchases by, 195–6; his daughters' portions, 196; Guy, his eldest son, d. 1359, bequest of books, 235

— Thomas, 4th earl, d. 1401, 24; loses Gower, condemned for treason, 189–90; purchases land, 196; building by, 196 and n. 7; income, 197 and n. 3; as Appellant, 200

— Richard, 5th earl, d. 1439, votive offerings by, 98, 200; household journal, 100–1; payments to retainers,